Program Development
in the
21st Century

To Gerri, Mom, Papa, and Paul—my family.
And to Denise Davenport, who would have been an
incredible program developer.

Program Development
in the
21st Century

AN EVIDENCE-BASED APPROACH TO
DESIGN, IMPLEMENTATION, AND EVALUATION

Nancy G. Calley
University of Detroit Mercy

Los Angeles | London | New Delhi
Singapore | Washington DC

For information:

SAGE Publications, Inc.
2455 Teller Road
Thousand Oaks, California 91320
E-mail: order@sagepub.com

SAGE Publications India Pvt. Ltd.
B 1/I 1 Mohan Cooperative
    Industrial Area
Mathura Road, New Delhi 110 044
India

SAGE Publications Ltd.
1 Oliver's Yard
55 City Road
London EC1Y 1SP
United Kingdom

SAGE Publications Asia-Pacific Pte. Ltd.
33 Pekin Street #02-01
Far East Square
Singapore 048763

Printed in the United States of America

Library of Congress Cataloging-in-Publication Data

Calley, Nancy G.
Program development in the 21st century: an evidence-based approach to design, implementation, and evaluation / Nancy G. Calley.
    p. cm.
Includes bibliographical references and index.
ISBN 978-1-4129-7449-3 (pbk.)
  1. Mental health planning. 2. Mental health services. 3. Community mental health services. I. Title.

RA790.5.C3155 2011
362.2068—dc22   2010029518

This book is printed on acid-free paper.

10 11 12 13 14 10 9 8 7 6 5 4 3 2 1

Acquisitions Editor:	Kassie Graves
Permissions Editor:	Adele Hutchison
Production Editor:	Jane Haenel
Copy Editor:	Megan Speer
Typesetter:	C&M Digitals (P) Ltd.
Proofreader:	Sarah J. Duffy
Indexer:	Maria Sosnowski
Cover Designer:	Bryan Fishman
Marketing Manager:	Stephanie Adams

Contents

About the Author

Nancy G. Calley, PhD, LPC, is associate professor and chair of the Department of Counseling and Addiction Studies at the University of Detroit Mercy. She is also the clinical director of Spectrum Human Services Inc. and Affiliated Companies. She has worked in the mental health and human services field for more than 2 decades, primarily in the areas of juvenile justice, child welfare, mental health, substance abuse treatment, and traumatic brain injury. She has developed several clinically based programs and has published numerous articles on program development and treatment modalities for specialized client populations, including juvenile sex offenders. As the focus of her clinical work has been on court-involved individuals and other marginalized populations, she is specifically invested in advocacy and social justice efforts to ensure access and equity in treatment for these specialized groups. She has received funding from several federal agencies and foundations to support her work and continues to be highly active in comprehensive program development efforts today.

Acknowledgments

First and foremost, I would like to acknowledge the individuals whom I have had the privilege of serving during my career as a mental health professional—each and every one of them has taught me so much. Second, I would like to acknowledge all the colleagues whom I have worked with in the human services field over the past 2 decades—this is indeed the best and most important work to be done, and I could not be more proud to be a part of such an esteemed group. I would also like to acknowledge my graduate students of the University of Detroit Mercy Counseling program—your spirit, thirst for knowledge, and determination bring me endless inspiration. I also must extend my deepest appreciation to my academic colleagues, who have provided me with incredible support throughout this process, most especially Lisa Hawley, Libby Blume, and John Staudemaier. I would like to thank my colleagues across the country who served as reviewers of the manuscript draft—your keen eyes and ears and erudite input contributed immensely to this text. Finally, I must express gratitude to my editor at Sage, Kassie Graves, whose strong belief in this project from the very beginning helped make it possible, to both Kassie and Veronica Novak for their expert editing and support, to Meg Speer for her diligent copy editing, to Jane Haenel for her thoughtful graphics and other production-related work, and to the rest of the team at Sage that participated in bringing this book out.

Publisher's Acknowledgments

SAGE gratefully acknowledges the following peer reviewers for their editorial insight and guidance:

David T. Beach, *University of Kentucky*

John R. Belcher, *University of Maryland*

Kevin W. Borders, *Spalding University*

Beulah Hirschlein, *Oklahoma State University*

Amy Galin Shulin, *Kennesaw State University*

Rosalie Smiley, *California University of Pennsylvania*

Karen VanderVen, *University of Pittsburgh*

Cirecie West-Olatunji, *University of Florida*

CHAPTER 1

Comprehensive Program Development in the Mental Health Professions

Learning Objectives

1. Define comprehensive program development

2. Increase understanding of the current climate in human services and mental health programming

3. Increase understanding of the role of today's mental health professional and how it has changed over the past 20 years

4. Identify the steps involved in comprehensive program development

COMPREHENSIVE PROGRAM DEVELOPMENT:
YESTERDAY VERSUS TODAY

1993	2010
Just having completed my master's degree in counseling and rather quickly been promoted into a program director position, I found myself suddenly responsible for the lives of 24 teenage girls—all of them survivors of physical and/or sexual abuse. I had spent 6 years working in juvenile justice, and I had indeed written my thesis on child sexual abuse—antecedents, protective factors, and treatment interventions—so, of course, I was fully prepared to direct a residential treatment program for young girls struggling to make sense of their world and understand why they were being punished for something that had happened to them.	I just completed a proposal for a residential substance abuse treatment program contract. If awarded, this will allow an existing program to accept clients from a new funding source. In developing this proposal, we were required to identify specific cultural identity characteristics (e.g., age) of our target population and explain precisely how treatment interventions would accommodate these unique needs. In addition, a large part of the proposal required that we articulate the models of addiction that the program was based on and the practice theories that would guide the clinical interventions. Specific evidence-based interventions also had to be identified. And the research supporting each of these had to be included.
Wrong! I was ill prepared for such responsibility. Whereas I had already begun to develop a background in supervision and management, I had not yet developed clinical program development skills—essential to my new role. However, little was asked of me in this area from my contractors/funders. In fact, as long as my program provided weekly individual therapy and biweekly group therapy, we were in compliance with our contract. The specific focus of the therapy (e.g., development, peer relations, abuse) was completely up to the therapist—who was under my supervision—to determine. My funders never asked if or how I knew the program was successful in treating abuse and helping these young ladies through their developmental years, but rather, they continued to send a constant stream of new clients as soon as we had a vacancy. Success, in the eyes of our funders, was measured by reuniting these girls with their	In order to demonstrate capability in operating such a program, we were required to include the results of a recent outcomes

families or placing them in a foster home once they had completed the treatment program. ***Successfully completing the program*** of course meant that the girls participated in therapy, attended school regularly, and generally abided by the house rules (easy expectations for 14- and 15-year-olds recently removed from their homes!). We—the treatment team—determined if and when success was achieved. We did not review the research to help us understand what expectations should exist for this particular population, nor did we use any formalized assessment to evaluate the degree and/or type of change that might have occurred, and we certainly did not engage in any type of outcomes evaluation. When the contract came up for rebid, we developed a new proposal articulating our notion of ***treatment*** (e.g., home schedule, school, recreation, therapy) with no accompanying research support, and we continued to be funded.*

evaluation that had been conducted on the program. And the design of the outcomes evaluation for the proposed program also had to be provided in addition to specific evidence of staff competency to effectively implement the program.

Finally, eligibility to apply for the funding was based on the organization having attained relevant national accreditation, and thus, evidence of such accreditation also had to be provided.

*Fortunately, and largely because of the incredible group of women with whom I worked and our need to provide the best treatment to our clients, we struggled, learned, and grew quickly.

Comprehensive Program Development

Today's Mental Health Professionals and Program Development

Although not that long ago—1993—times have changed dramatically in clinical program development. This is particularly evident in the expectations and emphasis placed on clinical program design and the use of evaluation methods—driven by rigorous and well-supported clinical design, accountability, and outcomes evaluation. In fact, I would never be allowed today to get away with what I did in 1993, specifically because today the stakes have been raised considerably (and necessarily), and as they have been raised, funding sources have continued to play an increasingly active role in ensuring that sufficient rigor and accountability exists. This is illustrated clearly in the requirements of my most recent program development project (i.e., 2010).

In addition to the changes that have taken place specifically in program development, the role of the mental health professional has become increasingly more expansive and the practice of counseling (i.e., therapy) has become increasingly more scientific. As such, mental health professionals are currently employed as clinicians, program managers, and administrators across a variety of settings (e.g., outpatient mental health clinics, juvenile justice facilities). And they must demonstrate both evidence-based practices and the ability to administer efficient operations. Additionally, as society continues to evolve, mental health professionals continue to find themselves treating an increasing number of specialized clinical issues (e.g., gambling addiction, self-mutilation, suicide). As a result of these significant changes, professional counselors and other mental health professionals must possess both scientific and business knowledge in order to develop efficient and effective specialized treatment programs that are not only viable but sustainable. With increasing emphasis on the use of evidence-based practices and efficient clinical program operations, mental health professionals must be competent in comprehensive clinical program development.

To further highlight the dramatic changes that have taken place over the past several years, I conducted an interview with Roger Swaninger, president and chief executive officer of Spectrum Human Services, Inc. and Affiliated Companies. Roger has been with Spectrum for 32 years. He was hired shortly after the company was founded, and as a result, he provides a necessary historic perspective on the mental health and human service industry. In addition, he leads a multifaceted nonprofit organization that has grown from an annual operating budget of approximately $2 million to approximately $56 million today, currently consisting of six companies specializing in adult mental health services and treatment, child welfare, juvenile justice, substance abuse prevention and treatment, vocational development, and an outpatient mental health clinic. Roger has witnessed the dramatic changes that have taken place over the past few decades and has been able to not only successfully navigate the changes but grow and develop exponentially despite myriad challenges. In fact, with so many mental health and human service organizations today finding it increasingly difficult to remain in business, the sustainability that Spectrum has demonstrated may offer significant lessons for today's mental health professionals.

INTERVIEW WITH ROGER I. SWANINGER, PRESIDENT & CEO

Spectrum Human Services, Inc. and Affiliated Companies (May 2010)

What are the greatest challenges or threats to human services today?

The most obvious challenge today is funding—today there are both shrinking dollars and more competition, which make this business tougher than ever before. The other great challenge today has to do with the talent factor—finding and keeping the most talented staff.

What are the most significant differences that you see today versus 30 years ago in human services?

Before, I could just go up to the state capitol and pitch my idea for a new program, and often they would go for it. Today, we have to demonstrate that a need exists, provide the research support for the program design, and demonstrate that we can achieve successful outcomes in order to gain and maintain funding.

How do you go about making decisions about new program development?

First we ask, is the idea related to programming that we currently do and/or will it enhance what we currently do? If it is an area that we are already in and it will allow us to expand in that particular area, it already has a natural lead-in. But there are also a number of due diligence activities that we have to consider that include both fully examining the finances of the program and the costs and benefits related to the new program, as well as considering if we have the appropriate infrastructure to support the new program. You have to always estimate risk-reward—you have to ask, how much can I afford to lose and what do I have to gain? You must do due diligence and carefully assess every aspect. All of these factors and more must be considered in every new venture.

To what do you attribute Spectrum's staying power—how has Spectrum managed to succeed despite the challenges that plague human services today?

Diversity of funding, talented staff, and the relationships our staff has built with contractors and others in the field.

We have an existing pool of talented staff that form the core of the organization—staff that have been with the agency for a number of years and that form the agency's executive leadership team. We have also taken calculated risk in expanding our business. I should add that we are very aggressive in going after new business. We have lost our share of contracts over the years, but it hasn't devastated us because we have built up a large continuum so that we have some degree of protection when we do lose specific funding. I think being aggressive has always been part of Spectrum's philosophy. Beginning with the founder, Jim Minder, who was

(Continued)

(Continued)

very aggressive in going after new business, we had had a tremendous growth spurt in the late 70s, early 80s, and then another in the late 90s.

The premise of this book is that today's mental health professionals must be extremely well rounded, having concrete knowledge and skills in comprehensive program development, including finance and human resource management. What do you believe today's mental health professionals need to be equipped with?

The best of both worlds is needed—you need to have both a clinical and a business background today. You must have business savvy and understand your budget as well as understand the relationship between the services you provide and the finances related to the services. You have to understand the politics of the business and develop effective relationships with funding sources and other key groups.

What types of characteristics do you look for when hiring someone today?

First and foremost, you have to have strong interpersonal skills—you have to be able to develop effective relationships with clients, colleagues, funders, et cetera. You also have to believe in our mission—in what we are trying to accomplish—understanding that serving individuals in need is the most important thing that we do.

I also look for someone who wants my job, someone who is hungry and really wants to do this work and gets excited about it.

Why should mental health professionals want to pursue this work today?

They have an opportunity to have a long-term impact on individuals—to provide input to program design, learn how to achieve effective outcomes, and understand the difference that they can make in the lives of others.

Note: Interview used with permission.

Current Climate in the Mental Health Professions

Much of the significant change that the mental health professions have experienced over the past 2 decades has been largely driven by the managed care movement and the more recent emphasis on the use of evidence-based practices (EBPs). Originally articulated by Sackett, Strauss, Richardson, Rosenberg, and Haynes (2000), and adopted by the Institute of Medicine in 2001, "evidence-based practice is the integration of best research evidence with clinical expertise and patient values" (p. 147). Applied to mental health professions, EBPs involve placing the client first, adopting a process of lifelong learning that involves continually posing specific questions of direct practical importance to clients, searching effectively and efficiently for the current best evidence relative to each question, and taking appropriate action guided by evidence (Gibbs, 2003).

The adoption of EBPs has been far-reaching and has had a considerable effect on mental health practices. In fact, Sexton, Gilman, and Johnson (as cited in Marotta & Watts, 2007) asserted that "the impact of EBPs is dramatic in that they are fundamentally changing the way practitioners work, the criteria from which communities choose programs to help families and youth, the methods of clinical training, the accountability of program developers and interventions, and the outcomes that can be expected from such programs" (p. 492). Also referred to as *empirically based practices*, EBPs are predicated on the use of scientific methods to evaluate clinical interventions. As a result, there is greater pressure on mental health professionals to either utilize clinical interventions that have established efficacy or engage in rigorous evaluation of unevaluated new practices.

Addressing this movement toward greater intentionality and accountability in the counseling profession, A. Scott McGowan, editor of the *Journal of Counseling and Development,* announced a "Best Practices" section to highlight evidence-based practices. Since then, a growing body of *best practice* literature has emerged addressing assessment of violence risk (Haggard-Grann, 2007), treatment of obsessive-compulsive disorder (Hill & Beamish, 2007), and treatment of depression (Puterbaugh, 2006). In addition, comprehensive clinical interventions for specialized populations of juvenile sex offenders (Calley, 2007) and adult male survivors of trauma (Mejia, 2005) have been articulated.

Within the broader mental health literature, specific types of research-based clinical interventions have been proposed, such as Wilderness therapy (Hill, 2007), rape survivor treatment (Hensley, 2002), and outreach strategies for female immigrants and refugees (Khamphakdy-Brown, Jones, & Nilsson, 2006). Finally, clinical interventions for such complex issues as dealing with developmental transitions of young women with attention deficit/hyperactivity (Kelley, English, Schwallie-Giddis, & Jones, 2007) have been proposed. Best practice literature typically summarizes research findings and, as a result, identifies etiological factors and proposes specific interventions for use in clinical treatment. In this manner, much attention is given to disseminating research findings for use in future clinical program development, ensuring that current research is fully utilized to inform practice.

Moving beyond best practice literature and its role in the development of clinical interventions, a very small body of work has begun to emerge exploring other factors related to clinical program development. Cost analyses of program development and implementation have been included (Chatterji, Caffray, & Crowe, 2004; Wilderman, 2005), thus promoting a practical understanding related to the financial implications in program development. In addition, the role of interagency collaboration in comprehensive program development has been examined (Donahue, Lanzara, Felton,

Essock, & Carpinello, 2006). Exploration of both these areas provides another layer of comprehensive program development that is not only complementary to clinically focused research but necessary to forwarding our understanding of *comprehensive program development.*

Whereas literature related to program development in the mental health professions has significantly increased over the past 5 years, limitations to utilizing this literature in practice continue to exist. The growing body of best practice literature provides necessary direction and guidance to treating various clinical issues; however, without a sound, comprehensive clinical program framework, these interventions may not be effectively implemented and evaluated on a broad scale. This causes a dilemma not only because it severely limits the use of such research but also because it creates challenges to perpetuating EBPs, the very issue it is seeking to address. In addition, literature examining factors such as cost and the role of collaboration in clinical program development enhance our understanding of program development but again fail to provide a more complete understanding of program development. To address each of these issues, mental health professionals need to be well versed in comprehensive program development. Moreover, by gaining competence in program development, mental health professionals will be able to effectively utilize existing knowledge to ensure that the most effective clinical interventions are provided to individuals in need.

Comprehensive Program Development Defined

Comprehensive clinical program development includes three major phases—program design, program implementation, and program evaluation—and reflects the entire developmental process from start to finish (see Figure 1.1).

Moreover, clinical program development refers to a systematic process that requires various stages of preplanning, planning, implementing, and sustaining effective mental health programming. A wide variety of highly focused and semisequential tasks compose comprehensive program development, including

- developing a program rationale,
- conducting a thorough review of the research for use in program design,
- addressing multicultural considerations in program design,
- designing the clinical program,
- developing the organizational structure,
- identifying relevant community resources,

Figure 1.1 Major Phases of Comprehensive Program Development

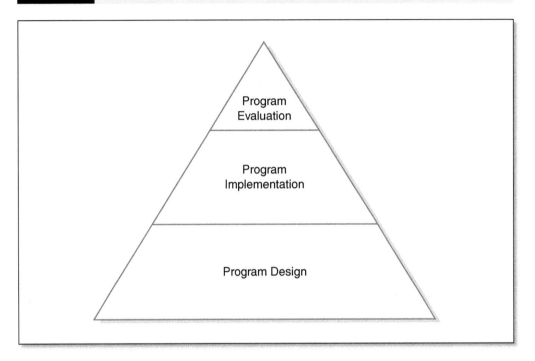

- identifying potential funding sources,
- developing a proposal,
- developing the initial budget,
- implementing the program,
- conducting the program evaluation,
- engaging community resources,
- developing a professional advocacy plan,
- identifying methods of data reporting, and
- developing plans to pursue accreditation.

Clinical program development occurs in many venues, including human/social service organizations; public systems specializing in mental health, criminal justice, or child welfare; and outpatient clinics. Clinical program development can be accomplished by mental health professionals with medium to large-sized staffs as well as those in small nonprofit clinics with very few staff members and other resources.

Fundamentally, program development in the mental health professions refers to comprehensive business planning. As such, several key business principles are used to guide the clinical program development process. These include such principles as

- identifying a need for services,
- identifying a gap in the existing market,
- utilizing research to guide product/service development,
- developing the most effective product/service,
- developing an effective and efficient infrastructure,
- effectively managing finances,
- continuously identifying customers,
- developing key relationships to support and sustain your business,
- employing a development specialist and a lobbyist to continue to promote your business interests,
- ensuring that you have the best product/service to offer,
- regularly sharing your success with *stakeholders*, and
- garnering national recognition.

Appreciating the inherent relationship or intersection of these key business concepts with clinical program development is critical to understanding precisely what clinical program development is in the 21st century.

Historically, a very small group of mental health professionals has been resistant to the notion that the mental health industry is indeed a business, often citing in their defense that the concept of business and that of helping individuals are diametrically opposed (Hansen, 2007). Mental health professionals cannot afford to think this way, particularly since our ability to continue to help individuals is significantly dependent on our business skills. If we bear in mind that a failure to effectively operate our business (i.e., mental health practice) may inevitably result in our inability to continue to help individuals, the compatibility of concepts related to both business and mental health practice should become quite clear.

Comprehensive Program Development Model

In order to guide mental health professionals through gaining competence in comprehensive program development, the *Comprehensive Program Development Model* was developed (see Figure 1.2). As you can see, the first eight steps comprise the components necessary for initial program development and implementation, whereas the final six steps illustrate the components necessary for implementation and ensuring long-term program success and sustainability. It is important to note here that the model is semisequential, insofar as some of the steps are purposely ordered. For

Figure 1.2 Comprehensive Program Development Model: Design, Implementation, and Evaluation

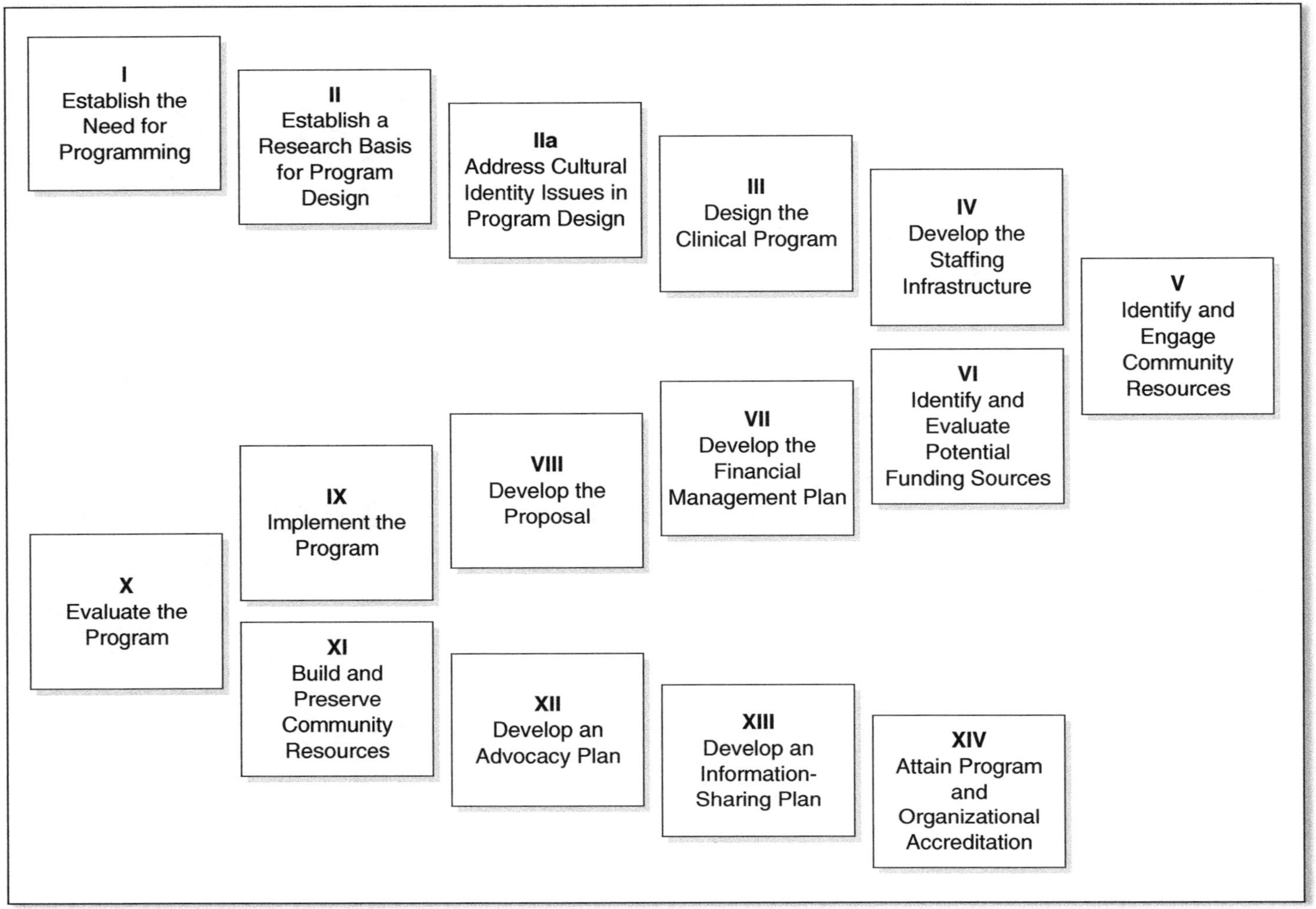

I
Establish the Need for Programming

II
Establish a Research Basis for Program Design

IIa
Address Cultural Identity Issues in Program Design

III
Design the Clinical Program

IV
Develop the Staffing Infrastructure

V
Identify and Engage Community Resources

VI
Identify and Evaluate Potential Funding Sources

VII
Develop the Financial Management Plan

VIII
Develop the Proposal

IX
Implement the Program

X
Evaluate the Program

XI
Build and Preserve Community Resources

XII
Develop an Advocacy Plan

XIII
Develop an Information-Sharing Plan

XIV
Attain Program and Organizational Accreditation

instance, establishing a *need* for programming must precede establishing a *research basis* in program design, since without sufficient justification of need, developing a program is futile. However, you may develop a program proposal and initial budget before identifying a potential funding source or vice versa, largely depending on proposal type and available funding opportunities. This is because there are both prescribed funding opportunities (opportunities in which the type of program needed is identified as well as the amount of funding available) and self-initiated or open funding opportunities (opportunities in which you propose the program and requested budget amount). In addition, some of the steps may occur simultaneously. A brief overview of each of the steps is provided below to begin familiarizing you with the model.

Step I: Establish the Need for Programming

The first step in program development is the identification of a broad region in which the program will be implemented. Once determined, the preplanning activities can begin. The results of this first phase result in identifying a *target population*, articulating a statement of the problem/primary needs of the population, and establishing the philosophical/ideological foundation for the program (e.g., juvenile justice is rehabilitation-focused).

Establishing the need for comprehensive programming in mental health counseling involves completing several planning activities that include conducting the following: a needs assessment, an *asset map*, a *community demography assessment*, and a *market analysis*. A needs assessment is used to identify and prioritize the clinical needs of a population. Conversely, an asset map identifies existing strengths (e.g., community organizing and cohesion) and resources in the *target region* (e.g., community organizing practices, human service organizations). A comparison of the results of the needs assessment to the results of the asset map can be used to address identified needs through existing resources. Complementing the needs assessment and asset map, the community demography assessment identifies the various population parameters and characteristics, including cultural identity aspects of community members (e.g., age parameters, prominent spiritual and/or religious faiths), and provides necessary preplanning data to ensure that program design takes into account any unique features of the target population.

Once the primary needs of the region are defined, a market analysis is conducted in the broader region in order to thoroughly examine providers that are already involved in working to address the identified problem(s). A market analysis should involve collecting detailed information about other providers that includes the following: scope and type of services provided, including treatment modalities, theoretical base, and use of best practices, and other relevant business information, including program history, capacity, staff credentialing, accreditation status, any limitations to service delivery, and any other relevant demographic information about the program and/or organization (e.g., other programs operated by organization). When conducting a market analysis, it is important to not only identify those providers that are engaged in direct interventions for the identified problem(s) (e.g., counseling services to battered women) but also those that may be involved indirectly (e.g., transitional housing for battered women), as these providers may be essential *community resources*. Taken together, these four activities provide comprehensive information about the target region and allow the program developer to systematically identify the problem(s) while becoming more informed about other relevant aspects of the region that will be critical in the program design. As such, a well-researched rationale is developed to provide evidence for the need for program development.

Step II: Establish a Research Basis for Program Design

Once effective justification for the program has been established, work can begin in developing the research basis for the program. This critical step is necessary to establish an empirical basis for the program and requires the completion of an extensive review of the literature. The literature review should minimally include three primary areas: scholarly research; best practice literature developed by professional associations, governmental bodies (e.g., Bureau of Justice), or other such bodies with relevant knowledge of the problem; and practice standards and other literature compiled by relevant accrediting bodies (e.g., Council on Accreditation).

In conducting a review of the scholarly literature for the purpose of new program development, the review should be comprehensive and include the exploration of several key areas. These include various types of data analyses regarding the identified problem (e.g., demographic issues related to sexual offending behaviors among adolescent males), empirically based studies related to the problem, research related to specific clinical interventions to address the problem, results of relevant program evaluations, literature reviews of research related to the problem, meta-analyses related to the problem, and position papers and other scholarship dedicated to examining and addressing the problem.

To complement the review of scholarly literature, best practice standards, white papers, and other literature developed by individuals, organizations (e.g., national task forces), and professional associations relevant to the problem should be examined. Whereas this type of literature is not typically published through traditional scholarly outlets, it is often the result of research findings and emphasizes practice and application. Conducting an exhaustive review of the current literature related to the problem that includes both scholarly research and other literature can be used to establish the empirical foundation for program design.

Step IIa: Address Cultural Identity Issues in Program Design

A significant subcomponent of the literature review involves specifically focusing on multicultural aspects. Addressing multicultural considerations in the program design does not constitute an independent step because it is simply part of the literature review; however, because of its significance and scope, it is specifically identified as a subset of Step II and a complete chapter is devoted to it.

Data gleaned from initial assessment activities (i.e., community demography assessment, community needs and assets assessment) are reviewed to ensure that the literature review addresses all unique aspects of the community population, thereby promoting culturally competent program design. For instance, if much of the research on the treatment of eating disorders focuses on white female adolescents and teens and your target population in need of treatment of eating disorders is Latino and white young adult males, specific attention must be given to program modifications that can effectively address the differential needs of your population.

Additionally, attention must constantly be given to exploring issues related to the target population's cultural identity throughout program implementation to ensure that program modifications are continuously made to support the dynamic nature of multiculturalism. For instance, whereas just 10 years ago it was more common to be married than single in adulthood, today it is more common to be single than married. In addition, whereas much research and literature has been devoted to African American studies in the past, the significant number of biracial and biethnic relationships producing bi- and multiracial and multiethnic children is again changing how race and ethnicity are perceived. Likewise, the increasingly global nature of our world is impacting the role that geography plays in cultural identity, while at the same time, the growing disparities between the upper and lower socioeconomic structures and diminishing middle class are creating new perceptions and meaning of class in the United States. These constantly changing patterns reflect what I mean by the dynamic nature of multiculturalism—there are always new and different cultural identity aspects that need to be considered and existing identity aspects that need to be reconsidered in order to understand precisely what meaning they have at any given time and to any given individual.

Because effective programs must be specifically designed for the individuals being served, multiculturalism and, more important, cultural competence (i.e., the use of specific knowledge and skills that effectively address the unique identity of the individual being served) are an inherent part of initial program design. In addition, cultural competence is a primary factor related to subsequent program modifications.

Step III: Design the Clinical Program

The program design consists of a comprehensive description of the program and utilizes specific design tools to illustrate the primary clinical components of the program. Articulated in the program design are the program vision and mission, clinical interventions, short- and long-term outcomes, and outcome measures.

The initial steps in program design involve revisiting both the philosophical/ideological foundations on which the program is built and the primary needs to be addressed by the program in order to articulate the program's vision and mission. These activities provide particular meaning to program design by allowing program developers to tie the primary needs and the ideological basis to the long-term vision of the program and broadly describe how and what the program attempts to achieve (i.e., mission). These initial design activities promote cohesion and provide direction for the more concrete steps of program design that follow.

Once the mission and vision of the program have been articulated, the core program design components consisting of clinical interventions, short- and long-term outcomes, and outcomes measures must be identified. The results of the literature review (Step II) provide the basis for program design and ensure that the identified clinical interventions have an empirical basis.

To assist in designing the clinical components of the program, a program planning tool such as a logic model (Alter & Egan, 1997) may be particularly helpful. A logic model is used to organize the design structure of the program and graphically should reflect a straightforward flow in program design. The logic model evolves forward from the identified need to the specific interventions to the intended outcomes of the interventions and the methods by which those outcomes will be measured. Using such a tool allows the program designer to effectively evaluate the coherence of the program design.

Step IV: Develop the Staffing Infrastructure

Once the program design has been determined, attention must be given to developing the appropriate *staffing infrastructure* necessary to implement the program. Considerations in this stage include identifying the *governance structure* (e.g., board of directors) if the program is being implemented as part of a new organization, administrative support positions (e.g., human resources, finance), program administrators (e.g., executive director, program director), management and supervisory staff, and direct service staff (e.g., counselors, case managers).

Several issues relative to the development of a staffing infrastructure that have particular significance to the program's effectiveness, efficiency, and sustainability should be considered. First, the results of the market analysis and logic model should be reexamined to determine the positions needed to implement each of the program's direct interventions. Second, the results of the market analysis should be reexamined to determine how similar program operations are structured. Finally, all key activities needed to fully operate the program must be identified (e.g., advocacy, oversight, finance). Each of these activities provides sound direction to decision making regarding each of the positions needed based on job duties.

The organizational chart provides a graph of the staffing infrastructure detailing reporting relationships, number of staff members employed, and specific duties of staff, thus making the various service components operational by identifying the responsibilities of the workforce. As a result, the use of an organizational chart is recommended to identify the necessary staffing infrastructure. Organizational structure provides the initial framework for organizational functioning and organizational behavior, and determining the appropriate structure requires consideration of organizational theory. Because this text cannot provide the level of detail needed for a full discussion of organizational theory, interested readers should pursue literature specifically on organizational theory to acquire deeper knowledge of this important topic. For the purpose of developing the organizational staffing structure in new program design, four issues should guide decision making: job duties of all positions, degree of need for supervisory and administrative support and oversight, organizational communication, and organizational decision making. Briefly, multiple layers of supervisory and management staff may prohibit efficient decision making and impact effective flow of communication throughout the program. Again, by allowing perceived effectiveness and efficiency in program operations to guide decision making regarding staffing infrastructure, the developmental process related to the staffing infrastructure should proceed smoothly.

Step V: Identify and Engage Community Resources

Initial community resource development involves the identification of various community resources consisting of like programs, organizations, or professionals and the identification of the methods by which such community resources will be utilized in program implementation. Some community resources may augment program service components as primary referral sources, whereas others may become part of a collective advocacy group.

The initial work in community resource development occurs as part of the asset map and market analysis that are conducted in the initial program planning step (i.e., establishing a need). At this point, precisely how the community resources will be utilized in program implementation (e.g., Marijuana Anonymous) or program sustainability (e.g., local juvenile courts) must be determined. Finally, relationships with community resources must be formalized. Formalizing relationships between the program and the various community resources involves finalizing all details of the relationship, minimally including the role of each party, responsibilities, and lines of communication. Ideally, community resource development should be guided by three key factors: utilization of current community resources to augment service array, coalition building with competitors and other invested stakeholders to increase advocacy strength, and development of strategic partners and supporters for long-term program sustainability.

Step VI: Identify and Evaluate Potential Funding Sources

Identifying potential funding sources requires extensive research that includes exploring all potential types of funding sources related to the specific type of mental health counseling program developed, including governmental sources at the local (e.g., county health department), state (e.g., state department of mental health), and national levels (e.g., National Institutes of Health) and nongovernmental sources (e.g., Annie E. Casey Foundation). During this phase, it is again necessary to revisit the market analysis to examine the funding sources related to all current providers and gain more specific information related to the parameters of funding (e.g., term, limitations) as well as any other pertinent information (e.g., success/lack of success with particular funders, lessons learned, relationships with funders).

In completing this phase, it is necessary to gather extensive information about each potential funding source. This information should minimally include the following: (1) primary focus of funding source (e.g., children's mental health), (2) amount of available funding, (3) length of funding (e.g., 1 year, unlimited), (4) terms and restrictions related to funding, (5) history of funding source, and (6) other pertinent information. Additionally, distinctions should be made between contractual funders and grant funders as two discrete, often noncompeting funding sources that may be used concurrently. Finally, all potential donors and types of potential donations should be identified.

Step VII: Develop the Financial Management Plan

Developing a financial management plan requires projections on both expenditures and revenues and comprehensive planning. The program budget details total annual expenditures that include both personnel (e.g., salaries, fringe benefits) and nonpersonnel costs (e.g., rent, insurance, professional development, evaluation instruments). Line-item budgets should be used to provide detailed information on all expenditures. Particular care must be taken to ensure a thorough examination of all real costs and potential related costs. Conversely, the revenue report should identify all actual and potential funding sources, amounts of funding and any terms or restrictions related to funding (e.g., term-limited, restricted to nonpersonnel costs), including monetary and nonmonetary donations (e.g., building space). It is recommended that great caution be given when identifying donations in the financial report, particularly because this type of funding may lack certainty and is often limited to one-time events. As a result, donations should be considered as extraneous to other forms of funding.

It is recommended that the financial management plan is developed for 3 to 5 years to reflect long-term planning and to promote increased understanding of the financial implications involved in program development. The financial management plan is intricately tied to other aspects of program implementation and program sustainability, directly reflecting expenditures related to organizational infrastructure and real and potential funding sources. Whereas funding sources are initially identified as specific to financial implications, the following step is dedicated to a broader exploration of potential funding sources.

Step VIII: Develop the Proposal

Developing a proposal for a clinical program requires pulling together what has been learned through the *comprehensive needs assessment* process and articulating the program design, staffing structure, and budget information. It is in the proposal development step that you are able to utilize the sum of work completed in program planning and craft the most effective argument for funding the program.

Because specific proposal development is extremely varied and based on the type of funding opportunity being pursued, the chapter on this step deals with essential considerations of proposal development. These include the use of a grant writer versus program developer, the use of internal reviewers, organizing the work of proposal development, and skills needed for proposal development.

Step IX: Implement the Program

Program implementation deals specifically with putting the program into place and the various tasks associated with initial implementation. Initially, this requires a thorough review of the contract/award and establishing an effective working relationship with the funding source/contract manager. On an ongoing basis, program implementation includes ensuring that the necessary structure exists to monitor and support the program throughout implementation. These activities include, but are not limited to, providing sufficient administrative and leadership support, acquiring and utilizing effective information systems, engaging in quality assurance activities, and ensuring contract compliance.

Step X: Evaluate the Program

Designing the evaluation program actually begins in the initial design of the clinical program phase with the identification and/or development of the clinical design, development of program outcomes, and the identification of measurement tools. At this later step dedicated to finalizing the program evaluation, three specific types of evaluation should be considered: fidelity assessment, process evaluation, and outcomes evaluation. Whereas both fidelity assessment and process evaluation deal with program implementation, outcomes evaluation focuses on the program's success or lack thereof. The relationship between interventions and goals is reexamined, and both short- and long-term outcome goals are finalized with identified time frames for attainment. Additionally, outcomes measures are reexamined to determine their appropriateness in assessing the established outcomes.

Selection of assessment tools should focus on the relevance of the tool to specific issues (e.g., depression inventory to screen for depression) and the efficacy of the assessment tools (i.e., reliability and validity of the measure). More than one method of assessment for each outcome is recommended to increase the reliability of the evaluation results. For instance, published standardized assessment tools (e.g., substance abuse assessment) in conjunction with observable or other concrete forms of assessment (e.g., urine screen) may be used concurrently to increase the strength of the evaluation results. Finally, data collection methods (e.g., initial intake interview), responsibility for data collection and analysis, and time frames (e.g., 6 months post-discharge) are determined in the evaluation design phase.

The evaluation plan promotes accountability, directly tying interventions to outcomes and identifying a process and time frames for outcomes to be evaluated. Moreover, evaluation planning allows clinicians to modify the original program design as a result of the evaluation. As such, evaluation planning and program design are dynamic activities that are often modified over time, contributing to the promotion of evidence-based practices.

Step XI: Build and Preserve Community Resources

Because community resource development is predicated on relationships between two entities (program and community resource), it is necessary to view community resource development as consisting of two essential components: identifying and engaging community resources (Step V) and building and preserving these relationships. By viewing community resource development in this manner, the significance of these relationships is reflected.

Whereas community resources were identified and the relationships were formalized in an earlier step, Step XI focuses specifically on continuous efforts to build and preserve these relationships. Establishing regular and frequent times for communication and instituting regular venues for information sharing are two examples of methods by which to continuously attend to relationships with community resources.

This type of community resource relationship building may yield concrete benefits of ensuring continued business *partnerships* when services are being provided by the community resource; however, there are also potential indirect benefits to such relationship building that cannot be overlooked. By promoting strong relationships with community resources, programs often may create new factions of support systems for use in community advocacy efforts, program promotion, and securing new and continued funding. As such, community resources play a pivotal role in developing, implementing, and sustaining successful clinical programs and, therefore, must be given focused attention throughout a program's life cycle.

Step XII: Develop an Advocacy Plan

Advocacy planning is critical to program sustainability, and continuous advocacy planning ensures that the program is responsive to environmental changes, as well as that the public remains aware of specific treatment needs being met through programming (e.g., child sexual abuse survivors). Advocacy planning includes the identification of all governmental and nongovernmental entities with whom the program will engage in advocacy efforts (e.g., increase funding for adolescent mental health), identification of community partners with whom advocacy coalitions might be formed—drawing directly from previous community resource efforts—and the articulation of multiple concrete methods of advocacy to be completed annually by the program (e.g., participation in public hearings, engaging a lobbyist). Depending on the type of program designed, advocacy efforts may be varied and include such activities as participating in public hearings, engaging a lobbyist, and facilitating regular forums to discuss advocacy issues with community partners. Ideally, multiple factions of advocates should be engaged and varied methods should be utilized to promote broad-based advocacy and to ensure that client needs continue to be promoted through public venues. Additionally, it is necessary to engage in advocacy efforts at the local, state, national, and international levels. Whereas initial advocacy begins in the program development phase, particularly in establishing the need for the program, program sustainability is often largely predicated on public awareness of specific treatment needs. As a result, advocacy efforts should be embedded throughout program operations in order to be systematically and continuously promoted.

Step XIII: Develop an Information-Sharing Plan

Once the evaluation program has been designed, it is necessary to develop plans for data reporting. Whereas outcomes data generated from the evaluation program are an integral part of a program data set, output data (e.g., number of clients served) and other relevant program data (e.g., staff credentials, operating costs) are also critical components that together provide a comprehensive picture of the program. It is therefore essential that this data is regularly shared with stakeholders. To accomplish this, a comprehensive data-reporting plan should be developed.

The data-reporting plan should minimally include types of data to be reported (e.g., outcomes evaluation, outputs), reporting time frames (e.g., quarterly, annually), individuals and entities to whom data will be reported (e.g., funding sources, community members, staff), and methods of data reporting (e.g., written report, meeting). Whereas all relevant program data and information should also be captured in the program's annual report, attention must be given to determining shorter and more frequent time frames for reporting data to promote increased accountability in program design. In fact, doing so may promote a culture of transparency and continuous evaluation, both of which are integral to the program's long-term sustainability.

Step XIV: Attain Program and Organizational Accreditation

The final step in comprehensive clinical program development involves accreditation planning. Whereas accreditation is a voluntary process and may be less relevant for certain types of programs than others, attainment of accreditation reflects the program's commitment to best practices and continuous evaluation. Accreditation standards are typically established as a result of current research and best practices. As such, accreditation can be used to guide ongoing program development as well as reinforce the integrity of the program.

Initial accreditation planning involves identifying an appropriate accrediting body(ies) and establishing a time frame by which to pursue accreditation. National accrediting bodies specific to clinical programs include but are not limited to the Council on Accreditation (COA) and the Joint Council on Accreditation of Health Organizations (JCAHO). Pursuit of accreditation is a lengthy process and, as such, requires long-term planning. Additionally, accreditation creates an ongoing expense incurred by the program and organization. As a result, thoughtful consideration must be given to determine when to pursue accreditation. Ideally, accreditation expenses should be reflected in the initial annual budget to prepare the program's stakeholders for the ongoing expenditures as well as to reflect the program's commitment to pursuing accreditation. Activities related to accreditation and reaccreditation impact all stages of program development and often strengthen the program by emphasizing the use of best practices in design, promoting a culture of evaluation and program accountability. Therefore, it is recommended that attention be given to accreditation planning throughout a program's life cycle.

Recall that at the beginning of the chapter, I raised the notion that comprehensive program development in the mental health professions is akin to business planning. I hope that this has become clearer from your reading so far. And to further clarify the relationship between basic business principles and comprehensive program development, take a moment to compare the basic business principles that were presented earlier with the comprehensive program development model in Figure 1.2. Table 1.1 illustrates this relationship.

Table 1.1 Comparison of Basic Business Principles and Comprehensive Program Development Model Steps

Basic Business Principles	Comprehensive Program Development Model Steps
Identifying a need for services	Establishing the need for programming
Utilizing research to guide product/service development	Establishing a research basis
Utilizing research to guide product/service development	Addressing cultural identity issues in program design
Developing the most effective product/service	Designing the clinical program
Developing an effective and efficient infrastructure	Developing the staffing infrastructure
Effectively managing finances	Developing the financial management plan
Continuously identifying customers	Identifying and evaluating funding sources
Developing key relationships to support and sustain your business	Building and preserving relationships
Employing a lobbyist	Developing an advocacy plan
Ensuring that you have the best product/service to offer	Evaluating the program
Regularly sharing your success with stakeholders	Developing an information-sharing plan
Garnering national recognition	Attaining program and organizational accreditation

As you can see, comprehensive program development and traditional business planning are not at all conflicting but, rather, are completely synonymous. It is in this way that I hope you may develop—if you have not already done so—a keen appreciation for the *business* that is the mental health profession.

About the Text

Terminology

What is meant by the term *mental health professionals*? Mental health professionals include master's- and doctoral-level practitioners in counseling, psychology (clinical and counseling psychology only), and social work. The primary objectives of each of these disciplines are to help individuals and groups through the use of various types of clinical interventions. Whereas the disciplines differ in specific areas, they share more commonalities than differences, and therefore, the inclusive term *mental health profession/professional* is commonly used today. This is the term most often used throughout this text. Marriage and family therapists are also included under the umbrella of mental health professionals, as are psychiatrists that engage in counseling.

The terms *program developer, program administrator,* and *mental health professional* are used throughout the text, primarily to denote the various roles that mental health professionals fulfill. *Mental health professional* refers to the primary identity of the professional, whereas it is indeed mental health professionals that serve in the roles of program developer, program administrator, program manager or supervisor, program evaluator, and chief executive officer in mental health and human services today.

The terms *human services* and *mental health programs* are also used interchangeably throughout the text. These refer to programs that are designed to address human, social, emotional, and behavioral needs. These programs are typically funded through governmental, foundation, or other philanthropic support and may exist as single-program organizations, part of multifaceted organizations, or within primary, secondary, and postsecondary educational institutions. Whereas the primary focus of this text is on nonprofit human service and mental health organizations, with the exception of funding and financial management, the material in the text is just as applicable to for-profit organizations.

Finally, the terms *counseling* and *therapy* are used interchangeably throughout the text. Both terms refer to the therapeutic practice in which master's- and doctoral-level mental health professionals (e.g., counselors, clinical/counseling psychologists, clinical social workers) engage.

Layout of the Text

The text centers on the *Comprehensive Program Development Model,* with a full chapter dedicated to each of the 14 steps (with a separate chapter devoted to multicultural considerations, which is actually a part of Step II of the model). Each of the chapters provides specific background information to increase understanding of each major task (i.e., step) involved in program development, and unique tools are provided to guide program development activities. Case vignettes are used at the beginning of each chapter to illustrate the importance of the specific step presented in the chapter, and case illustrations are used at the end of each chapter to highlight the material presented in the chapter. A summary chapter is provided as a brief review of the text and to offer significant issues for consideration in future program development efforts. A list of key words is provided in the back of the book, composed of key concepts presented throughout the text. A list of web-based resources is provided in the Appendix at the end of the book, composed of websites and specific resources discussed throughout the text.

Intended Users

The text is designed for master's- and doctoral-level practitioners and students in any of the major mental health professions (counseling, clinical and counseling psychology, and social work) as well as practicing mental health professionals and managers and leaders of mental health and human service organizations. The purpose of the text is to provide effective guidance and tools to current or future mental health professionals engaged in program development efforts. Such efforts might take place in a nonprofit human service organization, outpatient clinic, school, university, or governmental organization dedicated to serving individuals in need (e.g., state child welfare system, prison). Because of the nature of the framework provided in the text, the text has specific utility to the practical application of comprehensive program development.

Summary

Mental health treatment has changed dramatically, particularly in the past 2 decades. With the advent of managed care and the continued development of knowledge related to mental health treatment, the mental health industry has increasingly become more scientific and rigorous than ever before. As a result, the use of evidence-based practices is a standard requirement for counselors and other mental health professionals. At the same time, mental health professionals are increasingly responsible for the development of comprehensive mental health programs—programs that must be research-based. Therefore, mental health professionals must both understand and appreciate evidence-based practices but also the manner in which evidence-based practices are used in the development of comprehensive mental health and human service programs.

Comprehensive program development in the mental health professions involves design, implementation, and evaluation and, as a result, requires broad-based planning and a tremendous amount of work. Additionally, program development requires scientific, business, and clinical knowledge and skills. Because mental health professionals are often responsible for program design and program administration, it is essential that they are fully competent in comprehensive clinical program development. Clinical program design provides an essential component of program development; however, without completing due diligence to determine the viability of a clinical program (i.e., established need, funding) and possessing basic budget and management skills, it is almost impossible to implement a program. Moreover, without advocacy and leadership skills and program evaluation abilities, sustaining comprehensive mental health programs can be incredibly challenging.

The text provides a framework to guide mental health professionals in comprehensive program development. By using the text, it is hoped that mental health professionals will be better prepared to engage in clinical program development and gain increased appreciation for the complexities inherent in comprehensive program development. Furthermore, it is hoped that the use of such a framework will support mental health professionals in continuing to make even greater strides in the 21st century by responding effectively to a climate influenced by evidence-based practices that is wholly complemented by well-rounded business acumen.

REFLECTION AND DISCUSSION QUESTIONS

Please take a few minutes to reflect on the following questions before moving on to the next chapter:

1. What barriers might exist for you in developing a mental health/human service program?

2. Which of the steps involved in the comprehensive program development model do you believe might be the most challenging? Why?

3. What information provided in this chapter would be beneficial to you in developing a program? Why?

4. What are your thoughts and reactions about the *business* of the mental health professions and the notion that business skills are an essential requirement for today's mental health professionals?

References

Alter, C., & Egan, M. (1997). Logic modeling: A tool for teaching critical thinking in social work practice. *Journal of Social Work Education, 33,* 85–102.

Calley, N. G. (2007). Integrating theory and research: The development of a research-based treatment program for juvenile sex offenders. *Journal of Counseling and Development, 85,* 131–142.

Chatterji, P., Caffray, C. M., & Crowe, M. (2004). Cost assessment of a school-based mental health screening and treatment program in New York City. *Mental Health Services Research, 6,* 155–166.

Donahue, S. A., Lanzara, C. B., Felton, C. J., Essock, S. M., & Carpinello, S. (2006). Project Liberty: New York's crisis counseling program created in the aftermath of September 11, 2001. *Psychiatric Services, 57,* 1253–1258.

Gibbs, L. (2003). *Evidence-based practice for the helping professions: A practical guide.* Pacific Grove, CA: Brooks/Cole.

Haggard-Grann, U. (2007). Assessing violence risk: A review and clinical recommendations. *Journal of Counseling and Development, 85,* 294–302.

Hansen, J. T. (2007). Should counseling be considered a health care profession? Critical thoughts on the transition to a health care ideology. *Journal of Counseling and Development, 85,* 286–293.

Hensley, L. G. (2002). Treatment for survivors of rape: Issues and interventions. *Journal of Mental Health Counseling, 24,* 330–347.

Hill, N. R. (2007). Wilderness therapy as a treatment modality for at-risk youth: A primer for mental health counselors. *Journal of Mental Health Counseling, 29*, 338–349.

Hill, N. R., & Beamish, P. M. (2007). Treatment outcomes for obsessive-compulsive disorder: A critical review. *Journal of Counseling and Development, 85*, 504–510.

Institute of Medicine. (2001). *Crossing the quality chasm: A new health system for the 21st century.* Washington, DC: National Academy Press.

Kelley, S. D. M., English, W., Schwallie-Giddis, P., & Jones, L. M. (2007). Exemplary counseling strategies for developmental transitions of young women with attention-deficit/hyperactivity disorder. *Journal of Counseling and Development, 85*, 173–181.

Khamphakdy-Brown, S., Jones, L. N., & Nilsson, J. E. (2006). The empowerment program: An application of an outreach program for refugee and immigrant women. *Journal of Mental Health Counseling, 28*, 38–47.

Marotta, S. A., & Watts, R. E. (2007). An introduction to the best practices section. *Journal of Counseling and Development, 85*, 491–503.

Mejia, X. (2005). Gender matters: Working with adult male survivors of trauma. *Journal of Counseling and Development, 83*, 29–40.

Puterbaugh, D. T. (2006). Communication counseling as part of a treatment plan for depression. *Journal of Counseling and Development, 84*, 373–381.

Sackett, D. L., Strauss, S. E., Richardson, W. S., Rosenberg, W., & Haynes, R. B. (2000). *Evidence-based medicine: How to practice and teach* (2nd ed.). London: Churchill Livingstone.

Wilderman, R. (2005). A practical and inexpensive model for outpatient mental health evaluation. *Dissertation Abstracts International, 65*, 3734(B).

PART I

PROGRAM PLANNING AND IMPLEMENTATION

CHAPTER 2

Establish the Need for Programming

Developing the Rationale

Learning Objectives

1. Understand the significance of identifying a need in comprehensive program development

2. Identify and explain the methods and tools used in identifying a need for programming, including community demography assessment, asset map, and market analysis

3. Identify four strategies for use in the development of survey and/or focus group discussion questions

4. Explain how to effectively analyze the sum of data collected in order to use it in decision making related to program development

IF WE BUILD IT, THEY WILL COME

Tim's agency had been providing community-based juvenile justice services for the past 4 years, and Tim was anxious to grow the business more. Recently, at a conference out of state, he had learned about adventure-based interventions and had participated in a tour of a ropes course that one of the agencies had. Thinking about this more on the plane ride home, Tim realized that his state did not have anything like this, so he began planning in his mind how he might develop such a program. Energized, he drew up a basic outline of what the program might look like and discussed it with three of his key staff members. They, too, were excited about the possibility of new programming, so Tim scheduled an emergency meeting with his board to present the idea to them. Tim outlined his basic business plan, which included purchasing land and a small building or house that could be used for office space for a small staff. The land would be used to develop a ropes course and other outside activity areas so that the agency could begin providing adventure-based interventions for juvenile offenders. Tim stated that he would use a bank loan and a small portion of the agency's endowment to purchase the real estate, and he quickly showed how both the loan and the endowment monies could be repaid in less than 10 years as a result of the revenue that the new program would bring—using the numbers that the out-of-state program had presented. Everyone's ears perked up when they heard about these rates, especially in comparison with the relatively low per diem rate that the agency's community-based program currently generated. Tim further stated that he had spoken to a couple of the leaders of his funding agency—the state Department of Human Services—and they had expressed an interest in the program; so Tim was sure they would want to use the program as an additional treatment option for youth in the juvenile justice system. In addition, Tim thought there might be a market for other youth and/or adults in need of an alternative treatment to use the ropes course. After answering more questions about the new program, Tim had thoroughly convinced his board members and staff that this really was something that they needed to do. In fact, he stressed that since adventure-based interventions were very new, the agency had an opportunity to get in on the ground level by offering the state the first program of its kind, but they had to move quickly if they were going to do it. Without hesitation, Tim was given the green light, and he and his staff quickly got to work finding the real estate and developing the program. Six months later, they held the grand opening for the new adventure center. Tim had had several conversations with the Department of Human Services about the possibility of acquiring a contract for the services, but the state administrators stated that they had just instituted a moratorium on any contracts for new programs through the next fiscal year. As an aside, one administrator also shared with Tim that she had not seen the research support for adventure-based interventions and told him that the state would have to verify the program's evidence basis before considering it at a later date—as was standard practice for all new contracts. Tim began talking to other potential funding sources and assigned two of his staff members to immediately explore philanthropic foundation funding to see if there was an interest in supporting the program. A year later, Tim had only managed to get a contract with an insurance company so that his ropes course could be an option for their clients, and over the next 6 months, Tim had two clients referred from the insurance contract. Tim was sweating—his agency was going more in debt every day, and his great new idea was not amounting to anything but a great loss. Tim began wondering how he had gotten himself into this, and more importantly, he began wondering how he would get himself out of it.

CONSIDERING TIM

1. What mistakes did Tim make, and how could they have been prevented?

2. As the agency's leader, what is Tim's responsibility to his staff and his board?

3. What is the board's responsibility?

4. If you were Tim, what would you do now?

About This Chapter

As you can see in the above case vignette, identifying if a problem constitutes a *need* for new programming requires a significant amount of work. This work involves conducting a *comprehensive needs assessment*, including gathering community demography data, conducting a *problem analysis* and an asset inventory, completing a market analysis, and determining if a need exists. The comprehensive needs assessment process forms the basis of this chapter because it is the critical ingredient in establishing a rationale for new (or expanded) program development.

This chapter examines the initial step in comprehensive program development—*establishing the need for programming*. This step is viewed as the *preplanning stage*, since the outcome of this phase will determine if movement into actual program planning is justified. At times, the results of the comprehensive needs assessment may simply reinforce the need for programming, while at other times, the results will not support new programming.

And sometimes, the results will not indicate a need for the type of programming that had originally been thought to be needed, but another need for programming may emerge that directs your program planning energies elsewhere (such as the case that Gerri, Kari, and Jamie discovered, detailed in the case illustration at the end of this chapter).

We will explore the significance of data collection and analysis and the subsequent use of data-driven decision making throughout the chapter, just as illustrated in the above example. In addition, we will examine the comprehensive needs assessment thoroughly with specific tools provided to guide each component of the assessment process. Finally, we will explore methods by which to effectively summarize and report on all the data collected and analyzed, along with specific tips on data collection tools.

STEP I: ESTABLISH THE NEED FOR PROGRAMMING

Developing the Rationale

If you have worked as a mental health or social service practitioner, you have likely thought at one time or another, "If only there were a program for _____" or "We are in desperate need of a program for _____." Perhaps the space could be filled in with substance abuse prevention for preteens, autism, eating disorders, or traumatic brain injury, or with many of the myriad issues that currently impact our world. Other often emphatic statements you may have heard or shared personally might include "Violent crime is on the rise," "Teen pregnancy is an epidemic in urban areas," or "Anger management is desperately needed here." Whereas in some cases these statements may have some factual basis, often they are simply reactions to specific occurrences that cause us to believe that an issue is much greater than it actually is. For instance, during one of my most challenging times as a professional counselor working with juvenile offenders, within a 3-week span, one of my clients attempted to murder a woman during a carjacking, another client was placed under suspicion of murdering his mother and soon thereafter committed suicide, and a third was killed on his front porch by a gang just prior to my visit to his home. In addition to extreme stress and sadness, these events led me to believe that violent crime was indeed an epidemic. They reinforced my thinking that there was a desperate need for additional programs to treat young offenders and that the programs we were currently using did not seem to be working very effectively. However, these beliefs were directly based on my personal experience and, as such, represented only a very limited view of reality. My view was subjective rather than objective, and objectivity is an essential ingredient in establishing a need for programming. Without comprehensive, objective data collection methods that provide empirical evidence and support for new program development, new program development cannot be—or more significantly, is not—justified. The question then becomes, how can we be certain that comprehensive and objective data exists that provides sound justification to support the need for new program development?

Identifying the Need Through Data Collection

To answer this question, several activities must be accomplished, including (1) identifying a target region, (2) identifying a target population, and (3) conducting a comprehensive needs assessment. These activities compose the preplanning stage of program development, focusing specifically on gathering extensive amounts of data and analyzing the data to examine any needs that may exist. By engaging in this type of in-depth investigation at the preplanning stage, you are able to make sound decisions about initial program development that are supported by data. This is referred to as *data-based decision making* and may well be one of the most significant skills of a program developer. Ultimately, the results of the comprehensive needs assessment and analysis will provide evidence or justification as to what, if any, type of program is needed in a particular region. In addition, the results of the comprehensive needs assessment will tell you if new program development is a feasible pursuit when a need does exist.

Identifying a Target Region

Before moving into a deeper discussion of the needs assessment and analysis, it is necessary to first identify the broad region or area in which it is anticipated a new program may be implemented. This is considered the target region. The term *target region*, historically used in research efforts, today is also widely used by funding sources as an identifying factor related to service delivery.

When determining a target region, there are several factors that must be taken into consideration, including geographic size, population size, and population diversity. Each of these factors will likely have a direct impact on data collection and, subsequently, on the results of the data collection. Because geographic area does not necessarily impact population size, both geographic size and population size must be assessed individually and together. For instance, a city in rural South Dakota may be two to three times as physically large as an urban city such as Chicago and, at the same time, may have less than 1% of the population of Chicago. As a result, the diversity of individuals and needs will likely be limited to the number of individuals in a given area. This can have an impact on not only the types and range of needs and assets noted in a particular region but also the subsequent financial implications related to delivery of new programming (i.e., location of program, mileage considerations for clients and/or personnel).

Consider this for instance: Schizophrenia and other serious mental health disorders may be identified as a significant problem impacting 35% of the population in a town in rural South Dakota; however, 35% of the population is composed of just four individuals. As a result of this small number of individuals in need of specialized treatment, it may be financially (i.e., supporting a clinician to provide treatment, mileage costs incurred from driving to and from clients that are scattered throughout a broad region) and logistically challenging (i.e., finding someone to hire on a contractual basis with specialized skills and knowledge) to develop programming in the region to address these needs.

However, just as particular regions may prove challenging for program developers because of the number of individuals impacted by a specific problem and the geographic distances between individuals in need, mental health professionals/program developers must be fundamentally guided by the notion that all individuals have the right to access needed treatment. As such, the concept of social justice must be considered as an underlying force in all program development, working to ensure that equity and access to services are provided to all individuals in need. *In fact, did you not pursue this type of work precisely because you wanted to make a difference in the lives of those in need?* Therefore, specific regions should not be discounted simply because there are too few individuals or too few similar problems, but rather these areas must be considered in sum with other contiguous areas, and program design should be innovative enough to address any specific logistical challenges. So to ensure that the needs of the four individuals in rural South Dakota with serious mental health disorders are met, a program might be developed to include not only that particular region but two other contiguous regions that together account for a total of 12 individuals in need (i.e., 12 clients).

The program design may then consist of biweekly, home-based individual therapy (alternating weeks), biweekly multifamily support in a central location, and monthly medication monitoring (if needed). Staffing for the program may consist solely of one full-time clinical case manager (master's-level counselor or other master's-level clinician who has a blended role of therapist and case manager/resource coordinator) and one contractual psychiatrist. By structuring the program in this way with a minimal number of key staff, effective treatment can be provided (i.e., family support, individual interventions, psychiatric care) in a delivery format that consists of both home-based and center-based services, thus sharing transportation responsibilities while promoting broader community support (i.e., multifamily support sessions).

As I hope this example illustrates, there are indeed several innovative ways in which regional challenges can be addressed. The goal then for determining a target region is ensuring a broad enough area to yield various forms of diversity (e.g., problems, individuals) while simultaneously ensuring that individual needs are not ignored due to size constraints. Not limiting the target region by either geographic size or population size but, rather, treating the target region as flexible, with the ability to expand or reduce as needed, will allow for this to be accomplished.

Identifying a Target Population

Once a target region has been identified, a target population must be selected. Just as a number of factors must be considered in determining the target region, careful consideration must be given to determining the target population. The target population refers to the primary or core group of individuals to whom you ultimately plan to deliver services. Whereas it is important to not limit your target population to the point that you are unable to acknowledge significant needs of multiple groups, it is equally important to identify any specific population characteristics that you are most interested in treating. In making these initial decisions, the following questions may be helpful to consider:

- Is there a particular age group that I am targeting (e.g., teens, adults, elderly)?
- Is there a particular gender group that I am targeting (i.e., females, males)?
- Is there a special condition or circumstance that I am targeting (e.g., displaced workers, high school dropouts)?
- Is there a special need that I am targeting (e.g., mental health, addiction)?

As you can imagine, the degree to which a target population is identified may vary greatly. For example, here are some possible target populations in ascending order of specificity to illustrate the degrees to which you may specify a population:

- Elderly individuals (defines one age group)
- Elderly individuals with mental health care needs (defines one age group with broad clinical needs)
- Elderly individuals with major depression (defines one age group with a specific clinical need)
- Elderly individuals with major depression living independently (defines one age group with a specific clinical need in a particular living situation)

Whereas it is essential that both a target region and a target population be identified in order to conduct the needs assessment, both of these areas must be viewed as tentative since the results of the needs assessment may suggest otherwise. For instance, as you work through the needs assessment process, you might discover that there is a greater need for substance abuse treatment for adult women even though you had originally targeted male adolescents. Likewise, you may find that within your initially targeted region there is not a need for new program development to treat gambling as you had originally thought; however, two other nearby regions do have this need. This type of tentative thinking is another essential skill that you need to conduct an effective preplanning assessment since it allows you to be open to the data that is presented and able to flexibly change directions in new program development when warranted.

Comprehensive Needs Assessment and Analysis

Once the target region and the target population have been identified, a comprehensive needs assessment and analysis must be conducted. "A needs assessment describes the target population or community, including demographic characteristics, the extent of relevant problems or issues of concern, and current services" (Lewis, Packard, & Lewis, 2007, p. 29). A comprehensive needs assessment consists of a methodical and comprehensive evaluation of existing needs and assets and allows for sound initial decision making regarding new program development. Moreover, a needs assessment allows you to identify the gap between a target population's needs and existing services, providing essential information about how new programming can be designed to most effectively respond to needs (Darboe & Ahmed, 2007).

To conduct a comprehensive needs assessment, the following assessment and analysis activities must be completed:

1. Assessment of demographic characteristics of the community

2. Analysis of problem(s)

3. Analysis of existing treatment and service providers in the region

4. Identification of needs

5. An inventory of assets

To accomplish these assessment and analysis activities, five tools are needed. Table 2.1 illustrates each of these methods with its corresponding tool.

Table 2.1 Comprehensive Needs Assessment Methods and Tools

Data Collection Method	Data Collection Tool
Assessment of community demography	Community demography assessment
Analysis of problem(s)	Problem analysis tool
Analysis of current market	Market analysis
Identification of needs	Identification of need tool
Inventory of assets	Asset map

Taken alone, each of these five data sets provides important information about a given region but not enough information to effectively act on. However, taken together, these five data sets provide comprehensive information to help engage in decision making about new program development and allow a clear and accurate portrait of the region to emerge. I liken this process to shuffling through various sequences of letters during a visit to the optometrist. As you move up the chart, the lines become a bit more focused until you reach the line that provides you all the information needed to see clearly what is in front of you (see Figure 2.1).

The amount of work required to conduct a comprehensive needs assessment is tremendous and requires a great deal of attention to detail, objectivity, and trust in allowing the data to guide the decision-making process. In short, a scientific approach must be adopted in order to complete an effective needs assessment. Whereas the process may seem both tedious and challenging, the outcomes of the assessment and analysis easily justify the amount of work involved.

Figure 2.1 Ingredients Needed to Gain an Accurate Picture of the Region

Comprehensive Needs Assessment
Asset Map
Identification of Needs
Market Analysis
Problem Identification
Community Demography Assessment
Ndnigydgidios

Olndigkxoiwlighpwwog

Pfleoighwjgpopdt

Specific Challenges in Conducting a
Comprehensive Needs Assessment

To ensure the most accurate results, you must be sure to avoid specific challenges related to gathering comprehensive data. To aid in this, Finifter, Jensen, Wilson, and Koenig (2005) identified three key problems with conducting a needs assessment: (1) relying on intuition or anecdotal information rather than empirical evidence, (2) using one measure on a specific sector of the population that may not take into account the varying needs of specific subgroups (e.g., males vs. females, various ethnic groups) rather than collecting comprehensive data from various subgroups as well as the target population, and (3) completing a comprehensive needs assessment and failing to provide feedback to the various stakeholders and/or failing to implement programming to address any of the identified need(s) resulting from the assessment (stakeholders are all the various individuals, such as community members, officials, and various levels of professionals working in the region in schools, law enforcement, social service agencies, and other organizations, that are either directly or indirectly involved in the target region). Put another way, you must be careful to ensure that

- needs assessments are based on factual data,
- data collection is not limited to only the target population, and
- follow-up occurs to inform the various stakeholders about the results and next steps following completion of the needs assessment.

Strategies to Ensure a Successful
Needs Assessment and Analysis

Each of these challenges can be used to guide the development of a comprehensive needs assessment to ensure that such common mishaps can be avoided. In addition to avoiding these challenges, there are several specific recommendations that should be considered when designing a needs assessment:

1. Identify all the stakeholders in the target region.

2. Provide a full explanation of the needs assessment process to all stakeholders.

3. Garner stakeholder support prior to beginning the needs assessment.

4. Involve stakeholders in the design of the needs assessment process to ensure comprehensive data collection.

5. Gather multiple forms of empirical data from multiple sources.

6. Gather multiple forms of stakeholder input through a variety of tools.

7. Gather data on the broad population within the target area.

Briefly, the success of a needs assessment depends on its scope and accuracy, both of which are dependent on the involvement of a vast majority of the population or stakeholders. It is therefore necessary to first identify all the major stakeholders and provide a full explanation of the needs assessment process that includes the following:

- The reason for the needs assessment
- The types of data to be collected
- The types of data collection to be used
- The methods for ensuring the protection of the data and the privacy of individual participants
- The manner in which the data will be used
- The methods for reporting the results of the data collection process to the stakeholders

When conducting a comprehensive needs assessment, you must provide a full explanation of the needs assessment process to all participants in order to demonstrate ethical conduct; however, by fully explaining the purpose and the process, stakeholders may also become fully engaged in the process (an added benefit) and, as a result, may positively impact the data-collection process, increasing the scope of data collected. For instance, residents can inform you about the most effective methods to use to engage a broad part of the population and may suggest a visit to specific places of worship or informal clubs or associations as potential venues for reaching a diverse array of the population. Because residents and other stakeholders often have inside knowledge as to how their communities operate, they can provide significant guidance to you to ensure that no one is overlooked. It is in this manner also that stakeholders can be instrumental in further developing the needs assessment by identifying other potential methods for data collection that the program developer may not have considered and, thus, uncovering additional data.

The effective assessment of needs is crucial to any program development effort, and without it, effective planning is largely left to chance. In mental health and social service practice, a need refers to an existing social or clinical problem and an evident gap in services. Therefore, an untreated problem in a given area establishes a need for specific services. For instance, if a particular region has a high incidence of substance abuse among young adults and the community lacks substance abuse treatment programming, substance abuse is the identified problem and, subsequently, substance abuse treatment is the identified need. It is in this sense that social or clinical problems become translated into needs. A significant concern of program developers is ensuring the accurate identification of a problem and the subsequent accurate identification of a need. To accomplish this, an assessment of the region's problems must be conducted as well as an assessment of the existing market that is addressing the problems. Examined together, these two data sets will allow you to identify the existing gaps in treatment/services, thus identifying the needs. To further enhance the needs assessment and analysis process, two other data sets must be examined: demographic characteristics and assets of the community. Each of the five activities (i.e., methods) that compose the comprehensive needs assessment and analysis will be examined next, along with a discussion of each of the tools needed to complete each activity.

Data Collection Methods and Tools

Community Demography Assessment

The initial data to be collected involves broad-based demographic data about the target region and the target population. Demographic information about the community is essential to developing a clear understanding of the various population parameters and characteristics of the community. This type of data is some of the richest data available as it helps both broadly define a region/community as well as highlight some of the unique identity aspects of the community. Various types of empirical data are used to provide demographic information, often involving multiple data sources that include large-scale governmental data (e.g., U.S. Census, abuse and neglect data), state and regional data (e.g., local health department statistics, regional arrest rates), and region-specific data (e.g., high school dropout rate). I refer to this process of systematically gathering data sets, beginning with the largest data set (national data) and moving to the smallest data set (e.g., community data), as *data layering.* By collecting these various levels of data and comparing and contrasting the data through analysis, specific data begin to come into clearer focus and take on new meaning as it is compared with other data sets (as illustrated in the case study at the end of the chapter). For instance, national crime statistics may reveal a 28% drop in homicide rate over the past decade, but local crime statistics indicate a 32% increase in homicide over the past 3 years. This dramatic difference in data trends suggests that local crime is an area that may indeed represent a significant need and, as a result, must be further explored through data collection and analysis to increase understanding of the scope of the issue.

Demographic data typically is drawn from existing data sets; therefore, the task of the program developer is not to collect existing data sets but rather to collectively compile existing data sets in order to productively utilize the data through analysis. In short, the program developer must

1. identify an exhaustive list of the various types of data to be examined,

2. identify the corresponding data sources,

3. locate the data, and

4. conduct an in-depth examination and analysis of the data.

From the results of this endeavor, various types of trend data should begin to reveal detailed information and nuances about the region.

To gather the demographic information, a *Community Demography Assessment Tool* is used (see Box 2.1).

BOX 2.1

COMMUNITY DEMOGRAPHY ASSESSMENT TOOL

1. After identifying the target region and target population, determine the various types of empirically based demographic data needed to provide a comprehensive and accurate understanding of the region's population characteristics (e.g., age, gender, financial information) from all three levels: national, state, and local.

2. Identify the sources for each of the data sets: federal (e.g., U.S. Census data, U.S. Department of Health and Human Services data), state (e.g., state department of social services, state department of education), and local (e.g., county/city health department, police department, schools).

3. Identify the various aspects of cultural identity (e.g., religion/spirituality, ethnic groups, vocations, racial groups, first-generation immigrants) that are present in the environment through population characteristics, physical developments (e.g., places of worship, businesses), and other venues.

4. Gather the various data sets from the sources, accessing easily available published data electronically or in print format (e.g., governmental statistics) and communicate with state and local agency officials to acquire published data that is not easily accessible (e.g., schools, local agencies).

5. Comprehensively analyze the data sets, examining the data separately and in total, comparing the various data sets in order to note any trends (e.g., low socioeconomic status in region) or areas of significance (e.g., high regional incidence of high school dropout rate).

6. Following the analysis of all the demographic data, develop a brief community demography summary that highlights the various population parameters of the target region.

The guiding perspective of the community demography assessment is to collect enough data to ensure that an effective understanding of the population's characteristics can be achieved, especially as considered in conjunction with the region's unmet needs and assets/strengths.

Three types of data should be collected for the community demography assessment:

1. Federal governmental and other data collected at the national level (e.g., U.S. Census data, Centers for Disease Control data)

2. State governmental data and data collected by other organizations at the state level

3. Local data collected by local municipalities, schools, and other local organizations focused on the county, city, or town, including data related to specific physical structures relevant to various aspects of cultural identity

Whereas U.S. Census data should be gathered as part of any community demography assessment, other types of national data (e.g., child abuse and neglect data vs. addiction prevalence data) should be gathered as relevant to the target population and/or broad-based special condition or problem identified for future program development (e.g., children, addiction). The types of state and local data to be gathered should also be based on their relevance to the identified target population or initial target problem, with the perspective that more data is better than less data. If, for instance, the target population is children, demographic data from schools, state and local health departments, child welfare organizations, juvenile law enforcement and juvenile justice organizations, children's mental health and substance abuse organizations, schools, and other institutions dealing with children should be gathered.

The purpose of the *Community Demography Assessment Tool* is twofold, ensuring that comprehensive data is reviewed and allowing for the data to be organized in a meaningful manner to aid in data analysis. To ensure that the scope of the community demography data is inclusive, a list of specific national data sets that should be reviewed in most preplanning efforts is provided in Table 2.2.

With these initial data sets providing a sound starting point and the beginning foundation of demographic data, other essential data unique to the program development project must be identified and examined. For instance, if substance abuse has been identified as the broad-based need in a region, other essential demographic data may include items such as the prevalence of substance abuse in the community, primary types of illicit substances used, and primary age range of individuals that abuse substances. In addition, issues related to cultural identity must be explored to ensure that the various unique factors of the population are addressed in program design.

Cultural identity refers to the various aspects or characteristics that are assigned to us (what we have little to no control over/what we are born with or into), such as class, ethnicity, initial religious or spiritual beliefs, initial geography, language, class, race; the unique characteristics that we acquire on our own (e.g., education, class, religion/spirituality, intimate partner status); and the unique characteristics that impact us (e.g., historic events, chronic illness, death of loved ones; Arredondo & Glauner, 1992). By thinking

Table 2.2	Recommended Data Sets to Include in the Community Demography Assessment

Types of Data	Data Source	Data Source Location
Various types of demographic information per region/community that includes income, gender, age, etc.	U.S. Census Bureau	www.census.gov
National and state child abuse and neglect data	Child Welfare Information Gateway (Children's Bureau, Administration for Children and Families, U.S. Department of Health and Human Services)	www.childwelfare.gov
Physical health data	Centers for Disease Control and Prevention	www.cdc.gov
Mental health data	National Institute of Mental Health (National Institutes of Health)	www.nimh.nih.gov
Federal and state criminal justice data (crime, arrest, conviction)	Bureau of Justice Statistics (U.S. Department of Justice, Office of Justice Programs)	www.bjs.ojp.usdoj.gov
Federal and state juvenile justice data	Office of Juvenile Justice and Delinquency Prevention	www.ojjdp.ncjrs.gov
Educational data (elementary, secondary, postsecondary)	National Center for Education Statistics (U.S. Department of Education)	www.nces.ed.gov

about cultural identity in this manner, each of our unique cultural identities is composed of three dimensions or layers:

- That which we are born with or into
- That which we choose or direct
- That which happens to us that influences our identity development

These layers may converge with one another to create specific meaning at specific times (e.g., Arab American female in post-9/11 United States). As such, cultural identity is contextual—with certain aspects and/or the convergence of certain aspects giving unique meaning to us in specific places and at specific times. In fact, in the 1990s, I paid little attention to being Lebanese-American; however, after 9/11, I unfortunately found that much more attention was paid to me simply because of my Arabic background.

In terms of program development, cultural identity provides a rich source of information that often requires specific program interventions or modifications in order to respond effectively. For instance, age is one unique cultural identity variable that should be explored with relation to substance use, while other cultural identity aspects that should also be explored include employment status, marriage or intimate relationship status, ethnicity, and religion, to name just a few. Creating a culturally competent program requires gaining the awareness, knowledge, and skills necessary to effectively address various issues related to the cultural identity of clients. Whereas initial efforts toward increased understanding of multiculturalism occur in this preplanning stage of program development as a result of examining the population characteristics, effectively addressing these various cultural identity needs through treatment and service delivery occurs in program design (see Chapter 4).

Utilizing a variety of data collection tools that include, but are not limited to, telephone calls, data drawn from secondary sources (e.g., interviews with local social service providers/community developers), and focus groups, you must seek out specific information related to cultural identity and other demographic characteristics. When doing this, it is important to keep in mind that physical structures (e.g., places of worship, schools, nursing homes) and other data indicators (e.g., number of children receiving free lunch) are often rich sources of information about the characteristics of a region's population.

Using the *Community Demography Assessment Tool* helps organize your data-gathering process and allows you to examine the results of your efforts. Whereas the data is reviewed throughout the process individually, once all the relevant data has been gathered, you are able to view the sum of the community demography data and generate a rich portrait of the community.

Geographic information systems (GIS) may also prove helpful in the community demography assessment, as well as in other parts of the needs assessment process. In fact, the widespread availability of GIS software has proven useful in epidemiologic studies (Zandbergen & Green, 2007) and other community studies. As such, technologies such as this and others may continue to develop in the 21st century, providing us with ever more tools for use in better understanding communities.

Analysis of the Problem

After completing the community demography assessment, it is time to move to the next step in the needs assessment process: the analysis of problem(s) in the region. This second step draws directly from the community demography assessment, using the resulting data as foundational information about the region and thus providing a starting point for further investigation. Whereas the community demography assessment relies heavily on gathering large data sets from empirical data sources (e.g., governmental), the process of identifying existing problems in the region focuses on gathering more specific data sets (e.g., schools, health department) and gathering data from stakeholders (i.e., stakeholder input) through a variety of means. As discussed earlier in the chapter, stakeholders are critical to the success of the needs assessment process and, as such, great care must be taken in engaging stakeholders in the process, particularly during the problem analysis.

Stakeholder input can consist of various types of data such as perceived problems and needs of the target region, perceived changes in the target region (e.g., increase in the local homeless population), and opinions regarding methods to resolve potential issues. Whereas stakeholder data is an integral part of the problem analysis, a comprehensive array of both empirical and other data must also be collected to ensure accurate analysis. In fact, multiple forms of empirical data must be collected to enlarge the data picture and to ensure that specific data is not overlooked. A thorough problem analysis should yield a clear and accurate understanding of the problems and the scope of the problems in the region in the same manner that a thorough community demography assessment yields a complete picture of the community's population parameters. In order to maintain a systematic approach, the problem analysis must focus specifically on identifying and understanding the problem, not on generating solutions (Kettner, Moroney, & Martin, 2008).

To conduct the problem analysis, the *Problem Analysis Guide* can be used (see Box 2.2). To begin the analysis, data must first be gathered from various stakeholders. In fact, stakeholder input should be gathered from a broad faction of the population, again to ensure a comprehensive scope. Multiple methods should be used, including telephone, e-mail, face-to-face surveys and interviews, focus groups, and community forums.

BOX 2.2

PROBLEM ANALYSIS GUIDE

The problem analysis process is used to identify and prioritize the clinical needs of a population, allowing for a methodical and comprehensive evaluation of these needs. Ideally, the problem analysis process occurs immediately following completion of the community demography assessment so that the results of the community demography assessment are used to guide data collection in the problem analysis process.

1. Drawing from the community demography summary, identify any specific areas of particular relevance that require further information (e.g., drug[s] of choice among substance users, school dropout rate) in order to increase your understanding of the target population. Some of this data may not be readily available (e.g., primary behavioral issues witnessed in the school) and may require discussions with local officials and the development and use of various data-collection tools by the program developer (e.g., surveys, interview guides, focus group questions).

2. Identify the potential sources for each of the types of data needed.

3. Gather all available data from the sources.

4. Gain additional empirical/factual and informal input from agency officials about other characteristics of the target population and any perceived problems (e.g., increase in marijuana use among teens) and unmet needs in the region (e.g., lack of mental counseling services). Whereas it is ideal that this type of data be empirically based (drawn from existing records), if empirical data is not available regarding specific issues, gather as much informal data from credible sources (e.g., agency/institution officials, teachers) as possible to strengthen the data analysis process.

5. In addition to information regarding perceived problems and unmet needs, begin to gather data regarding existing assets and/or strengths within the region (e.g., community organizing, percentage of longtime residents).

6. Through communication with local officials (e.g., health department, schools, police), develop a plan for gathering additional informal information about any perceived problems, unmet needs, and assets/strengths in the region from various community members through focus groups, telephone or in-person interviews, surveys, or other venues.

(Continued)

(Continued)

7. Gather the informal data through the identified venues regarding perceived problems, unmet needs, and assets/strengths from various community members and other stakeholders (e.g., places of worship, business owners).

8. By carefully reviewing the results of the community demography summary with the various types of data gathered through the problem analysis process, identify each of the problems and then prioritize the problems, identifying two to four primary problems and the rationale for the prioritization.

9. Synthesizing the information about data types and methods from both the community demography assessment and the problem analysis process, develop a brief summary of findings outlining this. This summary—the *Data Collection Report*—should minimally include the following information:

- Types of data collected and rationale
- Data results
- Methods of data collection used
- Sources of data
- Data-collection time frames
- Limitations to data-collection methods (e.g., number of respondents, survey data vs. archival data)
- Exhaustive list of identified problems
- Two to four primary problems and the rationale for each

Because stakeholder input is gathered directly from individual stakeholders, it is imperative that tools used to gather such data are both efficient and effective—namely, that tools are able to generate the most necessary types of information in the shortest amount of time. Achieving both efficiency and effectiveness requires the development of specific questions that are designed to do just that. Unfortunately, survey/interview guide construction is an area that many struggle with, and as a result of poorly constructed surveys/interview guides, time may be spent collecting information that may not be highly useful. To avoid this and to promote the effective development of survey/interview questions, the following strategies may prove helpful:

- Limit the number of questions by ensuring that information generated from each question is absolutely necessary.
- Evaluate each question to determine if it is designed to generate the type of information that you are seeking.

- Identify the appropriate mixture of ranked question responses, closed-ended questions, and open-ended questions to yield both quantitative and qualitative data.
- When using ranked question responses, determine the type of scale to be used to yield the most effective data.
- Ensure that all questions are clearly focused on a single issue to reduce ambiguity in responses.
- Avoid double-barreled items that focus on more than one issue and, therefore, create challenges in interpreting results.
- Use age-appropriate language relevant to your participants.
- Capture any necessary demographic information about participants at the beginning of the survey.
- Provide informed consent to each of the participants and a full explanation of the rationale for gathering the data, privacy and confidentiality protections afforded to participants, and the manner in which the survey results will be used.

In addition to the strategies listed above, please refer to the *Survey Construction Tips* (Figure 2.2) for additional strategies to consider specifically when developing a survey, interview guide, or focus group questions.

Because informal data gathered through survey, focus groups, or interviews constitutes subjective data rather than empirical data, when summarizing the findings, it is essential that you fully explain the procedures and the findings to ensure an accurate understanding of the results. Minimally, in discussing the procedures, you should explain the method(s) by which the data was collected (e.g., survey, focus group, interview), the rationale for using the method(s), the rationale for selection of participants, the number of individuals participating (e.g., 62), and the percentage of the population of which the participant group is composed (e.g., 11%). In addition, you must identify the degree to which the participant group reflects an appropriate sample of the population and/or any limitations to this. In terms of reporting results, you should again seek to provide as much information as possible to ensure accurate interpretation of the results. You should provide both a brief narrative summary of the procedures and the results of the assessment as well as the actual assessment items with the corresponding response rates and the raw number of respondents per response (e.g., 48% [n = 398] of the respondents were between the ages of 18 and 24).

As stated earlier, multiple forms of empirical data must be collected to enlarge the data picture and to ensure that specific data is not overlooked. Common types of readily available empirical data consist of U.S. Census

Figure 2.2 Survey/Focus Group/Interview Guide Construction Tips

The following tips are strategies that may prove useful in ensuring effective survey construction as part of a comprehensive needs assessment process.

1. When developing the questionnaire, identify the major categories of inquiry and the rationale for each in order to organize the questions accordingly.

2. Limit the number of questions to no more than 15 items, with justification for each item, allowing for gathering the most essential information in the shortest amount of time being the guiding force (if a specific in-depth inquiry is warranted, the number of items may increase but, again, only with sound justification).

3. Determine the type of Likert scale to be used—3-, 4-, or 5-point—and if forced response should be used.

Example of 4-point scale with forced response (no option of "undecided"):

Strongly Disagree	Disagree	Agree	Strongly Agree
1	2	3	4

Example of 5-point, unforced response, allows for participant to remain neutral:

Strongly Disagree	Disagree	Undecided	Agree	Strongly Agree
1	2	3	4	5

4. Ensure all questions are clearly focused on a single issue to reduce ambiguity in responses.

Example: If I have a problem, I know there is someone that will listen to me.

5. Avoid double-barreled items that focus on more than one issue and create challenges in interpreting results.

Example: If I have a problem, I know there is someone that will listen to me, and I have talked to others before when I have had problems.

Strongly Disagree	Disagree	Agree	Strongly Agree

6. Use a variety of closed-ended and open-ended items to enhance results, providing both quantitative and qualitative data.

Example of closed-ended item: I had a choice in the development of my counseling goals.

Example of open-ended item: What activities (e.g., games, talking, journaling) that you participated in during counseling helped you learn the most about yourself?

7. Use age-appropriate language relevant to your participants.

8. Limit the number of questions to increase potential participation, and try to limit the survey to one page.

9. Use shading and/or other formatting techniques to increase the utility of the survey.

Example of shading to set off responses: If I have a problem, I know there is someone that will listen to me.

Strongly Disagree	Disagree	Agree	Strongly Agree
1	2	3	4

10. Provide a rationale for the survey to provide participants with reason for completion.

Example of rationale: Please take a few minutes to answer some questions about your satisfaction with our clinical services. Your responses will be confidential. Please *do not* put your name on the survey, in order to keep it anonymous. The purpose of this questionnaire is to help us improve our clinical services for our clients. Only aggregate data will be published; no individual data will be published.

11. Provide instructions for completing the survey, including anonymity status of participants.

Example of confidentiality and anonymity of participants: Your responses will be confidential. Please *do not* put your name on the survey, in order to keep it anonymous.

12. Include statement of informed consent on the survey.

Example of informed consent: Participation in completing this questionnaire is completely voluntary, and you have the right to refuse to participate. There are no known benefits or risks to you in completing this questionnaire. Completion of the questionnaire implies your consent. If you do wish to complete the questionnaire, please do so and place the completed questionnaire in the envelope provided. If you do not wish to complete the questionnaire, please place the questionnaire in the envelope provided.

13. Capture any necessary demographic information about participants at the beginning of the survey.

Examples of demographic information:

Gender: __ Male __ Female

Age: __ Under 13 __ 14–17 __ 18–24 __ 25–34 __ +34

Length of time in therapy with current counselor:

__ Less than 3 months __ 3–6 months __ 6–12 months __ More than 1 year data for regionalized demographic information related to residents (e.g., age, race, ethnicity, household income), various prevalence data from governmental sources (e.g., child abuse data, crime data), school-based data (e.g., graduation rate, student performance rates), and various forms of data collected by social service and other relevant providers (e.g., trend data in mental and medical health clinics)—some of which was gathered in the community demography assessment. Therefore, the results of the community demography assessment should be used to specifically direct other data collection needs so that you can identify specific problems. For instance, if the results of the community demography assessment indicate a 32% high school dropout rate, during the problem analysis, you would want to gather more detailed information to better understand this finding. To accomplish this, you would gather additional data from the schools related to this, such as time frame during which kids are most likely to drop out, demographic characteristics of kids that drop out (e.g., academic history, employment status at time of dropout, home situation, ethnicity, emotional/mental/physical disability status, class status, race), and any additional information that may be a perceived factor related to dropout rate or that might be perceived to be related in some other way to the dropout rate. By doing this, you are able to dig much deeper into understanding the meaning of various data, as well as better see the link between the data collected during the community demography assessment and data collected during the problem analysis.

The end result of the problem analysis—derived from analyzing the results of both community demography and problem analysis results—is the identification and prioritization of two to four problems. This supplies you with a specific direction as to how to move forward in the needs assessment process.

Assessment of the Existing Market

Whereas the problem analysis is designed to accurately identify problems in the target region, only problems that are not being addressed constitute needs and, thus, provide justification for new program development. Therefore, to determine if the identified problem does indeed constitute a need, a thorough assessment of existing providers in the region must be conducted. This type of assessment is a market analysis.

Market analysis is the identification and study of a market to determine if a particular good or service is needed (Emerson, 2008) and is based on the basic premise of supply and demand. By conducting a market analysis for clinical program development, you are able to determine (a) if the identified problem in the region is being addressed by existing providers and (b) the extent to which the problem is being addressed by existing providers. The results of this analysis are then used to indicate either that there is no need for new program development or that new program development is indeed warranted.

Whereas a market analysis is critical to providing evidence against or in support of new program development, the results are equally significant to the program design stage, particularly since the results of the analysis can provide information about how providers are addressing specific needs. By gaining this information about potential competitors, program developers may be able to differentiate their services and, thus, offer a unique product (i.e., treatment). Because the market analysis serves dual purposes, it is most effective as well as expedient to complete a full market analysis as part of this preplanning stage, gathering all the necessary data for both the needs assessment process as well as the program design process once and simply utilizing the data during the two different stages. This ensures that you gather data only once yet have all the essential data available for different types of decision making. To promote full understanding of the market analysis, I will first address the use of the market analysis in justifying new program development and then cover the use of the market analysis in program design (Chapter 5).

To accomplish an effective assessment of the existing market for use in preplanning, the following areas must be examined:

- The number of providers working to address the identified problem
- The scope of services of each provider
- Program capacity and any trends in program capacity
- Funding sources and trends in funding
- Length of time provider(s) has been working to address problem
- Other issues related to the continuation of services to address the problem

Each of these areas must be thoroughly explored to attain firm knowledge about the degree to which identified problems are being addressed by existing providers and to indicate if additional programming is indeed needed and is feasible for a new organization. Whereas the results of the market analysis may very well indicate that the existing providers are able to address only a fraction of the population's problems due to capacity constraints, the existing providers may have funding locked up for the next several years, with no additional funding available to address the problem, or there may be specific credentialing needed to be considered for new program development. Both of these issues speak to feasibility issues in regard to new program development. The first indicates that new program development is, at best, not justified for several years in the future, and the second indicates that other steps must be fully examined and evaluated to determine specific time frames and the ability to pursue additional credentialing.

There are four key benefits of a market analysis that should be discussed. First, acquiring critical information related to both clinical programming and business operations is essential to effective program design. As such, increased understanding of the various clinical interventions and program outcomes provides significant information for use in clinical program development (e.g., program capacity, clinical interventions and modalities). Likewise, increased understanding related to staffing patterns, organizational structure, and financial implications provides crucial information for operational issues in program development. Second, gaining such information about providers that have an established history of programming in the specific area promotes increased appreciation for the program development project and all that is involved in implementation and sustainability. Third, since other providers have previously experienced several challenges in programming, they may offer valuable insight into lessons learned that may be addressed in the initial program design to avoid similar fates. It is in this sense that new program developers should view competitors as having already piloted (i.e., tested) the programs and, thus, having much to offer in substantial knowledge that may help ensure early success with program implementation. Finally, providers that have prior experience offer valuable information by which your new program can be differentiated in design. This can be a significant factor in program design, particularly because you wish to emerge as a competitor. For each of these reasons and more, a market analysis is "arguably the most important element in understanding the competition" (Krentz & Camp, 2008, p. 64).

As a brief recap then, a market analysis should be conducted because it

1. is needed to dispute or support new program development,

2. is needed for effective program design,

3. increases appreciation for the scope of the program development project,

4. allows you to avoid similar mistakes in program development, and

5. provides information needed to differentiate your program from the competition.

For all these reasons, and likely several others, the market analysis is an essential tool for the program developer. To ensure thoroughness, the market analysis should include gathering the following information:

- Length of time the provider has been delivering the specific services
- Other information related to the program's history
- Relevant demographic information about the program and/or organization (e.g., other programs operated by the organization)
- The scope and type of services provided, including the specific service components and clinical interventions
- The *research basis*/evidence basis of the clinical interventions and service components (e.g., individual therapy, resource coordination)
- Any limitations to service delivery
- Program outcomes and program performance related to attainment of outcomes
- The annual average number of clients and program capacity
- Program vacancy trends and related factors
- The organizational structure (e.g., staffing patterns and hierarchy)
- Staff credentialing
- Financial information (i.e., annual budget, financial trends, revenue sources and amounts)
- Contractors, other funding sources, and related information
- Accreditation status and other credentialing information
- Any other information regarding program operations and/or sustainability

The *Market Analysis Checklist* serves as an aid to the market analysis process, ensuring that all necessary data has been collected (see Table 2.3).

In addition to the types of data collected, a market analysis should include all the existing providers in the region that are addressing the identified problem(s). If for some reason there are no existing providers in the region addressing the identified problem(s), the market analysis should be conducted on providers in similar regions (i.e., population characteristic and geographic similarities) for later use in program design. In this case, a minimum of three (3) organizations should be included in the market analysis to ensure a diverse representation of providers and programming.

As is the rule with most, if not all, assessment activities, the outcomes are only as good as the process. As such, a comprehensive market analysis will (a) provide essential information to direct initial decision making about new program development and (b) yield critical information for use in program design only when thoroughness and sufficient attention to detail have directed the process.

Table 2.3 Market Analysis Checklist

Data to Be Gathered	Status
Length of time the provider has been delivering the specific services	
Other information related to program history	
Relevant demographic information	
Scope and type of services provided	
Specific service components and clinical interventions	
Research basis/evidence basis of the clinical interventions	
Research basis/evidence basis of the service components	
Any limitations to service delivery	
Program outcomes	
Annual average number of clients	
Program capacity (clients)	
Program vacancy trends	
Factors related to program vacancy (e.g., maximum length of time paid by insurance company, increased competition)	
Organizational structure	
Staff credentialing	
Budget and revenue information	
Pay schedule information (e.g., capped rate, per diem)	
Contractors and other funding sources	
Accreditation status or other credentialing information	
Any additional relevant information	

Need Identification Process

Once you have completed both the problem analysis and the market analysis, you have sufficient data to determine if new program development is justified and the specific type of new program development that is needed. By examining the results of the market analysis in conjunction with the results of the problem analysis, evidence is provided indicating that the identified needs are currently being sufficiently addressed, and thus, new program development is not warranted, or that the identified problem is not being addressed/not being adequately addressed, and thus, new program development is warranted. This latter finding indicates a gap between problems and solutions to address the problems, thereby translating the identified problem into an identified need.

Of all the steps involved in the comprehensive needs assessment, the needs assessment provides specific sustenance to the process by allowing you to immediately view the fruits of your labor: necessary evidence that determines if new program development is justified or not. As a result, this step does not require completing any new activities but rather involves bringing together previously collected data to carefully examine it to

a. determine if the problem does indeed represent a need in the region and

b. if a need does exist, thoroughly examine the feasibility of moving forward in new program development.

Whereas the results of the community demography assessment and problem analysis are critical to determining *a,* the results of the market analysis should provide all the information needed to determine *b.* To determine if the problem does represent a need, the following types of questions will guide you:

1. Are there existing providers working to address the problem in the region?

2. Are there a sufficient number of existing providers to address the problem?

3. Are the existing providers unable to address the problem due to limited capacity?

4. Are the existing providers unable to address the problem due to poor performance?

5. If the existing providers are unable to address the problem due to limited capacity, what evidence exists that a new provider would be justified and welcome in the region?

6. If the existing providers are unable to address the problem due to poor performance, what evidence exists that a new provider would be justified and welcome in the region?

If a need does indeed exist, the following questions should be used to begin fully examining the feasibility of entering into new program development to address the need:

1. What are all the costs involved in new program development and implementation?

2. What is the overall investment needed for new program development (concrete expenditures, time, learning, etc.)?

3. What are the risks involved in new program development?

4. What are the benefits of new program development?

5. Do the costs outweigh the benefits of new program development?

It is in this manner that the results of a thorough market analysis are not only critical to determining if a need actually exists but also to providing the necessary information to decide if such new program development is feasible and beneficial to the organization. Discovering that a need does exist does not necessarily mean that new program development is warranted, particularly if the costs and risks to new program development outweigh the benefits to the organization. That is why the market analysis is so useful in allowing you to gain a much deeper understanding of the specific programming and all that it entails. Moreover, this is why the combined results of the community demography assessment, *Problem Identification,* and market analysis will provide you with the information required to determine if an actual need for new programming exists.

Inventory of Assets

The identification of existing assets and strengths of the region is just as critical to successful program development as the identification of specific needs. In fact, without an accurate understanding of the various assets that a region possesses, it is difficult to fully understand the needs of a particular region. Whereas the other steps of the needs assessment allow for the identification and prioritization of the clinical and related needs of a population, an asset map identifies existing strengths (e.g., community organizing and cohesion) and resources in the target region (e.g., community organizing practices, social service organizations), thereby providing a more balanced view of the region (Calley, 2009). In addition, because the assets of a region interact directly with the needs of a region, thereby contextualizing a region, assets provide an essential layer of information about the region/population/needs. Further, the strengths and internal assets of a community may prove particularly effective in resolving challenges and addressing the needs of the community (Yoon, 2009). As a result, an asset map (i.e., inventory of assets) is an essential part of the needs assessment process that provides additional information for use in preplanning.

Broadly, assets refer to strengths and/or resources that may exist within the target region or that may be characteristic of the target population. Examples of a target population's assets might include aspects related to cultural identity, such as close extended families, specific religious or spiritual beliefs, communication, and cohesion among community members. On the other hand, additional types of assets in the region may consist of social service organizations and the region's eligibility for specific governmental or other special funding status, among other issues. Mowbray et al. (2007) identify three specific types of *community assets* thought to contribute to resilient communities:

1. *Social assets:* community relationships built on friendships and other relationships with individuals as well as social ties to organizations such as schools, places of worship, and community centers

2. *Service agency assets:* community service providers with an institutional rather than social focus, such as hospitals and employers

3. *Economic and neighborhood resources:* resources that economically support families and communities, such as income and employment opportunities

Assets speak to the positive aspects of a population and a region and, as such, reflect the complexity that lies within populations and regions. By conducting an asset map, the program developer is forced to more thoroughly examine a population/region and, thus, gain a deeper sense of the population/region and again, hopefully, a more balanced view that recognizes both the challenges and strengths of a given population/region. This is of tremendous significance, particularly if a program developer believes he or she is very familiar with a population/region, since sometimes the closer we are to something, the less able we are to clearly see it. At times, mental health professionals become so entrenched in a given population/region that they see only the issues or problems that negatively impact the population and fail to acknowledge any existing strengths or resources.

For example, when I began working with physically and sexually abused teenage girls in residential treatment in a large, urban area, I was immediately struck by the degree to which these young ladies seemingly had the cards stacked against them. More often than not, there was not a family member interested in continuing to care for them, and few had any long-term friendships (due to myriad problems that often related to both concrete issues such as constant moves as a result of being in the child welfare system and psychological issues such as the inability to trust), and most had poor academic histories (again, often due to myriad issues, including lack of continuity in education as a result of child welfare system involvement). For obvious reasons, some of these young ladies felt hopeless, and after initially working intensely with them, I began to feel hopeless as well. What I failed to see was that these kids were survivors; they were resilient, adaptable, and typically able to negotiate new issues and environments in their quickly changing worlds. In essence, these girls had strengths and internal resources that few teens have yet to develop at the same stage of adolescent development. Because I was so entrenched in their everyday lives, I had become problem-saturated to the point that I could not see beyond what was wrong, and as a result, I was not aware of all the incredible assets that they each possessed. This is precisely the type of skewed perspective that can negatively impact any program development project, and that forces critical data to be overlooked. Moreover, this is precisely why conducting an asset map as part of a comprehensive needs assessment is so crucial to the preplanning process of program development.

In conducting the asset map, it is best to be as expansive as possible, making every effort to identify every existing asset (see Box 2.3).

BOX 2.3

ASSET MAP GUIDE

1. Gather asset data from regional stakeholders.

2. Reexamine the results of the community demography assessment to determine which characteristics constitute assets.

3. Identify all existing community resources (e.g., services, supports, networks).

4. Identify all existing providers of services.

5. Analyze the data by comparing the list of assets to the identified needs to determine ways in which assets might be used to address needs through new program development.

6. Identify the specific benefits to harnessing the various assets in new program development.

Data should be gathered from various sources, including regional officials, community members, and other mental health providers (some from sources with whom you have previously collected data). In addition, data from the community demography assessment must be reanalyzed to explore for assets and strengths that may not have previously been perceived as such. For instance, if the community demographic data indicated a preponderance of both children and individuals 60 years and older in the region and your interest was in developing a program for children, the aging population could be viewed as a critical asset. More to the point, you might develop an elder-child mentoring intervention/component or engage the aging population to serve as part of a community safety network, thereby establishing the elderly population as a critical asset in program design.

Similarly, the various cultural identity aspects of the demographic data must be thoroughly reviewed again to identify other existing strengths. For instance, if the majority of households in the target region are led by single females, the traits of fortitude and strength of women in the region should be considered obvious strengths. By using an enhanced, strengths-based lens (i.e., adopting an asset orientation) by which to view a region, many assets may begin to appear; however, doing so requires purposeful work, thus, the use of the asset map. In this manner, it is essential that you explore deeply so as to not overlook any existing strengths or resources.

In addition to identifying the various strengths of a population as assets, existing *community resources* must also be identified as assets. Because organizations within the region often can be utilized for a number of specific purposes in program development, they should be considered resources. Such resources should include all mental health and social service organizations, including school-based programs, and may include businesses (this may be of particular interest if program development is focused on vocational development) and physical health facilities (if particular interest is focused on health care or rehabilitation). Local organizations providing similar services or serving the same population will, in most cases, always be viewed as resources since they may be used in program development efforts for a number of purposes. Minimally, these organizations have specific historic knowledge and important data about the population and services. Such information is highly useful in program planning. As a result, it is imperative that program developers engage these organizations to learn and gain valuable data for use in new program development. Moreover, these organizations may serve as significant allies in advocacy and other collective efforts, as well as partners in collaborative efforts. The creation of collaborative *partnerships* is of particular interest as it may be critical to pursuing specific funding, and with the increasing emphasis on collaboration in funding opportunities, this has become increasingly important during the past decade. (The role of community resources and partnerships is explored thoroughly in Chapters 7 and 13.)

As you have probably noticed, there are typically numerous assets in a given region, and the challenge rests in working to identify all of them. Once an exhaustive list of assets has been identified, it should be compared with the identified needs. By comparing the region's assets with the region's needs, the program developer is able to determine how specific needs may be addressed through existing resources. This type of planning in program development, involving various existing systems and resources, is crucial as it implies that additional support is already available and simply needs to be creatively harnessed for comprehensive program development. This philosophy resonates with *multisystemic approaches*, originally developed by Henggeler and Borduin (1990), which utilize existing resources and create links with existing resources in treatment planning. More importantly, this type of approach has an established record of producing positive treatment outcomes (Henggeler, Clingempeel, Brondino, & Pickrel, 2002). It is because of these reasons and more that completing an asset map is so critical to program development efforts.

Summary: Pulling It All Together—Organizing the Data Collection Plan and Engaging in Data-Driven Decision Making

As you can see, establishing the need for programming is no small task. Rather, it involves identifying a target region and a target population followed by completing a five-pronged comprehensive needs assessment that includes

1. community demography assessment,

2. problem analysis,

3. market analysis,

4. need identification process, and

5. an asset map.

These activities focus on data collection and analysis for use in preliminary decision making about program development and, as such, collectively compose the preplanning stage of program development. The data gathered during this stage has tremendous significance to the entire program development process since this data provides the basis for decisions made about new program development. In short, this stage is arguably the most important stage in program development because every subsequent stage is based on decisions initially made during this stage, so that mistakes made here may have an enormous negative impact on program development efforts. In fact, failure to conduct a comprehensive and effective needs assessment based on all five components will likely lead to ill-conceived program development efforts. That is, if you complete a thorough community demography assessment but fail to conduct a comprehensive problem analysis, you may miss critical data that has a direct impact on a specific problem. Since the community demography assessment serves as the building block for the problem analysis, failing to fully utilize the results of the community demography assessment to dig deeper into specific areas during the problem analysis limits what you can learn from the data. For example, whereas the community demography assessment indicated an above-average rate of truancy among elementary school children, comparing this data to the rate of children receiving free lunch in the school, rather than investigating further, you might simply conclude a relationship between lower socioeconomic status and school truancy. However, by prematurely ending your investigation, you failed to learn that the majority of children with school truancy problems have caregivers that either work nontraditional hours or do not have transportation—two critical factors directly impacting their children's school attendance.

In addition, if you are successful in conducting an effective community demography assessment and problem analysis but fail to complete a thorough market analysis, your data may indicate a need for new program development that is already being met by other providers. As a result, you may move forward in new program development for a market that is already being served and, therefore, does not provide an opportunity for you to enter.

Indeed, the preplanning stage carries a heavy burden, as its implications are tremendous. However, nothing can substitute an effective comprehensive needs assessment. Indeed, completing an effective and comprehensive needs assessment yields the most significant results: evidence of new program development, when and where it exists. From a scientific perspective, this type of data-driven decision making is not only appropriate but required, and from a business perspective, it is often the difference between a successful entrepreneur and an unsuccessful one.

Moreover, solid data collection skills, effective analysis skills, and the unwavering ability to remain objective and allow data to drive decision making are each required ingredients of success in this stage. In addition, to effectively plan and carry out each of the preplanning activities, great attention to detail and effective organizational skills are needed. Effective planning must take into account the progressive nature of the data collection and decision-making process, appreciating that each activity provides an essential layer of information for the next. Therefore, the data collection process must be organized sequentially to allow for accurate data analysis and, ultimately, the most effective data-based decision making. The data collection plan should be organized as follows:

1. Identification of target region

2. Identification of target population

3. Community demography assessment

4. Problem analysis

5. Market analysis

6. Need identification process

7. Asset map

As a result of completing the needs assessment, you will have created a sound basis for decision making based on the effective use of data. To succinctly organize all the findings of the needs assessment and aid in decision making about new program development, a summary report that includes each of the assessment activities and findings should be developed.

CASE ILLUSTRATION

Gerri Scouton had been the executive director of Pyramid Social Services, an organization specializing in residential treatment for adults with serious mental health disorders, for the past 10 years. Although her agency was financially stable and had developed a strong reputation for quality services, her board of directors had been encouraging her to seek out new business over the past couple of years to grow the organization further. At the last board meeting, a discussion arose regarding the increasing number of individuals with traumatic brain injury (TBI) in the region. One board member stated that he did not feel there were enough residential facilities to treat all these individuals. Another board member claimed that he believed the large number of individuals with TBI in the region were involved in the criminal justice system and that often, these individuals were released from prison without any further treatment. As a result, he claimed, persons with TBI often continued to commit crimes.

He argued that to address this issue, there needed to be a residential program that could effectively treat these individuals upon their release from prison.

As the discussion continued, two of the board members suggested that this was an area that the agency should look to expand into (residential treatment for individuals with TBI) and that, by doing so, the organization would be able to expand its continuum of residential programming. Summarizing this discussion, the board president quickly directed Gerri to begin making plans for expansion in this area since this did indeed sound like a very good business opportunity. However, Gerri was not yet altogether convinced of the urgency of this directive.

Although Gerri had heard talk at monthly coalition meetings with other human service organizations that there seemed to be an increase in the number of individuals with TBI, it was not an area she had directly explored and, therefore, she was not comfortable that this argument was wholly founded. To be certain that this new program development effort was justified, Gerri responded that she would conduct a comprehensive needs assessment.

Gerri assigned the task of conducting a comprehensive needs assessment to a lead counselor, Jamie, and his clinical supervisor, Kari. Since the target region had already been identified (the region in which the organization currently operated) as well as the target population (i.e., adults with TBI), in order to get started with the community demography assessment, Jamie and Kari began brainstorming a list of all the data needed. They then split up the task of gathering the various data and made plans to meet at the end of the week to discuss their findings. After compiling all the data from the community demography assessment into a summary of findings, a clearer picture of the community emerged with the following key features:

- Increased prevalence of TBI in the region over the past 2 years—4% higher than the state rate and 6% higher than the national rate
- Increased prevalence of violent crime in the region over the past 2 years at 6% higher than the state level and 8% higher than the national level
- Racially diverse community: 48% black, 44% white, and 8% American Indian
- Ethnically diverse community: 37% African American, 11% Pacific Islander, 25% Euro-American, 19% Arab American, and 8% American Indian
- Adults composing the majority age population with 78% of the region's population between the ages of 18 and 65
- Economically impoverished area with 9% higher prevalence rate of poverty than state level and 12% higher than national level
- Population with limited postsecondary education, with 15% less of the region holding a bachelor's degree than the state level and 17% less than the national level

(Continued)

(Continued)

After discussing the community demography assessment summary in depth, Kari and Jamie decided that they had enough pertinent data to effectively move to the next preplanning step and begin a problem analysis. Finding that the region did indeed have a disproportionately high rate of both TBI and violent crime, they knew that they would need to investigate each of these areas further. Kari and Jamie again began by brainstorming the various types of data they would need to collect and then proceeded to identify the various sources of data. In addition, because some of their data would be coming from various stakeholders—in particular, the hospitals, local law enforcement, and providers of TBI treatment and services—they identified the methods of data collection that would be needed to gather the information. They decided that they would need to develop an interview guide and a survey to gather this specific data directly from these stakeholders. They also decided to use three methods by which to gather the data: telephone, electronic, and face-to-face—each based on the particular person(s) providing input (e.g., law enforcement, hospitals, providers). They had learned before in working with police that police officers were much more comfortable speaking in person than on the telephone or by e-mail, while providers typically preferred e-mail or other electronic communication. After constructing the survey and interview guide, Kari and Jamie split up tasks in order to maximize their time completing this next set of data collection activities and went to work.

Once they had successfully gathered all their information, they began the analysis process and compiled a report of the findings. The data yielded the following findings:

- Violent crime primarily consisted of homicide and male-to-female domestic violence.
- The trend in violent crime in the area appeared to be related to an increase in prisoners returning to the community prior to completing their full sentence as part of the state's plan to reduce its annual budget through the implementation of a prisoner reentry program (52% of the violent crime committed in the region over the past 2 years had been by repeat offenders).
- The reason for the disproportionate violent crime rate in the region may have been related to the fact that a specific location in the region served as a primary drop-off point for prisoners returning to the community.
- There was not a significant relationship between TBI and violent crime.
- Of the region's TBI population, 24% received their injury as a result of an automobile accident.
- Of the region's TBI population, 72% consisted of veterans of the recent war in the Middle East.
- The remaining 4% of the region's TBI population had received their injury as a result of accidental and nonaccidental events that were nonvehicular and not related to military involvement.

- The reason for the disproportionate rate of TBI in the region appeared to be a direct result of the state's Veteran's Administration (VA) hospital, which was located in the immediate region and at which the majority of TBI patients were treated for myriad issues, including TBI and related mental and physical health problems.
- In addition to the continuum of programming available from the VA hospital for TBI (providing residential programming only), there were three other providers of TBI treatment, two of whom provided both residential and community-based programming and one that provided only community-based programming.
- There was no evidence that TBI patients were not able to receive treatment due to a lack of available programming in the region.
- Over the past 5 years, the region had expanded its TBI services, including both residential and outpatient services, to the TBI population, largely in response to the increased prevalence rate related to the war in the Middle East.

After examining all the data that they had collected so far, Kari and Jamie were able to prioritize two primary problems existing in the community: (1) TBI and (2) violent crime among repeat offenders. Although the results of the problem analysis did not indicate that there was a lack of TBI treatment/services in the region, the results of the data collection were limited since Jamie and Kari had gathered data about this issue only from the VA hospital and from 38% of the TBI population. Kari and Jamie compiled the information that they had gathered as part of the problem analysis process, along with their previous findings from the community demography assessment, into a summary report—*Data Collection Report*. In their report, they explained the methods that they used to collect the data as well as specific limitations that they encountered in the data collection process (i.e., limited data on individuals with TBI). Knowing that they had not examined a large enough sample of the TBI population to fully understand the existing state of treatment needs or if any gaps in services existed, Jamie and Kari were not concerned since this would be fully explored in the next step, the market analysis; so they still had work to do.

Now knowing that the region did have a significant population of individuals with TBI, Jamie and Kari were anxious to get started with the market analysis to determine if this problem translated into a need. To begin the market analysis, Kari and Jamie identified all the existing TBI treatment providers within the immediate region as well as those within 1 hour of the region. The six TBI treatment providers offered the following treatment options:

2, residential treatment only

2, both residential and community-based programming

2, community-based programming only

(Continued)

(Continued)

Sufficiently equipped with the *Market Analysis Tool*, they set about to gather pertinent information about the existing providers. Although they could gather only a limited amount of data from three of the providers that did not include financial and vacancy information (providers unwilling to disclose some specific information), they had been successful in gathering a good deal of relevant data from the other three providers. After compiling all the results of the market analysis, Kari and Jamie came to the following conclusions:

- Two of the providers (one with both residential and community-based programming and one with residential programming only) had been providing TBI treatment for more than 20 years and had achieved significant positive treatment outcomes and developed strong reputations in the region for their treatment.
- The average vacancy rate for each of the residential providers was 35% (i.e., occupancy rate of 65%).
- None of the residential providers had been at full capacity during the past 2 years, with the exception of the VA hospital, which was the automatic initial residential placement for veterans returning from active duty with TBI (the VA hospital had been at full capacity for less than 2-week time frames over the past 2 years).
- Recent changes to the state's auto insurance industry limiting residential and outpatient treatment for TBI had decreased the client population for all the providers by approximately 15% during the past 2 years.

The results of the market analysis were clear: A need for additional TBI programming did not currently exist in the region. In fact, the market analysis indicated that there was already an excess of providers in the area. And this excess of providers, coupled with a shrinking market (individuals with TBI as a result of vehicular accidents for whom funding for treatment would not be provided), had already had a serious negative impact on each of the provider's market share.

Whereas Kari and Jamie had clearly found evidence that TBI was a significant problem in the region, the market analysis demonstrated that it was not a problem that represented a need—an opportunity for new or expanded program development. Further, because the results of the needs assessment process were conclusive and did not justify new program development for TBI, there was no reason to continue further in the assessment process by conducting an asset map. Instead, Kari and Jamie compiled their existing findings into a comprehensive needs assessment summary report and scheduled a meeting with Gerri to discuss the results of their comprehensive needs assessment.

After reviewing the findings with Jamie and Kari, Gerri, too, was convinced that a more than sufficient market currently existed to address TBI in the region and that, in fact, it appeared that the market may be saturated since none of the providers were operating at capacity. Gerri invited Jamie and Kari to present their findings at the upcoming board meeting. Following the presentation, the board, too, was convinced that as much as they were interested in growing the organization, new program development for TBI was not justified; however, the board was intrigued about the findings related to violent crime and an increase in the number of prisoners returning to the community. After some discussion, the board asked if Jamie and Kari could turn their attention to completing a needs assessment on prisoners returning to the community and violent crime among adults. The board members were impressed with the thoroughness of the work that Kari and Jamie had conducted to fully examine the needs related to TBI. As a result, they were anxious to see if their assessment and analysis work could be duplicated to determine if this other problem did in fact translate into a need for new program development.

Since they had already completed the community demography assessment in which some data related to this problem had inadvertently been gathered in the previous problem analysis, Jamie and Kari would be able to start midpoint in the assessment process and continue to collect more specific data related to the issue and then move to the market analysis. They, too, were anxious to get started, and more importantly, they were confident that by letting the data do the talking, their organization's future endeavors would be guided most effectively.

COMMUNITY DEMOGRAPHY ASSESSMENT EXERCISE

Identify a target region and target population, and use the community demography assessment tool to conduct a community demography assessment.

REFLECTION AND DISCUSSION QUESTIONS

1. What experience have you had in participating in new program development?

2. Having read this chapter, what most appeals to you about the preplanning/ establishing the rationale for program development phase?

3. What, if anything, surprised you about the preplanning phase of program development?

4. How could you use the results of a comprehensive needs assessment to impact governmental or philanthropic funding for new program development?

References

Arredondo, P., & Glauner, T. (1992). *Personal dimensions of identity model*. Boston: Empowerment Workshops.

Calley, N. G. (2009). Comprehensive program development in mental health counseling: Design, implementation, and evaluation. *Journal of Mental Health Counseling, 31*, 9–21.

Darboe, K., & Ahmed, L. S. (2007). Elderly African immigrants in Minnesota: A case study of needs assessment in eight cities. *Educational Gerontology, 33*, 855–866.

Emerson, D. M. (2008). Subdivision market analysis and absorption forecasting. *Appraisal Journal, 76*, 377–390.

Finifter, D. H., Jensen, C. J., Wilson, C. E., & Koenig, B. L. (2005). A comprehensive, multitiered, targeted community needs assessment model: Methodology, dissemination, and implementation. *Family and Community Health, 28*, 293–306.

Henggeler, S. W., & Borduin, C. M. (1990). *Family therapy and beyond: A multisystemic approach to treating the behavior problems of children and adolescents*. Pacific Grove, CA: Brooks/Cole.

Henggeler, S. W., Clingempeel, W. G., Brondino, M. J., & Pickrel, S. G. (2002). Four-year follow-up of multisystemic therapy with substance abusing and dependent juvenile offenders. *Journal of the American Academy of Child and Adolescent Psychiatry, 41*, 868–874.

Kettner, P. M., Moroney, R. M., & Martin, L. L. (2008). *Designing and managing programs: An effectiveness-based approach* (3rd ed.). Thousand Oaks, CA: Sage.

Krentz, S. E., & Camp, T. (2008). Taking a good look at the competition. *Healthcare Financial Management, 62*, 64–70.

Lewis, J. A., Packard, T. R., & Lewis, M. D. (2007). *Management of human service programs* (4th ed.). Belmont, CA: Thomson Learning.

Mowbray, C. T., Woolley, M. E., Grogan-Kaylor, A., Gant, L. M., Gilster, M. E., & Shanks, T. R. (2007). Neighborhood research from a spatially oriented strengths perspective. *Journal of Community Psychology, 35*, 667–680.

Yoon, I. (2009). A mixed-method study of Princeville's rebuilding from the flood of 1999: Lessons on the importance of invisible community assets. *Social Work, 54*, 19–28.

Zandbergen, P. A., & Green, J. W. (2007). Error and bias in determining exposure potential of children at school locations using proximity-based GIS techniques. *Environmental Health Perspectives, 115*, 1363–1370.

Establish a Research Basis for Program Design

Learning Objectives

1. Increase understanding of historical factors that have influenced clinical program design, including the federal government and accrediting bodies

2. Differentiate between evidence-based, emerging, empirically guided, and best practices

3. Identify the various areas to be explored in a literature review for use in program design

4. Increase knowledge of the key questions to be explored in the literature review

5. Identify key sources to be used in conducting the literature review

I DON'T HAVE THAT KIND OF TIME

Jack's boss, the agency's executive director, asked Jack to develop a proposal in response to a *Request for Proposal* (RFP) for a new short-term outpatient counseling program for individuals with substance abuse disorders. Jack had not developed a proposal independently before, but he thought that with his experience as the program supervisor of a long-term substance abuse program he could do it. Reading the RFP, Jack learned the program was to deliver treatment to adults with substance abuse disorders and co-occurring mental health disorders. Jack knew from working in the substance abuse field for the past 6 years that some clients did often have a mental health issue as well, but he also knew that substance abuse was always treated as the primary issue. He felt confident that he knew his stuff when it came to substance abuse treatment—after all, he was in recovery himself.

Jack moved through developing the proposal rather swiftly, and in response to questions regarding the program design, he used his current treatment model as the base, simply extending the length of time because the new program was long-term and his existing program was short-term. In response to the model and interventions that would be used to specifically treat co-occurring disorders, Jack discussed the use of psychiatric services and medication monitoring and even identified a contractual psychiatrist on the organizational chart that he was required to submit with the proposal. Jack articulated that the research basis for using psychotropic medication in the treatment of substance abuse was well founded and, therefore, did not require further discussion. Knowing that treatment of co-occurring disorders simply meant treating individuals with both substance abuse disorders and mental health disorders, Jack was confident he had covered both of his bases—identifying substance abuse treatment and psychiatric treatment as the two interventions that would be used in his program. He certainly did not need to review research to reinforce this since it was something he had known for a long time. Besides, he had only a week before the proposal was due.

After finalizing the proposed budget, Jack felt good about having finished his first proposal. Moreover, after briefly discussing it with his boss, Jack said he was ready to send it in and thanked his boss for trusting him to develop the proposal alone.

Six weeks later, Jack's boss received notice that Jack's proposal had been rejected. Among other comments, the reviewers had written that the proposal did not demonstrate an understanding of co-occurring disorders, nor did it provide an evidence-based treatment.

CONSIDERING JACK

1. How could Jack have prevented this from happening?

2. If you were Jack, what would you do now/how might you work to restore your boss's trust in you?

3. What role does research play in program design today?

About This Chapter

To fully understand how to establish a *research basis* in program design, it is necessary to first understand the various environmental changes that have helped get us to this point in program design. These include historical and influential factors impacting program design—namely, the role of the federal government and that of accrediting bodies, which is discussed in the next chapter. Next, we will examine the current climate of program design, beginning with a review of key concepts that include evidence-based, empirically based, emerging, and best practices. In addition to better understanding the forces that have propelled us forward in program design, it is equally essential to understand the various facets involved in developing a research basis for program design that includes the multiple sources needed to conduct a comprehensive literature review. These are composed of scholarly literature, best practice literature, reports from governmental bodies and other think tanks dedicated to research, professional conferences, and other sources—each of which will be explored. And, finally, we will discuss methods to identify significant findings from the research and effectively use these findings in program design efforts.

STEP II: ESTABLISH A RESEARCH BASIS FOR PROGRAM DESIGN

Research Basis for Program Design

As you witnessed in Chapter 2, deciding to move forward in program development requires a tremendous amount of work, primarily focused on comprehensive data collection. Once the rationale for new program development has been firmly established, the program design phase is ready to begin. Just as you had to provide a sound rationale for new program development by identifying the *need* through empirical investigation, you must now develop an equally sound rationale for program design. Establishing a firm basis in research is the first step in program design and, as such, must provide justification for the design. Whereas developing such justification for program design requires a different type of comprehensive investigation than conducted in establishing a need for the program, this process is not necessarily less intensive.

Over the past decade, increased accountability and a focus on effectiveness and outcomes have become guiding forces in program development. As a result, the integrity of program design is more critical than ever before, as program design is innately tied to program outcomes. This new era in program development has radically impacted not only how new programs are conceived but, more significantly, how new programs are designed— design that begins with establishing a sound research basis.

Historical and Influential Factors Impacting Program Design

Today, you cannot engage in a discussion about program design without being asked the basic question, "What evidence do you have that it works?" But this has not always been the case, and several factors and conditions have historically contributed to our current emphasis on evidence-based practices. Prior to the 1980s, programs were designed and implemented largely based on practices that had historical value—program models that had been used before. It was often the case that if your program or organization was known, did not commit any egregious acts, and could effectively manage both your client population and your staff, you could continue to receive funding. Whereas some form of accountability existed, often it consisted of little more than requiring an organization to demonstrate the ability to provide adequate, yet not rigorously evaluated services and achieve a balanced budget.

The Impact of the Federal Government

During the late 20th century, several historical changes occurred on the national level that had far-reaching influence on the state and local levels, and while it is difficult to target any one condition as *the* change agent, it is appropriate to conclude that a number of conditions contributed to varying degrees to where we are today. First, significant changes in the federal government occurred that reflected a shifting ideology about the importance of human services. In fact, beginning in 1930 with the inception of the National Institutes of Health and continuing through 1992 with the establishment of the Substance Abuse and Mental Health Services Administration, the 20th century was *the* era in which mental health and human services initially came into being.

In addition to the establishment of the major federal entities dedicated to mental health and human services, the late 20th century also witnessed a progressive focus on more and more specialized issues related to mental health and human services. For example, the Department of Health, Education, and Welfare (HEW) was created in 1953 to address issues related to each of these three major issues; however, in 1980, HEW became the Department of Health and Human Services, and the Department of Education was established as a separate entity (Department of Health and Human Services, n.d.).

This change is symbolic for many reasons but largely because it reflects increased understanding of the need for focused attention on health and social issues. As with most things, the more attention that is given to a particular issue, the more scrutinized it becomes, and thus, there is often a demand for greater accountability. Whereas the reorganization of the departments of health, education, and welfare offers one example of major shifts in the federal government related to the expansion of and increased focus on the human services, the timeline below (Table 3.1) provides a broader historical view.

As you can see, the changing ideologies about the need for research, increased funding, and attention to social issues are clearly illustrated by the

Table 3.1 Establishment of Federal Agencies

Year	Department Established
1930	National Institutes of Health
1946	National Institute of Mental Health
1953	Department of Health, Education, and Welfare
1974	Office of Juvenile Justice and Delinquency Prevention
1974	Alcohol, Drug Abuse, and Mental Health Administration
1980	Department of Education
1980	Department of Health and Human Services
1992	Substance Abuse and Mental Health Services Administration (previously the Alcohol, Drug Abuse, and Mental Health Administration)

establishment of new federal agencies. Whereas noting these shifts in government is integral to understanding the broad environmental changes that took place last century, none of these changes would likely have come about when they did without the emergence of the behavioral and social sciences. As each of the helping disciplines came into being and further developed, their collective influence on national legislation could not be ignored—beginning with the introduction of talk therapy to the field of psychiatry in the late 19th century (Trull & Phares, 2001) and followed by the emergence of the fields of psychology, counseling, and social work.

In addition, the influence of top-level politicians on the national conversation must not be underestimated. Indeed, the effect of the First Lady (e.g., Betty Ford) or the wife of a presidential contender (e.g., Kitty Dukakis, Tipper Gore) personally and publically confronting substance abuse and mental health issues was unprecedented. Obviously, we could spend a great deal more time ferreting out the myriad historical influences that contributed (and continue to contribute) to the changing landscape regarding mental health services, but this task is best left to other texts so that we can focus more specifically on what it all means today.

Whereas the development of a federal-level cabinet department or a subagency of a cabinet-level department, such as the Substance Abuse and Mental Health Services Administration, reflects national priorities, it also carries with it a vast increase in funding to support treatment to address and increase knowledge about the specific issue. Therefore, the major financial implications that these changes carry must be fully appreciated.

Over the past 30 years, federal expenditures have largely been dedicated to research and support direct services at the state and local levels. As with most trends, national changes beget state and local changes and, conversely, local and state changes are major drivers of national changes. Whereas local and state governments and private *philanthropic organizations* had previously provided funding for social service programs, when the federal government began providing funding to support direct services, the focus on accountability became greater. The reason behind this was no different than those that motivate us all as consumers—an innate need and a right to know that what we are purchasing works, and if it does not work, the right to not continue to pay for it. As the largest consumer in the United States, the federal government has the same need, only exponentially magnified! Therefore, as spending for mental health and social service programming has continuously expanded, accountability to deliver high-quality services has also increased.

But this increased scrutiny on mental health and human services did not evolve without conflict or without setting the stage for major political shifts in our nation. In fact, when the Nixon administration and other conservative politicians during the 1970s were initially instrumental in questioning the effectiveness of an array of social service programs, including the War on Poverty (Lewis, Packard, & Lewis, 2007), they were in part contributing to the undoing of some of the major philosophical tenets of Roosevelt's New Deal—such as a country providing for its own when they are in need. In this manner, the way was paved for the inception of managed care and the sweeping welfare reform legislation of the early 1990s. Fast-forward to 2010 and you are hard-pressed to find a contract to provide mental health or human services that does not specify required program outcomes and that does not result in loss of pay, loss of contract, or both for failure to meet such requirements.

In addition to the shifts resulting in the federal government's increased spending on mental health and human services, in the 1990s another trend emerged that also has had a significant impact on accountability: responsibilities for directly purchasing and monitoring programming at the state, regional, and local levels. The emergence of block grants enabling state, regional, and local governments to directly administer human service programs and dollars has increased the responsibility of these smaller governments. In addition to block grants, shifts in federal government spending have also allowed for increased privatization of specific services (e.g., juvenile justice). Both of these changes have contributed to a cultural move within human service programming toward increased innovation and a keener eye toward cost savings as the burden of fiscal control has increased in smaller levels of governments. This burden has been naturally translated into an increased need to ensure that each venture is worth the money that is supporting it. Whereas governmental spending composes the majority of funding for mental health and human service programming in the United States, the amount of financial support provided by private philanthropic organizations and foundations for such programming cannot be overlooked. As primary contractors of human service programming, private organizations have also been significantly influenced by governmental shifts, and as such, accountability in programming has become a key concern of private funders as well.

Various means have been utilized to address the issue of accountability in mental health programming, two of which require specific discussion here—national accreditation bodies and federal performance standards. The emergence of national accreditation bodies for mental health and social service programming and the promulgation of performance standards have each had a tremendous impact on raising the proverbial bar by continuously emphasizing standards of care and effectiveness. In short, these two areas have largely served as catalysts for moving mental health and human services through to an unwavering focus on the real bottom line—the client.

The Impact of Accrediting Bodies

While there are numerous national accreditation bodies dedicated to specific issues, arguably the three major accrediting bodies in mental health programming today include the Commission on Accreditation of Rehabilitation Facilities (CARF), the Council on Accreditation (COA), and The Joint Commission. Interestingly, the emergence of accreditation bodies very much reflects the trend toward more focused attention on specialized clinical issues noted in the development of various federal-level agencies. In fact, in the late 1960s (less than 15 years after the emergence of the Department of Health, Education, and Welfare), the first national accrediting bodies were established to provide voluntary accreditation for behavioral and human services in what are now The Joint Commission (formerly the Joint Commission on Accreditation of Healthcare Organizations) and CARF.

Since its inception in 1966, CARF has accredited rehabilitation facilities and has expanded to also include broader-based human services. Whereas CARF has historically specialized in residential facilities, the organization currently accredits programming in such diverse areas as dementia, brain injury, foster care, and opioid treatment (CARF, 2010). Whereas The Joint Commission was initially designed to accredit hospitals, in 1969, its scope expanded to include accreditation of programs for the mentally ill and developmentally disabled (The Joint Commission, 2010). Over the past several decades, The Joint Commission has continuously expanded its scope, while always maintaining a primary focus on health care facilities and programs.

Less than a decade later, in 1977, COA was created to establish service and administrative standards for an array of social service programs. Similar to both The Joint Commission and CARF, COA has progressively expanded its role in accreditation, accrediting a diversity of human service and mental health programs (COA, 2008a).

From the time that each of these three major national accrediting organizations arrived on the scene to today, changes in both the scope of programs eligible for accreditation and the major emphases of the standards provide another illustration of the significant increase in attention to mental and social issues. In fact, the trend toward more and more specialized services continues and is well reflected in the ever-increasing number of services/programs that COA accredits (40 as of 2010!). These programs include such diverse and specialized types as volunteer mentoring services, crisis response and intervention services, opioid treatment programs, and pregnancy support services, to name just a few. Just as accreditation bodies have continuously expanded their number of program standards to meet the growing need of specialized services, service standards have shifted significantly to emphasize the need for accountability in program outcomes. Since program outcomes are predicated on program design, these changes are clearly visible in program design standards. For example, consider this 2008 standard on psychosocial rehabilitation services:

> The program is guided by a philosophy that provides a logical basis for the services and support to be delivered to individuals, based on program goals and the best available evidence of service effectiveness. (COA, n.d.)

Providing evidence of a more fundamental shift toward increased rigor in program design and outcomes, a statement from COA (2008b) regarding the 2008 standards revisions articulates that the "standards are grounded in a long-standing, widely held belief that individuals who receive services are the direct beneficiaries when organizations invest in strong management practice, and can validate the impact of their services on those served." These most recent revisions to the COA standards clearly reflect the current landscape of national accreditation with a keen focus on the interconnected goals of quality, accountability, and effective outcomes.

Equally important in the move toward accountability is the promulgation of performance standards that have increased exponentially during the past 2 decades. Performance standards typically refer to the identification and tracking of *quality indicators* (e.g., client satisfaction), outputs (e.g., number of clients served), and outcomes (e.g., impact of intervention on client). Whereas outputs have particular significance, especially when funding is directly tied to capacity building, the past decade has witnessed an ever-increasing focus on outcomes and specifically measuring the impact of a program on the individual, the region, and the system. At the federal level, the Government Performance and Results Act (GPRA) of 1993, which requires federal departments and agencies to report their performance to Congress and to the president, has been a major driver of performance accountability (Kettner, Moroney, & Martin, 2008). The Government Accountability Office is charged with monitoring the GPRA in order to improve the performance and accountability of the federal government for the benefit of the American people (Government Accountability Office, n.d.). As you would expect, this increased accountability at the federal level has had tremendous impact on increased performance accountability at both the public and private levels of states and municipalities. In fact, 48 states currently have instituted performance accountability systems, and 50% of local and county governments have done the same (Melkers & Willoughby, 2005).

As you can see, numerous events and changes have occurred in recent history that collectively have had a tremendous influence on program development—namely, resulting in a primary focus on accountability. As a result, the current climate in clinical program development is predicated on established proof that the program design is effective in reaching tangible outcomes and that rigorous evaluation is built in to program implementation as an essential component to monitor and ensure effectiveness.

Thinking back to a not-too-distant past when I directed a mentoring and support program for kids with serious emotional disorders, my contractual agreements with funders were largely lacking in any requirements to demonstrate that the treatment and service interventions worked in any substantive way and, in fact, did not even require us to identify specifically what we were trying to achieve. This is not to say that since the clients were a part of the mental health system, functional stability was not the primary outcome, because it was. However, as a program specifically focused on the interpersonal and social skill development of children and adolescents, not only should we, as the provider, have been able to clearly identify and evaluate the clinical interventions that we used to address these issues, but moreover, our funding sources should have demanded that we do so. Thankfully, we have come a long way since then, much to the benefit (and respect) of those we serve, as well as the mental health profession itself.

In the 21st century, we are now fully ensconced in a mental health treatment culture that is keenly focused on clinical efficacy and accountability. That is to say, in terms of mental health programs supported through governmental or foundation funding, this is largely the case. Unfortunately, this continues to not necessarily be the case for individual clinicians working for private pay in outpatient clinics and private practices with individuals, families or groups, or with mental health professionals working in K–12 education or in higher education counseling centers. With the continued emphasis on clinical efficacy in mental health treatment, we may soon see more change in this area, but for now, we can only continue hoping for such change and take appropriate action to demand it.

Current Climate and the Adoption of a New Vocabulary

Now that we know *how* we arrived where we are today, let's look at exactly where "here" is. In our current climate, the focus on efficacy and accountability begins with a program design that is built on evidence and is evaluation-ready—able to measure performance throughout implementation and beyond. To aid us in moving into this new era in program design, a new vocabulary has continued to gain prominence in the behavioral and social sciences that includes terminology such as *evidence-based, empirically guided, best practices,* and *emerging practices.* While the terms have slightly nuanced differences, they share a common emphasis—a foundation in factual information. I prefer the term *research basis* because it is the most inclusive term, including both empirically based research and conceptual research that is factually based yet not fully empirically validated. Program design that falls into this latter category is also referred to as *emerging practices* to indicate that it is still under investigation; however, because of its research foundation, it offers significant promise as a future empirically based design. We will discuss each of these concepts briefly.

Evidence-Based Practices

During the past decade, the emphasis on evidence-based practices has grown at such a tremendous rate that it is now difficult to locate a funding source that does not demand the use of an evidence-based practice as a core part of a contractual agreement. Furthermore, each of the major scholarly journals is currently filled with articles expounding new evidence-based practices, detailing both the interventions and the evaluation findings. Finally, most governmental reports dealing with clinical issues dedicate a fair amount of space to defining evidence-based practices, as well as outlining various evidence-based practices with which to treat the issue.

As the term suggests, evidence-based practices simply refer to practices that have a basis in empirical evidence. Therefore, the use of evidence-based practices emphasizes that clinical programming is based on the best available evidence gathered from systematic research (Johnson & Austin, 2006). Concluding that an intervention has an evidence basis requires a formalized evaluation of the intervention. Thus, as the emphasis on evidence-based practice has continued to grow, the need for comprehensive evaluation has likely intensified. Today, the astute program developer does not consider program implementation without also developing a program evaluation.

There are numerous methods that may be used to evaluate a clinical program and/or the clinical interventions that compose a clinical program. These include

- randomized studies with random assignment of clients to either a treatment or control group;
- quasi-experimental study without random assignment of clients to either treatment or control;
- follow-up or cohort study—following an entire group of clients over a specified period of time;
- qualitative studies with statistical analyses;
- post-test studies;
- focus group, interview, or survey studies that draw from client self-report; and
- qualitative studies without statistical analyses.

In addition, a meta-analysis may be conducted to compare the results of multiple studies on a particular clinical intervention or clinical program. Because each of these evaluation methods differs in the amount of rigor required—with survey studies and qualitative analyses considered the least rigorous and meta-analysis and randomized studies the most rigorous—when identifying a particular evidence-based practice, you must carefully examine how the evidence basis was established. This is not to suggest that you will automatically reject a specific evidence-based model simply because an unsophisticated evaluation tool was used in determining this basis but, rather, that you must critically assess the type of evaluation as part of your decision making about types of interventions that you might adopt. This is important to note since there may be highly attractive reasons to consider the use of a particular evidence-based practice despite its lack of rigorous evaluation.

One example of an evidence-based treatment is multisystemic therapy (MST)—a comprehensive treatment approach that seeks to address the convergence of issues that impact the individual and takes into account the various systems within which an individual interacts. By working at both the family and community levels throughout the treatment process, successful treatment outcomes have been gained through fairly rigorous evaluation (Letourneau et al., 2009; Schoenbald, Heiblum, Saldana, & Henggeler, 2008; Sheidow, Henggeler, & Schoenwald, 2003). Whereas previous studies that had established the efficacy of MST with juvenile offenders were confronted with some methodological challenges, Letourneau et al. set out to address these challenges to determine if the approach was efficacious. In doing so, they used a comparison treatment that consisted of the most common treatment approaches provided to juvenile offenders, using a *Treatment as Usual* control group. By doing this, they were able to ensure a real-world comparison by which to effectively measure MST and, in so doing, found MST to produce similar successful outcomes, thereby reinforcing its evidence basis.

While still considered to be in its infancy, evidence-based practices in mental health treatment are likely very much here to stay and will only increase in use. To date, the use of evidence-based practices has had a significant effect on mental health treatment. In fact, Sexton, Gilman, and Johnson (as cited in Marotta & Watts, 2007) asserted that

> the impact of evidence-based practices is dramatic in that they are fundamentally changing the way practitioners work, the criteria from which communities choose programs to help families and youth, the methods of clinical training, the accountability of program developers and interventions, and the outcomes that can be expected from such programs. (p. 492)

Reflecting this new era of evidence-based practices, the Substance Abuse and Mental Health Services Administration (2007) launched the National Registry of Evidence-Based Programs and Practice. Funded by the federal government, the registry is a free searchable database of evidence-based practices in mental health and substance abuse that is designed to support program development efforts of community organizations and local and state governments. With this current momentum, the new climate is very much focused on accountability in program delivery and an evidence basis in program design.

Emerging Practices

Emerging practices refer to interventions that have not yet had time to be fully evaluated through rigorous means, that have a research basis, or that utilize innovative strategies. Emerging practices may also be termed *promising practices*, reflecting that there is more than just a hunch that these practices may be effective and that some preliminary evaluation has likely been done. In all cases, emerging practices imply the need for rigorous evaluation to effectively determine if they are, indeed, evidence-based.

Because there are a limited number of evidence-based practices currently available to treat an ever-growing number of clinical issues, emerging practices are often accepted for use in new program development by funders, given a rigorous evaluation plan has also been established to thoroughly test the intervention. Allowing for such piloting of new interventions while attempting to evaluate their merits is also very much in keeping with the spirit of research—continuous focus on creating new knowledge through application and testing.

Consider this example of an emerging practice: A mentoring and social support group for elderly individuals with chronic health issues was identified as an emerging practice to address social isolation and prevent depression. Mentoring had been successfully used to decrease social isolation among a small group of at-risk adolescents at post-test, and social support groups had been established as effective in expanding social networks for individuals with limited social resources. Neither of these interventions had yet been fully evaluated, but the merits of the interventions were apparent in that some preliminary evaluation had been conducted and there was some degree of knowledge that the interventions may prove efficacious. As a result, the interventions were identified as emerging practices, and a formal evaluation plan was designed to fully evaluate the interventions as they were implemented.

Emerging practices may indeed become evidence-based practices since most evidence-based practices begin as emerging practices. Thus, emerging practices have the possibility to become evidence-based if and when the anticipated outcomes are sufficiently proven and supported through rigorous evaluation. Conversely, an emerging practice may not ever become an evidence-based practice if such empirical evidence is not found.

Empirically Guided Practices

In addition to emerging practices emanating from preliminary studies, another form of emerging practice is conceptual in nature, rooted in empirical research yet not tested. These are typically referred to as empirically guided practices. For instance, the use of clinical interventions based on the core constructs of cognitive-behavioral therapy (i.e., the interrelationships between cognition, affect, and behavior) may be considered empirically guided because this theoretical base has been proven effective in treating a wide range of issues (Jungquist et al., 2010; Navarrete-Navarrete et al., 2010; Winokur, Rozen, Batchelder, & Valentine, 2006). By conceptualizing a specific clinical issue, such as self-mutilation, from a cognitive-behavioral perspective, you may be able to effectively argue that the use of cognitive-behavioral interventions may lead to successful treatment outcomes.

Best Practices

The term *best practice* has been used interchangeably with evidence-based practice, often signifying a program model with demonstrated success. However, whereas evidence-based practices typically refer to the clinical interventions that compose a program, best practices are more expansive and may include such program components as staffing characteristics (e.g., credentials, staffing patterns), length of treatment time, treatment continuum (e.g., residential, community-based, aftercare), and adjunctive services (e.g., support group, vocational support).

The identification of best practices often results from a thorough examination of research dedicated to a specific issue or evolves from rigorous evaluation. Often, best practice literature summarizes research findings and, as a result, identifies etiological factors and recommends specific interventions. Similar to evidence-based practices, today best practice sections are standard in the major mental health journals. In addition, best practices are often published by federal governmental (e.g., Substance Abuse and Mental Health Services Administration) and national nonprofit organizations (e.g., Child Welfare League of America) as guidance for new program development.

Research Basis

This new terminology in mental health practice (e.g., best practices, evidence-based practices) is not only relatively new and seemingly growing, but as a result, it can be somewhat confusing to practitioners and program developers. Table 3.2 provides a brief synopsis of each of these concepts.

Particularly since each term is more similar than different, with only slight nuances separating them, it is at times difficult to distinguish among the terms. As a result, I prefer to use the broader concept of *research basis*, as I believe it to be more inclusive, capturing evidence-based, emerging, empirically guided, and best practices and allowing for utilizing both research that has been proven and that which has been logically proposed but not yet fully tested. Moreover, I believe it is in this manner that the essential core of program design is captured—the utilization of empirical knowledge in program design and the dynamic nature of program design as a fluid and ever-changing process, constantly developing as new knowledge emerges. After all, it is not the precise concept that is used in program design that is of utmost importance but, rather, that programs have a firmly established research basis that serves as the foundation by which clinical interventions are anchored. This can be accomplished by the use of a specific evidence-based practice, the utilization of an emerging practice with promising preliminary research, the use of an empirically based conceptual design, or the integration of best practices into program design.

Table 3.2 Key Concepts in Program Design

Evidence-Based Practice	Emerging Practice	Empirically Guided Practice	Best Practice	Research-Based Practice
Proven successful through rigorous evaluation	Not yet sufficiently evaluated; promising, yet requires more rigorous evaluation	Theoretical or conceptual framework based in empirical research; has not been evaluated	Includes evidence-based practices as well as other essential program components; summarized research findings	Inclusive term used to refer to practices that may be evidence-based, emerging, empirically guided, or best practices

Knowing that the current climate of program design requires a firm basis in research is of great use to beginning program developers, and gaining a better understanding of the various factors that have led to the current focus on accountability provides an effective context for working within the current climate. More importantly, this knowledge alerts us to the amount of attention to detail and work required in program design. This work begins with utilizing our own research skills and involves conducting a comprehensive review of the literature.

Conducting a Comprehensive Literature Review

As stated earlier, building a research-based program design requires a tremendous amount of attention and significant work. To accomplish this, a comprehensive literature review must be conducted that allows for a careful examination of all current relevant literature. The literature review must minimally include scholarly research (i.e., journals, academic texts), best practice literature, governmental reports and bulletins, and research from other sources such as national advocacy groups or professional associations dedicated to a particular clinical or social issue (e.g., Child Welfare League of America). For the majority of clinical program development efforts, scholarly research typically provides the most wide-ranging source of information; however, there often is overlap between traditional scholarship, best practice literature, and governmental publications.

In conducting a review of the literature for the purpose of new program development, what is most necessary is that the review is thorough, allowing you to gain as much knowledge as possible about all the various aspects of the particular issue you are seeking to address through programming (e.g., elderly depression, substance abuse). This is definitely a case in which *more is better,* since your fundamental program design tool comes directly from the literature review. As a result, it is essential that you explore all relevant nooks and crannies in the literature so that you can become fully equipped with the knowledge necessary to effectively inform your program design. Before moving into a broader discussion about each major type of literature to be examined, let's first discuss strategies to focus or guide the review.

Guiding the Literature Review

The vast amount of research that must be examined in a thorough review of the literature can be daunting, and as with all tasks that might at first blush seem bigger than life, it is necessary to break things down so that they are both manageable and effective. In this case, you must ensure that you examine all relevant information while drilling down to focus on what is most essential in the literature. To organize your review, you will need to focus on the key issues (see Box 3.1) and the key questions (see Box 3.2).

BOX 3.1

KEY ISSUES TO GUIDE LITERATURE REVIEW

1. The population and its specific needs to be addressed through program design

2. Counseling theory

3. Clinical interventions

4. Adjunctive and nonclinical interventions and/or supports

5. Multicultural issues

BOX 3.2

KEY QUESTIONS TO GUIDE LITERATURE REVIEW

1. What are the specific risk factors of the target population?

2. What specific protective factors have been found to mitigate risk?

3. What specific theories have proven effective in addressing the need?

4. How has successful treatment been defined?

5. What major clinical interventions have proven effective in addressing the need?

6. What types of nonclinical or adjunctive interventions have proven effective in addressing the need?

7. What are the frequency and number of interventions that have proven effective in addressing the need?

8. What specific delivery method or continuum of care (e.g., residential, home-based) has proven effective in addressing the need?

Whereas there may be additional questions that can be used to further focus your review depending on the specific topic, the objective here is to ensure an efficient inquiry; so simply utilize guiding questions that allow for this. With the guiding questions in hand to organize the literature review, attention can be turned to the various types of literature for review.

Sources of Research for the Literature Review

Scholarly Literature

Scholarly literature provides the starting point for the research review; however, because of the breadth and diversity within scholarship, it is necessary to organize your search to ensure that specific key areas are explored. These include, but are not limited to, various types of data analyses regarding the identified problem, such as demographic variables, risk and protective factors, and other compiled statistics and empirically based studies related to the problem, including outcomes evaluations, research related to specific clinical interventions, compiled literature reviews of research related to the problem, meta-analyses of interventions and/or programs, position papers, theoretical articles, and other scholarship dedicated to examining and addressing the problem (Calley, 2009).

Published literature reviews and meta-analyses of program outcomes related to the problem often are extremely valuable to the research review process because they contain summaries of the scholarship published on the topic. While I find these particularly helpful since a good part of work has already been done for me, I also have to be careful not to overly rely on these summaries at the neglect of reviewing equally significant single studies that have not been included in the compilation. To ensure that you, too, avoid this potential pitfall, published literature reviews and meta-analyses should be used only *in addition to* single studies and independent articles focusing on the issue at hand.

The other important facet to bear in mind when conducting a review of scholarly literature is to search widely across the literature, appreciating that relevant knowledge is often promoted across various disciplines. Therefore, rather than focusing solely within your own particular discipline (e.g., counseling), make certain to conduct your literature search across disciplines to ensure the necessary breadth of the literature review. Particularly today, areas of specialization within professions are vast and overlapping. As a result, it is not uncommon to find research on depression in counseling and clinical psychology journals as well as in medical journals and criminal justice literature.

In addition to scholarship that is published through professional journals, empirically based books published by scholarly presses or as academic texts also should be examined. Often, collections of previously published articles on a single topic may be bound in a text and/or the results of a comprehensive study may be published in book format to include more details than could be provided in a scholarly journal. These types of scholarship often provide a great deal of knowledge on a particular topic and can be as significant to the literature review as journal articles.

Best Practice Literature

To complement the review of scholarly literature, best practice literature must also be examined. Whereas the scholarly literature does publish various best practice literature, best practices are often published through a variety of other venues as well. Typical venues for publishing best practice literature include professional associations of major disciplines (e.g., American Counseling Association, American Psychiatric Association), professional associations of specialty areas (e.g., Association for the Treatment of Sexual Abusers), and national task forces designed to address a specific area. Although this type of literature is not always published through traditional scholarly outlets, it is often the result of research findings and emphasizes practice and application (Calley, 2009).

Governmental Publications

Because we are so fortunate in the United States to have so many governmental agencies dedicated to a variety of mental health and social service issues, the federal government is a tremendous resource for program development efforts. In addition to the vast Departments of Health and Human Services and Education, the National Institute of Mental Health, the Substance Abuse and Mental Health Services Administration, and the Office of Juvenile Justice and Delinquency Prevention, as specialty agencies, provide focused attention to their respective issues. As a result, these and similar governmental agencies house extensive archives and publish comprehensive bibliographies as well as a variety of literature. Published literature may be the result of national task forces established to make recommendations regarding a specific issue or may summarize the findings of various research efforts. In addition, compiled statistics and essential data are housed by the federal government and can be freely organized to meet the needs of a given project. Briefing books and bulletins are also regularly published to provide information quickly and in simple formats that serve as handy references, while white papers often provide executive summaries addressing a particular issue. Finally, because so much mental health and human service programming is funded by the federal government, a significant number of publications are the direct result of funded programs and projects.

I find that I rely heavily on the resources produced by the federal government not only for my work in new program development but as an integral and incredibly vast resource for my day-to-day work. The resources are indeed extensive and, as such, require time to fully examine all that is available and become familiar with the various types of existing knowledge. However, governmental resources can also present their share of challenges, particularly as the publishing process is largely dictated by fiscal health and can be slow at times, sometimes limiting the amount of material available while other times delaying the release of pertinent information and resources. In addition, there is always the risk of politicization that can occur with regard to the types of resources that are published.

Conferences

Conferences sponsored by professional associations or other professional groups may provide yet another forum through which to obtain research for use in the literature review. Unlike scholarly publishing, which is often dogged by incredibly lengthy time periods between submission of research findings and publication of the research findings, conference presentations enjoy a much shorter shelf life, allowing research findings to be disseminated fairly quickly. As a result, some cutting-edge research may be easily accessible through conference presentations.

However, obtaining research through conference presentations may also bring its fair share of challenges. First and foremost of these challenges is the type of research presented at conferences, which may run the gamut in terms of the degree of rigor involved in the original evaluation, from survey data to experimental design. In addition, there are far more opportunities for researchers to share their research at conferences than through scholarly journal articles, making conference participation far less competitive. Finally, and tied directly to both of these issues, is the type of vetting process employed by the conference organizers, which may impact the type of research presented. The use of a peer review or juried process to select conference presentations may provide an increased level of scrutiny, but it in no way guarantees that only scientifically sound research is presented. Because of these reasons, when gathering research from conference presentations, you must critically evaluate the degree of scientific rigor applied in the research design.

Summary

As you can see, the era of program development in which we now live has quite a long and multifaceted history. In fact, it is the result of more than

40 years of small yet significant changes, myriad factors, and external forces that collectively have led to a climate in which accountability and effectiveness are the core principles driving program development. This has fundamentally changed the way in which we do business today, and it is difficult, if not impossible, to survive as a program developer without an innate commitment to accountability and effectiveness in the 21st century.

Both accountability and effectiveness in program development begin with a program design that is based on empirical evidence. As such, the existing body of research must be fully utilized to inform and guide program design. By conducting a comprehensive literature review and using the various principles and practices that have been identified in the research, a research-based program design can be established, thus accomplishing the second integral step in comprehensive program development.

CASE ILLUSTRATION

A Request for Proposals was issued by the state for a juvenile sex offender treatment program. The human services agency that Joseph worked for was interested in applying for the program as a result of its experience with juvenile offenders. Joseph, a clinical supervisor in the agency's community-based program for juvenile offenders, was charged with developing the program design description for the proposal. To begin to develop the design, he headed to the local university library, where he secured a visitor pass to utilize the library's research database.

To organize his search, Joseph began by limiting research to peer-reviewed scholarly journal articles published within the past 5 years and utilized two comprehensive databases that focused on the behavioral and social sciences and criminal justice. He then began searching for information about the population by using *juvenile sex offender* as the key words. As he became more familiar with the type of research available, he conducted advanced searches focusing on both assessment methods for juvenile sex offenders and treatment efficacy for juvenile sex offenders. These advanced searches allowed him to locate specific information regarding these two key aspects of treatment—assessment and effectiveness. Moving further into the treatment aspect, Joseph began to search for articles focusing on theory and the relationship between theory and clinical programming for juvenile sex offenders. After reading through either the abstracts or the full-text articles (when available), he selected those articles that were relevant to his needs so that he could either obtain copies of the articles that were not available through interoffice library loan or save them to his jump drive for full review later.

(Continued)

(Continued)

As Joseph was reading through some of the articles, he ran across several references to sex offender legislation and other legal issues, prompting him to conduct an advanced search on *juvenile sex offender legislation* and *legal issues related to juvenile sex offending*. In addition, Joseph expanded his search to include two legal databases.

He then expanded his search of databases to include books and other documents dealing with juvenile sex offenders, marking those most relevant for full examination later. After identifying three books and two white papers on the topic, Joseph conducted a broad search using an Internet search engine to get a better sense of who else was publishing information about juvenile sex offenders. This resulted in Joseph locating three credible resources: the National Criminal Justice Resource Center, a comprehensive resource of research archives hosted by the federal government; the Center for Sex Offender Management, a consortium dedicated to disseminating knowledge about sexual offending; and the Association for the Treatment of Sexual Offenders, a professional association for individuals working with juvenile sex offenders. Joseph visited each of the entities' websites and was able to locate a number of relevant documents, including white pages, fact sheets, and specific bibliographies related to juvenile sex offenders.

After concluding his research, Joseph gathered all the documents available to him directly from the library, including one of the books, and then went about acquiring the other documents that were not available from the library. With all the research in hand, Joseph set about learning all he could about juvenile sex offenders, closely reading through everything he had. His comprehensive review of the literature resulted in identifying the primary clinical needs of juvenile sex offenders, including but not limited to identification of pattern/cycle of abuse, resolution of victimization in the juvenile sex offender's history, identification of cognitive distortions and thinking errors that support sex-offending behaviors, and development of empathy (Andrade, Vincent, & Saleh, 2006; Calley, 2007; Righthand & Welch, 2001; Worling, 2005). In addition, Joseph learned that cognitive-behavioral theory had established efficacy as a theoretical base for treating juvenile sex offenders (Winokur et al., 2006) with several cognitive-behavioral therapy techniques such as behavioral rehearsal, examining the interrelationships between thoughts and behaviors and the affect of changing one to impact change in another, and controlling stimuli used in treatment. He also learned about the evidence related to the use of various clinical modalities, including individual, group, and family counseling for juvenile sex offenders, as well as differences in treatment outcomes related to length of program and program types (i.e., residential, clinic-based, home-based). After thoroughly culling all the research relevant to community-based programming for juvenile sex offenders, Joseph was prepared to begin designing the treatment program. Moreover, Joseph was confident that his design was well justified, with a solid foundation in empirical research.

References

Andrade, J. T., Vincent, G. M., & Saleh, F. M. (2006). Juvenile sex offenders: A complex population. *Journal of Forensic Science, 51*, 163–167.

Calley, N. G. (2007). Promoting an outcomes-based treatment milieu for juvenile sex offenders: A guided approach to assessment. *Journal of Mental Health Counseling, 29*, 121–143.

Calley, N. G. (2009). Comprehensive program development in mental health counseling: Design, implementation, and evaluation. *Journal of Mental Health Counseling, 31*, 9–21.

Council on Accreditation. (2008a). *About COA.* Retrieved September 9, 2010, from http://www.coastandards.org/about.php

Council on Accreditation. (2008b). *Introduction: Private standards.* Retrieved July 17, 2010, from http://coastandards.org/standards.php?navView=private

Council on Accreditation. (n.d.). *Standards.* Retrieved September 9, 2010, from http://www.coanet.org/front3/page.cfm?sect=55&cont=4191

Council on Accreditation of Rehabilitation Facilities. (2010). *Quick facts about CARF.* Retrieved September 9, 2010, from http://www.carf.org/About/QuickFacts

Department of Health and Human Services. (n.d.). *Historical highlights.* Retrieved September 9, 2010, from http://www.hhs.gov/about/hhshist.html

Government Accountability Office. (n.d.). *Welcome to GAO.* Retrieved April 28, 2010, from http://www.gao.gov/index.html

Johnson, M., & Austin, M. (2006). Evidence-based practice in the human services: Implications for organizational change. *Administration in Social Work, 30*, 75–104.

Joint Commission, The. (2010). *A journey through the history of The Joint Commission.* Retrieved September 9, 2010, from http://www.jointcommission.org/AboutUs/joint_commission_history.htm

Jungquist, C. R., O'Brien, C., Matteson-Rusby, S., Smith, M. T., Pigeon, W. R., Xia, Y., et al. (2010). The efficacy of cognitive-behavioral therapy for insomnia in patients with chronic pain. *Sleep Medicine, 11*, 302–309.

Kettner, P. M., Moroney, R. M., & Martin, L. L. (2008). *Designing and managing programs: An effectiveness-based approach* (3rd ed.). Thousand Oaks, CA: Sage.

Letourneau, E. J., Henggeler, S. W., Borduin, C. M., Schewe, P. A., McCart, M. R., Chapman, J. E., et al. (2009). Multisystemic therapy for juvenile sexual offenders: 1-year results from a randomized effectiveness trial. *Journal of Family Psychology, 23,* 89–102.

Lewis, J. A., Packard, T. R., & Lewis, M. D. (2007). *Management of human service programs* (4th ed.). Belmont, CA: Thomson Learning.

Marotta, S. A., & Watts, R. E. (2007). An introduction to the best practices section. *Journal of Counseling and Development, 85,* 491–503.

Melkers, J. E., & Willoughby, K. (2005). Models of performance-measurement use in local governments: Understanding budgeting, communication, and lasting effects. *Public Administration Review, 65*, 180–190.

Navarrete-Navarrete, N., Peralta-Ramirez, M. I., Sabio-Sanchez, J. M., Coin, M. A., Robles-Ortega, H., Hidalgo-Tenorio, C., et al. (2010). Efficacy of cognitive behavioural therapy for the treatment of chronic stress in patients with lupus erythematosus: A randomized controlled trial. *Psychotherapy and Psychosomatics, 79,* 107–115.

Righthand, S., & Welch, C. (2001). *Juveniles who have sexually offended: A review of the professional literature.* Washington, DC: Office of Juvenile Justice and Delinquency Prevention.

Schoenbald, S. K., Heiblum, N., Saldana, L., & Henggeler, S. W. (2008). The international implementation of Multisystemic Therapy. *Evaluation Translation of Health Behavior Research Innovations, Part I,* 211–225.

Sheidow, A. J., Henggeler, S. W., & Schoenwald, S. K. (2003). Multisystemic therapy. In T. L. Sexton, G. R. Weeks, & M. S. Robbins (Eds.), *Handbook of family therapy* (pp. 348–370). New York: Brunner-Routledge.

Substance Abuse and Mental Health Services Administration. (2007). *SAMHSA launches searchable database of evidence-based practices in prevention and treatment of mental health and substance use disorders.* Retrieved September 9, 2010, from, http://www.samhsa.gov/newsroom/advisories/0703013707.aspx

Trull, T. J., & Phares, E. J. (2001). *Clinical psychology: Concepts, methods, and profession* (6th ed.). Belmont, CA: Wadsworth.

Winokur, M., Rozen, D., Batchelder, K., & Valentine, D. (2006). *Juvenile sex offender treatment: A systematic review of evidence-based research.* Fort Collins: Colorado State University, College of Applied Human Sciences.

Worling, J. R. (2005). Assessing sexual offense risk for adolescents who have offended sexually. In B. K. Schwarz (Ed.), *The sex offender: Issues in assessment, treatment, and supervision of adult and juvenile populations* (Vol. 5, pp. 18-1–18-17). Kingston, NJ: Civic Research Institute.

CHAPTER 4

Address Cultural Identity Issues in Program Design

Learning Objectives

1. Discuss the significance of cultural competence in program design

2. Identify two resources that can be used to provide guidance in delivering culturally competent services

3. Discuss the various factors that have influenced the current climate related to cultural competence in program design

4. Identify two methods for use in identifying aspects of an individual's cultural identity

DETENTION IS DETENTION

Larry had been managing a shelter program for boys in the child welfare system for a year when his contract manager informed him that the county wanted him to begin serving girls as well. After working out the logistics with his staff and his executive director, Larry was able to confirm that the shelter would be ready to begin accepting female clients in the next 30 days. Larry and his staff then moved quickly to rearrange the building so that the living spaces would be separated between the sexes, completing some minor renovations. More importantly, having worked only with male clients in the past, Larry was looking forward to the change that female clients would bring. He and others at his agency were also excited that the county had specifically asked them to take on this new business that would result in an increase of revenue for the agency and further demonstrate the agency's good standing with its funding source.

Five months after the program began serving females, the county's licensing consultants came for their regular review/audit. When asked about the new program that had been developed specifically for the female clients, Larry looked back at the consultant, not quite understanding what she was referring to. Larry shared with the consultant that the program they had in place for the boys had been successful, and so they did not make any changes to the program when they began serving girls. The consultant further pushed Larry, inquiring if he was aware of *gender-specific treatment*, to which Larry responded that of course he was. In fact, he stated that the agency had made significant—and costly—changes to the facility in order to separate the living spaces between the girls and boys, and he further shared with the consultant that he had directed the staff to purchase dolls and sewing kits for the girls.

When the licensing review report arrived 2 weeks later, Larry had been given a noncompliance for failing to provide gender-specific treatment in the shelter. As a result, he was required to submit a corrective action plan within 30 days stating how this issue would be addressed.

CONSIDERING LARRY

1. What did Larry fail to do?

2. In addition to the licensing citation, what other ramifications might this issue have caused Larry/the agency?

3. If you were Larry, how would you go about determining how to develop a program for female children versus male children?

About This Chapter

Because cultural competence is an essential component of program design, part of the literature review must be specifically devoted to examining culturally competent interventions. While this does not constitute an additional step in the program development model because of its significance and scope, it is important that it be given particular attention in the literature review. Thus, it is considered Step IIa—a specific subcomponent involved in establishing a research basis in program design.

Because cultural competence is such an integral part of clinical programming, the first part of the chapter is devoted to a review of some of the major concepts of cultural competence. Next, we will examine historical and influential factors related to the current climate of multiculturalism, with a specific focus on the role of professional associations, scholarship, academic preparation, accreditation, and funding. Finally, we will explore methods by which to identify cultural identity aspects of client populations. An exercise is provided at the end of the chapter to assist you in focusing the literature review on cultural competence and in identifying culturally competent treatment strategies for use in program design.

STEP IIA: ADDRESS CULTURAL IDENTITY ISSUES IN PROGRAM DESIGN

Culturally Based Concepts: The Building Blocks of Our Current Vocabulary

As you witnessed in Chapter 3, the manner in which clinical programs are developed has changed dramatically over the past couple of decades. In addition to the increased emphasis on program effectiveness and accountability in program design, in more recent history, there has been an increasing call for cultural competence in program design. Also, just as a new vocabulary has been adopted for program design focused on enhanced business practices and accountability (e.g., evidence-based practices, best practices), other new concepts have come into more frequent use to reflect an ever-increasing emphasis on cultural competence in program design. Spurred on by the growth and development of the human service and mental health fields and increased recognition and understanding of diversity, the commitment to cultural competence has expanded tremendously.

To aid in our understanding of multiculturalism and its intersection on program design and implementation, concepts such as diversity, multiculturalism, cultural self-identity, and cultural competence have reemerged or been introduced into our vocabulary. These concepts provide us with a sound foundation for understanding issues related to cultural identity, as well as illustrating the progress that has been made in this area. In fact, I like to think of these terms as building blocks, each concept dependent on the previous one and each one reflecting our increased knowledge and growth in this area (see Figure 4.1). Although entire graduate courses today focus on multiculturalism and related issues, a brief summary of each of these major concepts is necessary to frame the discussion on incorporating multicultural considerations into program design.

Diversity

Fundamentally, diversity refers to differences. In the mental health professions, diversity refers to working with individuals who are different from us. In our rather short history of identifying and understanding diversity, we have come quite a long way, moving from a small and exclusive definition of diversity into a broad, encompassing view. Early forays into diversity in the mental health professions focused primarily on race, with an underlying assumption that racial differences constituted the primary differences between individuals. It was not until the 1970s that empirical studies on

Figure 4.1 Building Blocks of Culturally Based Concepts

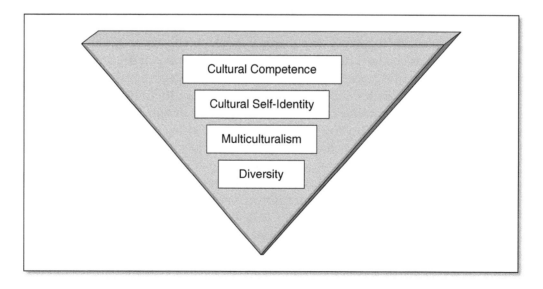

ethnicity began to significantly increase (Baruth & Manning, 1999). Interestingly, this expanding view of diversity occurred at quite a slow pace, particularly given that Erikson (1950) began urging the mental health professionals to enlarge their view of diversity by looking beyond mainstream America as far back as 1950.

Regardless of how long it has taken to get here, today we understand a much broader concept of diversity—one that goes well beyond both race and ethnicity. Currently, we understand diversity as being highly inclusive of an endless number of traits, encompassing an individual's unique differences that might be related to class, physical or mental ability, sexual orientation, religion, gender, national origin, race, geography, ethnicity, or other aspects (Lum, 2007). Moreover, as we have come to understand diversity as broad and expansive, we have come to associate diversity with richness—understanding that differences between individuals provide a unique source of benefit to others and to humankind.

Corporate America was one of the first to pick up on the inherent value of diversity, and thus, businesses began making strategic hiring decisions designed to achieve a diverse workforce. As a result, diverse workforces were often able to achieve greater success in business. It is not difficult to understand the logic behind embracing diversity in the workplace, particularly when considering decision-making processes. For instance, decisions made by a group of individuals of similar backgrounds and experiences often reflect nothing unusual or different to any of the members. This results in *business as usual* decision making. However, decision making by a group of individuals from varied backgrounds and experiences often promotes new ways of thinking and doing business, thus enriching the outcomes and allowing the business to try something new—a near necessity in today's rapidly changing business world.

Whereas the business world has long understood the benefits and strengths that diversity offers in the workplace, the mental health professions have continuously worked to better understand specifically how to support individuals with diverse needs and from diverse backgrounds. At the basis of this understanding is the notion of diversity as fundamental to all of us as human beings. As a result, understanding and appreciating diversity requires that in order to most effectively treat and serve individuals in need, we must first understand what makes each individual who and what s/he is.

Multiculturalism

First identified as the fourth force in counseling by Pedersen (1990), multiculturalism refers to an appreciation and acceptance of differences/ diversity and specific needs and strengths that exist among and between groups. As such, multiculturalism embraces unity and diversity (Flowers, 2009). Multiculturalism assumes that there are multiple forms of diversity without hierarchal structures or values ascribed to any one type of diversity over another. Multiculturalism promotes an understanding that differences between individuals and groups are not only essential but are to be embraced and celebrated. Further, multiculturalism—or more specifically, cultural relativism—requires us to view differences from their unique perspective rather than by using ourselves as the measuring stick by which to evaluate differences. In so doing, we are forced to learn about differences from the inside out rather than by applying a subjective or encapsulated view of what constitutes a difference and what that difference means.

Whereas diversity taught us to identify differences and begin to understand the value of differences, multiculturalism taught us how to not only acknowledge the nuances of differences but celebrate those differences. As such, multiculturalism serves to limit egocentricity and expand our thinking about what diversity is by forcing us to look beyond ourselves and appreciate the richness of others.

Cultural Self-Identity

Cultural self-identity refers to the extent to which individuals perceive themselves as included and aligned with others through various shared aspects of diversity (e.g., gender, generation, ethnicity, class). Growing out of multiculturalism, cultural identity picked up where multiculturalism left off, allowing for an understanding that a variety of cultural differences exist within each individual, collectively shaping the individual's self-identity. It is in this regard that cultural identity is highly complex, with identities having varying levels of prominence, often contextually influenced. For example, whereas the socioeconomic status of a 40-year-old cashier at a fast food restaurant may not be something of which he is largely aware when he is among friends in his neighborhood, it can become the most prominent aspect of his identity when he is at a function with a group of wealthy individuals. Similarly, the fact that one is agnostic may have little bearing on how one feels about oneself day to day; however, when attending religiously affiliated events, one's agnosticism may suddenly have quite significant meaning. These examples highlight the manner in which aspects of identity converge to create a specific meaning to the individual as well as the contextual nature of cultural identity wherein certain aspects achieve greater prominence as a result of environmental factors.

Moving our understanding of cultural self-identity forward, Arredondo and Glauner first presented their framework for understanding cultural identity in 1992. The framework categorizes aspects of identity into three groupings: identities that are assigned to us/that which we cannot control (e.g., initial geography, class, ethnicity, initial religion), identities that we have some control over (e.g., vocation, class, geography), and historical or other issues that impact our self-identity (e.g., chronic illness, living through a recession). Through this framework, cultural self-identity promotes an enriched understanding of individuals in which the individual is the sum of his or her parts and, as such, requires mental health professionals to understand and appreciate the convergence of identity aspects. Moreover, the framework suggests that whereas there are three major methods by which our cultural identities can be shaped, the prominence and meaning of each is determined by the individual. Therefore, whereas for some individuals, initial socioeconomic class has significant meaning to how they perceive themselves, for others, the class that they achieve later in life may have greater influence on their self-perception.

Cultural Competence

Cultural competence (also known as multicultural competence) is defined as the counselor's development of awareness of her or his cultural identity and belief systems and the knowledge and skills to work with diverse individuals (D. W. Sue, Arredondo, & McDavis, 1992). As a means of making the standards operational and to promote an inclusive view of cultural identities, Arredondo et al. (1996) identified a set of competencies for counselors to achieve in practice that built on the previous work of D. W. Sue et al. These competencies have been endorsed by the Association for Multicultural Counseling and Development and can be found both on its website (www.amcdaca.org) and on the website of the American Counseling Association (www.counseling.org).

Similarly, the National Association of Social Workers (2007) has promulgated standards for cultural competence in practice to provide specific guidance to social workers in this area. *Indicators for the Achievement of the NASW Standards for Cultural Competence in Social Work Practice* can be found on their website (www.socialworkers.org).

Briefly, cultural competence requires mental health professionals to fully understand their own cultural self-identity, confront their own biases or limitations, and effectively deal with any beliefs that may impact their professional ability to support an individual of differing identity. Second, cultural competence requires individuals to gain deep knowledge and understanding of various identity aspects in order to be well informed and achieve a general framework while at the same time learning from each client about his/her cultural self-identity and its personal meaning. For instance, possessing knowledge that for many African Americans, extended family is a critical support system does not necessarily imply that each African American client is significantly connected to his/her extended family or that extended family has significant meaning to that particular individual. Finally, cultural competence requires mental health professionals to attain specific skills that are necessary to effectively work with individuals from diverse backgrounds or with unique aspects of identity. This includes the use of assessment instruments that have been appropriately tested or normed on diverse groups (e.g., you would not use a self-efficacy assessment tool with an Asian youth that has been normed on a population of African- and Euro-American youth). In addition, this requires the use of specific clinical interventions that are culturally sensitive or that take the client's cultural identity into account.

Seeking cultural competence—a primary objective of all mental health professionals—requires working with clients in a state of *constant curiosity*. By this, I mean that understanding the multifaceted layers and unique meaning of a client's cultural identity requires the counselor to be open to continuous learning about how the client perceives him/herself. At the same time, it means that the counselor must be continuously committed to learning all there is to know about how to provide the most effective treatment to the client as a result of his/her cultural identity.

As you can see, we have come quite a long way in how we think about differences among persons and the impact of those differences on clinical treatment. Whereas we had to first understand that differences among individuals need to be acknowledged and thoughtfully considered, thus ushering in studies of diversity, we soon shifted our focus beyond simply looking at differences between individuals and groups to increasing our understanding of the value of such differences. From this framework, an emphasis on cultural self-identity emerged that then led us to our current focus, which ties all three of these areas together in the concept of cultural competence.

Cultural Competence and Clinical Program Design

Brief History

The brief review of terminology related to multiculturalism provides one level of understanding the history of cultural competence in clinical programming and should also provide an effective map to better understanding the developmental path that cultural competence has taken. Whereas we witnessed significant growth in the area of diversity and multiculturalism over the past 2 decades, it was not until much more recently that particular shifts toward cultural competence in clinical program development began to emerge.

Initially, this shift led to the development of programs focused on a specific cultural identity aspect. This led to a much clearer focus on developing programs not only that were gender-focused/gender-specific and developmentally appropriate but also that focused on specific subgroup populations, such as child-welfare–involved Latino youth and female prisoners with primary substance abuse problems. These shifts toward thinking about treatment for specific subpopulations had tremendous impact as they challenged the status quo by demanding that treatment take into account an individual's unique attributes when relevant to treatment.

Prior to this, while it was common for males and females to be housed separately in residential programs, the focus of clinical treatment was most often the same, regardless if the treatment issue was addiction, a serious mental health issue, or homelessness. As such, the risk factors for a female addict, the manner in which she experienced addiction, the unique meaning that she derived from being a female with an addiction problem, and the methods by which she could be successful in treatment were not necessarily considered since often the treatment approaches had been originally developed for male addicts. This is not to say that early treatment programs for males did a much better job integrating gender as a focus of treatment but that because programs were largely facilitated by men, they may have had somewhat of an innate predisposition to incorporating male gender into treatment.

This very issue of the convergence of cultural identity with a treatment need (e.g., Asian-American mental health treatment) continued to gain ground as a body of research was developed addressing these issues. Studies on topics such as treating single adults in homeless shelters (Baggerly & Zalaquett, 2006), treating bereavement and coping among South Asian families post-9/11 (Inman, Yeh, Maden-Bahel, & Nath, 2007), and counseling clients that are deaf (Peters, 2007) began to appear, investigating the significance of incorporating specific cultural identity aspects into treatment. Not only did these studies produce significant knowledge for the mental health professions, but they served to further reinforce the necessity of addressing cultural identity in treatment.

All this may seem perfectly logical today, considering that the experience of a female who is homeless is often significantly different than that of a homeless male, particularly with regard to safety, risk factors that led to homelessness, and resources needed to move out of a transitional state.

However, a tremendous amount of effort by many mental health professionals was expended to get us to this current place of understanding that for each individual, the convergence of various identities creates unique meaning and treatment needs.

Current Climate

Knowing how far we have come always helps us better understand where we are today, which is a place wherein cultural competence is not only an aspirational goal of mental health professionals but both an intrinsic value and mandatory objective of our profession. In addition to the multicultural competencies that guide the work of professional counselors and other mental health professionals, the stature of cultural competence in the mental health and human service fields is widely evident through a multitude of factors. In particular, six factors likely serve as the most effective indicators of the current climate. These include

1. the number of professional associations specifically committed to both broad and specific aspects of multiculturalism,

2. the amount of scholarship dedicated to cultural competence,

3. cultural competence as a core part of academic preparation in mental health disciplines,

4. the promulgation of national standards of cultural competence by the federal government,

5. the inclusion of cultural competency-specific accreditation standards for mental health and human service programs, and

6. the requirement of addressing cultural competence in proposals for funding new program development.

Professional Associations

The number and diversity of cultural identity issues that are the focus of divisions of both the American Counseling Association and the American Psychological Association provide a snapshot of the current stature of multiculturalism in the mental health professions. In fact, currently, there are four divisions of the American Counseling Association and five divisions of the American Psychological Association specifically dedicated to one or more aspects of multiculturalism (see Table 4.1).

Table 4.1	Professional Mental Health Associations With a Specific Focus on Multicultural Issues

Divisions of the American Counseling Association	Divisions of the American Psychological Association
Association for Adult Development and Aging	Society for Child and Family Practice
Association for Lesbian, Gay, Bisexual, and Transgender Issues in Counseling	Society for the Psychological Study of Ethnic Minority Issues
Association of Marriage and Family Therapy	Society for the Psychological Study of Lesbian, Gay, Bisexual, and Transgendered Issues
Association for Multicultural Counseling and Development	Society for the Psychological Study of Men and Masculinity
	Society for the Psychology of Women

Whereas these professional associations serve multiple purposes such as providing scholarly and collegial outlets for professionals working with issues of diversity, they each also serve to ensure that both specific (e.g., men and masculinity) and more broad-based issues of diversity (e.g., multicultural counseling and development) retain a central focus in the mental health professions. The work of the associations is wide-ranging, including the promotion of professional dialogue, conferences, dissemination of scholarly and nonscholarly information through various venues, and professional advocacy, to name just a few. What each association shares, regardless of its particular focus on multiculturalism, is an emphasis on increasing knowledge and skills of mental health professionals to better support individuals of varying identities. Moreover, professional associations serve as collectives of behavioral change agents to clients nationwide and serve as national leadership forums in dialogue and teaching about diversity issues.

In addition, the Codes of Ethics of both the American Counseling Association (2005) and the National Association of Social Workers (2008) provide further reinforcement of the central role that cultural competence has in mental health treatment today. To illustrate this, Table 4.2 provides a snapshot of the specific ethical standards related to culturally competent practice.

Table 4.2 Ethical Standards Related to Culturally Competent Practice

American Counseling Association	National Association of Social Workers
Standard B.1.a. Counselors maintain awareness and sensitivity regarding cultural meanings of confidentiality and privacy. Counselors respect differing views toward disclosure of information. Counselors hold ongoing discussions with clients as to how, when, and with whom information is to be shared.	*Standard 1.05 (a)* Social workers should understand culture and its function in human behavior and society, recognizing the strengths that exist in all cultures.
Standard E.5.b Counselors recognize that culture affects the manner in which clients' problems are defined. Clients' socioeconomic and cultural experiences are considered when diagnosing mental disorders.	*Standard 1.05 (b)* Social workers should have a knowledge base of their clients' cultures and be able to demonstrate competence in the provision of services that are sensitive to clients' cultures and to differences among people and cultural groups.
Standard E.8. Counselors use with caution assessment techniques that were normed on populations other than that of the client. Counselors recognize the effects of age, color, culture, disability, ethnic group, gender, race, language, preference, religion, spirituality, sexual orientation, and socioeconomic status on test administration and interpretation, and place test results in proper perspective with other relevant factors.	*Standard 1.05 (c)* Social workers should obtain education about and seek to understand the nature of social diversity and oppression with respect to race, ethnicity, national origin, color, sex, sexual orientation, gender identity or expression, age, marital status, political belief, religion, immigration status, and mental or physical disability.

Scholarship

As a key function of professional associations, the dissemination of knowledge through scholarship has long been served via the professional journals published by various associations. Today, each of the major behavioral and social science disciplines publishes journals dedicated solely to multicultural issues. More telling a sign of the significance that multiculturalism and cultural competence has today in the behavioral and social sciences, though, is the number of scholarly articles pertaining to such issues published across various journals within disciplines. For instance, whereas all the articles in the *Journal of Multicultural Counseling and Development* are directly related to issues of multiculturalism and cultural competence and the *Journal of Lesbian, Gay, Bisexual, and Transgendered Issues in Counseling* and the *Journal for Social Action in Counseling and Psychology* focus on specific subareas of diversity, journals with a much broader scope such as *Professional School Counseling* and the *Journal of Counseling and Development* often contain multiple articles focused on various aspects of cultural competence. Moreover, multiculturalism and diversity cut across most if not all scholarship today. In fact, you would be hard-pressed to find a major journal in any discipline, from accounting to zoology, not addressing some aspect related to cultural identity.

The breadth of scholarship dedicated to multiculturalism and cultural competence in the United States is highly indicative not only of the immense diversity of our country but, more so, of our commitment to knowledge as we continue to grow and expand. Likewise, the integration of multicultural issues across a vast number of disciplines speaks to the universal regard for cultural competence as one of our core values.

Academic Preparation

Related to both professional associations and scholarship is the current focus of academic preparation in mental health fields specifically on cultural competence. As a result, there is significant emphasis on the teaching of cultural competence as part of standard pedagogical practice.

At the graduate level, academic programs are often largely influenced by academic accreditation standards, as graduate programs often strive to attain accreditation. Because these accrediting bodies are largely influenced by the major activities of the field, while professional associations have evolved to specifically focus on multiculturalism, unique academic program standards dedicated to multiculturalism have also been promulgated. And it is in this way that the interactions between these factors are evident.

For instance, the Council for Accreditation of Counseling and Related Educational Programs (CACREP) guides the teaching of graduate-level counselors. This type of discipline-specific academic program accreditation concentrates on all aspects of academic programming, from the university infrastructure to the program-level administration and from the admissions process to the curricular experiences and academic objectives. Mirroring the current values of the counseling profession, these accreditation standards reflect the prominence of cultural competence within the broader mental health field. As such, Social and Cultural Diversity is one of the eight core curricular areas of CACREP accreditation standards, focusing on academic experiences that promote understanding of the cultural context of relationships, trends, and issues currently impacting the profession of counseling (CACREP, 2009). Core curricular areas provide the foundation of the counseling curriculum, serving as the underlying objectives of all counselors rather than focusing on a specific specialty (e.g., addiction counseling, school counseling). As such, these objectives focus on broad aspects of cultural competence such as theories of identity development and social justice and the counselor's role in eliminating biases, prejudices, discrimination, and oppression (CACREP, 2009). Whereas issues related to multiculturalism compose one of the core standard areas, aspects of cultural competence are also a part of other core areas such as assessment and evaluation and research and program evaluation. Finally, standards related to cultural competence are again evident in the standards of each specialty area under the heading of *Diversity and Advocacy*. Within the specialty areas, standards related to cultural competence are more practice-specific, taking into account issues relevant to the specific specialty, such as recognizing the various types of families that may be counseled by specialists in Marriage and Family Counseling—which might include same-sex couples and/or families in transition. Table 4.3 provides examples of these academic program standards.

Academic program accreditation standards ensure that cultural competence is an essential part of academic training and preparation. As a

Table 4.3	Integration of Multiculturalism and Cultural Competence Across CACREP Standards
Core curricular area—Social and Cultural Diversity	II.G.2.e. Counselors' roles in developing cultural self-awareness, promoting cultural social justice, advocacy and conflict resolution, and other culturally supported behaviors that promote optimal wellness and growth of the human spirit, mind, or body
Inclusion of cultural competence in other core curricular objectives	II.G.8.f. Ethical and culturally relevant strategies for interpreting and reporting the results of research and/or program evaluation studies
Practice standards of specialization areas—diversity and advocacy	Career Counseling—E.4. Understands the changing roles and responsibilities of women and men and the implications of these changes for employment, education, family, and leisure

result of the influence of academic preparation, new clinicians are fully aware of the significance of cultural competence in mental health treatment and human services.

National Standards

Providing another form of guidance on a national level, the standards promulgated by the Department of Health and Human Services' (2007) Office of Minority Health focus specifically on cultural and linguistic competencies for health care providers (see Box 4.1). In addition, the National Center for Cultural Competence at Georgetown University provides a host of resources for integrating cultural competence in mental health program design (http://nccc.georgetown.edu). Both of these may prove significant resources in comprehensive program development to ensure that cultural competence remains a central part of services and treatment.

BOX 4.1

NATIONAL STANDARDS ON CULTURALLY AND LINGUISTICALLY APPROPRIATE STANDARDS (CLAS)

Health care organizations should take the following actions to meet CLAS standards:

1. Ensure that patients/consumers receive from all staff members effective, understandable, and respectful care that is provided in a manner compatible with their cultural health beliefs and practices and preferred language

2. Implement strategies to recruit, retain, and promote at all levels of the organization a diverse staff and leadership that are representative of the demographic characteristics of the service area

3. Ensure that staff at all levels and across all disciplines receive ongoing education and training in culturally and linguistically appropriate service delivery

4. Offer and provide language assistance services, including bilingual staff and interpreter services, at no cost to each patient/consumer with limited English proficiency at all points of contact, in a timely manner during all hours of operation

(Continued)

(Continued)

5. Provide to patients/consumers in their preferred language both verbal offers and written notices informing them of their right to receive language assistance services

6. Assure the competence of language assistance provided to limited English proficient patients/consumers by interpreters and bilingual staff; family and friends should not be used to provide interpretation services (except on request by the patient/consumer)

7. Make available easily understood patient-related materials and post signage in the languages of the commonly encountered group and/or groups represented in the service area

8. Develop, implement, and promote a written strategic plan that outlines clear goals, policies, operational plans, and management accountability/oversight mechanisms to provide culturally and linguistically appropriate services

9. Conduct initial and ongoing organizational self-assessments of CLAS-related activities and, ideally, integrate cultural and linguistic competence-related measures into internal audits, performance improvement programs, patient satisfaction assessments, and outcomes-based evaluations

10. Ensure that data on the individual patient's/consumer's race, ethnicity, and spoken and written language are collected in health records, integrated into the organization's management information systems, and periodically updated

11. Maintain a current demographic, cultural, and epidemiological profile of the community as well as a needs assessment to accurately plan for and implement services that respond to the cultural and linguistic characteristics of the service area

12. Develop participatory, collaborative partnerships with communities and utilize a variety of formal and informal mechanisms to facilitate community and patient/consumer involvement in designing and implementing CLAS-related activities

13. Ensure that conflict and grievance resolution processes are culturally and linguistically sensitive and capable of identifying, preventing, and resolving cross-cultural conflicts or complaints by patients/consumers

14. Try to regularly make available to the public information about the organization's progress and successful innovations in implementing the CLAS standards and provide public notice in their communities about the availability of this information

Accreditation Standards for Mental Health and Human Service Organizations

In addition to the above national standards of the Office of Minority Health and the National Center for Cultural Competence, some of which are mandated for subcontractors receiving federal funding, the major national accrediting bodies for human services and mental health programs have also promulgated specific standards addressing cultural competence in program design and service delivery. By doing so, organizations that voluntarily seek accreditation are required to comply with such standards, thereby effectively addressing cultural competence as a primary aspect of programming. For instance, Adoption Standard 2.02 of the Council on Accreditation (COA; 2008) requires that "assessments are conducted in a strengths-based, culturally responsive manner to identify resources that can increase service participation and support the achievement of agreed upon goals."

Each of the specific accreditation standards for the Council on Accreditation of Rehabilitation Facilities (CARF) and COA can be found on their websites (www.carf.org and www.coanet.org), while the accreditation standards of The Joint Commission are available for purchase at their website (www.jointcommission.org). Taken collectively, these accreditation standards that specifically address cultural competence constitute another major influence on current mental health and human service programming in the 21st century.

Funding

Just as scholarship has informed academic preparation programs and national accrediting bodies as to the significance of cultural competence, funding bodies have not ignored this call. In fact, some requests for new program development are directed specifically toward diverse populations. To illustrate this, consider these recent funding opportunities targeting specific cultural identity aspects and treatment needs:

- Urban and nonurban homeless veterans' reintegration program (Office of the Assistant Secretary for Administration and Management, Department of Labor, 2010)
- Technical assistance for national minority aging organizations (Administration on Aging, 2010)
- Women's mental health in pregnancy and the post-partum period (National Institute of Health, 2009)

As you can see, funders have begun to emphasize a *need* for programs and research that addresses unique treatment needs of special populations.

In addition to directly targeting specific subpopulations through specialized funding opportunities, funders may also require that applicants address various unique needs of populations within more general grant applications. In doing so, the funding source may provide information in the application summary that speaks to some of the unique issues of the population in order to provide background information to applicants. This information, based on current research, is crucial to the applicant as it provides necessary information that needs to be addressed in the application. For instance, take a look at the following excerpt from a recent federal Request for Proposal summary for projects to provide substance use services to United States veterans:

> Younger service members with combat exposures had increased rates of new-onset heavy weekly drinking, binge drinking, alcohol-related problems and increases in smoking initiation and relapse (Jacobson et al., 2008; Smith et al., 2008). . . . In addition to deleterious effects of deployment on the military member, there is emerging evidence of the effects on the family. (Department of Health and Human Services, n.d., "Deployment," para. 1)

By articulating this information in the Request for Proposal, the funder is specifically emphasizing the significance of culturally competent treatment. As such, the funder is providing critical information related to the specific needs of (1) younger military personnel and (2) families of military personnel and two specific types of unique treatment needs of these populations— (1) substance use and abuse and (2) deployment-related issues. Moreover, the funder explicitly requires that the unique needs of the identified special populations must be addressed by applicants.

In both instances, when funding is provided for special populations and when funding is provided for a general population with targeted subpopulations, applicants are often required to stipulate their plans to work with these populations and to state specific methods by which the treatment needs of the populations will be met. The astute program developer is wise to pay close attention to delineating the relevant aspects of cultural identity and unique treatment needs to ensure that s/he is fully equipped to address these critical issues through programming, thus articulating one's cultural competence.

As you can see, scholarship, professional associations, academic preparation, national standards, accreditation bodies, and funding trends have each had a significant influence on the current climate related to cultural competence in program design. These influences have not occurred in isolation but rather, in many ways, are highly interconnected, with a change in one influencing a change in another. Moreover, it is because of the collective force that has been brought to bear by the convergence of these influential factors that today cultural competence is a central tenet of mental health and human service programming.

However, whereas the current climate reflects this shift toward increased knowledge related to cultural identity, research focused specifically on treatment interventions for diverse groups is still very much in its infancy. We must therefore be cautious not to mistake this growth in awareness and knowledge of multiculturalism as growth in cultural competency. Rather, we must continue to focus our energies toward increasing our knowledge and skills to ensure that we can indeed most effectively address diverse needs through culturally competent program design.

Cultural Identity Aspects and Client Populations

Building programs that are culturally competent begins with fully understanding cultural identity and the vast aspects that compose cultural identity. As stated originally by Arredondo and Glauner (1992) and as reiterated by Lum (2007), cultural identity is both multifaceted and complex, with various layers and dimensions that individually and collectively influence a person's perceptions of self and the world in which s/he lives. To provide a sense of some of the aspects that contribute to one's cultural identity, see Table 4.4.

I should note that Table 4.4 provides just a sample of cultural identity aspects and subtypes and that the aspects and subtypes are not organized with any type of hierarchy or implied value. This is important to keep in mind when remembering that the value that any aspect of cultural identity has is determined by the individual, not by others (this deserves repeated mention). Whereas this is only a sample, it illustrates just how complex cultural identity is and, as a result, just how much we as program developers need to understand all the various nuances that compose cultural identity. Although the table is designed to provide a snapshot of some of the identity aspects that belong to a particular category (e.g., Ableness: paraplegic, visually impaired, traumatically brain-injured, physically abled), to gain a sense of the complex identities of individuals, move across the table from left to right, considering that one row reflects five identity aspects of an individual. For instance, one individual is a gay Muslim from a poor, urban area whose vocation is in mining and who views extended family members as his/her primary family members. The complexity of this

Table 4.4 Cultural Identity Aspects and Subtypes

Class	Ethnicity	Gender	Ableness	Race
Lower socioeconomic class	African American	Female	Paraplegic	Black
Middle socioeconomic class	Maltese	Male	Visually impaired	American Indian
Lower upper-socioeconomic class	Hmong	Intersexed	Traumatically brain-injured	White
Upper lower-socioeconomic class	Hispanic	Transgendered	Physically abled	Pacific Islander

Sexual Orientation	Religion	Geography	Current Family	Vocation
Gay	Islam	Poor, urban city	Extended family as primary	Miner
Straight	Buddhism	Rural Midwest farming community	Same-sex parents	Professor
Bisexual	Catholicism	Rural, poor south	Foster or adoptive family	Fast food worker
Questioning	Seventh Day Adventist	Wealthy, urban city	Nuclear family with opposite-sex parents	Customer service representative

individual's cultural identity is easily evident, but only s/he can tell us what particular meaning this identity holds for him/her.

Like understanding the various meanings that are made from cultural identities, understanding the various aspects that fall into each category is no easy task. This is especially true since new aspects of cultural identity are constantly emerging and new meaning is formed by the convergence of multiple aspects of identity. Particularly relevant in the United States, with our continuously expanding diverse population, one of the primary challenges in developing culturally competent interventions again lies in one's ability to remain constantly curious—ensuring that you are indeed receptive to continuous learning about new needs related to cultural identity and to designing programs that are flexible enough to accommodate needs as they arise.

Identifying Cultural Identity Aspects of Client Population

Ensuring that you are adequately prepared to address the diverse needs of client populations begins with comprehensive planning that has a focus toward cultural competence. Ideally, this results in a culturally competent program design and a treatment milieu that is conducive to ongoing modifications to meet the needs of individual clients. There are two specific activities that need to be conducted to accomplish these objectives, one that is used to identify multicultural considerations needed in the initial program design and the other that is used to identify additional issues related to cultural identity that may require ad hoc program modifications. As such, the first is necessary for initial program design and is considered part of the *preplanning stage*, whereas the second is considered an ad hoc feature of program design, utilized when necessary as new prominent aspects of cultural identity emerge.

The first activity involves revisiting the results of the community demography assessment. Because the community demography assessment results provide broad information about the population parameters, they are especially useful to this stage. Since this assessment was conducted previously (in Step I), the work has already been completed; so the objective at this stage is now twofold: (1) Review the information to use in developing knowledge about the population's diversity and attendant needs, and then (2) use this new knowledge to identify multicultural considerations that will need to be addressed in program design (Step III). To accomplish this, you must return to the summary report compiled as part of the comprehensive needs assessment process (Step I) in order to cull the cultural identity information of the population. Having done this, you are effectively prepared to research specific clinical needs that are related to cultural identity.

For instance, if the results of your needs assessment and market analysis justify the development of a program targeting adolescent males, and there are majority groups of Mexican and Chaldean youth among your target population, research must be conducted to learn more about the unique experiences and/or special needs of adolescent Mexican and Chaldean youth. Examining the research on these two ethnic groups would likely clarify that both groups may be characterized by strong familial ties (Nydell, 2006; Szapocznik et al., 1997), a belief in Fatalism (Arredondo, Bordes, & Paniagua, 2008; Hakim-Larson, Kamoo, Nassar-McMillan, & Porcerelli, 2007), the Catholic faith (Matovina & Riebe-Estrella, 2002; Nydell, 2006), and difficulty attached to seeking outside help (Abudabbeh & Aseel, 1999; McCabe, 2003). Whereas this knowledge should not be used to pigeonhole any population (indeed, no characteristics can be applied to all individuals within a subgroup), it does ensure that program designers have some level of general knowledge about their specific target populations, and that knowledge should be used to provide some guidance to program design. As such, gaining this information about these groups allows you to determine what, if any, unique features should be built into the program design in order to address these multicultural considerations when relevant to the individuals being served.

In order to accomplish the second objective related to making program accommodations to address specific culturally related needs, culturally focused assessment must guide this process, often built into the client intake process. Unlike the first activity that involves research to gain broad knowledge related to cultural identity, making program modifications relies on gaining specific information through assessment directly from clients who may indicate such a need. Assessment questions may be focused on such areas as religious and/or spiritual traditions, family dynamics, or communication style, to name a few. These questions of inquiry should be designed both to promote sharing significant personal information with the clinician and to inform the clinician about important client characteristics that may require specific accommodation. As with all questions posed as part of a therapeutic experience, each question must be fully justified and, therefore, must add specific value to the treatment process. To illustrate this type of assessment, Table 4.5 provides sample questions and how they may be used to accommodate the client.

These questions can be easily embedded in the intake questionnaire so that they simply become a part of the initial client assessment process—an essential part, at that. By doing this, accommodations can easily be made for the client, and in this way, cultural competence is demonstrated not only as a programmatic value but as a construct that

Table 4.5	Sample of Culturally Focused Assessment Questions, Objectives, and Potential Accommodations

Question	Objective	Potential Accommodations
Do you subscribe to any particular religion and/or spirituality, and if so, what would you like me to know about the type of meaning that religion and/or spirituality has in your life?	Provides broad information related to client's belief system and informs the clinician about the degree of significance that religion/spirituality has in the client's life	Incorporate beliefs into treatment process; assist client in conceptualizing issues from a religious or spiritual perspective
What types of religious and/or spiritual practices do you engage in and when, if any?	Provides information about types of activities that provide meaning to the client and may indicate times that the client may be unavailable	Avoid scheduling treatment or treatment-related activities during religious/spiritual practice times
How do you typically go about making decisions?	Informs clinician about client's decision-making process and may indicate if the client involves other individuals in the decision-making process	Include in treatment decision-making process

requires consistent and deliberate attention in order to be achieved. It probably goes without saying that program developers who appreciate cultural competence are fully attuned to their responsibility to create flexible programs and work diligently at program modifications as needs arise.

Developing Culturally Competent Treatment Interventions

Despite the fact that we have an advanced understanding of cultural competence today and understand that cultural competence is a core expectation for all mental health professionals, we have yet to fully understand if and how cultural competence impacts treatment outcomes.

In fact, in a climate in which empirical evidence must guide clinical practice, there is a dearth of research on culturally competent empirically supported mental health interventions (Roberts, Yeager, & Regehr, 2006). While this does not necessarily indicate that there is not a relationship between cultural competence and treatment outcomes, it does mean that without doing more work in this area, we can only discuss cultural competence from a *best practice* perspective and not an *evidence-based* perspective.

The reasons for the dearth of research in this area are highly valid and easy to understand, based directly on how an evidence basis is established in the first place—through rigorous research with appropriate sample sizes. And more importantly, through the use of randomized controlled studies (S. Sue & Zane, 2006). Speaking specifically of cultural competence with regard to ethnic and/or racial differences, Conner and Grote (2010) summarize these challenges:

> The ability to effectively develop and conduct randomized controlled trials to test mental health interventions in racial/ethnic minority populations has proven to be particularly challenging. Given that the population sizes of racial/ethnic minorities in America are relatively small when compared to Whites, it is not uncommon for racial/ethnic minorities to be concentrated in particular geographic regions in the United States. Thus, it may take additional resources to gain access to these communities in order to engage them in research. (p. 590)

In order to begin to understand precisely how cultural competence can be integrated into treatment in order to produce effective outcomes, we must work to overcome these barriers. To provide a starting point for this, Conner and Grote (2010) suggest incorporating culturally competent interventions into existing evidence-based practices (e.g., cognitive-behavioral therapy) and conducting rigorous evaluation to determine the outcomes. Applying Bernal, Bonilla, and Bellido's (1995) cultural framework that includes language, persons, metaphors, content, concepts, goals, methods, and context, the authors demonstrate how this can be done (see Conner & Grote, 2010). Whereas there may indeed be other methods by which to begin this research, the fact remains that particularly because we have come so far in our understanding of cultural competence, we must now examine it with specific regard to evidence-based practices.

Summary

As you can see, cultural competence is a critical component of clinical program development today, and one that is arguably a most essential factor in the ongoing health and quality of human services. However, it has taken quite a bit of time to reach this current state, and fully appreciating where we are today requires an understanding of the various historical factors that prompted us to arrive here. As a starting point, the basic concepts of diversity, multiculturalism, cultural identity, and cultural competence have both provided a framework for understanding issues related to culture and moved us forward from transforming knowledge and understanding into action. But the progressive use of these concepts did not occur outside the context of other changes occurring in the field, and in fact, changes in professional associations, scholarship, academic preparation, accreditation standards, the promulgation of national standards, and funding requirements were each instrumental in creating the current climate. Working symbiotically, these factors—as well as others—have converged to increase our understanding of cultural identity and propel us toward cultural competence. As knowledge in this area has increased, program developers have been more concerned with addressing cultural identity in initial program design and in ongoing program implementation efforts.

However, whereas the current climate in program development does indeed emphasize attention to cultural identity, we still have quite a long way to go to achieve cultural competence in program design. This will likely require both greater pressure from funding sources and rigorous evaluation that includes an emphasis on the impact of cultural competence by program developers and other evaluators. So, just as we have made significant strides in increasing understanding of the role that culture plays in program design, our energies must now be focused more specifically on the development of culturally competent interventions that are empirically supported through rigorous evaluation. By shifting our focus to an action orientation now, we will continue to move forward in integrating cultural competence into program design. Whereas this is the ideal objective of all efforts related to multiculturalism, it is obviously no easy task. Just as it has taken more than 30 years to create the current climate that includes an expansive and complex understanding of cultural identity, it will require concerted efforts by program developers and practitioners, funding sources, and researchers to continue to propel us toward this ideal end—an end that, when achieved, will mark an entirely new dimension of growth in clinical program development.

CASE ILLUSTRATION

Hank and Janet have received funding to implement an outreach program for elderly persons with serious mental health issues. While working to establish a research basis through a review of the literature, they realize they need to reexamine the results of the community demography assessment in order to better understand the specific cultural identity aspects of their target population. In doing so, they find that the target population is largely composed of elderly women and that the majority of persons—both men and women in the region—are highly impoverished and economically poor. In addition, the region itself is large, urban, and highly challenged by a significant lack of resources, high rates of both unemployment and crime, and a large population of homeless individuals. The demographic information of the region provides a necessary context for developing the program, and the four most prominent aspects of cultural identity that have been identified include

- age (i.e., elderly),
- gender (i.e., women),
- mental health status (i.e., serious mental health issues), and
- socioeconomic status (i.e., poor).

Each aspect requires specific consideration in program design, so Janet and Hank turn to the scholarly literature to learn some of the specific needs related to elderly women with serious mental health issues in poor economic circumstances. Through this review, they learn that serious mental health disorders among this population may include depression, dementia (including Alzheimer's), and psychosis. In addition, they learn of other risk-related issues, such as

- heightened sensitivity to psychotropic medication,
- lifestyle and age-related risk factors for depression (e.g., loneliness, bereavement, poverty),
- nighttime restlessness,
- suicide risk, and
- homelessness risk.

As a result of this knowledge, Hank and Janet design specific program features that will take into consideration the unique needs of the population and, as such, may serve to guard their population against further risk. As part of the program's assessment activities that they have built into the program design, they identify specific assessment instruments designed to evaluate depression, psychosis, and dementia. In addition, they decide to incorporate assessment tools that evaluate substance use, including prescription drugs, because of the potential for co-occurring disorders involving substance-use disorders and depression, psychosis, or dementia. To address some of the other unique needs, they then incorporate the following activities into the program design:

- Increase of psychotropic medication monitoring from monthly to weekly
- Creation of a buddy system (elder to elder) to provide ongoing one-to-one, in-home social support (in addition to the Community Support Network that is part of the basic program design)
- Nighttime activity options
- Enhanced case management activities to sustain housing and basic living needs

By adding these culturally focused activities to their basic program design, Janet and Hank are able to thoughtfully and effectively plan for the unique needs that some of their clients may have. In keeping with culturally competent practice, the individual needs of each client must be continuously assessed to ensure appropriate treatment.

To address other unique needs more relevant to specific individuals rather than reflective of the group, Janet and Hank add a series of culturally focused initial assessment items to the intake interview guide. These include such questions as the following:

- When you are feeling good, what types of things do you most like to do?
- What times of day, if any, are particularly difficult for you?
- Whom do you most like to talk to if you have a problem?

By adding items like these to the interview, Hank and Janet believe they will be able to focus more on some specific needs of their clients and be better equipped to make individual modifications. For instance, additional activities and monitoring will be added midday for clients who report most difficulty during this time of day, and these clients may not participate in nighttime activities (unless desiring to do so).

Adding culturally focused assessment items to the initial intake process and incorporating additional activities into the initial program design based on the literature pertaining to the target population allows Hank and Janet to implement a culturally focused program that is empirically guided. As such, their program design is enhanced at the outset and, hopefully, has greater potential to fully engage the target population in the treatment process. Moreover, Janet and Hank are postured to deliver effective treatment that places unique identity factors at its center, reflecting a commitment to culturally competent program design. But determining if the program is culturally competent will require rigorous evaluation, and Hank and Janet have already begun thinking about this step (fully covered later in this book).

DESIGNING CULTURALLY COMPETENT INTERVENTIONS EXERCISE

You have been awarded a federal grant to work with single adult males who are homeless or in transition. After reviewing the results of your community demography assessment, you note that the target region consists of a large population of first-generation Latino men, primarily of Mexican heritage, with a sizeable portion who are in their early 20s.

1. Identify four prominent aspects of cultural identity related to this target population.

2. Review the scholarly literature and identify a minimum of six unique characteristics related to the target population that should be considered in program design.

3. Develop specific activities or interventions to address each of the unique characteristics in the initial program design.

4. Develop four to five questions to be added to the initial intake process that are designed to capture additional culturally based information about each individual client.

References

Abudabbeh, N., & Aseel, H. A. (1999). Transcultural counseling and Arab Americans. In J. McFadden (Ed.), *Transcultural counseling* (2nd ed., pp. 283–296). Alexandria, VA: American Counseling Association.

Administration on Aging. (2010). *National minority aging organizations technical assistance centers.* Retrieved September 10, 2010, from http://www.grants.gov/search/search.do?mode=VIEW&flag2006=false&oppId=47070

American Counseling Association. (2005). *ACA code of ethics.* Alexandria, VA: Author.

Arredondo, P., Bordes, V., & Paniagua, F. A. (2008). Mexicans, Mexican Americans, Caribbean, and other Latin Americans. In A. J. Marsella, J. L. Johnson, P. Watson, & J. Gryczynski (Eds.), *Ethnocultural perspectives on disaster and trauma* (pp. 299–320). New York: Springer.

Arredondo, P., & Glauner, T. (1992). *Dimensions of personal identity model.* Boston: Empowerment Workshops.

Arredondo, P., Toporek, R., Brown, S. P., Jones, J., Locke, D. C., Sanchez, J., et al. (1996). Operationalization of the multicultural competencies. *Journal of Multicultural Counseling and Development, 21,* 42–78.

Baggerly, J., & Zalaquett, C. P. (2006). A descriptive study of single adults in home-less shelters: Increasing counselors' knowledge and social action. *Journal of Multicultural Counseling and Development, 34,* 155–167.

Baruth, L. G., & Manning, M. L. (1999). *Multicultural counseling and psychother-apy: A lifespan perspective* (2nd ed.). Upper Saddle River, NJ: Prentice-Hall/Merrill.

Bernal, G., Bonilla, J., & Bellido, C. (1995). Ecological validity and cultural sensitivity for outcome research: Issues for cultural adaptation and development of psychosocial treatments with Hispanics. *Journal of Abnormal Child Psychology, 23,* 67–82.

Conner, K. O., & Grote, N. K. (2010). Enhancing the cultural relevance of empirically supported mental health interventions. *Families in Society, 89,* 587–595.

Council for Accreditation of Counseling and Related Educational Programs. (2009). *CACREP accreditation manual.* Alexandria, VA: Author.

Council on Accreditation. (2008). *Private standards.* Retrieved April 30, 2010, from http://www.coastandards.org/standards.php?navView-private&core_id-912

Department of Health and Human Services. (2007). *National standards for cultur-ally and linguistically appropriate services in health care.* Retrieved September 10, 2010, from http://minorityhealth.hhs.gov/templates/browse.aspx?lvl=2&lvlID=15

Department of Health and Human Services. (n.d.). *Substance use and abuse among U.S. military personnel, veterans and their families.* Retrieved September 10, 2010, from http://grants.nih.gov/grants/guide/rfa-files/RFA-Da-10-001.html

Erikson, E. (1950). *Childhood and society.* New York: Norton.

Flowers, L. R. (2009). *The ACA encyclopedia of counseling.* Alexandria, VA: American Counseling Association.

Hakim-Larson, J., Kamoo, R., Nassar-McMillan, S. C., & Porcerelli, J. H. (2007). Counseling Arab and Chaldean-American families. *Journal of Mental Health Counseling, 29,* 301–321.

Inman, A. G., Yeh, C. J., Maden-Bahel, A., & Nath, S. (2007). Bereavement and cop-ing of South-Asian families post-911. *Journal of Multicultural Counseling and Development, 35,* 101–115.

Lum, D. (2007). *Culturally competent practice: A framework for understanding diverse groups and justice issues* (3rd ed.). Belmont, CA: Thomson Higher Education.

Matovina, T. M., & Riebe-Estrella, G. (2002). *Horizons of the sacred: Mexican tradi-tions in U.S. Catholicism.* Ithaca, NY: Cornell University Press.

McCabe, K. M. (2003). Factors that predict premature termination among Mexican-American children in outpatient psychotherapy. *Journal of Child and Family Studies, 11,* 347–359.

National Association of Social Workers. (2007). *Indicators for the achievement of the NASW standards for cultural competence in social work practice.* Washington, DC: Author.

National Association of Social Workers. (2008). *Code of ethics*. Washington, DC: Author.

National Institutes of Health. (2009). *Women's mental health in pregnancy and the postpartum period*. Washington, DC: Author.

Nydell, M. K. (2006). *Understanding Arabs: A guide for modern times* (4th ed.). Boston: Intercultural Press.

Office of the Assistant Secretary for Administration and Management, Department of Labor. (2010). *Urban and nonurban homeless veterans' reintegration program*. Retrieved September 10, 2010, from http://www.grants.gov/search/search.do?oppId=41279&flag2006=false&mode=VIEW

Pedersen, P. (1990). The multicultural perspective as a fourth force in counseling. *Journal of Mental Health Counseling, 12*, 93–95.

Peters, S. W. (2007). Cultural awareness: Enhancing cultural understanding, sensitivity, and effectiveness with clients who are deaf. *Journal of Multicultural Counseling, 35*, 182–190.

Roberts, A. R., Yeager, K. R., & Regehr, C. (2006). Bridging evidence-based health-care and social work. In A. R. Roberts & K. R. Yeager (Eds.), *Foundations of evidence-based social work practice* (pp. 3–21). New York: Oxford University Press.

Sue, D. W., Arredondo, P., & McDavis, R. J. (1992). Multicultural counseling competencies and standards: A call to the profession. *Journal of Counseling and Development, 70*, 477–486.

Sue, S., & Zane, N. (2006). Ethnic minority populations have been neglected by evidence-based practices. In J. C. Norcross, L. E. Beutler, & R. F. Levant (Eds.), *Evidence-based practices in mental health: Debate and dialogue on the fundamental questions* (pp. 329–337). Washington, DC: American Psychological Association Press.

Szapocznik, J., Kurtines, W. M., Santisteban, D. A., Pantin, H., Scopetta, M., Mancilla, Y., et al. (1997). The evolution of a structural eco-systemic theory for working with Latino families. In J. Garcia & M. Zea (Eds.), *Psychological interventions and research with Latino populations* (pp. 166–190). Boston: Allyn & Bacon.

Design the Clinical Program

Learning Objectives

1. Discuss the relationships between Steps I and II and Step III

2. Discuss the objectives of a program mission and vision

3. Identify the components of the core clinical program

4. Differentiate between outputs and outcomes

5. Differentiate between short- and long-term outcomes

6. Develop a logic model

WHO ARE WE ANYWAY?

Donald had been the executive director of a mental health agency for the past 5 years. The agency had been founded on the premise of serving individuals in need and specializing in mental health treatment. Over the years, they had built up a sizeable continuum of care that included outpatient counseling, crisis services, and an in-home care program for adults. After seeing some of his colleagues succeed in operating methadone clinics in the region, Donald began talking to his staff about the possibility of the agency opening one. After laying the groundwork, getting authorization from his board, and putting a team together to develop the program, Donald finally witnessed the opening of his new methadone clinic. The program was successful financially and was now entering its second year. Donald then was approached by one of his neighbors about beginning a financial planning clinic for individuals in debt. Donald liked the idea and again worked through the plans to open the clinic. While his board had questioned how financial planning fit into the agency's broader mission, Donald claimed that it simply provided another mechanism by which to help people, and therefore, it fit nicely with the agency's mission. Plus, Donald added that the mission was intended to change over time and that he had to bear that in mind so that the agency could continue to grow and adapt. And since they had named the financial planning program a *clinic*, it sounded more like the agency's other programs.

A couple of months later, after the financial planning program was up and running, Donald had overheard some of his staff talking in the lunchroom, saying they didn't know what the agency was anymore. Making her point, one of the supervisors had stated: "Who are we anyway? A meth clinic, financial planners, or mental health professionals?" Donald dismissed this as typical employee grumbling.

Donald and his board had to gear up and begin their next round of fundraising activities for the agency. And during various campaigns, one of the questions from potential funders that kept coming up was, what is your business? Donald continued to claim that, as the agency's mission stated, the agency was committed to *helping people in need*, primarily through mental health programming. When questioned about the two new programs, Donald stated that he saw both as offshoots of broader mental health programs and he stressed how the programs augmented the agency's service array. But most of the agency's previous funders had a hard time buying this, claiming they didn't feel connected to the agency as they had before. They further shared that they had previously provided their support because the agency's mission had specific meaning to them; however, this was no longer the case, and they felt the mission had been diluted. Donald thought to himself, *People put too much emphasis on mission—maybe we should just change it and everything will be okay again.*

CONSIDERING DONALD

1. What, if anything, do you believe Donald did wrong?

2. If you were Donald, what next steps would you take and why?

3. As the agency's leader, what responsibility does Donald have to the agency mission?

4. What relevance do organizational identity and mission have to staff and other stakeholders?

About This Chapter

This chapter marks the beginning of the program design phase, specifically dedicated to the development of the clinical program. The first part of the chapter deals with the mission and the vision, with an in-depth examination of each and an exploration of specific issues to consider in the development of mission and vision statements. After tackling these two initial program design tasks, the chapter moves into a discussion of the core program design elements, including ideological foundations, interventions, outputs, short- and long-term outcomes, and outcome measures. We will thoroughly examine each of these core design elements, with examples provided throughout the chapter. Then, we will discuss two essential design tools—the logic model and the project timeline. Examples of each of these are also provided. Finally, a case study illustrates and further reinforces the major concepts of the chapter, and an exercise is provided to allow you the opportunity to construct your own core program design.

STEP III: DESIGN THE CLINICAL PROGRAM

Comprehensive Program Design

After the target population and primary needs have been identified, a thorough review of the literature has been conducted, and the multicultural needs of the population have been identified, the preplanning stage has been officially completed and the planning phase is ready to begin. The planning phase begins with program design. Program design includes

- articulating the program mission and vision,
- identifying the core components of the program (ideological foundations, interventions, outputs, outcomes, and outcome measures),
- organizing the plan for program implementation, and
- organizing the program evaluation.

Each of these aspects of program design is critical, and they all serve unique yet interrelated purposes. And by bringing each of these aspects together, the program developer is able to achieve effective coherence in program design—a most significant necessity. More importantly, Step III is directly tied to Steps I and II and cannot be completed without these previous steps being effectively completed first. That is, the program's objectives and what it seeks to achieve (i.e., mission, vision, outcomes) are based on the needs that are identified in Step I. At the same time, the interventions and outcomes are designed to directly address and resolve the identified needs. In addition, the design is based specifically on research that was identified in the literature review, and modifications to the design are based on demographics of the target population and research supporting such modifications—each of which is based on achieving specific short- and long-term outcomes. As a result, at Step III, you are able to clearly begin to see the sequential nature of these initial three steps and how each acts as a building block to the next—providing precisely the type of guidance needed in comprehensive program development.

Program Mission and Vision

The mission and vision of a program or organization are brief statements that are developed to capture the essence of a program and that serve two different purposes: The mission communicates the core purpose of the program, while the vision communicates the aspirational goals of the program. Because the mission and vision are vitally interconnected, they are typically considered together. Ideally, the mission and vision are collaboratively constructed by program leaders, staff, and other key stakeholders and, ultimately, are approved by an organization's governing board. Completed as part of the initial program design, the mission and vision provide an opportunity during this early program development phase for leaders and staff to articulate the purpose of the program and look toward future goals, thus further justifying the program's existence while inspiring future growth.

The program mission and vision can be among the most powerful programming development tools available to the program developer but only if used effectively and to their full potential. Failing to effectively use the mission and vision can alternatively result in creating statements that are tossed around at meetings and other events that have little substance and limited meaning to program personnel, clients, and the public. Used to their full potential, the mission can effectively communicate the program's rationale and core objectives, while the vision can articulate the future goals of the program. As such, the mission and the vision are essential communication tools—sending critical messages to all stakeholders (i.e., staff, clients, public) about *why the program exists* and *what the program and its personnel seek to achieve in the long term.* Moreover, the mission and vision have the potential power to engage stakeholders to invest in the program and to contribute to the success of the program. Unfortunately, missions also are vulnerable to becoming no more than empty words that convey little to no meaning. And because missions can become so easily obscured in the day-to-day work, Gray and Kendzia (2009) urge nonprofit organizations to continuously revisit and strengthen their missions to ensure that they remain relevant.

The most significant stakeholder to any program is the client population; therefore, the mission must reach this group. However, this may not often be the case. In fact, a study of mission statements from 40 state-administered child welfare agencies found that 30 of the statements required 12th-grade reading comprehension (Busch & Folaron, 2005). As a result, a portion of the people that the organizations were serving was unable to understand the mission of the organization serving them. Thus, the agencies created barriers between themselves and their clients. Conversely, and as the authors point out, effective missions not only provide essential information to clients but also may provide essential guidance to employees.

In addition to providing guidance and direction to the program both initially and on an ongoing basis, there are several other objectives that can be accomplished by the development of the mission and vision statements. These include

- improving outcomes by providing clear direction (Busch & Folaron, 2005);
- defining and communicating the meaning of the program to staff, clients, and the public;

- engaging staff, clients, and the public in the program;
- directing short-term and long-term planning and operational decision making;
- providing coherence and continuity for the program;
- setting the stage for long-term strategic planning;
- differentiating the program from competitors while highlighting common objectives; and
- providing an initial branding opportunity to program developers for use in marketing and future program identity development.

Again, while the potential exists for the mission and vision to have a positive and far-reaching impact on the program, achieving maximum benefits from a mission and vision requires strategic efforts and constant commitment from program developers and program leaders. For instance, the mission and vision must be actively and continuously assessed as part of ongoing program planning and used as the foundation for branding and other marketing activities. By actively using the mission and vision as a core part of initial and ongoing program development, they remain not only relevant but essential to the sustainability of the program. And it is in this manner that the mission and vision are brought to life—not simply written words but living guides.

Constructing the Mission Statement

According to Brody (2005), an effective mission statement is concise, inspiring, and understandable. More pointedly, Lewis, Packard, and Lewis (2007) suggest that a good mission statement be approximately two sentences in length or brief enough to fit on the back of a business card. Further, the authors suggest that the mission statement should answer these key questions:

- What social needs does the program address?
- What are the primary services of the program?
- What makes the program unique?

In addition, the mission should also identify the type of organization (e.g., human service, advocacy, food service). Whereas this may be less relevant when this information can be easily deduced from the type of services provided, when this is not the case, the type of organization should be identified. By answering these basic questions, the mission statement should easily communicate the purpose of the program, operations of the program, and unique features of the program—basically, it should communicate the program's identity.

In addition to being concise and providing a clear picture of the program, there are some other key recommendations to consider in the construction of the mission statement. These include the following:

1. *Create a mission that is easily accessible to clients and that clearly reflects the program objectives and practices* (Busch & Folaron, 2005). Because the primary target group that should be reached through a mission statement is the client population, it is imperative that the mission is accessible through both the reading level at which it is written and through the means by which it is provided. In addition, the mission must be able to communicate in straightforward terms what is to be expected from the program.

2. *Create a mission that is enlarged enough to grow with the program while focused enough to clearly communicate the core purpose of the program.* This is particularly important because a mission serves to communicate the identity of the program, and as such, it needs to have lasting power lest it be easily forgotten.

3. *Avoid language that may have specific meaning with a particular group while alienating others.* Whereas a program may be specifically developed to address the needs of one particular population, the mission statement must be easily understood and have the ability to connect a broad range of individuals that include funding agents, donors, and the public. If a mission includes language from a religious text, it may resonate deeply with some while not engaging others. I should add that this consideration must be carefully weighed, particularly in light of programs/organizations that value connecting with a unique primary group at the expense of losing a broader audience. For instance, a human service organization that is specifically designed to address the needs of a particular ethnic group, such as Maltese Americans, should strategically include the target ethnic group in the mission statement as it is a core part of the program's identity.

4. *Use language that can be easily adapted for use in marketing and branding.* Because the mission statement has such potential for various uses, it is important to fully consider its utility as a marketing tool. For a mission statement to be easily adapted, it is best to have

key language that can serve as sound bites. For instance, language such as "one family at a time" or "functional independence" may be easily culled from a broader mission statement and used in various venues to further promote the program.

In order to examine a mission statement to determine if it is indeed communicating the unique identity of the organization and articulating the primary objectives of the organization, consider the current mission statement of my employer:

> The University of Detroit Mercy, a Catholic university in the Jesuit and Mercy traditions, exists to provide excellent student-centered undergraduate and graduate education in an urban context. A University of Detroit Mercy education seeks to integrate the intellectual, spiritual, ethical, and social development of our students.

As a highly subjective reviewer of this mission (since I am paid by the institution), it seems to me that several key pieces of information are communicated in this mission that together form a broad, yet focused identity. These key terms include the following:

- University
- Catholic
- Jesuit and Mercy
- Education
- Student-centered
- Undergraduate and graduate
- Urban context
- Intellectual, spiritual, ethical, and social development

Further, the primary objective of the mission seems to be clearly communicated—*to provide excellent student-centered undergraduate and graduate education.* Whereas this particular mission has personal significance to me since I am charged with carrying it out on a daily basis, consider the mission of your organization and what it communicates to you.

Now, take a moment to review the mission statements from various organizations to determine if you can link the mission with its corresponding organization in the *Name That Organization Exercise*. Select from the list of organizations below and match each with its mission statement by providing the organization's name in the box beside the statement.

NAME THAT ORGANIZATION EXERCISE

Mission Statement	Organization
a. The mission of the _____ is to prepare young people to make ethical and moral choices over their lifetimes by instilling in them the values of the _____ Oath and Law.	
b. Eliminating racism, empowering ____–it's what we are about and what we intend to do.	
c. To make, distribute and sell the finest quality all natural ice cream and euphoric concoctions with a continued commitment to incorporating wholesome, natural ingredients and promoting business practices that respect the Earth and the Environment	
d. ____ builds _____ of courage, confidence, and character, who make the world a better place.	
e. The mission of the __ is to ensure the political, educational, social, and economic equality of rights of all persons and to eliminate racial hatred and racial discrimination.	

Organizations (please note that there are more organizations listed than included in the exercise):

Girl Scouts of America

Florence Crittenden Homes for Girls

Greenpeace International

Haagen Daas

Young Women's Christian Association (YWCA)

Boy Scouts of America

National Association for the Advancement of Colored People (NAACP)

Ben & Jerry's

(The answers are located at the end of the chapter.)

How did you do? I am guessing that you may have easily been able to match some of the organizations with their mission statements while others may have posed a bit of a challenge for you. Did any of the mission statements communicate a unique identity to you? Did any of the mission statements surprise you or resonate with you for any particular reason? Whereas a product such as ice cream is the same at its most basic level (i.e., milk, sugar, eggs), the manner in which the company produces the ice cream and seeks to differentiate the ice cream in design can make it unique from the products of other ice cream makers. In the same manner, outpatient treatment programs for individuals with gambling addiction may be fundamentally based on the same general treatment principles but may be uniquely different than their peer programs as a result of specific design features. It is these unique factors that should be communicated in a mission lest the mission fail to reach its full potential.

Typically, when I do this exercise with my students, awareness levels related to mission statements are raised a bit and sometimes a deeper understanding of a specific organization is realized. But, whereas being able to match organizations with their mission statements may increase awareness of mission statements to a small degree, close examination and deconstruction of the mission statement is needed to gain a much more thorough appreciation of the power of a mission statement.

And just as with all activities that are part of business planning, it is essential to learn from other organizations before you tackle your own work. Therefore, before constructing your own mission statement, it is essential that you gain the knowledge and experience of critically evaluating the mission statements of other companies. The *Mission Analysis Tool* was developed to assist in this process. Use the *Mission Analysis Tool Exercise* to critically evaluate the mission statements from the companies listed in the exercise above.

MISSION ANALYSIS TOOL EXERCISE

Organization: _____   Type of Business: _____

Area of Analysis	Yes/No	Evidence
Does the mission identify the type of program/ organization?		
Does the mission identify the needs that are being addressed by the program/organization?		

Area of Analysis	Yes/No	Evidence
Does the mission identify its primary services/products?		
Does the mission identify what makes the program/organization unique?		
Is the mission effectively enlarged to allow for growth yet focused enough to clearly communicate its primary focus?		
Does the mission contain any specific language that may inadvertently alienate specific groups?		
Does the mission contain language that can be easily adapted for use in marketing and branding?		

Use the findings of this exercise to further think about how you would go about developing a mission. And most importantly, since a mission is innately tied to program design, keep in mind that the ability of the mission to communicate a program's unique identity ultimately lies in the ability of the program developer to design a unique program.

Constructing the Vision Statement

Whereas the mission statement should emphasize concise language that clearly communicates the program/organization's primary objectives, the vision statement should look well beyond the mission to what the program/organization aspires to in the future. As such, the vision should be grand, lofty, idealistic, and far-reaching, yet attainable. Because of its aspirational nature, the vision should be used to motivate and increase the momentum of staff and other stakeholders as they collectively work toward this ideal outcome.

Constructing the vision can serve to initially bring staff and other stakeholders together to determine where they would ultimately like to take the program/organization, and as a result, constructing the vision can be used to harness the energy of program stakeholders. In addition to the benefits involved in initially constructing the vision, the ongoing benefits of the vision should not be overlooked. For instance, when programs/organizations are experiencing particularly difficult times or growing pains, revisiting the vision can be used to center stakeholders and provide renewed energy as staff work through challenges.

Take a moment to consider the examples of vision statements below (Box 5.1).

BOX 5.1

VISION STATEMENT SAMPLES

We will be the model system for comprehensive and effective juvenile sex offender management throughout the state and the nation (Comprehensive Juvenile Sex Offender Management Initiative, 2009).

We envision a society characterized by a strong commitment to universal civil rights; safe communities, workplaces, and schools; stable families; and self-reliant LGBT individuals (Triangle Foundation, 2009).

To be the food company of choice (Kellogg Company, 2010).

Each of these vision statements reflects aspirations and goals, and each provides a vision of a future not yet arrived at but, to some degree, one that is clearly identified. Phrases such as "the model system" and "company of choice" illustrate the ultimate goal of the organization; however, so does "communities of service," as it reflects a better place for individuals, a place in which individuals are truly interdependent. This is the test of the vision statement: Does it provide a picture of the future that the program/organization is dedicated to achieving? If it does, it is likely to have been effectively written, but if it does not, it probably requires revisiting.

One of the things you have probably realized is that the concept of the mission and vision is well aligned with the mental health professions and the business principles that guide our work. As an industry that is inherently purpose-driven and outcomes-oriented, the vision and mission serve to provide us with direction while communicating who we are and exactly how much of an impact we are striving to make. Since the work that we do has the potential to significantly impact lives, our mission and vision carry enormous weight and require careful consideration and continuous attention.

Core Program Design

By far, the most important aspect of program development is the core clinical program design. Without an effective design, mission and vision statements really are little more than words, but with an effective program design, mission and vision statements serve as useful and complementary tools of communication. Simply put, the design of the program is the nuts and bolts—the program's essence.

Comprehensive program design comprises

- philosophical foundations,
- clinical interventions,
- adjunctive services,
- outputs,
- short- and long-term outcomes, and
- outcome measures.

As stated earlier—but well worth repeating—the program design is completely dependent on the work completed in Step II (Establish a Research Basis for Program Design). In fact, if a thorough and effective literature review has been conducted, designing the program can be easily completed by using the research findings to guide the design. More importantly, the research basis provides empirical justification for the program design—a critical issue for all stakeholders, particularly as each has a right to know that the program is designed to reach its stated outcomes. And by incorporating evaluation into the program design, you are able to effectively measure if the interventions are able to achieve the outcomes previously identified in the research and, if not, quickly make any necessary modifications and continue the evaluation process.

Program design requires specific structure and is a directional process in which each major design aspect (e.g., philosophical foundations, interventions, outputs, outcomes, outcome measures) is related to the others. It is in this manner that program design has a particular flow, with each core component directing the next.

Philosophical Foundations → Interventions → Outputs → Outcomes → Outcome Measures

Philosophical Foundations of Program Design

Comprehensive program design must begin with establishing the philosophical or ideological foundation that guides the program design. The philosophical foundation is the basic premise on which the program is developed and, as such, describes the guiding belief justifying why the program has been developed. Because philosophical foundations are broad-based and not necessarily specific to a particular program but more likely related to specific types of programs, philosophical foundations may not be unique to a program but rather to types of programs. For instance, several foster care programs may operate on the philosophical foundation that *all children deserve to live in a family environment,* thus sharing the same basic belief.

Other examples of philosophical foundations include the following:

- Family-based treatment is necessary to sustain successful treatment outcomes of juvenile offenders.
- Substance abuse is a community issue that must be addressed at the community level.
- Individuals with serious mental health issues have the same rights to community living as does everyone else.

As you can see, philosophical foundations really reflect the underlying values of a program, further reinforcing the program's purpose. This is an area that must not be underestimated, particularly because articulating the philosophical foundation of a program provides the basic rationale of why you do what you do and, as such, can be instrumental in gaining support for the program from all stakeholders. Moreover, the philosophical foundation reflects a core part of the program's identity and one that can be used to provide ongoing direction and reinforcement to clients, staff, leaders, and other key stakeholders—reminding them precisely why they do what they do.

Program Interventions

The program interventions are at the center of the program design and are designed to directly address the clinical needs of the population. Clinical interventions may consist of various types of treatment (e.g., counseling, psycho-education, relapse prevention), treatment modalities (e.g., individual, family, group counseling), and activities or other key components (e.g., structured play, simulated communication, family support networks). Typically, clinical interventions derive directly from theory (e.g., cognitive-behavioral, multisystemic); therefore, clinical interventions largely have a basis in theory, providing further justification for the use of the intervention. More significantly, though—and worth restating—determining program interventions is not a result of brainstorming or other types of pondering but, rather, is based on the empirical research that was reviewed in Step II.

In addition to clinical interventions, program interventions also may include adjunctive interventions. These interventions are composed of additional interventions and activities that complement the clinical interventions and that are necessary to address the complex issues of the client population. Also, unlike clinical interventions, adjunctive interventions may not require a clinician for implementation. Adjunctive interventions may consist of such activities as case management, monitoring, job coaching, and educational support services. Table 5.1 provides examples of potential clinical and adjunctive interventions that might be used to address specific treatment issues.

Each of the examples in Table 5.1 illustrates common evidence-based interventions used to address specific issues. However, one issue to bear in mind when determining which interventions to use in the program design is that simply because an intervention has a research basis does not mean that you will incorporate it into your design. This is because there may be several different and somewhat conflicting approaches that may each have been found to be effective in addressing a particular treatment issue. As a result, you would not simply incorporate each intervention into the design but, rather, thoroughly examine the research to understand precisely how each intervention has been used and if each was used in isolation or concurrent with another intervention. This relates to the *fidelity* of a clinical program—the degree to which an intervention/program is implemented as originally constructed. In the case of incorporating an evidence basis into the program design, fidelity refers to the degree to which the intervention/program is implemented as it was when it was found to be effective. (Fidelity is discussed in much greater depth in Chapter 12.)

For instance, one treatment model that has been found to be effective in addressing the treatment needs of youth with marijuana use problems is composed of therapeutic sessions based on motivational interviewing

Table 5.1 Clinical and Adjunctive Interventions per Treatment Program

Treatment Program	Clinical Interventions	Adjunctive Interventions
Children with autism	Behavior modification; social cue training; interpersonal skill development	Family support; educational support; recreational activities
Juveniles who sexually offend	Cognitive-behaviorally based individual and group therapy; multisystemic interventions; family therapy	Family support; academic and/or vocational support; social support network development
Adults with substance use disorders	Motivational interviewing techniques; cognitive-behaviorally based individual and group therapy; 12-step programming	Community resource linkages; family support; support system development; employment support

followed by cognitive-behaviorally focused therapeutic sessions (Dennis et al., 2004). If you had a similar target population and wished to base your treatment program on this approach, you would need to ensure that you followed the instructions provided for the model—specific therapy session topics, time frames, and other essential details—in order to ensure treatment fidelity. In this case, which is part of the Cannabis Youth Treatment project sponsored by the Substance Abuse and Mental Health Services Administration, it would mean facilitating a total of 14 therapeutic sessions as prescribed by the treatment manual outlining the entire intervention. It would also mean ensuring that the credentials of the individuals delivering the treatment are consistent with the guidelines of the treatment, as well as attending to all other aspects of the model.

Whereas the clinical interventions form the crux of any treatment program, adjunctive services are typically a necessary component of any comprehensive program and serve to enhance the process. Therefore, the selection of adjunctive interventions must also be guided by sound research and/or empirical guidance and, equally important, must contribute to the overall coherence of the program. For example, when implementing a substance abuse program, the use of community-based 12-step meetings is also often essential to ensuring long-term community support for individuals post-treatment. Similarly, the establishment of additional community supports and an enhanced social support network is often necessary to promote long-term success as individuals work to overcome myriad treatment challenges (e.g., mental health, criminal activity, homelessness).

Outputs

Outputs evolve directly from the interventions and, according to Brody (2005), indicate the volume of work accomplished. Outputs provide important information about the program design and may directly impact client outcomes. However, unlike outcomes, outputs do not indicate a change in quality of life for clients or reflect the impact of an intervention. The difference between outputs and outcomes can be difficult to grasp, especially since, historically, there have been times when outputs were conceptualized as outcomes (Rossi, 1997). Today, it is generally accepted that outputs and outcomes are distinctly different and each is significant to program design.

There are two types of outputs—intermediate and final. Intermediate outputs refer to the number and frequency of interventions, whereas final outputs refer to measurements such as the number of clients served, client completion rate, and average length of time for program completion. In this way, one way to think of outputs is that they are often numeric and focused on units or other types of measurements. Measuring outputs is critical to program evaluation because outputs provide essential details related to the program that may directly impact program outcomes. For instance, you may find that client success is directly related to the number of family counseling sessions provided or that client success is directly impacted by program completion. Moreover, measuring outputs allows you to determine exactly how much of a specific intervention a client actually received (Kettner, Moroney, & Martin, 2008) and to what degree the program was implemented as originally designed. Returning to the Cannabis Youth Treatment intervention discussed above, both the order of the interventions and the number of sessions of each intervention are outputs. Making a change to one or more of the outputs, such as limiting the number of cognitive-behaviorally based (CBT) sessions from 12 to 7 or changing the order by using CBT followed by motivational interviewing, may impact the treatment outcomes. And such modifications to a prescribed treatment model reflect nonadherence to fidelity—indicating that the fidelity of the treatment model was not maintained. As a result, the treatment cannot be evaluated in comparison with the original model, nor should similar treatment outcomes be expected to result from the modified treatment.

Outcomes

As stated above, outcomes are the impact or effect that the interventions (or treatment program) have had on the client. Outcomes are treatment-focused, referring to the efficacy and effectiveness of a given treatment (Mours, Campbell, Gathercoal, & Peterson, 2009). Further, outcomes in the mental health professions typically reflect changes in quality of life as a result of treatment. In this way, it is hopefully easy to differentiate outcomes from outputs. Identifying specifically targeted outcomes means identifying the anticipated effects on clients resulting from treatment interventions. Outcomes must be observable, attainable, and measureable. Outcomes should be evidence-based, if possible, deriving from the literature review and directly associated with previous findings from similar treatment interventions. Additionally, outcomes should be ambitious and agreed on by all stakeholders as important and feasible. Further, because the anticipated outcomes provide the basis for most subsequent decision making, the development of the right outcomes is critical (Lewis, Lewis, Daniels, & D'Andrea, 2003). Table 5.2 provides specific examples of outcomes for common treatment programs.

Table 5.2 Sample Outcomes for Common Treatment Issues

Treatment Program	Sample Outcomes
Adults with serious mental health disorders	Independent living; functional improvement
Juvenile offender treatment	No recidivism/reoffending; improved family functioning; improved academic/vocational functioning
Substance abuse treatment	Sobriety; enhanced support network; employment maintenance
Foster care	Family reunification; improved family functioning
Outreach for homeless/individuals in transition	Stable housing; employment; independence

According to Mours et al. (2009), there are several reasons for conducting outcome assessments, including

- to enhance the science behind clinical work,
- to improve treatment,
- to provide accountability, and
- to maintain the ethical responsibility of clinicians to examine quality.

Particularly today, in an era of clinical accountability, understanding and evaluating outcomes is a primary responsibility of all mental health professionals.

There are two types of outcomes—short-term and long-term. Short-term outcomes may be targeted for achievement during active treatment or shortly after treatment ends, while long-term outcomes may be targeted for achievement shortly after treatment ends or within as many as 2 years following treatment cessation. However, there are no standard rules regarding when short-term versus long-term outcomes occur. In fact, time frames for achievement of targeted outcomes must be program-specific since there are several factors that may influence the attainment of outcomes, such as type of clinical issue being addressed, type of intervention, length of intervention, treatment milieu, and other factors (e.g., client supports, environmental risks).

Determining the length of time associated with short- and long-term outcomes has particular ramifications for evaluation since outcomes evaluations are conducted to examine a program's success or lack of success. If time frames for achieving short- and long-term outcomes have not been thoughtfully established with both a research basis and relevance to the program time frames, the program may not be effectively evaluated. Therefore, again by fully utilizing the knowledge gained from the literature, establishing outcomes can be fairly straightforward but requires rigor and careful consideration.

Outcome Measures

Establishing outcomes is one thing, but once established, appropriate measurement tools must be identified by which to evaluate the outcomes. Outcome measures typically fall into one of three categories—standardized assessment, level of functioning scales, and status evaluations/numeric counts. In addition, as measuring client satisfaction has become standard practice, it too has been considered an outcome. Briefly, standardized assessment refers to assessment instruments that have been validated to measure specific issues. Standardized assessment instruments are often used to measure more sophisticated treatment needs such as depression and family functioning.

Because of the rigor with which standardized assessment tools have been tested and validated, the findings generated from some of these measures are highly reliable and, as such, particularly attractive to funders concerned with the treatment of specific clinical issues. Some well-known assessment instruments used in the mental health professions include

- the Substance Abuse Subtle Screening Inventory (Miller, 1997);
- the National Institute of Mental Health Diagnostic Interview Schedule for Children IV (Shaffer, Fisher, Lucas, Dulcan, & Schwab-Stone, 2000);
- the Millon Adolescent Clinical Inventory (Millon, 1993);
- the Beck Depression Inventory II (Beck, Steer, & Brown, 1996); and
- the Family Assessment Device (Epstein, Baldwin, & Bishop, 1981).

Interestingly, even though standardized outcome assessment has been viewed as a standard part of clinical research for some time (Ogles, Lambert, & Fields, 2002), its use is no longer limited to clinicians working in large systems (e.g., human services, hospitals) but, rather, is widespread. In fact, most recently, Hatfield and Ogles (2004) found that 37% of independent private practice clinicians used standardized outcome assessments, while Phelps, Eisman, and Kohout (1998) had earlier found that 40% of psychologists working in a medical facility used standardized assessment instruments, followed by 34% of those working in government-based programs. While there is a lack of more recent studies related to the utilization rate of standardized outcomes, these two studies reflect the trend that continues today: Standardized outcome assessment is a basic requirement for all clinicians, regardless of work setting.

Great care should be used in the selection of standardized assessment instruments. First and foremost, you must ensure that the instrument does indeed possess strong psychometric properties and that the evaluation to determine the instrument's effectiveness has been both rigorous and independently conducted (not simply conducted by the developer). Findings related to an instrument's effectiveness are most likely found in scholarly journal articles, and so, as part of the selection process, the research literature must be revisited. Second, in reviewing the literature about a specific instrument, consideration must be given to the population for whom the tool was initially developed, the population on which the tool was normed, and the population for whom you wish to use the instrument. These issues relate to cultural competency (as discussed in Chapter 4), and use of the tool may have significant ramifications if the differences between the populations are too great. Additionally, it is important to keep in mind that an instrument's popularity in terms of widespread use (e.g., Beck Depression Inventory) does not necessarily imply its efficacy or relevance to your target population. This is always a good rule of thumb in any business venture: Be as thorough as possible and do your homework diligently to ensure that you know everything about every aspect of your venture. Doing so will not only save time and money in the long run but also allow you to experience tremendous professional growth throughout the program development process.

At the core of most, if not all, mental health interventions is the objective of improving the functional ability of individuals treated. Level of functioning scales is based on the premise that an individual's ability to fully engage in a positive and fulfilling manner in the various aspects of lifestyle (e.g., home, work/school, personal relationships) is predicated on one's mental health. Conversely, the degree to which stress or symptoms impact one's ability to function in a healthy manner in one or more areas is an indicator of some degree of mental distress or symptoms. To measure this, level of functioning scales have historically been widely used.

Likely the best known and most widely used level of functioning scale is the Global Assessment of Functioning, which is a standard part of both psychological and psychiatric evaluations and is indicated on Axis V of a multiaxial assessment. More recently, the Child and Adolescent Functional Assessment Scale, which was originally developed in 1991 (Hodges, 2000), was developed to specifically evaluate children and youth ages 7 to 17 years, whereas the Functional Assessment Rating Scale was developed to specifically assess adults (Ward, Dow, Penner, Saunders, & Halls, 1998). Because level of functioning scales are designed to assess a sophisticated treatment issue, any instrument built for this objective must be standardized. As such, the same issues identified in the above paragraphs regarding rigorous selection of assessment tools must be applied—again, regardless of how well known an instrument is.

Client status or numeric counts are commonly used as a type of outcome measure. Numeric counts are nominal measures typically requiring a "yes" or "no" response to specific questions (Kettner et al., 2008). Questions such as "Did the client reoffend within 2 years of discharge?" or "Were there any new reports of child abuse?" constitute nominal measures. Numeric counts require other data collection, but they are typically easy to define and, when converted into percentage scores, provide stakeholders with crucial outcome information that is both tangible and straightforward. More significantly, client status typically reflects the primary outcome of a given program (e.g., family reunification, sobriety, employment) and, as such, is typically the most valued by funding organizations. Measuring and collecting client status data often requires the use of various methods such as urine screening to evaluate continued substance abuse, but it also requires reviewing other data sets. For instance, a review of paystubs and/or other employment verification documents may be used to evaluate employment outcomes, whereas court records may be used to evaluate any new criminal activity. Therefore, evaluating client status outcomes requires that you have specific follow-up measures in place to allow for gathering the necessary data.

Finally, client satisfaction surveys are a standard part of most mental health and human service programs and largely reflect a client-centered philosophy that prizes the client as the primary stakeholder. Client satisfaction surveys are typically developed by the program developer and program staff and include questions pertaining to both general (e.g., overall satisfaction) and unique issues about the program (e.g., resource coordination and access to new resources). Because of the manner in which client satisfaction surveys are developed and their primary purpose in assessing satisfaction, these tools often do not have tremendous rigor. This may not necessarily pose a problem since client satisfaction is most often viewed as an additional, but not primary, aspect of treatment. However, with all types of assessment, general rules regarding assessment construction must be followed to ensure that the most effective tools are used. Moreover, client satisfaction may directly impact more significant client outcomes (e.g., sobriety) and, as a result, must be carefully assessed with an eye toward understanding the potential impact of satisfaction on treatment efficacy (Van der Haas & Horwood, 2006). It is worth emphasizing here that client satisfaction surveys *complement* other types of outcome measures—they do not replace them.

Each of these types of outcome measures has specific utility and contributes to program design. Identifying precisely how a particular outcome will be measured during the program design phase allows the program developer and all stakeholders to better understand these critical relationships and ensure that the evaluation program is effectively established prior to program implementation. Moreover, the selection of outcome measures during program design serves as a checkpoint for the program developer to ensure that outcomes (program objectives) are written in terms that are measureable. Each of these measures is covered more thoroughly in Chapter 12, which deals with program evaluation.

Design Tools

As you can see from each of the components that make up the program design, when done correctly, the process itself is very structured and quite fluid. The challenge, I believe, is taking advantage of the directional nature of the process and allowing the inherent structure to work for you. This can be accomplished through the use of program design tools—most notably, the logic model.

Logic Models

A logic model is an essential tool for the program developer and has specific utility at every major phase of program development (i.e., design, implementation, and evaluation). The purpose of the logic model is to "depict the sequence of events that identifies program resources, matches them to needs, activates the service process, completes the service process, and measures results" (Kettner et al., 2008, p. 6). As such, a logic model connects the needs/problems to the interventions/treatment methods and anticipated outcomes, demonstrating the necessary links between each of these major program design components. Put another way, a logic model depicts the path from resources to operations to outcomes (Torghele et al., 2007). A logic model illustrates these interdependent relationships in a short, easy-to-follow graphical format, allowing the program developer and stakeholders to quickly examine the basic treatment program, including rationale (i.e., need/problem), interventions, outcomes, and evaluation plan. Figure 5.1 provides a sample logic model that illustrates a portion of a residential treatment program for juveniles who have sexually offended. The sample contains both clinical and adjunctive/nonclinical interventions.

Figure 5.1 Sample Logic Model: Juvenile Sex Offender Residential Treatment Program

Problem	→ Interventions	→ Outputs	→ Short-Term Outcomes	→ Long-Term Outcomes	→ Outcome Tools
Juvenile sex offending	**1** Group therapy using an evidence-based cognitive-behavioral treatment model (clinical) **2** Family counseling using a multisystemic family systems approach (clinical) **3** Independent living skill development (nonclinical)	**1** Group therapy five times per week over 12 months **2** Biweekly therapy with an increase to weekly 30 days before discharge **3** Biweekly independent living skill development workshops	**1a** Reduction of 80% in dynamic risk factors at discharge **2a** Increase of 70% in family functioning at discharge **3a** Demonstrated increase in independent living skills from 80% of youth	**1b** In first year post-discharge, 85% will not reoffend **2b** Of families with children 17 or younger, 70% will remain living together during first year post-discharge **3b** Of youth17 and over, 70% will be employed within 6 months post-discharge	**1a** J-SOAP II **1b** Criminal history record audits **2a** Family Assessment Device **2b** Family follow-up **3a** Daniel Memorial Independent Living Skill assessment **3b** Client follow-up

149

It is the scope of information contained in the logic model that makes it a primary tool in not only program planning but program evaluation. Because the logic model should contain all the pertinent elements that go into a program and the expected benefits of each, demonstrating the interactions between each component—interventions, outputs, outcomes (Torghele et al., 2007)—the logic model provides the crux of the evaluation and is, therefore, the first evaluation tool that program developers have available to them. By using a logic model, one of the historic challenges related to program evaluation can be resolved: linking program design to program evaluation (Hernandez, 2000).

Because logic models are simple in their design yet convey such complex information about social and mental health problems, they not only are of great use in guiding program design and program evaluation but also can be used in other venues. In fact, one use of particular meaning is that of educating policymakers regarding specific community problems and methods by which to effectively address them (Lewis et al., 2007). Additionally, in today's era of accountability, logic models are often required by funding sources as part of a proposal for program development.

To aid in the development of logic models, an excellent guide is the W. K. Kellogg Foundation (2004) *Logic Model Development Guide*. The guide provides examples of various types of logic models, providing information regarding how best to use them, and discusses the various audiences that may benefit from using them. (The guide can be found at www .wkkf.org/knowledge-center/resources/2010/Logic-Model-Development-Guide.aspx.) Additionally, the Office of Juvenile Justice and Delinquency Prevention (OJJDP; 2009) provides useful information about the logic model, a sample illustration of a logic model, and a template by which to develop your own logic model. Whereas the logic model template is provided for applicants preparing to submit a grant proposal, the information that the OJJDP provides can also be of great help. (You can find this information at http://ojjdp.ncjrs.org/grantees/pm/logic_models.html.) Because the information pertaining to logic model development and use is provided freely by both the W. K. Kellogg Foundation and the OJJDP, I encourage you to take the time to review both of these resources.

Project Timelines

Whereas the logic model is an essential tool for program design, a project timeline is an effective tool for organizing program implementation. This is because thorough planning must be completed well in advance of program implementation (ideally 6–12 months prior), and to effectively accomplish all that's necessary in the most efficient manner, a high degree of organization is necessary. Without the use of strong organizational skills at this point, program implementation may be jeopardized. And it is in this initial program design step that the actual implementation process begins. Unfortunately, I have too often witnessed well-designed programs quickly close down or not receive continued funding due to ineffective implementation planning.

Today, with the highly competitive climate of mental health and human service programming that exists, implementation must often occur immediately after funding has been awarded. Therefore, time is of the essence, and those who are not prepared well in advance of award notification create not only an unnecessary but often insurmountable challenge to the program implementation process. As such, any reduction in the program's operating time cycle could negatively impact the program's success. Unfortunately, because of the time frames in which award notices are often given compared with the initially outlined time frames for program implementation, time frame challenges are often an inherent part of receiving funding.

To illustrate the tight time frames that can exist between notification of award and program implementation, consider my past two projects (shown in Table 5.3). Both of these projects were based on 2-year funding cycles, each of which—ideally and as designed in the original proposals—required the projects to operate for 2 full years in order to achieve anticipated program outcomes.

As you can see, notification of the award was provided well beyond the project implementation dates for both of these projects. Whereas funding was provided for one project to begin more than 3 months prior to notification of the award and the other more than 5 months before notification, you cannot retroactively begin a program that was not begun—unless, of course, there is a physicist out there prepared to take on this challenge. As a result, you are forced to move rapidly to implement the project, realizing that regardless of the speed by which implementation occurs, a significant part of real time can simply not be recovered.

Table 5.3 Time Frames for Notification of Funding and Implementation of Projects

	Award Notification Date	Original Project Funding Dates for Implementation	Loss of Implementation Time
Project 1	9-14-06	6-1-06 to 5-31-08	−104 days
Project 2	9-29-08	4-1-08 to 3-31-10	−152 days

Whereas these examples illustrate extreme challenges with program funding and implementation cycles, they are not uncommon. However, there are significant differences between state, federal, and foundation funding, and it is unusual when state or foundation funding timelines actually have begin dates prior to notification of the funding award. Unfortunately, though, it is not uncommon for even these types of funding sources to make awards with as little as a 60-day implementation time frame. As a result, you must *have a plan for implementing the plan* (Lewis et al., 2007) so that you are prepared well in advance and can efficiently implement the program.

It is because of each of these reasons that a project timeline is indeed a necessity to the program developer. There are a range of project timeline formats with varying levels of details that may include the time frames during which each major activity should be implemented, the individual(s) responsible for implementing each activity, and any associated outcomes, when relevant. Because there are so many facets involved in program implementation—from recruiting staff and developing marketing materials to admitting the first clients and beginning the program evaluation—timelines should be used to map out each of these. Two examples of timelines are provided, with Table 5.4 illustrating a timeline for program implementation that includes many of the associated activities that occur both before and during program implementation and Table 5.5 illustrating a specific timeline for one aspect of the program development process—program evaluation.

As you can see from the two sample timelines provided, there are different methods you can use in formatting timelines. Additionally, timelines can include all program implementation activities or you may use timelines that are limited to specific implementation activities (e.g., program evaluation). I find it best to develop one *master* timeline that includes all the major program activities and use additional timelines that focus on specific major activities (e.g., staff training program, program evaluation). By doing this, my colleagues and I are able to view an inclusive map to program implementation that can straightforwardly and efficiently illustrate all the various activities that need to occur as well as when they need to occur. In addition, by developing additional timelines for subprojects, I gain more detailed directions to guide major activities that are a part of the larger implementation plan. I have found this incredibly helpful to organizing my own time as well as helping others appreciate the concept of time involved in effectively implementing a program. Moreover, I am a firm believer that the more we can break down major projects into their various parts, the more tangible the whole process becomes. This is integral to the success of program development. Because

Table 5.4	Sample Program Implementation Timeline: Outreach Programming for Homeless Women

Activity	Responsibility	Week											
		1	2	3	4	5	6	7	8	9	10	11	12
Develop marketing materials	Marketing director	—	—	—									
Finalize program manual	Program director	—	—	—									
Recruit staff	Human resources director	—	—	—									
Train staff	Training director				—	—	—	—					
Program start date									—				
Client intake assessment and initial treatment planning	Intake coordinator								—	—	—		
Physical exam and initial health plan development	Physician and nurse								—	—	—		
Weekly group counseling	Assigned counselor									—	—	—	—
Resource coordination	Assigned social worker									—	—	—	—
Begin data collection for program evaluation	Counselors and supervisors								—	—	—	—	—

program development requires such a tremendous amount of work and attention to so many details, it can easily be intimidating if considered in its entirety. Therefore, by separating each of the various components into tangible projects via timelines, a degree of psychological relief is provided that often mitigates any sense of being overwhelmed by the incredibly important and large-scale work inherent in program development efforts.

Table 5.5 Project Timeline: Program Evaluation of Juvenile Sex Offender Program

Month	Project Goal	Related Objective	Activity	Expected Completion Date	Person Responsible
1	Enhance understanding of the efficacy of the current residential treatment model for juvenile sex offenders	Assess efficacy of existing model	Develop data collection tools and consent forms	Month 2	Research coordinator and research assistant
2	Acquire oversight of research project involving human subjects	Ethics related to research	Complete application for Institutional Review Board (IRB) review of study and submit to university IRB for study oversight and approval	Month 3	Research coordinator
4	Identify benefits, challenges, and efficacy related to each program component and the risk and protective factors present in subjects and the relationship of each to treatment outcomes	Assess efficacy of existing model	Recruit participants in study Implement evaluation and begin data collection Train staff in data collection	Ongoing	Research coordinator and research assistant
9	Increase understanding	Assessment of current	Conduct analysis of initial data set	Month 9	Research coordinator

Month	Project Goal	Related Objective	Activity	Expected Completion Date	Person Responsible
	of the demographic variables of client population and risk and protective factors	residential treatment model with current evidence-based research	Prepare paper for internal guidance		and research assistant
9	Enhance understanding of the demographic variables of client population and risk and protective factors present in population	Assess efficacy of existing model	Prepare initial paper on demographic variables, risk and protective factors, and program model	Month 11	Research coordinator
16	Enhance understanding of the relationship of each program component, adjunctive service, and major clinical component on treatment outcomes	Assess the process by which core treatment components are implemented and the impact of these on treatment outcomes	Conduct data analysis of second data set Prepare second paper examining the major components of the treatment model and relationship to client success	Month 18	Research coordinator

Summary

The program design process is akin to putting a puzzle together—a puzzle for which most of the pieces have already been identified and simply require positioning, while other aspects involve a more thorough search for new pieces to complete the whole. By allowing the previously collected data to guide the program design (identification of need, research basis for program design that includes a specific focus on culturally based interventions), developing the mission simply means articulating how the research is used in your program design and why you are working to address an identified need. Developing the vision provides the opportunity to establish just how far you wish the program to reach and succeed, while designing the core program design relies on data found in all three of the previous steps (i.e., identifying the need, establishing a research basis in program design, and identifying multicultural considerations) and requires assembly into a coherent design.

It is precisely in this way that the initial part of the program development process is data-driven and unidirectional, each step building from the previous one. Moreover, it is in this way that program development is a scientific endeavor, one that requires a great deal of rigor and research skill and, when conducted effectively, one that results in a strong foundation for success—not to mention a significant degree of satisfaction.

CASE ILLUSTRATION

Joan and Cynthia had volunteered to design a new program model for adolescent substance abuse treatment that they were going to present as part of a proposal to request funding from a philanthropic foundation. They had already done due diligence and completed a comprehensive needs assessment, thus justifying the *need* for the program, and they had also conducted a market analysis as part of the preplanning process. In addition, they had conducted an extensive review of the literature and had identified an evidence-based treatment model. In order to design the program, they developed a logic model illustrating the various components of the program. Because the program was a community-based, family-focused program, the clinical interventions included family therapy, family problem solving, and individual sessions based on motivational interviewing and cognitive-behavioral interventions. The program's adjunctive or supportive interventions included case management focused on identifying and linking the family with needed community resources and academic support and involvement in the treatment planning process. After establishing several short- and long-term outcomes based directly on the treatment interventions and the research, Joan had identified improved family functioning, improved academic performance, decreased substance abuse–related risk factors, and sobriety as four of the outcomes. Cynthia then began to investigate appropriate assessment instruments to measure each. After reviewing the research, Cynthia identified the Family Assessment Device to assess family functioning, knowing that it had demonstrated strong psychometric properties. Academic progress reports that focused on several aspects of academic performance, including improvements in homework submission, class participation, assignment grades, and overall achievement, and report cards would be used to assess change in academic performance. The Substance Abuse Subtle Screening Inventory for Adolescents would be used to assess change in substance abuse risk factors, and random drug screens would be used to assess sobriety. Both Joan and Cynthia established the outcome targets after a further review of the research on the evidence-based model and the target thresholds that its population had achieved. A snapshot of the partial program design included the following:

Needs	Clinical Interventions	Adjunctive Interventions	Outcomes	Outcomes Measures
Effective family functioning and family independence	Family therapy	Linking the family to needed community resources	Improved family functioning following 4 months of treatment	FAD pre/post-test at admission and 4 months post-treatment
Academic support and success	Individual and family therapy	Academic support and involvement of school personnel in treatment planning	Improvement of 20% in overall academic performance following 3 months of treatment	Monthly teacher progress reports; report cards
Reduced risk for substance abuse	Individual and family therapy		Decrease of 30% in overall substance abuse–related risk factors following 3 months of treatment	SASSI-A2 pre/post-test at admission and 3 months post-treatment
Sobriety	Individual and family therapy		Following 3 months of treatment, 80% of youth would experience one relapse or less	Random drug screening

(Continued)

(Continued)

Joan and Cynthia chose to identify the needs in need language rather than as problems since this fit more with their philosophical thinking of helping. They used the five categories of needs, clinical interventions, adjunctive interventions, outcomes, and outcomes measures to diagram their program design, knowing that there were different ways to develop logic models and that what was most important was articulating a clear understanding of the relationships between these five areas. After finalizing their program design and adding it to the proposal that included the results of their comprehensive needs assessment, Joan knew they had developed a strong proposal. She and Cynthia had not only built a firm case establishing the need for the program, they had used the most current research to design what they knew was not only a comprehensive but highly cost-effective program. The program's evidence basis was well established, and they had proposed the use of assessment methods that would allow them to effectively evaluate the program. Cynthia and Joan praised each other on their collaborative efforts, worked to put the finishing touches on the proposal, and submitted it to the foundation the following week.

LOGIC MODEL EXERCISE

To reinforce your knowledge of the logic model, complete the following exercise:

1. Consider a local human service, mental health, or school-based program with which you are somewhat familiar.

2. Using the sample logic model that I provided, identify the following information related to the program:

   - A minimum of three interventions (two clinical, one nonclinical)
   - One output for each intervention
   - One short-term outcome goal for each intervention
   - One long-term outcome goal for each intervention
   - One outcome measurement tool for each short- and long-term goal (total of six measures)

3. Contact a program representative to gain any missing information.

4. Once the logic model has been completed, critique it by examining the following issues:

   - Are the clinical interventions evidence-based?
   - If not, identify a minimum of one evidence-based intervention.

- Are outputs clearly defined?
- If outputs are not clearly defined, identify alternative outputs.
- Is there evidence that the clinical interventions may lead to the identified outcomes?
- If there is not evidence that the clinical interventions may lead to the identified outcomes, develop alternate outcomes that are related to the clinical interventions.

ANSWERS TO NAME THAT MISSION EXERCISE

a. Boy Scouts of America

b. Young Women's Christian Association

c. Ben & Jerry's

d. Girl Scouts of America

e. NAACP

References

Beck, A. T., Steer, R. A., & Brown, G. K. (1996). *Beck Depression Inventory II*. Upper Saddle River, NJ: Pearson Assessment.

Brody, R. (2005). *Effectively managing human service organizations* (3rd ed.). Thousand Oaks, CA: Sage.

Busch, M., & Folaron, G. (2005). Accessibility and clarity of state child welfare agency mission statements. *Child Welfare, LXXXIV*, 415–430.

Comprehensive Juvenile Sex Offender Management Initiative. (2009). *Mission statement*. Retrieved April 25, 2010, from http://www.cjsom.com

Dennis, M., Godley, S. H., Diamond, G., Tims, F. M., Babor, T., Donaldson, J., et al. (2004). The Cannabis Youth Treatment (CYA) Study: Main findings from two randomized trials. *Journal of Substance Abuse Treatment, 27*, 197–213.

Epstein, N. B., Baldwin, L. M., & Bishop, D. S. (1981). *The McMaster Family Assessment Device, Version 3*. Providence, RI: Brown University & Butler Hospital Family Research Program.

Gray, G. C., & Kendzia, V. B. (2009). Organizational self-censorship: Corporate sponsorship, nonprofit funding, and the educational experience. *Canadian Review of Sociology, 46*, 161–177.

Hatfield, D. R., & Ogles, B. M. (2004). The use of outcome measures by psychologists in clinical practice. *Professional Psychology: Research and Practice, 35*, 485–491.

Hernandez, M. (2000). Using logic models and program theory to build outcome accountability. *Education and Treatment of Children, 23*, 24–40.

Hodges, K. (2000). *Child and Adolescent Functional Assessment Scale (CAFAS)*. Ann Arbor, MI: Functional Assessment Systems.

Kellogg Company. (2010). *Vision and mission*. Retrieved July 23, 2010, from http://www.kelloggcompany.com/company.aspx?id=888

Kettner, P. M., Moroney, R. M., & Martin, L. L. (2008). *Designing and managing programs: An effectiveness-based approach* (3rd ed.). Thousand Oaks, CA: Sage.

Lewis, J. A., Lewis, M. D., Daniels, J. A., & D'Andrea, M. J. (2003). *Community counseling* (3rd ed.). Pacific Grove, CA: Brooks/Cole.

Lewis, J. A., Packard, T. R., & Lewis, M. D. (2007). *Management of human service programs* (4th ed.). Belmont, CA: Thomson Learning.

Miller, F. (1997). *Substance Abuse Subtle Screening Inventory (SASSI) manual*. Bloomington, IN: SASSI Institute.

Millon, T. M. (1993). *Millon Adolescent Clinical Inventory (MACI) manual*. Minneapolis, MN: National Computer Services.

Mours, J. M., Campbell, C. D., Gathercoal, K. A., & Peterson, M. (2009). Training in the use of psychotherapy outcome assessment measures at psychology internship sites. *Training and Education in Professional Psychology, 3,* 169–176.

Office of Juvenile Justice and Delinquency Prevention. (n.d.). *Performance measures: Logic models*. Retrieved September 10, 2010, from http://ojjdp.ncjrs.org/grantees/pm/logic_models.html

Ogles, B. M., Lambert, M. J., & Fields, S. A. (2002). *Essentials of outcome assessment*. New York: Wiley.

Phelps, R., Eisman, E. J., & Kohout, J. (1998). Psychological practice and managed care: Results of the CAPP practitioner survey. *Professional Psychology: Research and Practice, 29,* 31–36.

Rossi, P. (1997). Program outcomes: Conceptual and measurement issues. In E. Mullen & J. Magnabosco (Eds.), *Outcomes measurement in the human services* (pp. 20–34). Washington, DC: NASW Press.

Shaffer, D., Fisher, W. P., Lucas, C., Dulcan, M., & Schwab-Stone, M. (2000). The NIMH Diagnostic Interview Schedule for Children (NIMH DISC-IV): Description differences from previous versions and reliability of some common diagnoses. *Journal of the American Academy of Child and Adolescent Psychiatry, 39,* 28–38.

Torghele, K., Buyum, A., Dubruiel, N., Augustine, J., Houlihan, C., Alperin, M., et al. (2007). Logic model use in developing a survey instrument for program evaluation: Emergency preparedness summits for schools of nursing in Georgia. *Public Health Nursing, 5,* 472–479.

Triangle Foundation. (2009). *Our organization*. Retrieved March 14, 2010, from http://www.tri.org/our-organization.html

Van der Haas, M., & Horwood, C. (2006). Occupational therapy: How effective do consumers think it is? *New Zealand Journal of Occupational Therapy, 53,* 10–16.

Ward, J. C., Dow, M. G., Penner, K., Saunders, T., & Halls, S. (1998). *A manual for using the Functional Assessment Rating Scale (FARS)* (Rev. ed.). Tampa, FL: Department of Mental Health Law and Policy, FMHI/USF.

W. K. Kellogg Foundation. (2004). *Using logic models to bring together evaluation and action: Logic model development guide*. Battle Creek, MI: Author.

Develop the Staffing Infrastructure

Learning Objectives

1. Explain the difference between process and structure in organizational design

2. Identify three types of process factors related to organizational design

3. Discuss the purpose and role of the governing board in nonprofit organizations

4. Explain the relationship that both the market analysis and the logic model have with the design of the staffing infrastructure

5. Illustrate a staffing infrastructure through the use of an organizational chart

BUT I NEED MORE SUPPORT

Annette had been managing two programs for batterers—one for female batterers and one for male batterers—for the past 2 years and had increased her client load considerably since the program's inception. She told her executive director that she needed more staff. In particular, she requested two clinical managers—one for each program—an administrative assistant, and an additional intake coordinator. And she produced a revised program organizational chart to illustrate the new staffing infrastructure, stressing how much the program had grown. After briefly reviewing the program's financial records with Annette and the chief financial officer, the executive director agreed to the new positions, each of which was a full-time, salaried position.

The human resources manager was told to develop new job descriptions in accordance with Annette's modified organizational chart.

After having each of the positions in place for 6 months, the programs experienced a 40% reduction in referrals. Annette was not too worried, accepting that her business often experienced peaks and valleys; however, 4 months later, the programs were still operating at approximately 60% of their previous capacity. Finally, with no change occurring, Annette's boss and she met and discussed the fact that she would have to reduce her staffing costs by half within the next 30 days. Annette admitted that she had not fully examined the financial implications of the new hires nor had she thought about the program's future revenue—she really thought the program would continue to operate at the same client/revenue levels as it had in the past. After reviewing the recent financials on the program, Annette realized that the new hires had cost the program in excess of $210,000, including salaries and fringe benefits, and now the program would incur additional costs as a result of severance and unemployment-related fees.

Annette was astounded at the costs but knew she now had to make tough decisions about how she would go about downsizing. In fact, she realized that the sooner the downsizing occurred the better, as she needed to act quickly now to stop the bleeding lest she face losing her program altogether.

CONSIDERING ANNETTE

1. What mistakes did Annette make?

2. How could she have prevented this from happening?

3. What, if any, responsibility do Annette, the chief financial officer, and/or the executive director have in creating this problem?

4. If you were Annette, what steps would you take now to attempt to remedy this, and how might you go about making decisions related to staffing and hiring in the future?

About This Chapter

Whereas the previous chapter dealt with clinical program design, this chapter moves into a discussion of the other primary part of program design—*staffing infrastructure* design or organizational structure. The chapter begins with an examination of the two key elements of organizational design—structure and process—and a discussion about the ingredients needed for effective organizational design. Examining the various structural issues related to staffing, we will discuss each of the various levels of staff—including the executives, managers, supervisors, and line staff. In addition, we will explore the purpose and role of the governing board. Next, we will discuss the major process components, including communication, supervision and accountability, work flow, types of staffing options and their impact on organizational processes, and scheduling.

To again illustrate the sequential process of comprehensive program design, we will revisit two previously discussed program planning tools—the market analysis and the logic model. We will reexamine both of these essential tools to illustrate the impact that each has on the development of the organizational infrastructure design. Finally, we will fully explore the organizational chart—the key tool used in organizational staffing infrastructure design. An organizational chart exercise is provided at the end of the chapter to further reinforce learning.

STEP IV: DEVELOP THE STAFFING INFRASTRUCTURE

The Organizational Structure

The clinical program design constitutes roughly half of the design process, while the organizational structure constitutes the other half. Therefore, after the comprehensive program design is complete, the organizational design must be devised. Effective organizational design must minimally do the following:

1. Address units, departments, roles, and responsibilities

2. Promote the most effective use of resources, open communication, and expedient decision making

3. Reflect the goals, needs, size, theoretical orientation, and philosophy of the organization/program

Organizational design consists of two major components—structure and process. Structure refers to how the program/organization is organized, primarily with regard to staffing. Structure is typically overt and visible throughout the organization, referring to staffing hierarchies and the grouping together of various staffing functions. Process, on the other hand, is more subtle, existing within the structure. Organizational processes often describe what is going on within the structure, such as communication patterns and decision making.

Designing the organization/program begins with designing the organizational structure—namely, the staffing infrastructure. The staffing infrastructure refers to all the human resources that are needed to implement the program and monitor the program's operations. Developing the right staffing infrastructure is directly tied to the program design since the type and scope of interventions dictate program staffing needs. Additionally, developing the right staffing infrastructure is equally critical to program implementation since successful program implementation is dependent on both effective program design and effective staffing to implement the program design. There are several factors that O'Looney (1996) originally proposed for consideration in organizational design, including

- design must be consistent with organizational objectives (if creativity is desired, promote autonomy and reduce constraints);
- design around outcomes;
- promote freedom in design;
- promote open communication;
- allow easy access to resources for those in need;
- link parallel activities;
- capture information once (e.g., client database that is used by all relevant staff); and
- examine how you look to the client (e.g., are you accessible 24 hours a day?).

In addition, activities that may also be useful to the organizational design process include

- thoroughly exploring all the tasks needed to implement the program,
- separating activities for specific individuals and/or groups,
- determining levels of responsibility needed per staff position,
- determining the degree to which staff positions relate to one another,
- determining the decision-making process and structure,
- determining internal and external lines of communication,
- garnering top-level support for organizational/program design,
- developing a steering committee to lead the process to promote collaborative decision making in design,

- involving all levels of staff in design,
- focusing on efficiency in operations—each step must be justified and add value—and
- designing for future climate and changes by orienting all staff toward flexible thinking regarding process issues.

Because clinical program design dictates organizational staffing infrastructure needs, staffing infrastructures vary from program to program, with some programs composed of just two levels of staff (e.g., supervisors, clinicians) and others composed of six or more levels (e.g., manager, supervisors, clinicians, case managers, behavior specialists, direct care workers). Likewise, human service organizations vary greatly, with some organizations consisting of a singular program while others are multifaceted, consisting of a variety of programs working across multiple systems (e.g., workforce development, substance abuse, children's mental health). These differences between programs and organizations highlight the dynamic nature of staffing infrastructures by illustrating that there is no one model of staffing infrastructure but rather that staffing needs are modulated based on programming.

To illustrate the possible breadth of a human service organization's infrastructure, Box 6.1 provides a near-exhaustive list of potential staff positions as well as the organizational oversight body (i.e., governance structure).

BOX 6.1

SAMPLE OVERVIEW OF GOVERNANCE AND STAFFING

Governing board

Executive leadership

Executive management

Administrative support staff

Supervisory staff

Clinical staff

Case management staff

Direct care staff

Paraprofessionals

Other program staff

Whereas each of these staff groups serves unique purposes, there is also some degree of overlap between certain positions. For instance, administrative support staff from the finance department and program managers may both be involved in program accounting activities; however, the program manager is largely responsible for managing the program budget, while the financial coordinator is responsible for program billing and financial record keeping. It is this type of structuring of both unique responsibilities, as well as overlap associated with various work groups, that reflects the symbiotic nature of work flow, in which multiple factions are required to collaboratively produce and support the goals of the organization.

Whereas numerous characteristics of organizational structures have been examined throughout the literature, Pleshko and Nickerson (2008) identify four major structural dimensions—formalization, integration, centralization, and complexity—that have historical roots (Dalton, Todor, Spendolini, Fielding, & Porter, 1980; Ford & Slocum, 1977; Frederickson, 1986; Fry, 1982; Miller, 1988; Miller & Droge, 1986). Pleshko and Nickerson provide a brief synopsis of each of these organizational structures, which serves as a good primer on the topic.

Formalization: Policies and procedures are widely used to prescribe the manner in which tasks should be performed (Frederickson, 1986). Opposed to promoting employee autonomy, formalization in organizational structure restricts employee activities to only those activities proscribed in advance.

Integration: Activities are coordinated so that various specialized groups work together (Miller, 1988). Integrated organizations often promote contact with experts across departments as well as contact with top executives, promoting integrated work activities.

Centralization: Decision-making power is concentrated in the hands of a few (Frederickson, 1986), with critical decisions made only by top executives.

Complexity: This term describes the various interrelated parts of an organization. Complexity includes the scope of an organization, power structures, and number and geography of multiple-site organizations.

Whereas these four organizational structures provide a schema by which to better understand the science of structure, by examining each, you may also begin to notice how organizational structure and processes interact in organizational design. For instance, formalized organizations operate more like a dictatorship, whereas integrated organizations function more like democracies—both of which have obvious implications for employees and how they play their roles within the organization.

Organizational designs in the human services and mental health settings can differ enormously from one organization to the next, with flatter organizations (i.e., fewer hierarchical levels) and more collaborative decision making (i.e., integrated structures) much more common today than in previous decades. However, hierarchical structures (i.e., formalized structure) continue to be necessary, particularly to depict lines of authority and *organize* the organization, and as a result, you would be hard-pressed to find an organization today without some degree of formalization. But probably the most important point regarding organizational structure was put forth by the management guru Peter Drucker (1999), who argued that "the best structure will not guarantee results and performance. But the wrong structure is a guarantee of nonperformance" (p. 440). There are many texts devoted specifically to organizational structure and theory, and I suggest you look to those for a more in-depth examination of this topic. For now, our discussion will focus on the staffing infrastructure.

Governance Structure

The board of directors comprises the *governance structure* of an organization and, as such, serves to monitor the organization and represent the organization to the public. In this sense, boards are both overseers of business operations as well as ambassadors of the organization. Boards of human service and public organizations may be termed *board of directors, board of trustees,* or *board of regents,* depending on the type of institution and its organizational structure.

For-profit boards differ in some ways from nonprofit human service boards, particularly in the degree of public scrutiny that they receive; however, all boards share ultimate accountability for organizational activity and accomplishment (Carver, 2006). Because the board does hold ultimate accountability for the organization, it is always placed at the top of the organizational structure. Accountability in the extreme sense means that boards are charged with fiduciary responsibility for the organization and for dissolving the organization should it need to cease operations. Over the past decade, with the introduction of the Sarbanes-Oxley Act of 2002, the role of corporate governance has become even more significant, and as a result, there is now greater responsibility and accountability for boards.

At a structural level, boards operate to set organizational objectives, allocating necessary resources to meet objectives, monitor the organization's performance, and ensure that the organization acts as a responsible member of the larger community (Kessler & Schuster, 2009). On a daily basis, boards monitor the organization, working primarily with the organization's leader and top administrators, regularly receiving information and participating in various levels of organizational decision making. Board activity varies tremendously from organization to organization. On one end of the spectrum, board members may participate solely in board meetings that are no more than information dissemination forums in which they receive information from the organization's leadership team and are asked to do little else for the organization. Conversely, in some organizations, board members serve as strategic organizational representatives, engaging in advocacy, fundraising, and other public activities to increase support for the organization as well as participating in key decision making about the organization. In the latter case, board members are often viewed as an instrumental support and leadership arm of the organization.

Because it behooves every organization to have a board that enhances the organization, the astute organizational leader works to develop the most productive board that s/he can. Unfortunately, limited time and other scarce resources, as well as perceived threats to executive power, may at times prohibit organizational leaders from committing the necessary time and energy to developing a dynamic, productive board. This truly is unfortunate since the benefits gained from the work of an effective board can exponentially increase the value of the organization with very little associated cost. This is because board member time is the primary cost of board participation, and since board members are volunteers, this cost is incurred by the individual and not the organization. As such, an effective board simply offers another layer of no-cost support and value to the organization—a critically needed commodity in the current climate of shrinking resources.

Executive Leadership

The executive of the organization is the top official, the individual responsible for overseeing the organization's day-to-day operations. In human services organizations, the top official typically has the title of executive director, president, and/or chief executive officer. This individual reports directly to the board and is charged with the responsibility of overseeing all aspects of the organization. Because the executive leader is responsible for not only running the organization but also ensuring the ongoing health of the organization, it is critical that this individual possess highly effective leadership skills. In particular, the executive leader must minimally be able to

- engage staff in the mission of the organization,
- represent the organization to the public,
- effectively work within the political system and other systems that impact the organization,
- be able to produce successful organizational outcomes, and
- be able to visualize well into the future and act to posture the organization for success in years to come.

In his discussion of learning organizations, Senge (2006) characterizes leaders as designers, stewards, and teachers responsible for building organizations in which all individuals commit to learning by continuously expanding their capabilities. As he asserts, in order to achieve this, leaders must first be able to inspire. In a similar vein, Bolman and Deal (2008) reframe leaders not as authority figures but as individuals who must work within the context of multiple relationships within the organization and pay attention to developing relationships in order to move organizations forward. In particular, Bolman and Deal define leadership as a subtle process based on mutual influence that fuses thought, feeling, and action to produce cooperative efforts that meet the needs and are consistent with the values of both the leader and the led. Leadership then must be viewed not as something that is done to the staff and other stakeholders of an organization but rather as what is accomplished collaboratively by the staff and stakeholders of an organization.

While extremely significant and relevant to today's climate, these sentiments in no way represent new thoughts in leadership; however, when discussed today, these arguments are often made in the context that a shift in thinking must occur—that we must now conceptualize leaders not as authority or control figures but as collaborators. This is particularly interesting since historically leadership has indeed been viewed in much the same manner. For example, consider these views on leadership from some prominent historical figures (Box 6.2).

BOX 6.2

HISTORICAL QUOTES ON LEADERSHIP

I must follow the people. Am I not their leader?

—Benjamin Disraeli, prime minister of England
(1804–1880; as cited in Bernays, 2005)

If your actions inspire others to dream more, learn more, do more, and become more, you are a leader.

—John Quincy Adams, sixth president of the
United States (1767–1848; as cited in Department of the Interior, 2009)

A leader is best when people barely know he exists, when his work is done, his aim fulfilled, they will say: we did it.

—Lau Tzu (600 BC–531 BC),
Chinese Taoist philosopher and founder of Taoism

When viewing the major thoughts on leadership from this much broader historical view, it seems that whereas the emphasis on leaders as co-constructionists—collaboratively creating a vision of the organization and working collectively to fulfill its mission—is not a new concept, it is indeed timeless. And to be an effective leader first and foremost requires an unwavering commitment to the organization and all that the organization represents. Without such commitment, no degree of inspiration, political capital, or administrative competence will be enough to effectively lead.

Another critical aspect of leadership has to do with the ability of the leader to motivate and influence individuals with different needs to attain the goals of the organization. This most often requires modifying the leadership approach. Indeed, effective leaders must adapt their style to meet the needs of their subordinates (Hur, 2008).

In addition to the chief executive, several other employees may serve in leadership roles, such as those who are directors, managers, or supervisors. Therefore, several of these basic principles of leadership apply to them as well.

Management Staff

Depending on the size and structure of the organization, there may be one level or multiple levels of management staff. In mid- to large-sized human service organizations, there may be three levels of management staff that include executive-level management, divisional management, and program management. In this context, I am referring only to operations/program management and not to administrative support management (e.g., finance), which will be discussed later.

Executive-level managers often carry the title of *chief operating officer, deputy director,* or *vice president* and report directly to the chief executive of the organization. These individuals function as part of the *executive leadership* team, working closely with the organizational leader, providing broad-based leadership, engaging in organizational development, and overseeing the operations of the organization.

Members of the second level of management—division-level managers—typically operate in organizations that are composed of multiple programs that have been grouped together into divisions through similar services. These managers are responsible for overseeing more than one program, directly supervise program managers or directors, and report to the executive-level manager. Because this level of manager works between the program manager and the executive-level manager, her/his activities often overlap with those of the other two levels. As such, division-level managers may be directly involved in managing program operations to some extent, as well as being involved in comprehensive organizational development. In addition, division-level managers ideally focus their energies on division-level development, working to ensure the quality of existing programs for which they are responsible, representing their programs to the public, working to ensure continued funding, and engaging in new program development, to name just a few key activities.

Members of the third level of management—program managers, also known as program directors—are responsible for directly overseeing the program. These individuals report directly to the division-level manager (or the executive-level manager in a flatter organization) and oversee program supervisors. An all-important though heavy burden to carry, it is typically the program manager who is directly charged with ensuring the most effective treatment of program clients and protecting the welfare of clients being served by the program.

These individuals are considered the program administrators because they are charged with fulfilling all the duties associated with the operations of a program. These duties can include

- supervising program supervisors and staff;
- hiring and training staff;
- attending to the financial aspects of programming, including budgeting and financial reporting;
- representing the program to stakeholders and the public;
- working directly with funding sources;
- engaging in new program development;
- managing program improvement activities, including program monitoring and evaluation, and engaging in program advocacy efforts; and
- working directly with program clients.

Regardless of management level (executive, division, program), all managers must possess mastery of a wide range of skills, including short- and long-term planning, human resource development, supervision, finance management, and evaluation, and they must possess a keen understanding and competency to work effectively within the context of the organization, given its values, beliefs, and customs (Lewis, Packard, & Lewis, 2007). In addition, managers must possess essential leadership skills and work to continuously enhance the program/organization in a spirit of collective engagement and productivity.

Administrative Support Staff

Administrative supports include departments such as finance, research and program development, human resources, fund development, training, and information systems. *Administrative support staff* are often as critical to the organization as are direct care staff because administrative support staff make it possible for direct care staff to carry out their duties. Administrative support staff members typically work behind the scenes of the organization, tending to all the essential duties that allow an organization to continue its work. It is in this sense that mental health professionals and other program staff may not be aware of the role and value of administrative support until it does not exist. For instance, if the Internet connection in your office went down or if the organization's server could not be accessed and there were no information systems support staff available, your work and the work of the organization could temporarily cease. The same is true for finance support and human resources support. If financial support staff did not manage and coordinate the finances to ensure that billing was received, employees may not be regularly paid. Likewise, if human resource department staff did not gather proper documentation as part of the hiring process to ensure the eligibility of all workers as well as compliance with state and federal employment mandates, the livelihood of the organization could be in danger. It is in this manner that a highly interdependent relationship exists between program personnel and administrative support personnel in an organization. Without program personnel to carry out the program operations, there is no need for administrative support personnel, and conversely, without administrative support personnel, program personnel may be unable to effectively carry out program operations.

Depending on the size of the organization, each department may consist of one individual (e.g., controller) or comprise large staffs with various levels of internal leadership (e.g., chief financial officer, controller, finance manager, finance coordinators). The number of staff members within each administrative support department may also be an indicator of the organization's values. For instance, a one-person research and development department and a five-person fund development department may indicate an organization that values charitable fundraising over research and programmatic innovation.

Supervisory Staff

Supervisory staff typically report to managers and are responsible for directly supervising program staff. However, again, the number of layers within any organization may vary greatly, with some programs composed of only one level of management staff (e.g., manager) and others with both supervisors and program managers. Because program staff consists of individuals who actually deliver the program interventions, supervisors have the most direct line of oversight to program implementation and, thus, carry a tremendous responsibility. It is in this manner that *supervisory staff* is differentiated from *managerial staff*. However, supervisory staff may also be involved in program development activities and other activities that are a primary part of the managers' responsibilities.

Because there are different types of direct service workers, which may include clinicians, case managers, and paraprofessionals, different types of supervisors often oversee each group. Just as is true in big industry, supervisors in human service organizations often are former direct service workers. As a result, supervisors have prior experience in the work performed by those whom they are supervising and, more often than not, have been promoted to a supervisory position based on their performance as direct care workers. Additionally, supervisors may have previously been direct care workers who have achieved an advanced degree and have been promoted to supervisor as a result of this advanced standing. This is more unique to supervisors of case managers and paraprofessionals than clinical supervisors, because clinical supervisors typically share the same or similar academic credentials as those whom they supervise (i.e., master's degree in clinical field).

Clinical Staff

Clinical staff may be composed of mental health and/or substance abuse therapists who possess either a master's degree or doctorate in counseling, clinical social work, or clinical psychology and who hold state licensure in their respective discipline. In addition, clinical staff may include psychiatrists who hold medical degrees and board certification in either child or adult psychiatry.

Clinical staff play a unique and incredibly significant role in programming and in the organizational operations as a whole. Because the success of clinical programming is first and foremost based on the quality of the clinical interventions, the work that these individuals perform is integral to the value of the program/organization. Indeed, it is this group of individuals that is responsible for delivering the therapeutic interventions that lead to the program's clinical outcomes.

The therapeutic interventions may include individual, group, and/or family therapy, assessment, referral and resource coordination, comprehensive treatment planning, and psychiatric care. In addition to their primary functions, clinicians often provide direct input for program development and participate in program evaluation and other forms of research.

Because clinicians possess advanced knowledge about various treatment issues, they are viewed as program leaders, responsible for teaching and training other levels of staff in specific treatment issues. As is true for all mental health clinicians, regardless of type of clinical practice, clinicians also have a specific responsibility to advocacy—for clients, treatment issues, and the public.

Case Management Staff

Case management staff typically work very closely with both the clinicians and the direct care workers, serving as somewhat of a binding agent holding together the critical members of the treatment team. Case managers are usually charged with leading the treatment planning process and identifying and addressing all the clients' nonclinical and support needs while at the same time working to gain the input of clinicians regarding the clients' clinical needs. A large part of what case managers do is coordination—coordinating resources, coordinating dialogue between treatment team members, and coordinating meetings and other planning processes, to name a few. As a result, case managers must possess effective communication and organizational skills and be well versed in resource coordination.

Case managers are typically required to have bachelor's degrees, and some may have master's degrees. Historically, case management jobs were filled primarily by individuals holding master's or bachelor's degrees in social work, but today, case managers may have degrees in human services or another of the newer disciplines, and some may also have master's degrees in a traditional mental health discipline (e.g., counseling, psychology).

Direct Care Staff

Direct care is the broad-based term given to the individuals responsible for providing basic services to clients. *Direct care staff* perform different functions depending on the type of treatment setting (e.g., residential, school-based, home-based). For instance, in residential treatment programs, direct care staff provide continuous supervision and support to clients, ensuring that all primary needs are met, often cooking, cleaning, and providing transportation to clients. In home-based programs, direct care staff may provide mentoring or other types of social support services to the client/family.

Because of the broad scope of work and responsibility that direct care staff have, they have the greatest amount of direct interaction with clients. As a result, direct care staff are particularly critical to the treatment process. This is particularly true in residential or inpatient programs, where direct care staff function as primary caregivers to clients. Because placement in a residential program is often extremely challenging for clients, direct care staff are charged with supporting and helping clients adjust to what is a difficult and temporary living environment at best.

Typically, direct care staff are considered paraprofessionals, as their role supports the primary work of other professionals. Often, these workers are minimally required to have a high school diploma, with some organizations requiring some postsecondary education, up to a bachelor's degree. Additionally, direct care staff are typically required to participate in specialized training to further support their work.

Other Program Staff

There are two other types of program staff that may be a part of the organization, both professional staff and other nonprofessional staff. In terms of professional staff, some programs may employ behavior specialists, nurses, or other medical professionals as well as occupational therapists. These individuals specialize in a specific area, often holding a bachelor's degree and/or professional credentials.

Other nonprofessional staff may include individuals who perform specific client support functions such as providing transportation or monitoring/tracking client progress in the community. These staff support the work of the direct care workers or, in some cases, are in place of direct care workers and, as such, hold similar credentials.

As you can see, a diverse array of individuals may compose the staffing infrastructure in a human service organization, each possessing a specific set of skills and each playing a unique role within the organization. At the same time, there is often overlap between positions. This is precisely why organizations that value deep knowledge and skills as well as flexibility in roles and responsibilities are often successful. Current mental health organizations must promote staffing positions that are highly focused yet adaptive to assuming new and different responsibilities, since one of the key factors today is constant change within the broader mental health service industry.

Organizational Processes

There are a multitude of process elements that must be considered in designing the organizational structure. These include communication, supervision and accountability, culture, and staffing options. Each of these elements contributes to the organizational structure and, more specifically, to the way that the organization functions both subtly and overtly.

Communication, supervision and accountability, and culture are considered processes because they reflect specific aspects of the organization that influence its underlying processes. For instance, in organizations in which open communication is promoted, employees are more prone to engage in critical thinking and collaborative decision making. As a result, this type of communication pattern illustrates the way in which the organization functions. Although staffing options and scheduling do not reflect a specific process, they do influence other processes. For instance, organizations with a majority of contractual staff may have a culture that is highly competitive, with employees more concerned about their own work and less engaged as a collective workforce.

Communication

As Moss Kantor (1983) put it in her seminal text, *The Change Masters,* a communication system, depending on the kind adopted by a given corporation, can either constrain or empower the effort to innovate. Unfortunately, though, as fundamental and significant as that communication is to the success of an organization, little attention is paid to communication processes and functions, resulting in neglect of this critical process (Lewis et al., 2007).

Whereas it is difficult to discuss communication patterns without a broader discussion of organizational theory, few human service organizations today operate from a strict theoretical foundation but, rather, are hybrids of various theories. Organizational theories from which specific aspects are most often reflected today include classical, learning organizations, quality management, and open systems. Table 6.1 provides a simple illustration of how aspects of specific organizational theories are reflected in today's human service organizations.

Table 6.1 Organizational Theories in Today's Human Service Organizations

Organizational Theory	Theoretical Aspects Used in Today's Human/Social Service Organizations
Classical theories (bureaucracy, scientific management)	• All employees work toward overall goals of the organization • Employees are organized around specialized functions (e.g., counselors vs. case managers) • Employees work toward same goal • Hierarchical reporting; little employee autonomy
Learning organizations	• Shared vision among all employees • Team learning
Quality management	• Employee commitment to continuous improvement • Client satisfaction as key objective
Open systems	• Organization responds directly to its internal and external environment

As you can see from Table 6.1, organizational theories have a strong influence not only on communication but also on other aspects of organizational functioning. While this snapshot provides you with only a brief view of organizational theory, a multitude of organizational theory texts are available to provide you with a firm foundation in this important area.

With regard to specific types of communication patterns in a program/organization, communication patterns can range broadly from having primary features of information hoarding and top-down communication, directive and strategic communication, open exchange of communication, and open exchange and productive use of communication, among others. These communication patterns and their relationship to the major organizational structures discussed previously are outlined in Box 6.3.

BOX 6.3

POTENTIAL COMMUNICATION STYLES RELATED TO ORGANIZATIONAL STRUCTURE

Information Hoarding and Top-Down Communication (Formalization)

- Authority is centralized at the top of the organization.
- Information is viewed by authority as power and, therefore, information sharing is limited.
- Communication is one-way, from the top to the rest of the organization.

Directive and Strategic Communication (Centralization)

- Communication is viewed by authority as a tool to be used strategically with the rest of the organization.
- Formal communication throughout the organization is managed by the authority.

Open Exchange of Communication (Integration)

- Whereas communication and dialogue are promoted throughout the organization, it often may not impact decision making.

Open Exchange and Productive Use of Communication (Integration)

- Open communication and dialogue are promoted as a means of enlarging decision-making processes and enhancing organizational functioning.
- Open communication may be facilitated for specific purposes and result in specific outcomes.

Whereas outlining these broad categories of communication patterns allows for broad characterizations of communication patterns, organizations are composed of human beings. As a result, organizations are extremely complex and often difficult to accurately characterize. More often than not, communication patterns are nuanced and somewhat flexible, becoming modified by other forces both within and external to the organization.

In terms of the significance of communication to the program developer, the manner in which communication patterns support or prohibit effective program/organizational functioning is a critical issue. More to the point, the program developer must be concerned with ensuring that communication processes are consistent with the goals and objectives of the program. In addition, program developers must bear in mind that creating an effective work environment begins with knowing and frequently communicating with employees (Fodchuk, 2007); therefore, a great deal of attention must be given to communication style and processes.

Supervision and Accountability

Supervision in any organization implies some degree of accountability, as the existence of a supervisor indicates the need for specific monitoring and, thus, some degree of responsibility for the actions of the supervisee. In accordance with Standard F.1.a. of the American Counseling Association (2005),

> A primary obligation of counseling supervisors is to monitor the services provided by other counselors or counselors in training. Counseling supervisors monitor the welfare and supervisees' clinical performance and professional development. To fulfill these obligations, supervisors meet regularly with supervisees to review case notes, samples of clinical work, or live observations. (p. 13)

Supervision is a vast area, encompassing such aspects as roles, responsibilities, styles, legal issues, and ethical issues, to name just a few. And because many organizations may have multiple layers of supervisors, including first-line supervisors, program directors, middle managers, and executive-level managers—including the chief executive—each of these positions is accountable to some degree for the organization. It is the manner in which supervisory roles and accountability are practiced within the organization that relates to organizational design. This is because supervisory roles and functions reflect the underlying processes of an organization.

Whereas most human service/mental health organizations today have some degree of supervisory hierarchy, this may vary quite a bit depending on the type of organization/program. For instance, in a community-based mental health organization consisting of programming for seniors with co-occurring mental health and substance abuse issues, specific types of workers may be separated by their functions (e.g., clinicians, case managers, paraprofessionals)—each group with specific supervisors assigned to it as well as one layer of management and executive leadership. A different supervisory schema may exist within a school-based counseling program in which counselors and other mental health clinicians may report directly to a lead counselor for supervision that is largely consultative while indirectly reporting to the school principal or other administrator for nonclinical/administrative issues. In other types of mental health organizations, there may not be any direct supervisors, but rather because of the professional credentials of each employee, employees function as accountable to the organization rather than to a specific individual. This is most common in clinical private practice environments in which professional counselors and other mental health clinicians function as owner-employees or independent contractors.

Supervision and accountability are just as tied to organizational structure and organizational theory as are communication patterns. Organizations based on classical theories often are designed hierarchically, with managers and supervisors at various levels providing direct monitoring and supervision of staff below. Conversely, learning organizations may be characterized by supervisory relationships that reflect collaboration and mutual learning through support and teamwork. Actually, much can be learned about an organization's theoretical bend by observing supervisory practices. In fact, I remember when one of the organizations that I worked for began introducing some of the principles of quality management and learning organizations throughout the organization, beginning with the executive management team. This created some degree of tension within the organization as executive-level managers began sharing meeting space and engaging in more enhanced teamwork and decision making with subordinate staff. Because the organization had been accustomed to relying more heavily on classical theories in which power was largely situated in the hands of top-level managers, sharing power and increasing the autonomy of others in the organization presented a significant change—creating new friction as the organization worked through the change process.

This example is not at all uncommon, particularly because most organizations are constantly changing—expanding and reducing in size and scope, being influenced by new and different individuals and thought, and reacting to external and internal pressures. Further highlighting this, Bolman and Deal (2008) contend that organizations are highly complex, constantly changing, organic pinball machines in which decisions, actors, plans, and issues continuously move through an ever-changing field of barriers, supports, and traps. And, like all organisms, changes in one area most often cause changes in another, and at times, these changes impact how supervision and accountability are interpreted and practiced within an organization.

With regard to program development, the developer must again pay attention to the primary objectives of the program/organization and ensure that attainment of objectives is supported through existing accountability and supervisory processes. As such, lines of supervision and all aspects related to supervision and accountability within the organization must be carefully considered when designing the organization.

Culture

The concept of organizational culture is one that has been widely discussed, particularly as it relates to the inner climate of an organization. Just as the concept of culture refers to people, the culture of an organization can be defined as the values, beliefs, and traditions of the organization. Culture also speaks to the underlying orientation of an organization—the ways in which employees of an organization think, act, and react and the norms that guide behaviors within the organization. In addition, culture may also be referred to as the work environment. Culture is difficult to quantify and make tangible yet enormously significant to the operations of an organization. In fact, Deal and Kennedy (1982) may have most succinctly summed it up almost 3 decades ago as "the way we do things around here" (p. 4).

The culture of an organization is highly influential, as it often sets the internal tone of the organization. The culture of an organization often dictates how change is interpreted, how success or failure is perceived, and how engaged employees are in the organization. Whereas it is not always highly evident to outsiders, employees are often subtly or overtly indoctrinated into the organization's culture. Speaking about the tremendous power of culture, Moss Kantor (1983) discusses how one company credited its ability to fully indoctrinate new employees to the organizational culture with its success in working through a significant organizational change process. Through this indoctrination process, employees became fully integrated into the organization and completely engaged in the organization's ultimate goals. Seasoned employees spent much time sharing stories and legends about the organization with new employees, and new employees were sent through boot camp–like venues to attain the history and specific perspectives of the organization. This example illustrates the importance that this organization ascribed to culture and the subsequent lengths to which the organization went to ensure that its culture was effectively transmitted to new employees.

Along these same lines, there are other cultural or work environment factors that may have a positive influence or promote *organizational citizenship behavior* (OCB; Conlon, Meyer, & Nowakowski, 2005; Dalal, 2005). OCB basically refers to being a good citizen of the organization—engaging in activities that are not directly rewarded but that ultimately are in the best interest of the organization (e.g., obeying rules, efficiently completing tasks, fully participating in processes). Historically, OCBs have been found to be related to job satisfaction (Whitman, Van Roody, Viswesvaran, 2010), organizational justice (Konovsky & Pugh, 1994), and organizational commitment (O'Reilly & Chatman, 1986). While it seems only logical that promoting OCBs should be an objective of all leaders and managers, research has found that average levels of OCBs are linked to overall organizational performance (Koys, 2001)—further highlighting its significance!

Conversely, just as OCBs exist in organizations, so too can *counterproductive work behaviors* (CWBs; Marcus & Schuler, 2004). CWBs are employee behaviors that can harm an organization either through actions that directly impact the organization or through actions directed at individuals. Just as specific antecedents to OCBs have been identified, so too have factors that influence CWBs. These include sensation seeking (Marcus & Schuler, 2004), motives (Rioux & Penner, 2001), and self-control (Marcus & Schuler, 2004). Ideally, leaders and managers wish to eliminate counterproductive work behaviors while promoting organizational citizenship behaviors. And the key mediating factor to achieving this seems to be organizational justice (Fodchuk, 2007)—the perception that employees are treated in a just and fair manner. In order to positively increase a culture of justice within an organization, various activities may be critical, including the use of effective interpersonal skills when delivering bad news, ensuring selection procedures are job-related (Truxillo, Bauer, Campion, & Paronto, 2002), and training managers in interpersonal justice (Skarlicki & Latham, 2005).

Mental health professionals might be predisposed to promoting organizational justice since most have chosen their discipline because of an innate need to help others and most are preternaturally disposed to working collaboratively. Moreover, most are not only accustomed but are particularly oriented to contributing to overarching goals. As a result, leaders of mental health organizations may be able to simply tap into the existing shared values and beliefs of their employees and use them to reinforce a positive organizational culture.

Staffing Options and Scheduling

Staffing pattern is another process-related issue in organizational design. There are basically three types of staffing patterns in most human service and mental health organizations: full-time, part-time, and *contingent/ contractual employees*. Whereas it most often stands to reason that organizations largely composed of full-time employees may have an easier time engaging their workforce with the organization, it is not uncommon for human service organizations to maintain contingent paraprofessional staff as well as contingent professional staff. In fact, hiring contingent workers allows the organization greater flexibility and control over its long-term financial commitments (Gibelman & Furman, 2008) and may be used to ensure fiscal stability. Depending on the type of work being done, the contingency plan, and how the contingent workforce fits into the rest of the organization, contingent/contractual employees in human service organizations may be equally engaged in the organization.

While staffing patterns can impact organizational culture, program developers must be highly concerned with developing the most effective staffing pattern for the work being done within the program/organization. For example, inpatient substance abuse treatment programs have much different staffing requirements than community-based substance abuse prevention programs. Minimally, inpatient treatment programs require paraprofessional staff to be available around the clock and require full-time professional counselors/mental health professionals, full-time case managers/social workers, and immediate access to medical personnel (e.g., physician, nurse). This may result in staffing patterns that include full-time, part-time, and contingent paraprofessionals, recreational and other support staff, full-time mental health professionals, full-time case managers, and contingent or part-time medical personnel, as well as program supervisors, managers, and administrators. In addition, client-staff ratios for paraprofessional/direct care workers and caseload size for clinicians and case managers must be considered in residential programs with regard to best practice standards articulated by accrediting bodies, licensing bodies, or other contractual requirements. Depending on the program capacity, residential programs may have as few as 40 employees for a 12-bed program and as many as 150 for an 80-bed program. Conversely, a community-based substance abuse prevention program may consist solely of full-time staff that may minimally include clinicians and other professional staff as well as a program supervisor and/or manager. In this case, depending on the number of target clients, a community-based prevention program may have as few as three employees, including clinicians and a program administrator.

As a result of the vast differences in required staffing patterns based on program type and program capacity, program developers must pay particular attention to identifying the right staffing pattern for their program. Because staffing patterns are directly tied to program outcomes and have significant financial implications, it is essential that the right staffing pattern be put in place at initial implementation. In fact, failure to do so may result in treatment failure and financial loss, either of which could cause the program to lose continued funding and, ultimately, cease operations.

As you can see, each of these organizational processes and design issues (i.e., communication, supervision and accountability, culture, staffing, and scheduling) require critical thinking by the program developer to ensure the development of a sound design. The *Organizational Design Process Issues Checklist* may aid you in initially working through these design issues (see Table 6.2).

Table 6.2   Organizational Design Process Issues Checklist

Process Issue	Question
Communication	What organizational theories guide the program/organization?
	What communication styles most reflect our organizational theory?
	What types of communication patterns most effectively support our program objectives?
	What types of communication patterns may be detrimental to the program's success?
	How does the program/organization need to be structured to support the most effective communication patterns?
	How is information disseminated within the organization?
	How is communication accounted for within the organization?
Supervision and accountability	What types of supervision and accountability patterns are most effective given our type of program and staffing options?
	What types of supervision and accountability patterns are most effective to carry out the program's objectives?
	What type of supervision and accountability patterns will help us achieve our desired organizational culture?

(Continued)

Table 6.2 (Continued)

Process Issue	Question
Culture	What type of organizational culture will most effectively help us achieve our program objectives?
	What type of organizational culture should we expect as a result of our organizational theory, communication patterns, supervision and accountability patterns, and staffing?
	What will need to be purposely done in order to promote the desired organizational culture?
	What type of culture is transmitted through this design?
Staffing options	Is every staff position justified?
	What credentials and experience are needed to implement the program?
	What are the accreditation standards and licensing and contractual requirements for staffing this type of program?
	What type of staffing structure has been found to most effectively support the program objectives?

Each of the questions focuses on specific issues related to design and, as such, should prompt further exploration into specific areas, generating more information for use in decision making about design. However, this list is in no way exhaustive, and likely you will generate new questions as you begin thinking about each of these issues.

Designing the Staffing Infrastructure

Designing an effective organizational infrastructure is no small feat. On the contrary, it requires a great deal of time, focused attention to detail, and an ability to look beyond the nuts and bolts of staffing to how you wish the organization to function well into the future. Because of the complex issues that both influence and are influenced by organizational infrastructure, it is imperative that extensive consideration be granted to this phase of program design. And as with all other aspects of program design, this work must be guided by data. In fact, when designing the organizational staffing infrastructure, you must first revisit the program design, research review, and market analysis, as each will provide guidance to the infrastructure development.

Revisiting the Program Design, Research Review, and Market Analysis

The program design provides the most relevant information needed for designing the staffing infrastructure. This information includes

- target population,
- program type,
- program size/capacity,
- clinical and nonclinical interventions, and
- length of treatment.

Each of these design aspects influences decision making related to staffing. Whereas program type, size, and interventions provide basic information related to the type and number of staff needed, program type also guides thinking about staffing options (full-time, part-time, contractual).

After identifying the various types of staff positions needed based on the program design, the results of the literature review should again be consulted. However, the review at this juncture should be specifically focused on program evaluation and other research related to achieving program outcomes—identifying the type and number of staff needed to successfully carry out the program.

In addition to learning about the effect that staffing patterns have had on program outcomes through a focused research review, you should also review national accreditation standards related to the program type for guidance. Accrediting bodies often articulate best practices related to staff credentials, number of staff members needed, client-staff ratio and caseload size, and any specialized training needs, among other aspects. It is best to not limit the review of accreditation standards but rather review the standards of each of the major accreditation bodies that have promulgated standards for your particular type of program, regardless if you are planning to pursue accreditation with only one accrediting body. I say this because, as you hopefully recall from Chapter 3, most accreditation bodies today provide standards for a broad and highly diverse group of programs. By taking advantage of this and reviewing the standards of each body related to your type of program, you can gain more information for use in decision making about staffing infrastructure development.

In addition, regional or state licensing rules and/or other oversight or contractual bodies must be consulted for their specific staffing requirements. Often, these types of oversight agencies also articulate staff credential needs, staff-client ratio and caseload size, and specialized training needs.

Last but not least, the results of the market analysis should again be utilized. Because the market analysis provides detailed information about regional and national competitors, this data can be highly meaningful in designing the staffing infrastructure. Learning from what others who have been operating similar programs have done is often critical to successfully designing your own program. When considering staffing design, understanding what has worked well and what has not worked for competitors can assist you in ensuring that you take advantage of the best of what they have produced while avoiding similar failures. At the same time, you must consider how your program will differentiate itself from the competition, and the staffing infrastructure may be a likely component by which to further make your program unique or enhanced so that it is set apart from the competition. For instance, if your competitors use a treatment team approach in a community-based program for adolescents with substance abuse issues that includes a case manager and a clinician, you may add a paraprofessional to your treatment team to work specifically with the client and family in effectively linking them to various community supports and providing direct support to them as they begin and/or continue these relationships. By doing so, you may enhance your treatment approach while differentiating your program from the competition. And if you share one paraprofessional position between three work teams, the added cost that you incur may be minimal, particularly if better program outcomes can be achieved.

Organizational Chart

The organizational chart is one of the program developer's principal tools for use in designing the organizational infrastructure and constitutes the first and arguably most critical step of organizational design. Organizational charts provide an illustration of the staffing infrastructure of a program/organization and, as such, communicate program/organization structure to staff and other stakeholders. In addition, organizational charts clarify the chain of command and illustrate the expected flow of communication within an organization at a basic level (Lewis et al., 2007). Similar to logic models, the organizational chart is an integral program planning tool.

Although organizational charts are an effective tool for designing the staffing infrastructure, the organizational chart is not intended to, nor does it, overtly articulate deeper levels of organizational processes (e.g., communication, decision making, culture). Moreover, organizational charts do not clearly illustrate the manner in which responsibilities are delegated, and organizational charts alone cannot explain the functions of a position. As a result, organizational charts must be used in conjunction with written job descriptions (Lewis et al., 2007). Regardless of its limitations, the power of the organizational chart must not be overlooked. Namely, organizational charts illustrate chains of command/hierarchy within a program/organization, and this in turn has a great deal of influence on communication, decision making, and culture. So, whereas the organizational chart will not provide information about specific organizational process issues, it is an essential component underlying the organizational processes. Moreover, developing the organizational chart aids in the initial program planning, implementation, and evaluation of the organizational structure and processes. For instance, when a program experiences difficulty with communication among staff, a review of the organizational chart may assist in ferreting out where communication may be breaking down and how hierarchical reporting patterns may influence communication, both negatively and positively. As such, the organizational chart not only serves as critical to the initial organizational design but also as the first line of defense in addressing organizational design issues that emerge later during program implementation.

In addition to the significance that an organizational chart holds for the organization, it is often equally significant to funders. In fact, organizational charts are often required by state and regional funding agencies as part of the proposal process to bid for human service programs. Because funders have an integral stake in the success of a given program, organizational charts are often required to demonstrate an appropriate staffing infrastructure—lending further support to the overall proposal.

Because organizational charts reflect the type, number, and scope of a program and/or organization, the charts vary drastically based on each of these factors. In single-program organizations, one organizational chart may be used that reflects the organization and includes the program. However, single-program organizations that are highly complex may require both an organizational chart for the program and one for the organization's administrative structure. This is the standard for multifaceted organizations whereby an organizational chart should be developed for each program, detailing all the staffing components contained in the program, as well as a separate one for the organization that includes the administrative structure and basic information about programs. Probably the most important issue to remember regarding the use of an organizational chart is that it is a tool for use by the program developer, manager, or other leaders. As a tool, it is flexible and works with the program developer as needed. Therefore, you must determine the most effective use of organizational charts, detailing as much as you wish and using as many charts to illustrate various components of the program/organization as needed. The organizational chart provided in the case illustration at the end of the chapter (Figure 6.2) reflects a single program structure and includes the total administrative structure (i.e., president, office support coordinator) and program structure. Figure 6.1 illustrates an additional type of organizational chart—a program-specific chart.

Figure 6.1 depicts the staffing infrastructure of a community-based psychiatric program for adults with serious psychiatric disorders—similar to an Acute Community Treatment model. As such, the primary staff are clinicians. This is because this is a clinically based program and, therefore, the bulk of expenditures are used to support the primary workers. In this program, the program director holds either a master's degree or a doctorate (counseling, clinical psychology, clinical social work). The same is true for the clinicians, and the case managers may have a master's in social work or a bachelor's degree in one of the helping professions with advanced

Figure 6.1 Program-Specific Organizational Chart for a Community-Based Psychiatric Treatment Program

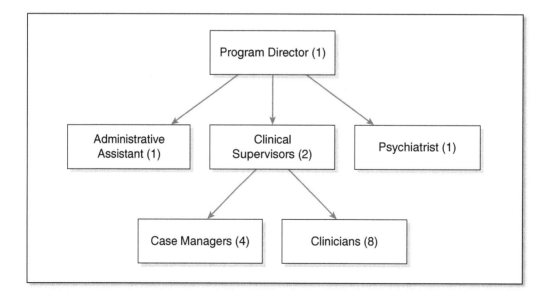

training in psychiatric treatment. Additionally, the number of positions per category is based on the type and intensity of work performed by each position. As such, the staffing pattern includes the following:

- One program director to oversee the program operations, with responsibility for the direct supervision of the psychiatrist, clinical supervisors, and administrative assistant
- One psychiatrist to provide monthly medication reviews and consultation as needed (smallest workload)
- Two clinical supervisors who each have a small supervisory load of four clinicians because of the type of services provided
- Eight clinicians to provide the key treatment and most intensive services with weekly individual therapy and biweekly group therapy
- Four case managers to provide once-per-week home visits and resource coordination as needed
- One administrative assistant to provide office support to the 16 members of the staff

Summary

Achieving an effective organizational design is no small feat and, in fact, requires a tremendous amount of knowledge and skill as well as a commitment to continuous evaluation. In the helping professions in particular, the success of our business depends on the individuals providing the services, and therefore, finding the right people to fill the right roles is an essential objective. However, before we can even consider the right people, we must ensure that we have identified the right positions to implement the various components of the program. This, like all other aspects of comprehensive program development, involves no guesswork but, rather, effectively using research, knowledge, and data to guide the planning process. Namely, the results of the market analysis, literature review, and the program logic model must be used to guide the development of the organizational/program structure.

In addition to developing the right staffing infrastructure, the various process issues that influence program/organizational functioning (e.g., scheduling, communication patterns, supervision and accountability, culture) must be thoroughly considered. More to the point, there must be a deep appreciation for the interdependent relationships between staffing infrastructure and process issues and the need for the program developer to thoughtfully and strategically influence the organizational design so that the program can not only thrive but be sustained over time.

CASE ILLUSTRATION

Allied Mental Health Services had been in operation for 9 years, providing outpatient counseling to children, adults, and families with a variety of presenting issues, including grief and loss, addiction, and serious mental health disorders. This mental health agency was small, with 11 staff members, including Marge, who served as the president (also a full-time clinician); a full-time receptionist/bookkeeper; three full-time clinicians; and six contractual clinicians. The agency had successfully operated over the past several years in the community, expanding its client population and increasing revenue as a result of increased recognition for the quality of its work. Most recently, the county mental health board had released a Request for Proposal for comprehensive counseling and support services for veterans and their families, and a representative of the mental health board had encouraged Marge to submit a proposal on behalf of Allied.

Marge called a meeting for all the staff to discuss the possibility of developing a proposal for this new program. The group engaged in quite a bit of dialogue regarding how taking on such a program might alter the current organization, both in terms of structure and in terms of process (e.g., culture, decision making). This was particularly at issue since the agency operated as an employee-owned organization, with therapists responsible for generating specific levels of revenue and a cost- and revenue-sharing plan in place. This arrangement had historically promoted a high degree of autonomy for the clinicians and uniquely engaged them in the organization since all were equally responsible for the agency's health.

After spending a good deal of time outlining the pros and cons of pursuing this new business, the group decided that it was in their best interest to develop a proposal. While working on the proposal, the group began thinking about how the new program would be staffed and how the new program structure would differ from their existing structure—and how this might impact the organization. The existing structure was almost flat—consisting of two levels, with Marge occupying the top level and all the clinicians and the receptionist/bookkeeper sharing a level directly beneath her.

Because Marge assumed a quasi-leadership role in the organization, she had a larger financial stake in the business and, because of this, ultimately carried more risk and subsequent responsibility for the business (e.g., physical space, business taxes). However, Marge's hierarchical standing had more to do with business-related liabilities and expenditures than with decision-making authority since the clinicians largely operated autonomously yet collectively. However, with the addition of a traditional human service program with multiple levels of staff, contractual obligations, and a need for varying levels of accountability, the program staffing infrastructure would need to look quite different from the existing structure. And as the organization's leader, Marge would likely have to assume more direct oversight of the program—attending to program operations details that she did not currently need to scrutinize.

The staff felt strongly that the current success of their organization was largely based on the organizational structure that they had in place and were fearful of letting go of some of the ownership that they perceived they had in the business operations, and this remained in the back of their minds as they moved forward in planning for the new program. After charting out the various positions needed in the proposed program based on the program design, market analysis, and literature review, they were able to identify four levels of positions needed: program director, clinicians, family support coordinators, and an office support staff person (see Figure 6.2). The thinking behind this design was that the program director would be responsible for the administrative aspects of the program, while the clinicians would focus primarily on the program implementation and, as such, would oversee the work of the family/community support coordinators. Because the office support coordinator would provide administrative support to all program staff, this position would report directly to the program director so that the clinicians would be able to focus solely on the program. Marge would provide executive leadership to the program, directly supervising the program director.

Figure 6.2 Proposed Program Organizational Chart for Comprehensive Counseling and Support Services for Veterans and Their Families

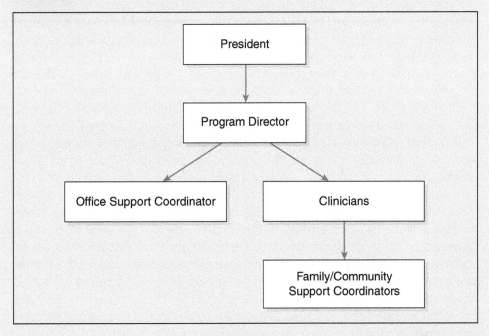

(Continued)

(Continued)

Having completed the design of the staffing infrastructure, the work group turned its attention to the various process issues that needed to be addressed through design. The group most wanted to take steps to not disrupt the current functioning of the organization through any radical changes. So they decided that the program director and clinician positions would be offered first to current part- and full-time clinicians, if they were qualified and interested. It was thought that by doing this, the organization would be less negatively impacted since existing staff would simply take on new roles, thus ensuring some degree of continuity for the entire organization during its time of transition. In addition, it was also hoped that this would allow for the existing climate and culture, which was very positive, to naturally influence the new program since much of the culture resided within and was influenced by the existing staff.

In addition to planning to move existing staff into key positions in the new program, the group also planned for decision making, supervision and accountability, and other issues related to organizational culture. To this end, the group decided that although a program director was in place, team-based decision making would be practiced. This meant that family/support coordinators and clinicians would engage in collaborative decision making regarding programming and operational issues, with the program director weighing in but with the majority ruling in decisions, as relevant. In addition, peer review and team consultation practices would be in place to promote a climate in which all staff would be accountable to one another and to the program. By putting these two significant process strategies in place, the work group believed that a culture of staff empowerment, autonomy, and healthy engagement within the program could be gained. In many ways, this schema would mirror the existing organizational structure. This would ensure organizational coherence and a smooth transition as the organization experienced this expansion and change process.

After finalizing the detailed organizational design for the proposed program, which would be maintained as a guide for program implementation if the contract was awarded, the group completed the proposal for the new program and submitted it to the funding agency. In debriefing the work group activities as a follow-up, members reported feeling even greater engagement in the organization and much more investment in winning the proposal—another benefit of involving staff in any type of change project. More significantly, though, group members discussed making it a priority to regularly debrief and check in as a large group about their organizational process issues if and when the new program was implemented, as well as if it was not. As they had learned throughout this initial planning process, successful organizational structures do not simply happen but, rather, are well orchestrated and continuously tended to. This was a lesson that they agreed could not simply be taken for granted within the organization.

ORGANIZATIONAL CHART EXERCISE

To put your own organizational staffing infrastructure design skills to work, complete the following exercise either independently or in a small group:

1. Identify a program of particular interest to you that you would like to develop to address a specific issue (e.g., elder abuse, depression, gang violence), and review the research related to this type of programming.

2. If the program is a clinical program, consider that the program capacity is 40 clients (total number of clients served at a given time), and if the program is a school-based program, consider that the total number of students is 300. Or simply determine another relevant capacity level based on your particular program so that you can use this information to determine the number of staff needed and relevant caseload sizes.

3. Develop a program-only organizational chart identifying all the program-specific staff positions needed to operate the program at full capacity.

4. Identify the types of minimal credentials needed for each staff position and provide an explanation for each.

5. With the exception of program administrative assistant/office support staff, if needed, do not include any other support positions (e.g., finance, human resources, information systems) in this chart.

6. Identify the hours of program operations and the scheduling patterns for the various staff positions.

7. Identify the desired communication patterns, supervision and accountability processes, and culture that you hope to achieve within the program.

8. In small or large groups, present your findings, providing all the following information:

   • Justification for each position in the staffing infrastructure
   • The rationale for staff qualifications
   • The caseload size and rationale
   • The relationship between the organizational chart and the logic model
   • The relationship between the desired communication patterns, supervision and accountability processes, and culture and the staffing structure
   • Any necessary modifications to the organizational chart as warranted based on lack of effective justification or other issues that emerge from your presentation

References

American Counseling Association. (2005). *ACA code of ethics.* Alexandria, VA: Author.

Bernays, E. L. (2005). *Propaganda.* Brooklyn, NY: Ig.

Bolman, L. G., & Deal, T. E. (2008). *Reframing organizations: Artistry, choice, and leadership* (4th ed.). San Francisco: Jossey-Bass.

Carver, J. (2006). *Boards that make a difference: A new design for leadership in nonprofit and public organizations.* San Francisco: Jossey-Bass.

Conlon, D. E., Meyer, C. J., & Nowakowski, J. M. (2005). How does organizational justice affect performance, withdrawal, and counterproductive behavior? In J. Greenberg & J. Colquitt (Eds.), *Handbook of organizational justice* (pp. 301–328). Mahwah, NJ: Lawrence Erlbaum.

Dalal, R. S. (2005). A meta-analysis of the relationship between organizational citizenship behavior and counterproductive work behavior. *Journal of Applied Psychology, 90,* 1241–1255.

Dalton, D., Todor, W., Spendolini, M., Fielding, G., & Porter, L. (1980). Organization structure and performance: A critical review. *Academy of Management Review, 5,* 49–64.

Deal, T. E., & Kennedy, A. A. (1982). *Corporate cultures.* Reading, MA: Addison-Wesley.

Department of Interior. (2009). *Federal outreach and leadership development program.* Retrieved May 10, 2010, from http://www.doi.gov/febtc/files/FOLD brochure.pdf

Drucker, P. (1999). *Management: Tasks, responsibilities, practices.* New York: HarperCollins.

Fodchuk, K. M. (2007). Work environments that negate counterproductive behaviors and foster organizational citizenship: Research-based recommendations for managers. *Psychologist-Manager Journal, 10,* 27–46.

Ford, J., & Slocum, J. (1977). Environment, technology, and the structure of organizations. *Academy of Management Review, 2,* 561–575.

Frederickson, J. (1986). The strategic decision-making process in organizational structure. *Academy of Management Review, 11,* 280–297.

Fry, L. (1982). Technology-structure research: Three critical issues. *Academy of Management Journal, 25,* 532–551.

Gibelman, M., & Furman, R. (2008). *Navigating human service organizations.* Chicago: Lyceum.

Hur, M. H. (2008). Exploring differences in leadership styles: A study of manager tasks, follower characteristics, and task environments in Korean human service organizations. *Social Behavior and Personality, 36,* 359–372.

Kessler, G., & Schuster, M. H. (2009). Design your governance model to make the matrix work. *People and Strategy, 32,* 16–25.

Konovsky, M. A., & Pugh, S. D. (1994). Citizenship behavior and social exchange. *Academy of Management Journal, 37,* 656–669.

Koys, D. J. (2001). The effects of employee satisfaction, organizational citizenship behavior, and turnover on organizational effectiveness: A unit-level, longitudinal study. *Personnel Psychology, 54,* 101–114.

Lewis, J. A., Packard, T. R., & Lewis, M. D. (2007). *Management of human service programs* (4th ed.). Belmont, CA: Thomson Learning.

Marcus, B., & Schuler, H. (2004). Antecedents of counterproductive behavior at work: A general perspective. *Journal of Applied Psychology, 89,* 647–660.

Miller, D. (1988). Relating Porter's business strategies to environment and structure: Analysis and performance implications. *Academy of Management Journal, 31,* 280–308.

Miller, D., & Droge, C. (1986). Psychological and traditional determinants of structure. *Administrative Science Quarterly, 31,* 539–560.

Moss Kantor, R. (1983). *The change masters.* New York: Simon & Schuster.

O'Looney, J. (1996). *Redesigning the work of human services.* Westport, CT: Quorum.

O'Reilly, C., & Chatman, J. (1986). Organizational commitment and psychological attachment: The effects of compliance, identification, and internalization on prosocial behavior. *Journal of Applied Psychology, 71,* 492–499.

Pleshko, L., & Nickerson, I. (2008). Strategic orientation, organizational structure, and the associated effects on performance in industrial firms. *Academy of Strategic Management Journal, 7,* 95–110.

Rioux, S., & Penner, L. A. (2001). The causes of organizational citizenship behavior: A motivational analysis. *Journal of Applied Psychology, 86,* 1303–1314.

Senge, P. M. (2006). *The fifth discipline.* New York: Doubleday.

Skarlicki, D. P., & Latham, D. P. (2005). How can training be used to foster organizational justice? In J. Greenberg & J. Colquitt (Eds.), *Handbook of organizational justice* (pp. 499–524). Mahwah, NJ: Lawrence Erlbaum.

Truxillo, D. M., Bauer, T. N., Campion, M. A., & Paronto, M. E. (2002). Selection fairness information and applicant reactions: A longitudinal field study. *Journal of Applied Psychology, 87,* 1020–1031.

Whitman, D. S., Van Roody, D. L., & Viswesvaran, C. (2010). Satisfaction, citizenship behaviors, and performance in work units: A meta-analysis of collective construct relations. *Personnel Psychology, 63,* 41–81.

Identify and Engage Community Resources

Learning Objectives

1. Discuss the importance of community resource development in comprehensive program development

2. Explain how community resources can be used to augment the service array, build advocacy coalitions, and garner funding

3. Explain the relationship between community resource development and program sustainability planning and strengthening communities

4. Discuss the relationships between the results of the asset map, community demography assessment, market analysis, and logic model to community resource development efforts

5. Investigate and identify relevant community resources by completing the community resource development exercise

WHY ENGAGE THE COMPETITION?

Ryan and Adrienne recently celebrated the third anniversary of their outreach and shelter program for female survivors of domestic violence. Their shelter program had consistently remained at 95% capacity over the past 2 years—unfortunately, reflecting the continued scope of the domestic violence problem in the region—and they had expanded their outreach program to include a domestic violence prevention program for high school and college students. In addition, the programs had recently gained accreditation through the Council of Accreditation—something they were very proud to have attained.

While Ryan and Adrienne had become familiar with some of the staff of the local hospital as well as an attorney's office, they had had only brief encounters with the other two major providers working with domestic violence survivors in the area. Moreover, Ryan and Adrienne had taken few steps to identify other resources that existed in the community, believing that they would be better off trying to address the needs of their clients directly rather than referring their clients to other providers. Their fear, of course, was that if they referred their clients to other providers, they might put their own program at risk of losing its relevance and potentially going out of business. So far, this method had served them well—their business was thriving, and they successfully expanded their core business—demonstrating that they could be involved not only in shelter services but also in primary prevention efforts.

However, not soon after they celebrated their 3-year milestone, their shelter contract was up for bid. Whereas the original contract focused primarily on the services provided on-site at the shelter, the contract had been significantly modified with a new emphasis on the creation of linkages to an extensive community network. The contractor's intent was to more effectively support the long-term needs of the client population by assisting them in accessing various resources. As such, applicants interested in applying for the contract were required to identify a community network, consisting of multiple organizations that offered adjunctive services (e.g., vocational development, housing) and extended core services (e.g., domestic violence support). With the proposal due in 3 weeks, Adrienne and Ryan had to quickly begin speaking with various leaders of community organizations (i.e., resources) in an attempt to get them to participate as part of a community network. They began by approaching their two main competitors; however, they quickly learned that these two organizations had worked collaboratively for the past several years, using each other as a referral source to augment their own services as well as working together to pass new legislation on behalf of domestic violence survivors. The competitors further shared that they were also planning to pursue the contract and would be doing so in a partnership with several other community organizations with whom they had previously done business.

Without being able to establish a key partnership with one of the two providers offering core services, Ryan and Adrienne knew their chances of securing the contract were slim. And after spending a considerable amount of time trying to line up potential adjunctive partners, Ryan and Adrienne consistently received the same message: They were simply not known to other community resources, and therefore, there was no desire for others to partner with them, particularly given such a short time frame in which to make a decision.

They were able to get the attorney's office to provide a *letter of support*, and they were able to secure a letter from one of the high schools where they provided outreach services, but they knew that their proposal was weak—not demonstrating their ability to offer an extensive community network. Needless to say, when they received notice that they did not win the contract, they were not surprised. Rather than wallow in this failure for long, Adrienne and Ryan decided to put their energies into getting to know their competitors in domestic violence prevention, as well as developing relationships with other community resources—having directly learned the significance of these relationships.

CONSIDERING ADRIENNE AND RYAN

1. What mistakes did Ryan and Adrienne make, and how could they have prevented them?

2. Beyond gaining a letter of support, what other benefits might you receive from developing a relationship with your competitor?

3. Are relationships between competitors in human services different from those between different types of for-profit businesses? Why or why not?

About This Chapter

This chapter focuses specifically on community resource development and the key role that community resource development can play in program development efforts. In the comprehensive program development model, there are two steps involving community resources—identifying and engaging community resources and building and preserving relationships with community resources. This chapter covers Step V of the model and involves the initial work with community resources—resource development and, specifically, identifying and engaging community resources.

The chapter begins with defining community resources and discussing the role of community resource development in program development efforts. Further highlighting the significance of community resource development, we will examine five major purposes related to community resource development that include augmenting the service array, developing an advocacy coalition, garnering funding, planning for sustainability, and strengthening communities. In order to illustrate how this step builds on work previously completed in the preplanning and planning stages of program development, we will revisit the results of the community demography assessment, asset map, market analysis, and logic model for use in identifying community resources. In addition, we will initially discuss the need to not only engage but begin to preserve community resources, particularly as this need links to Step XI (Build and Preserve Community Resources). Finally, the *Community Resource Snapshot* tool is provided for use in community resource development, and an exercise is provided to further reinforce the topic.

STEP V: IDENTIFY AND ENGAGE COMMUNITY RESOURCES

Community: Defined

A discussion about community resources must begin with a discussion about community and exactly what is meant by the concept of community. Providing a focused definition of community, Bookman (2005) views it as a "real geographical community that shapes family life and work" (p. 144). In contrast, according to Lewis, Lewis, Daniels, and D'Andrea (2003),

> The word community means different things to different people. To some it may refer to people living in a specific geographic area (e.g., rural versus urban community). To others it may mean a group of people related by their unique cultural, ethnic, or racial background, such as the Asian American community. Still others may use the term to refer to the interdependence each has to one another as members of a much broader "global community." (p. 6)

Taking the concept of community a step further, Homan (2004) offers the perspective that a community is similar to an individual, insofar as a community may have strengths and limitations, specific challenges that it faces (e.g., ethnic conflict, crime), feelings of powerlessness, unique skills that come from its members, and the ability to engage in collaboration/ supportive activities. Whereas these definitions reinforce Gareis and

Barnett's (2008) assertion that there still is not a well-established consensus definition of community in the mental health professions, for the sake of the discussion on community resource development, an even more focused definition of community will be used. Community will be defined as the geographic region in which client populations reside—consistent with the concept of a target region discussed in Chapter 2.

Community Resources: Defined

Community resources are assets that the community possesses. Or simply, "resources are what a community has going for itself" (Homan, 2004, p. 55). As discussed in Chapter 2, resources can include services, other treatment providers, knowledge, and other assets that are available within the community. Because the strength, self-preservation, and sustainability of a community are often based on the degree to which a community can be self-supporting, the resources that a community has are integral to achieving this. In fact, communities themselves often play a critical role in helping individual community members overcome major stressors and successfully adapt in the face of severe challenges (Yoon, 2009). However, it is not simply the fact that a community has available resources that makes it healthy but, rather, that the community fully utilizes its available resources in order to achieve greater health and self-sufficiency.

Community Resources: Brief Review of the Literature

Unfortunately, research in the area of community resource development has been scattered and noncumulative (Gareis & Barnett, 2008), with the bulk of the literature still in its infancy. Studies that have been conducted in this area have focused on the peripheral issue of needs assessments in identifying service needs for specific populations, such as elderly African immigrants (Darboe & Ahmed, 2007); the use of neighborhood mapping techniques to identify community assets and other community characteristics, including specific resources (Aronson, Wallis, O'Campo, & Schafer, 2007); and the resilience of particular communities as a result of various existing community assets (Maybery, Pope, Hodgins, Hitchenor, & Shepherd, 2009).

In addition, one recent study sought to move into new territory by investigating perceived community resource fit compared with individual community members' needs and by developing a quantitative tool by which to assess this (Gareis & Barnett, 2008). In this work, the authors examined a residential community of employed families, exploring community members' satisfaction with their personal values, desires, or goals as matched with the community's existing resources. Their findings illustrated the significance of effective community resource fit in school and work in particular and its relationship to overall well-being, reinforcing previous findings (Gareis, Barnett, & Brennan, 2003; Voydanoff, 2004). As such, the greater the perceived satisfaction with work and school resources, the less family conflict and psychological stress there is. This work also resulted in the development of a standardized measure to assess community resource fit that has promising psychometric properties (Gareis & Barnett, 2008), which may be instrumental in future studies in this area.

Whereas research in this area is beginning to evolve, much more attention will need to be paid to ensure that studies related to community resource development focus on all types of communities, particularly those facing serious challenges (e.g., working poor and impoverished, largely unemployed, high-crime areas). It is often these types of marginalized communities that provide the context of work in human services, and therefore, it is precisely these types of communities in which we need to better understand the role that community resource development plays.

Community Resource Development

Mental health professionals and individuals with chronic needs typically know precisely what resources exist in their communities. This is because they have an innate need to know. The former know because their success as clinicians often rests on this knowledge, while the survival of the latter often depends on such information. In fact, I have often thought the measure of a truly effective clinician can be found in his/her awareness of and proximity to an array of community resources. Clinicians today must not only know what resources are available, but they also must be able to skillfully ensure that access to such resources is unrestricted. More often than not, that means that they have to have already developed strong working relationships with the individuals managing the resources. Whereas resource coordination is a core part of the clinicians' job, individuals with chronic needs are motivated by sheer survival skills to identify and access necessary resources for themselves. As such, individuals with chronic needs are often the most incredibly resilient people, with an enormous amount of knowledge and skill related to available resources—not to mention inner strength and perseverance—from which we all can learn.

The availability and array of community resources are integral to any community's health, required for community development, and indicative of a community's sustainability. Because of this, community resources are a necessity for any clinical or human service program's development efforts and must be viewed as a key ingredient of comprehensive program development.

Community resource development refers to three main issues:

1. The existence of resources within a community to meet specific needs

2. The ability to access needed existing resources

3. The development of new resources designed to address existing needs

The Sooke Navigator project (Box 7.1; Anderson & Larke, 2009) provides an excellent example of the need for comprehensive community resource development.

BOX 7.1

THE SOOKE NAVIGATOR PROJECT

The objective of the project was to improve mental health and addiction services to individuals in a rural region in British Columbia. Led by a collaborative team of mental health professionals and community leaders, the project focused on identifying and engaging existing community resources in order to increase access to available services in the region.

After a thorough investigation of all the existing community resources, two Navigator positions were developed that would function as direct links to needed community resources. One Navigator was assigned to youth, and the other Navigator was responsible for adults.

Navigators were mental health workers that were responsible for

- conducting a strengths-based assessment and initial plan,
- connecting individuals to necessary resources,
- providing focused support and guidance to individuals in need,
- educating community members and other professionals about the existing community resources, and
- following up with individuals to determine the outcomes related to community resource linkages.

In addition, Navigators were required to have specialized knowledge of the primary treatment issues, collaborate with both the individuals and participating community resources in the development of the initial assessment plan, and provide or coordinate ongoing linking services to ensure that the individual could indeed access any necessary resources.

By implementing the Navigator system, the region was able to increase community member access to necessary mental health and addiction treatment.

One of the key factors that motivated the Sooke project was that even though the region had various resources, individuals in need of the resources often were unable to access them because they were not aware of them or because other barriers stood in their way. Unfortunately, this problem is in no way unique to British Columbia, but rather it is a highly common problem that many, if not most, communities face. However, through a coordinated planning and action process, the Sooke Navigator project demonstrated that it was able to produce a significant impact in linking individuals in need with existing community resources. And it is precisely these types of linkages on which community resource development efforts are based.

Objectives of Community Resource Development

In addition to ensuring that individuals in need are able to gain access to necessary community resources, there are several other purposes for utilizing community resources in comprehensive program development. These include, but are not limited to, the following:

- Augmenting the service array
- Building an advocacy coalition
- Garnering additional and/or new funding
- Promoting long-term sustainability planning
- Strengthening communities from within by recognizing and utilizing existing resources

Because each of these issues is of particular significance to program development efforts, each will be discussed further below.

Augment Service Array

As you have likely already witnessed in each of the previous steps of the program design process, a tremendous number of needs must be met when addressing a clinical or social issue. This is because no clinical or social problem exists in isolation, but rather each is connected to a highly complex individual—moreover, a highly complex individual who is multifaceted and who interacts within a broad social context. For instance, treating depression relies only partially on treating the clinical symptoms of depression and should address all aspects of the individual's lifestyle (e.g., work, hobbies, family, friends), social systems, and intra- and interpersonal aspects, among other issues. Because some of these issues can be addressed therapeutically and others require additional types of intervention, it is necessary to coordinate additional services to ensure that the problem is truly addressed in a holistic manner.

Therefore, achieving a comprehensive approach to program development requires not only directly addressing a host of related issues and treating the whole client but also demonstrating the ability to provide enhanced services and treatment through the use of other available resources. This was one of the key factors related to the Sooke project (Anderson & Larke, 2009)—the need to ensure that residents could take advantage of the various resources that existed within their community. From the program developer's perspective, the ability to tap into existing community resources allows for augmenting the service array, thus enlarging the continuum of services for use by the target population. In doing so, the program developer is able to focus more specifically on the core treatment program since other providers are able to offer enhanced treatment options.

In addition to being a smart business practice—using what already exists rather than re-creating what is already there—this approach provides the added benefit of strengthening the community by recognizing its existing attributes. Doing so ensures not only an effectively encompassing treatment approach but also greater potential for sustaining treatment gains as a result of tapping into the community's existing riches.

Advocacy Coalition Development

Equally important to utilizing existing community resources in program development efforts is engaging existing community resources as a means to begin building an advocacy coalition. An advocacy coalition refers to a group of individuals and organizations dedicated to a specific treatment issue or social need that works collectively to increase awareness and knowledge of the issue. Advocacy coalitions may become involved in lobbying efforts— efforts designed to increase funding—and/or may engage in other methods that seek to increase recognition of specific issues and in other activities designed to ensure that the issues can be most effectively addressed. In addition, advocacy coalitions may organize public forums or campaigns to garner support for specific issues, and the work of advocacy coalitions may result in increased pressure on elected officials (Roberts-DeGennaro, 2001). Developing an advocacy coalition may prove essential to sustaining a new program, as the coalition can function to ensure that attention is continuously paid to the types of issues being addressed by the program.

Lewis et al. (2003) outline the coalition-building process as one that includes three stages of development:

1. *Planning*: In the planning stage, counselors must identify those constituency groups that might link with their organization to address an issue of common concern. This task includes making sure that those invited to attend the first coalition-building meeting really do have a common interest and stake in the given issue(s).

2. *Consultation*: Coalition building involves more than simply presenting an issue to each organization in a way that makes the members appreciate its importance and value. During the consultation stage, representatives from various organizations must discuss the ways in which joining a coalition with other groups will benefit each constituency.

3. *Planning and implementation*: The planning and implementation stage of the coalition-building process determines the level of interest and commitment that individuals genuinely have regarding the issues of common concern to them. This is critical because individuals will likely demonstrate an increased commitment to a coalition when they feel they have been directly involved in the planning and implementation of beneficial strategies. Given their training and expertise in human relations, counselors are well equipped to deal with the challenging task of facilitating group discussions that involve all participants during the planning and implementation stage. (p. 238)

By simply utilizing and working collaboratively with existing community resources in initial program development efforts, you have an opportunity to begin to develop your own advocacy coalition. And it is through this work of getting out and ensuring that you are aware of all the existing resources that you can begin to build your resource knowledge base. In addition, this work allows you to meet and engage your neighbors and potential business partners on a meaningful level. Moreover, by developing close relationships with competitors that offer mutual benefits, you can decrease the possibility of operating at cross purposes (Homan, 2004)—thus, keeping your competitors with you serves to also ensure that they are not working against you. The role and function of advocacy coalitions is further explained in Chapter 13 as part of the broader discussion related to preserving community resources.

Garner Additional and/or New Funding

Now more than ever before, collaborative efforts in mental health and human service programming are demanded. In fact, rare is the call for proposals for new programs that does not require collaboration between at least two organizations. Two program proposals on which I recently worked might be helpful in illustrating this current trend.

The first Request for Proposal was for a contract to provide an array of children's mental health services and required that the applicant organization identify an established panel of community providers that could provide additional and enhanced services to the target population. The second, from a federal funding agency, required that the applicant organization identify two primary partners—one psychiatric care provider and one medical health provider—that would provide necessary linkages to clients to ensure the availability of comprehensive treatment. In addition, this particular proposal required identifying two additional support service providers (e.g., employment, education) that could be used to further complement the core services provided by the applicant organization.

Both of these sets of requirements outlined by the funding sources accurately reflect the current climate in programming—a climate that is highly focused on developing broad-based systems of care. This is largely based on the notion that by developing a broad-based system of care through collaborative efforts, communities can further develop their internal abilities to respond to the needs of their residents, thus strengthening communities from within.

Whereas developing such comprehensive systems is often necessary to effectively treat individuals, without established relationships with a variety of community resources, such systems are almost impossible to build. Pragmatically, organizations that do not fully appreciate the need for developing relationships with other existing community resources may find that they have been effectively eliminated from potential new funding. However, with appropriately developed community resource partnerships, programs/organizations can find that they are well postured to seek additional and/or new types of funding—thus, possibly allowing for new opportunities and opportunities that may have a direct impact on sustainability.

Sustainability Planning

Whereas both of the above issues have already alluded to long-term sustainability planning, this notion also deserves mention on its own. Sustainability planning refers to the ability of any organism (e.g., program, organization, community) to continue its existence well into the future. This term has come to be a critical part of our vocabulary in the 21st century, particularly as it relates to sustaining the earth that we inhabit. However, thoughtfully focusing on sustainability has been a primary business objective throughout history since, arguably, all new businesses begin with the hope of lasting well into the future and, more so, of experiencing continuous and vast growth.

Since mental health and human services are indeed businesses, program developers must design and implement programs with an initial focus on long-term sustainability. Doing so is often a result of multiple factors that will be discussed in detail in the final part of the text, specifically with regard to the importance of evaluation, information sharing, and accreditation. However, sustainability is another significant benefit related to community resource development. That is, by initially engaging and determining how community resources can be utilized in new program development, you are in fact moving toward ensuring that your program can be sustained over time. This is because any program that utilizes existing and alternative resources—not drawing solely from within the program itself—has greater staying power simply because it draws its strength and support from multiple sources rather than relying only on its own. This is no different than individual health and wellness—the richer one's social support network, the more resilient one is when dealing with hardship.

Strengthen Communities From Within

Developing relationships with community resources, further developing community resources, and maximizing the relevance of existing resources each have the potential benefit of strengthening the community from within, as was previously noted. Indeed, the more available resources are at the local level, the greater the likelihood that the needs of community members can be addressed at the local level. This type of relationship between a community and its resources serves to empower community members as they realize that they have a community infrastructure within which their needs can be effectively met. As you can imagine, this has tremendous significance to most of us—after all, at the most basic level, we all want to know that we have immediate access to needed resources.

Strengthening communities from within is akin to making a community more resilient. And in fact, there are three types of resources that are believed to contribute to a community's resilience:

1. Social assets—relationships with neighbors and/or affiliations or ties to schools, places of worship, and other community-based organizations

2. Service agency assets—human service organizations that have an institutional rather than a social focus, such as child welfare organizations, hospitals, etc.

3. Economic and neighborhood assets—includes such aspects of a community as family income and employment opportunities (Mowbray et al., 2007)

By utilizing community resources in new program development, you are able to reinforce the value of existing community resources to community members. In addition, you have the opportunity to develop new support networks that can be accessed and that may more effectively serve community members. As a result of engaging in community resource development, you have the potential to strengthen communities from within, thus increasing the community's potential for resilience.

Identifying Community Resources: Revisiting the Asset Map, Community Demography Assessment, Market Analysis, and Logic Model

Identifying existing community resources is the obvious first step in community resource development. But this is not necessarily an easy task, and it really depends on the program developer's ability to cast the widest net in exploring existing community resources. Fortunately, if you already completed the preplanning activities as part of the initial step in program development—including an asset map, community demography assessment, market analysis, and logic model—much, if not all, the work has been done by this point. As a result, the task now becomes revisiting the results of each previous activity to determine how to move forward in community resource development.

This begins with reviewing the community resources listed on the asset map to become more familiar with each of the existing resources and delve deeper into gaining more specific information about each. As a guide to ensure that you have captured basic standard information for each resource, use the *Community Resource Snapshot* (Table 7.1). Completing the *Community Resource Snapshot* may help guarantee that you have adequate information pertaining to each resource that will be necessary in making decisions about potential partnerships. For instance, whereas you may have initially identified an outreach center for homeless adults as a resource, you now will need to know about all the types of services provided there (e.g., warming center, breakfast and lunch served, Alcoholics Anonymous and Narcotics Anonymous meetings held on-site, basic medical exams), as well as any specific limitations that might exist (e.g., meals not served on Sundays, medical exams available once per month). Possessing information about the

Table 7.1 Community Resource Snapshot

Program/Organization: _____

Resource Aspects	Details
Type of programming provided	
Location(s) and contact person	
Hours of operation/availability	
Client eligibility and funding	
Staff qualifications	
Adjunctive services (e.g., transportation)	
Length of time as a provider	
Accreditation status and other organizational credentialing information	
Other information	

outreach center will be essential if you are to recommend this center as a resource for your clients. In addition, this should help guarantee that you have enough general and specific information about each resource to begin making decisions about any potential partnerships that you wish to form with community resources.

Completing the *Community Resource Snapshot* requires conducting additional research on each of the existing community resources. By doing so, you are able to gain an in-depth understanding of the precise types of existing community resources, thus gaining a better understanding of the demographic makeup of existing community resources and more effectively posturing yourself to make key decisions regarding how you might work directly with specific community resources.

After you have thoroughly researched each of the community resources initially identified on the asset map, you must once again take a broad look at the community to ensure that you have captured all its existing resources. By doing this, you are able to account for any new resources that might have emerged following completion of the asset map, guaranteeing that your work in this area has been exhaustive. This level of attention to detail— while at times tedious—can make a world of difference to new program development efforts. By fully understanding the landscape of the community with regard to available resources and by thoughtfully identifying resources with which to potentially partner or align prior to program implementation, you can save yourself a tremendous amount of time during implementation. This time can then be used to oversee all that is involved in program implementation since you will be well equipped with a host of community partners and potential referral sources for your client population. Moreover, this type of long-term planning allows you to better position your program for initial implementation. This is important to both introducing your program/ organization as a new participant in the community as well as starting up with a support system of resources that will interact directly with your program in some way.

Next, the results of the community demography assessment must be reviewed again. Because this data set provides you with a rich understanding of the characteristics of the community population, you will need to use this to identify specific existing resources that may prove essential partners to your program. For instance, if the majority of the community is Arab-American—Lebanese and Syrian—with a sizeable subpopulation that does not speak English, you will need to identify which community resources exist that can provide translation and other support services to this population.

Identifying exactly how you would like to interact with existing community resources also requires revisiting the results of two other key planning activities—the market analysis and the logic model. Because the market analysis provides critical information about competing programs, this information can be especially helpful in deciding how you might expand your treatment and/or services through the use of specific community resources. Such expansion serves to further differentiate your program from the competition while enabling you to better serve your target population. In addition, by utilizing existing community resources, you can play a key role in strengthening the community from within by helping it become more self-sufficient.

Because the logic model articulates the initial program design, it too must be reviewed to determine if any of the identified services or interventions can or should be provided by existing community resources. For instance, consider that you have designed a treatment program for elderly women with substance addiction. Included in the design is an activity-based component to promote social connections through recreation and other types of interpersonal activities. In order to meet this need, you may decide to explore a partnership with a local daycare organization so that your elderly clients can choose to participate as volunteers or as employees to facilitate a variety of recreational (e.g., reading, play) or other types of activities (e.g., feeding). By partnering in this way with the local daycare, your clients are able to take advantage of another type of treatment intervention while both your program and the daycare receive mutual benefit. Because this type of partnership is mutually rewarding, it can be adopted with no additional cost to your program. More importantly, by facilitating this type of partnership within your community, you expand the social support networks of both the elderly population that you are treating and the children being served by the daycare. This type of community collaboration is often essential to community development efforts that may further strengthen a community. The challenge then is gaining an expansive enough view of community resources to recognize all the possible partnership opportunities currently existing within the community.

As the above examples are meant to illustrate, there are numerous ways in which your program may interact with existing community resources. Possibilities include, but are not limited to,

- direct partnerships wherein the community resource provides an intervention or service to your clients through a collaborative arrangement,
- formally linking your clients with a community resource through direct referral to provide additional treatment and/or services that you do not provide, and
- informally providing information about the community resource to your clients as an additional resource.

Each of these allows your clients to receive enhanced treatment and/or services as a result of an extended scope of treatment and/or services, and this is precisely what is needed in the 21st century as we continue to fulfill the charge of creating comprehensive treatment and service systems.

Engaging Community Resources

Initial Relationship Building

Engaging community resources means approaching the leader(s) of each organization that holds the desired resource(s) and discussing the various ways in which you believe your organizations may work together. As with any potential partnership, the key lies in ensuring mutual benefit to both organizations, thus the term *partnership*. Therefore, a major part of the initial discussion should focus on potential benefits of the partnership. Because in most cases new efforts to work specifically with a community resource result in new business for the organization holding the resource, this is not a difficult message to convey. In addition to the straightforward benefit of increased business that the organization seeks to gain, other significant benefits of such partnerships should also be illuminated.

These other benefits include three of the five issues identified at the chapter's beginning, which consist of building an advocacy coalition, engaging in long-term sustainability planning, and strengthening communities from within by recognizing and utilizing existing resources. Whereas these were initially discussed as benefits of incorporating community resources into new program development efforts, they apply almost equally to benefits provided to the organizations holding the community resources. As such, a minimum of two organizations in the community (i.e., yours and the community resource) can gain from these types of partnerships, while the community itself continues to be further strengthened. In addition, while the partnership may result in financial growth for the other organization, it may also lead to opportunities for the partnership to garner additional funding—another of the key benefits listed previously.

Once adequate work has been done to initially develop the partnership, concrete methods for how the two organizations will interact should be clearly identified. In addition, plans for maintaining regular communication between program coordinators and other relevant staff should be established. The frequency of meeting times should be dependent on the type of partnership (core programming partner vs. referral source).Whereas you can likely imagine that making time to maintain regular contact should be one of the easier tasks to manage, it is the one most often neglected. This probably has little to do with program leaders and staff not wanting to maintain regular contact and more to do with prioritizing this as having similar value to other operational activities. As a result, the significance of such contact must be reinforced, and the program developer/leaders must take full responsibility for ensuring that this happens.

The benefits of regular contact can be many. At the basic level, frequent communication can promote open communication and a climate in which any potential issues can be quickly resolved. This type of quick resolution not only reduces stress on both organizations but often has the added effect of strengthening the partnership. In addition, regular contact can ensure that the partnership is proceeding as leaders initially anticipated, and it provides a venue for discussing new opportunities or threats, need for specific advocacy, and other potential shared goals or activities. Most significantly, regular communication promotes preservation of the relationship/partnership and may work to strengthen the relationship in its earliest stages, when it's needed most.

Initial Preservation Efforts

Efforts at preserving relationships with community resources are often imperative to maintaining a program's success; therefore, more work must often be invested in preserving these relationships than was initially required to develop them. The manner in which the partnership was initially developed may indeed set the stage for the long-term relationship, and as mentioned above, maintaining regular contact is often a necessity to preserving the relationship.

However, there are many other issues that must be kept in mind to ensure that these relationships are preserved. In addition to each of the benefits identified earlier in the chapter, preserving relationships with community resources allows your organization to maintain its own support network, keeps you connected to other issues that may indirectly or directly impact your business, and may provide you with ongoing opportunities for new business. Each of these benefits is of significant value, particularly in a business that is characterized by all the stress related to constantly shrinking dollars and frequent—and often tumultuous—change. Indeed, with the attendant challenges that often accompany this equally rewarding work, close relationships with those that share in your community may be exactly what sustains you, both literally and figuratively.

Because preserving relationships with community resources has specific relevance to program implementation and sustainability, an entire chapter is devoted to this second part of community resource work (Chapter 13). So we will leave the discussion about preserving relationships here for now and pick it up again later.

Summary

Community resource development is essential to program development efforts. More to the point, engagement with community resources may prove one of the most valuable activities in which you engage during the program planning phase. There are various types of relationships that you may develop with community resources. These include developing direct partnerships wherein the community resource provides an intervention or service to your clients through a collaborative arrangement, formally linking your clients with the community resource through direct referral to provide treatment and/or services that you do not provide, and providing information about the community resource to your clients as an additional resource. Engaging in any of these types of relationships constitutes a partnership of some form in which both organizations benefit from the relationship. As such, there is a good deal of significance generated from such relationships.

Moreover, there are numerous benefits that may be achieved through engagement with community resources, including augmenting your program's service array, contributing to the development of an advocacy coalition, better equipping your program/organization to garner new and/or additional funding, contributing to the long-term sustainability of your program, and strengthening the community from within.

Consistent with the previous steps in this model, community resource development builds on work completed in earlier steps. Therefore, information generated by the community demography assessment, asset map, market analysis, and logic model is used to guide resource development efforts. This again illustrates the program development process as a highly structured, data-driven activity—one in which chance and guesswork have no place but in which purposeful and methodical work guide the process.

CASE ILLUSTRATION

Ranee and Paul had just completed the entire design of a program (i.e., program design, staffing structure) for children with serious emotional and mental health disorders and their families. The program objectives were to provide comprehensive family-focused treatment to these children and their families through an integrated approach that involved both in-office and community-based interventions. Both had worked in the community for some time—Ranee in an outpatient clinic and Paul in a foster care program. In addition, they had each previously worked with the target population—not as part of their primary work but, more often, when children's mental health was a secondary treatment issue of a child and/or family being treated. As a result of their past experience in the community and their at least minimal exposure to the target population, they felt that they were aware of several of the community's existing resources. More importantly, having completed the asset map earlier, they now felt confident that they had a comprehensive view of all the current resources that might be useful to their new program.

But they needed to consider the manner in which specific resources might directly interact with their program, and they also needed to gain deeper knowledge about each of the most relevant resources. To begin to explore this much more thoroughly, Paul and Ranee sat down together to review the initial list of resources and cull all the ones that they considered potential candidates with whom to develop specific

(Continued)

(Continued)

relationships. Ranee found herself needing to really think broadly about each resource and its potential interactions with their program, thus causing her to be cautious in not simply eliminating a resource because of the apparent differences it might have. For instance, Ranee initially had automatically reached to eliminate an animal shelter because neither she nor Paul could see the relevance of it to their program. However, after allowing a moment to think it through, they both realized that the shelter may indeed have a pivotal role to play in augmenting their treatment program. Specifically, Paul began to explore the idea of interpersonal skill development through caring for animals—an emerging treatment strategy for work with at-risk children (Cole, 2005). They realized that the animal shelter might provide the venue in which some of their clients could engage in this type of intervention as part of their individualized treatment plan. As a result, they identified the shelter as a possible partner.

During this review of existing community resources, Ranee and Paul also revisited the results of the community demography assessment and market analysis. From this previously compiled data, they culled specific resources that were relevant to the primary target population based on community demographics (e.g., Jewish, Hmong-American) to ensure that they would be able to link clients to culture-specific resources, if needed. After again reviewing the results of the market analysis, they reviewed the existing resources with an eye toward ensuring that their program offered the same minimum services as the competition as well as additional services or aspects that differentiated it from the current providers. As a result of reviewing the list of existing community resources with both of these data points in mind, several additional community resources were culled and added to the list of resources for follow-up. These included such organizations as the local Jewish Community Center, Jewish Vocational Services, several synagogues and Hmong churches, the local Hmong Economic and Social Services Agency, and several other culture-specific organizations. In addition, a few organizations dealing specifically with mentoring services were also identified, particularly because these were part of the enhanced service array provided by one of the main competitors. The previously developed program logic model was also revisited to ensure that community resources that might be used as referral sources could be identified, as well as those that might be used to provide an enhanced service (e.g., recreational facility). Finally, Paul and Ranee did a quick review of the community to ensure that all existing resources had been captured in their initial data collection work and that no new ones had emerged since they completed their work. They were surprised to find that two new resources had indeed emerged in the past 3 months—a group home for developmentally disabled adults and an existing park that had expanded with the addition of outdoor picnic areas and another basketball court.

After compiling their list of existing community resources for follow-up, Ranee and Paul split up the list, each agreeing to complete the *Community Resource Snapshot* for their assigned resources. They then reviewed the information and began to prioritize the resources based on their program needs. In addition, they made preliminary decisions about how they would likely interact with the various resources. From this process, Ranee and Paul were able to identify 23 community resources with whom they were interested in engaging in a more formal relationship for the purposes of working directly in service delivery, mutual use as a referring agent and referral source, providing information about the resource to clients informally (not formal referral), and as part of an initial advocacy coalition.

To maintain efficiency, Ranee and Paul split up the job of contacting those organizations about whom they envisioned simply being able to share basic informal information with their clients. They each discussed this with the contact person at the other organizations and requested brochures and other materials that they could make available to their clients. During these conversations, Paul and Ranee also took the time to reintroduce their own program and communicate that this initial business relationship may open potential future opportunities. They assured the other organization leaders that they would keep in close communication.

Because of the more partnership-oriented relationships that Ranee and Paul wished to establish with the remaining organizations' leaders, they decided it was best to meet individually with each of these leaders to discuss these plans. After meeting with leaders from each organization and discussing potential working relationships, Ranee and Paul now had partnerships established between their program and eight of the other organizations. Of these eight partnerships, one had been formed with the Hmong Economic and Social Services Agency, one had been formed with the local animal shelter, and another with the Jewish Community Center. As a secondary treatment intervention when warranted, the clients in Ranee and Paul's program would be able to spend time playing with and caring for animals in the shelter, an activity that would be cofacilitated by the case manager and a shelter staff person. The Jewish Community Center personnel would work directly with Ranee and Paul to develop a network of support families that would be available for matching client families to provide additional support and mentoring during the treatment program, as well as to expand the families' existing social support networks well beyond involvement in the program.

Throughout the course of these initial engagement meetings, Paul and Ranee were also able to lay out their plans for holding regular forums with the group of involved organizations. These forums would allow for continuous monitoring of the relationships and promote open exchanges of information and would provide the basis of an initial coalition for advocacy and other pursuits.

(Continued)

(Continued)

Having completed this step of identifying and engaging community resources, Ranee and Paul felt confident not only that they had an effective plan for utilizing a variety of existing resources but that their program design had been significantly improved as a result. In addition, they felt a sense of empowerment—largely due to the fact that they now had a professional support network of their own. Equally significant, Paul and Ranee felt that their program now was well positioned to pursue funding as a result of this broad-based community collaboration. And while they needed to work first toward securing initial funding for their program, they couldn't help but realize that as a result of their community resource development efforts, they would likely be able to explore other business opportunities as well.

COMMUNITY RESOURCE DEVELOPMENT EXERCISE

Using the *Community Resource Snapshot*, identify and investigate five existing local community resources that you might use in your own program development project. After you have investigated each resource, answer the following questions:

1. Exactly what type of relationship will you pursue with this resource?

2. In what ways will your program benefit from this relationship?

3. Given the five resources you have identified for developing a specific relationship, how will you maintain communication with each?

4. In addition to your response to Question 1, in what other ways do you envision working with these resources?

References

Anderson, J. E., & Larke, S. C. (2009). The Sooke Navigator project: Using community resources and research to improve local service for mental health and addictions. *Mental Health in Family Medicine, 6,* 21–28.

Aronson, R. E., Wallis, A. B., O'Campo, P., & Schafer, P. (2007). Neighborhood mapping and evaluation: A methodology for participatory community health initiatives. *Maternal and Child Health Journal, 11*, 373–383.

Bookman, A. (2005). Can employers be good neighbors? Redesigning the work-place-community interface. In S. M. Bianchi, L. M. Casper, & R. B. King (Eds.), *Work, family, health, and well-being* (pp. 141–156). Mahwah, NJ: Lawrence Erlbaum.

Cole, D. L. (2005). Horse and youth: A not so typical approach to at-risk programming. *Journal of Extension, 43*, 1–6.

Darboe, K., & Ahmed, L. S. (2007). Elderly immigrants in Minnesota: A case study of needs assessment in eight cities. *Educational Gerontology, 33*, 855–866.

Gareis, K. C., & Barnett, R. C. (2008). The development of a new measure for work-family research: Community resource fit. *Community, Work, & Family, 11*, 273–282.

Gareis, K. C., Barnett, R. C., & Brennan, R. T. (2003). Individual and crossover effects of work schedule fit: A within-couple analysis. *Journal of Marriage and Family, 65*, 1041–1054.

Homan, M. S. (2004). *Promoting community change: Making it happen in the real world.* Belmont, CA: Brooks/Cole.

Lewis, J. A., Lewis, M. D., Daniels, J. A., & D'Andrea, M. J. (2003). *Community counseling: Empowerment strategies for a diverse society* (3rd ed.). Pacific Grove, CA: Brooks/Cole.

Maybery, D., Pope, R., Hodgins, G., Hitchenor, Y., & Shepherd, A. (2009). Resilience and wellbeing of small inland communities: Community assets as key determinants. *Rural Society Journal, 19,* 326–339.

Mowbray, C. T., Woolley, M. E., Grogan-Kaylor, A., Gant, L. M., Gilster, M. E., & Shanks, T. R. (2007). Neighborhood research from a spatially-oriented strengths perspective. *Journal of Community Psychology, 35*, 667–680.

Roberts-DeGennaro, M. (2001). Conceptual framework of coalitions in an organizational context. In J. E. Tropman, J. L. Erlich, & J. Rothman (Eds.), *Tactics and techniques of community intervention* (pp. 130–140). Belmont, CA: Wadsworth/Thomson Learning.

Voydanoff, P. (2004). Implications of work and community resources and demands for marital quality. *Community, Work, & Family, 7,* 311–325.

Yoon, I. (2009). A mixed-method study of Princeville's rebuilding from the flood of 1999: Lessons on the importance of invisible community assets. *Social Work, 54,* 19–28.

CHAPTER 8

Identify and Evaluate Potential Funding Sources

Learning Objectives

1. Identify and differentiate the three primary types of funding sources that support mental health and human service programs

2. Explain the difference between a Request for Proposal and a Request for Quote

3. Discuss methods by which you can learn about potential funding opportunities

4. Identify three funding sources for clinical and/or human service programs

5. Explain three advantages of diversified or mixed funding

6. Identify five aspects of a potential funding source that should be evaluated

7. Apply the knowledge gained in this chapter by using the *Funding Opportunity Evaluation Tool*

WHAT FINE PRINT?

For the past 8 years, Ivana had been managing a program for adults returning to the community from prison, and she loved her work. But she also was becoming more and more interested in pursuing other types of programming. She had been searching various directories and websites for potential funding opportunities when she came across a *Request for Quote* (RFQ) from the Bureau of Prisons (BOP). Even though she was not familiar with the BOP and had never pursued or received funding from them, she was intrigued by the opportunity.

The RFQ was to provide prison-based counseling services at a local prison. All the services that were to be provided were listed, including individual, group, and family counseling; psychological evaluation; psychiatric evaluation; and psychiatric monitoring. Because the funding source was interested in not only an organization's ability to provide the services but also the cost at which the organization would provide them, the RFQ had been issued as part of a competitive bid process driven by the government securing the most effective services at the lowest cost.

After doing a quick review of the RFQ, Ivana felt confident that her organization could effectively implement the program, and although she did not currently work with a psychiatrist, she knew two who were interested in contractual work. Knowing she had only 2 weeks to prepare the proposal, Ivana quickly got to work, informing her executive director that since the proposed program seemed like such a good fit to further expand the agency's continuum of care, she felt they should definitely go for it. Moreover, she felt she could develop the proposal relatively quickly since it mostly involved working with the finance staff to determine the proposed fee schedule.

Ivana spent most of the following week and the beginning of the next working on the proposal and finally felt she had made a strong argument for the organization's ability to carry out the program. Moreover, she felt that the fee schedule they had devised would be highly competitive while allowing the agency to adequately support the program. After having others review her work and going through her proposal several times herself, Ivana felt confident that they had a good shot at acquiring this funding.

Three months later, when the awards were announced, she was surprised and upset to learn that her proposal had not been selected. She immediately contacted the contract manager to inquire. The contract manager shared with Ivana that, while her proposal had been fully reviewed, the review team had been surprised by the submission since the funding opportunity was limited to businesses with less than $1 million in annual revenue—Ivana had disclosed in the proposal (as required) that the annual revenue of her business was $5.6 million. Therefore, her agency was not eligible to apply. The contract manager asked Ivana if she had not fully reviewed the RFQ, including the fine print that clearly stated this limitation. Locating the RFQ, Ivana did find the stipulation and sheepishly ended the call.

CONSIDERING IVANA

1. How could Ivana have prevented this from happening?

2. In addition to carefully reviewing a funding opportunity in its entirety, what other steps might you take to ensure that you fully understand it before investing time in developing a proposal?

About This Chapter

This chapter is specifically dedicated to bringing a program to fruition through the acquisition of funding. The chapter focuses on identifying and evaluating potential funding sources in order to increase your knowledge of the various types and parameters of funding opportunities and to provide you with additional knowledge and tools for use in rigorously evaluating potential funding opportunities. The chapter begins with an examination of the major types of funding sources available in mental health and human services, which include public, philanthropic, and fee-for-service. Next, we will explore types of funding opportunities, including governmental, business, and philanthropic, along with the various parameters associated with each. This is followed by a discussion of pursuing short- versus long-term funding and mixed funding and the pros and cons related to each.

Next, the discussion will focus on methods by which to identify potential funding sources and includes an introduction to some of the available tools that may aid in this work. In addition, we will once again revisit the market analysis in order to determine if its results provide additional guidance in identifying potential funding sources. Finally, comprehensive methods for evaluating potential funding opportunities are presented that include such issues as the philosophical foundations of the funding source, funding parameters, eligibility criteria of applicants, history of funding, and the length of the funding opportunity. An evaluation tool is provided, and an exercise provides you with the opportunity to apply your funding opportunity evaluation skills.

STEP VI: IDENTIFY AND EVALUATE POTENTIAL FUNDING SOURCES

Funding the Program

Moving the program development process from the planning phase to the implementation phase is completely dependent on acquiring financial support for the program—a process that begins with identifying and evaluating potential funding opportunities and that successfully ends in securing funding. While this is no easy task, this step is made much easier by the previous work completed in the preplanning and planning stages. Specifically, having completed due diligence in the preplanning stage (i.e., needs assessment, community demography assessment, market analysis, asset map), there is strong justification for the program. This coupled with designing a research-based program and developing a highly effective and efficient staffing infrastructure provides the bulk of information needed to identify potential funding options.

Because identifying funding opportunities and developing the financial management plan are highly interrelated, the order of Steps VI and VII should not necessarily be viewed as fixed—in some cases, Step VI may precede Step VII, while in others, Step VII may precede Step VI. As such, the sequence in which these steps occur may differ for each new project depending on how you set about the program development process. Particularly with regard to these two steps, the program development process may be *responsive* or *proactive*—responsive meaning the program development process is initiated in response to an announcement of available funding (i.e., you begin to develop a program after learning about available funding opportunities), or proactive meaning that the program was developed in an effort to explore and subsequently secure funding. Even though there are obvious benefits to developing a program in which concrete funding is readily available (i.e., responsively), there are equally good reasons for developing a program in hopes of identifying and securing funding. Particularly for program developers working in human service organizations, there may be an evident gap in the existing service and/or treatment continuum that the developer wishes to fill and, thus, does so through the development of a proposal that may be pitched to existing contractors or new funding sources or both. Because the finance-related steps in the comprehensive program development model may need to occur either at the end or at the beginning of the program planning phase, simply be aware of this and adapt this part of the model to best fit your circumstances.

As you can well appreciate by this point, program development requires a tremendous amount of energy, hard work, and perseverance throughout each major phase (planning, implementation, and evaluation). Whereas perseverance is a prerequisite at every step, it may be particularly necessary when it comes to pursuing funding. This is because there is a limited amount of funding available to meet the needs of a tremendous number of individuals. As a result, securing funding is a highly competitive venture. This is more the case today than ever before. Historically, nonprofit organizations were competing only against one another for the same funds, whereas today, for-profit organizations are also part of the competition. This is most often notable in competitions for government and managed care contracts (Gibelman & Furman, 2008)—which, unfortunately for nonprofits, constitutes a significant portion of available funding. In addition, electronic technology has significantly impacted access to funding opportunities. Indeed, with the most recent developments of funding source directories and databases, access to information about funding opportunities has increased exponentially, thereby creating further competition for such opportunities.

Because of the incredible amount of work that goes into new program development, coupled with the highly challenging task of identifying and securing funding, this type of work is certainly not for those who cannot effectively forge ahead, even in the face of defeat—or in this case, rejection of your proposal. In fact, I would bet that anyone who has developed five or more program proposals has had at least one proposal rejected, if not several. It is in this manner that the program development process mirrors the research and writing process for scholarly journals. Indeed, I also cannot imagine any scholar claiming that s/he has never had an article rejected for publication by a journal editor. The rejection process is not only a rite of passage but also a feature of the competitive process—which both program proposals and scholarship share. This rejection is so much affiliated with scholarly writing that a professor once coined the term *pre-jection,* referring to developing his own rejection letter at the time of submitting his manuscript for review in order to mentally prepare himself for the probable rejection letter from the editor (Montgomery, 2003). Whereas this struck me as very funny—not to mention extraordinarily clever—it also seems to perfectly reflect the challenging terrain that is an inherent part of developing work for a competitive review process, and most significantly, it captures the emotional component involved in this work.

Because of this highly competitive type of work, program developers must be prepared for possible rejection. But more importantly, wise program developers use the rejection process to their advantage—taking the feedback provided by the reviewers and using it to revise and strengthen the proposal for a subsequent submission or to refocus their energies in a different direction.

Whereas many funding sources will automatically provide written and/or verbal feedback to the applicant, the Freedom of Information Act allows you to access this information from governmental funding bodies via written request.

In addition to preparing yourself for the competitive nature of the initial proposal process, you also must understand that you will likely be involved in this type of process over and over again—thus, this is where perseverance is most needed. Unfortunately, simply because you are successful in securing funding for your program, there is no guarantee that you will not have to compete again for funding in a very short time (recall the case of Ryan and Adrienne in the previous chapter). This is because the majority of funding opportunities are time-limited, typically with funding cycles that are for 1, 3, or 5 years, some with renewable clauses and others without. Whereas maintaining funding for an existing program constitutes one way in which the search for new funding will continue, each time there is a new funding opportunity that you wish to pursue or a new program that you developed for which you wish to secure funding, another need to pursue funding will be created. And it will continue on and on so that you grow to realize that identifying and securing funding will be an ongoing part of your work in program sustainability and new program development.

This means that program developers/mental health professionals must be highly proactive, always keeping an eye on the horizon, not only focused on when funding will expire but also focused on exploring new funding sources, new funding opportunities, and any sociopolitical or other environmental factors that may influence existing or future funding. Indeed, successful program developers and program administrators must possess long-term strategic thinking, particularly with regard to the critical funding aspect of comprehensive program development. This is arguably one of the key reasons for the sustainability of most mental health and human service organizations, and unfortunately, the lack of such proactive and strategic efforts may be the cause for the demise of other such organizations. Sustaining funding support is further covered in Chapter 13, but what is most important to bear in mind for this discussion is that *securing* funding is indeed a continuous part of comprehensive program development.

Types of Funding Sources: Public, Philanthropic, Fee-for-Service

There are three major types of funding sources typically used in mental health and human services: public, philanthropic, and fee-for-service. Public funding is provided by the government at the federal, state, or local level. Philanthropic funding is made available by charitable organizations and foundations, often in support of various types of programming and related aspects. Finally, fee-for-service funding is based on programming in which individuals (or insurance or other businesses) pay the organization directly for services provided. Whereas both public and philanthropic funding are most associated with nonprofit human service organizations and for-profit organizations may at times be excluded from pursuing public and philanthropic funding, fee-for-service funding may be sought by both nonprofit and for-profit organizations. Each of these sources of funding is discussed below.

Public/Governmental Sources of Funding

As stated previously, the U.S. government is the largest funding source for human services in the United States. Governmental funding is typically made available through the legislative process in which allocations are dedicated to support specific types of programming and/or research. Depending on the specific focus of the funding, the funds may be offered through various routes. At the cabinet level, agencies such as the Department of Health and Human Services, Department of Education, Department of Justice, and Department of Housing and Urban Development provide funding for a variety of programming directly and through their subagencies (e.g., Centers for Disease Control and Prevention, Office of Juvenile Justice and Delinquency Prevention). In addition, funding may trickle down from the federal level to be allocated directly at the state or local level. In this case, statewide departments of human services, community mental health organizations, and criminal justice systems provide funding for specific areas, often at both the state and regional levels, while county and/or city organizations, such as the health department, often provide funding at the most local level.

Philanthropic Sources of Funding

Whereas the number of governmental entities providing funding is extensive, the number and diversity of philanthropic organizations is also fairly tremendous. Philanthropic organizations typically have a specific identity and seek to fulfill the organization's mission through offering funding in specific areas. While the breadth of the mission may be of varying degrees, with some extremely focused on very specialized issues (e.g., autism), others might be more broad-based but still focused in a single area (e.g., children). In addition, some philanthropic organizations are specifically dedicated to a geographic area as part of their mission (e.g., greater Chicago, Detroit), and therefore, funding opportunities are limited to a particular region. To get a sense of the diversity of philanthropic funding and the recent levels of funding available from each, see Table 8.1.

Table 8.1 Philanthropic Organizations

Organization	Funding Scope	Focus	Annual Funding
Annie E. Casey Foundation	National and international	Foster care	$350 million (2008)
John D. and Catherine T. MacArthur Foundation	National and international	Human rights Global conservation Community improvement Children and technology	$252 million (2008)
W. K. Kellogg Foundation	National and international	Early childhood development Class and race disparities	$190 million (2008)
Hogg Foundation	Statewide (Texas)	Mental health service Research Public education Policy projects	Less than $10 million (2007)
Skillman Foundation	Local (Detroit, MI)	Community and school improvement and development	$23 million (2009 budget)

As you can see in Table 8.1, philanthropic organizations differ quite a bit, from large international, broad-based organizations to small local organizations. The good work that is supported through these types of philanthropic organizations often has its roots in highly energetic and creative business people. In fact, delving into the origins of philanthropic foundations can be a fascinating journey and one that I recommend all program developers take. This is particularly necessary for those foundations that you may wish to approach for future funding, but you also will find that exploring the various histories of these organizations may prove helpful to simply enlarging your view of the important organizations that support such a large part of our work today.

To give you a brief illustration of what I mean, consider Jim Casey and Robert and Rose Skillman. As illustrated in both of the brief sketches below, the transformative business minds and the unwavering commitment to do good that each of them possessed is reflected in the philanthropic legacies they created.

JIM CASEY, UNITED PARCEL SERVICES FOUNDER

Jim Casey founded the United Parcel Service (UPS) in the first half of the 1900s. Having amassed a fortune, in 1948, he began the Annie E. Casey Foundation with his siblings in honor of their mother, who had raised them as a widow. The mission of the foundation reflects Jim's belief that the future of children is largely determined by what their families can provide to them emotionally, ethically, and materially.

In 2009, the Annie E. Casey Foundation, located in Baltimore, Maryland, was the 17th largest private foundation in the United States with assets of more than $2.3 billion. The Annie E. Casey Foundation (n.d.) ranks 24th in the nation for charitable giving and is dedicated to improving the lives of children and families, with a specific focus on foster care.

ROBERT AND ROSE SKILLMAN

Robert Skillman was an early pioneer at the Minnesota Mining and Manufacturing Company (3M), responsible for transforming a Detroit facility into an adhesive plant in the 1940s. Robert worked for 3M until his death in 1945. Remaining in Michigan, where the couple had lived most of their married life, Rose was increasingly committed to the welfare of vulnerable children, making charitable contributions to organizations that served children. In 1960, Rose developed the Skillman Foundation.

In 2009, the Skillman Foundation, located in Detroit, Michigan, budgeted more than $23 million for grants focused specifically and almost exclusively on the children of Detroit. The Skillman Foundation (n.d.) remains committed to Rose's mission of helping vulnerable children by providing funding and using its clout to be a voice for children.

In addition to philanthropic organizations, many for-profit corporations, such as Starbucks and Verizon, offer formal giving programs. Some of these function similarly to the philanthropic organizations listed above, but others function as mini-foundations—providing small amounts of funding to support a variety of programming and projects. Because many for-profit corporations seek to also fulfill a social mission, these giving arms work to accomplish this. Often, some of these types of funding opportunities are limited to local applicants to reflect the business's commitment to the local community through planned giving to the community. For example, Microsoft Corporation has provided specific funding to programming and other types of support services in King County, Washington, where many of the company's employees reside.

Fee-for-Service Sources of Funding

Fee-for-service funding is rooted in traditional business wherein a service is provided to an individual and, in turn, the individual pays directly for the service. In mental health and human services, payment may be made by the individual or by the individual's insurance. This type of payment schema is most often associated with outpatient clinics and individual private practices in which clinicians establish a fee for their service (e.g., counseling, clinical assessment) and charge clients accordingly.

Fee-for-service programs may be funded by participating on a number of insurance boards, gaining authorization as a payee. In addition, fee for service programs may be paid by a public insurance company (e.g., Medicaid) to support counseling as well as psychiatric services. Whereas insurance companies traditionally limit funding to mental health services, human service organizations may offer specific services to be paid on a fee-for-service basis, such as daycare.

Fee-for-service payment schedules are used by both nonprofit and for-profit mental health providers. One of the challenges to using a fee-for-service payment schedule is that of receiving varying amounts for the same service. For instance, you may set the fee for an individual counseling session at $65, but one of the insurance providers that you work with may pay only $55 for a session while another reimburses $50. In this case, you may be able to charge $65 only to individuals who are paying out-of-pocket— which in and of itself may present a moral dilemma, since the privileged population that has insurance will have their treatments funded while those who do not will be penalized even further by possibly paying even more for the same service. However, a good many mental health practitioners— especially professional counselors—who hold social justice as a core practice value offer sliding scales for payment. A sliding scale means that the clinician creates a fee schedule that accommodates the individual client by charging only what the client can afford.

Working solely with fee-for-service funders can prove quite challenging, particularly because fee-for-service contracts are typically small in relation to governmental or philanthropic contracts. In addition, grants or contracts from the government and grant funding from philanthropic organizations typically provide a specific amount of funding (e.g., $300,000, $1.2 million) over a particular amount of time, whereas a contract with an insurance company may be capped at $70,000 a year and any funds received from the contract are based on the number of clients seen. As a result, a contract like this may yield only $22,000 a year if only a small number of clients are referred or choose to utilize your services. Equally challenging, simply being on an insurance panel of providers does not necessarily mean that any revenue will be generated from this particular endeavor. These types of payment schemes have obvious implications for financial management and also sustainability; however, depending on the specific area of mental health and human services that you wish to pursue, fee-for-service may be the primary means of funding, and for many mental health professionals, this has proven highly successful.

Types of Funding Opportunities

The types of funding opportunities available to nonprofit mental health and social service programs through the government and philanthropic organizations have many things in common, particularly with regard to the types of funding they each may make available. Beginning with governmental funding opportunities, I would like to explore some of the most common types of each.

Governmental Funding Opportunities

Governmental funding opportunities can be enormously diverse and have changed dramatically over the past several decades, especially as governmental agencies have increasingly elected to purchase services from nonprofit agencies opposed to directly administering programs. In fact, in the 21st century, purchasing services from the private sector has become a favored means of delivering human services (Gibelman & Furman, 2008).

Governmental funding opportunities may be offered directly by the federal government through a cabinet-level department (e.g., Department of Health and Human Services) or through one of the subagencies of a cabinet-level department (e.g., Bureau of Justice Programs). Typically, federal agencies will issue a Request for Proposals (RFP) indicating that funding is available to address specific needs. There are two primary types of RFPs for program delivery: (1) one in which the treatment and/or service needs are identified and applicants must articulate how they will address the needs as part of the proposal and (2) another in which both the needs and the treatment and/or service interventions have been identified or prescribed by the funding source and applicants must articulate how they will implement the interventions. In both of these types of proposals, applicants must also stipulate the cost of implementing the proposed programming, staying within the stated funding parameters.

The first type of RFP—in which a specific treatment need is identified by the funding source and applicants must determine how they will address these needs—is one of the most common types of funding opportunity. In comparison with other types of RFPs and Requests for Quotes (RFQs), this by far offers the most autonomy for the applicant. Examples of this type of RFP include announcements for funding to address reentry issues among juvenile offenders or to address the vocational needs of returning veterans. Proposals for these types of RFP require that the applicant identify an accessible target population and target region, justify the need, design a treatment program and evaluation plan, and identify the requested amount of financing to support program design and implementation.

The second type of RFP—in which the need has been identified and the specific treatment is prescribed—is typically offered when a specific type of program has been found to be effective and, thus, the governmental body has a desire to implement the program in multiple regions. This type of RFP could also be issued as part of a pilot program in which multiple applicants implement the same program as part of a national comprehensive program evaluation project. For instance, a family-based behavioral program may have been developed for the treatment of children with autism, and an RFP is issued that stipulates the minimum number of individuals that must be treated as part of the funding award and provides training manuals detailing the complete interventions and time frames for each. Applicants must identify the accessible target population and region and justify the need and then must specify how the treatment will be implemented as prescribed.

Another type of funding opportunity offered by the federal government is an RFQ. Similar to an RFP, in which the identified needs and treatment and/or services are stipulated by the funding source, RFQs are issued when the competition for the funding is largely based on the *cost* requested by the applicant. In these types of funding competitions, the award is again based on the organization that can provide the best proposal for successfully implementing the program; however, the cost of the program is also considered. This is one aspect in which the RFQ can differ slightly from an RFP competition, since the RFP competition may be slightly less focused on cost than an RFQ competition.

An example of what may be involved in developing a proposal in response to an RFQ can be found in one that was issued by the BOP in 2009. This RFQ entailed providing mental health and substance abuse services for adult male prisoners residing in a halfway house in a specific region (similar to the RFQ in the case of Ivana). Each of the required services was identified in the announcement of funding issued by the BOP and included individual, group, and family counseling and clinical evaluation. In addition to stipulating each type of intervention, the number of units to be provided was also stipulated. Therefore, in order to respond to the RFQ, applicants simply completed the application forms, included copies of organizational and professional qualifications, and provided a cost for each service along with a total annual cost.

In addition to governmental funding for clinical and human service programming, the federal government also offers funding for clinical and social science research. These types of opportunities typically stipulate a broad-based area (e.g., mental health, violence) and allow for varying degrees of freedom with which the applicant can propose specific research projects. Although academics typically compete for research grants, nonprofit organizations may be invited to bid as well.

Whereas a variety of funding is available directly from the federal government, federal monies also are issued to state and local governments for disbursement at those levels. Through RFPs and RFQs issued by state and local governments, mental health and human service organizations can compete for funding to provide substance abuse prevention and/or treatment, mental health treatment, mentoring, and family preservation work and address a number of other issues. Whereas federal funding opportunities involve geographic regions competing with one another, in-state and local funding opportunities involve local providers competing with one another.

In addition to traditional RFPs and RFQs, state and local governments also directly purchase services in a variety of areas from nonprofit organizations. Child welfare programs such as foster care and semi-independent living, juvenile justice programs such as community-based treatment and detention, and mental health programs such as residential programs for individuals with Alzheimer's disease and supported living environments for adults with developmental disabilities are just a handful of program funding opportunities made available through purchase of service agreements between state and local governments and nonprofit organizations. Whereas purchase of service contracts also can be competitive, they typically differ from RFPs and RFQs in that they are longer-term (5 years or more) or may not be time-limited.

When interested in pursuing governmental funding, you must not only have a firm understanding of how funds are secured, but you also must have a clear understanding of specific current trends and be aware of what is on the horizon. This is particularly significant since you may have only 3 to 4 weeks to prepare a proposal in response to an RFP, and without having a sound framework from which to begin developing the proposal, the opportunity may pass you by. To be aware of what current trends exist and what may be on the horizon, several strategies are suggested:

- Study the current research in your areas of interest.
- Stay informed of any relevant legislative changes.
- Attend conferences.
- Remain connected to the governmental agencies that support funding in your area(s).
- Stay connected to colleagues.

By using several methods to stay informed, you may be much better postured to pursue governmental funding.

In terms of examining trends, take a moment to consider some of the recent trends in governmental funding in the 21st century that have included funding for Alzheimer's, autism, and sexual offender treatment. Twenty years ago, none of these three areas were even widely discussed, but today, each has become a topic of national dialogue and funding for treatment and research into each has increased exponentially. In fact, funding for research grants supporting autism increased 15% from 1997 to 2006 (Singh, Illes, Lazzeroni, & Hallmayer, 2009). To provide a sense of just how much funding has been provided for autism, the National Institutes of Health have increased from $22 million to $108 million during this time frame (Vitiello & Wagner, 2007). In addition to the dramatic increase in funding to support programming for individuals with autism, these most recent trends also illustrate a shift from basic science to clinical and translational research—integrating research into practice (Singh et al., 2009). This trajectory is a common one in which research findings often prompt new funding for programming, again reinforcing the need to keep abreast of current research.

Conversely, federal funding for aging services has declined sharply over the past 3 decades, with funding today at about 70% of what it was in 1980, a highly unfortunate trend (Payne & Applebaum, 2008). Interestingly, this decrease in funding for aging support services is occurring at the same time that the aging population is growing most rapidly—at a 44% increase from the same time period. Fortunately, while federal funding for aging has decreased, philanthropic funding for aging has increased (Farquhar, Lowe, & Campbell, 2007)—possibly making up for some of the gaps left by the government funding reductions in this area. Whereas there is much to learn from the myriad trends in funding, what is most important is that adequate time is taken to become fully informed of these trends.

Philanthropic Funding Opportunities

Funding opportunities that are made available by philanthropic organizations generally fall into one of two categories: solicited and unsolicited. Solicited funding opportunities typically include an RFP process in which a specific area is identified; however, generally, these types of RFPs are much less structured in their requirements than those issued by the government and allow for even greater autonomy on the part of the applicant to determine precisely how problems can most effectively be addressed. This is often because philanthropic organizations are most interested in connecting individuals and organizations with specific expertise to funding in order to support advancements in these areas. This is not to say that the government is not also interested in doing this, but since the government's responsibility as a steward may be perceived as much greater than that of a philanthropic foundation, it stands to reason that such differences should exist.

Governmental funding opportunities are reflective of the governmental agencies that make the funding available. Therefore, funding for veteran services most often derives from the Department of Veterans Affairs, just as funding for mental health programs typically originates from the Department of Health and Human Services and flows into the National Institutes of Health or the Substance Abuse and Mental Health Services Administration. Similarly, types of funding opportunities made available by philanthropic organizations (i.e., foundations) are reflective of the mission of the organization. As stated previously, the scope of issues targeted by foundations may vary greatly, with some focusing on very specific issues (e.g., foster care) in a variety of regions (e.g., nationally and internationally) and some focusing on broad-based issues (e.g., children) in specific regions (e.g., Detroit).

For instance, the W. K. Kellogg Foundation (2009)—administratively housed in Battle Creek, Michigan, and founded by the maker of Kellogg cereals—was developed in the 1930s to "serve humanity for generations to come." Currently, the foundation is focused on early childhood development and issues related to social divides around race and class. This broad-based mission allows the foundation to offer funding in a variety of areas and, most significantly, to be highly adaptive to environmental changes.

The John D. and Catherine T. MacArthur Foundation (n.d.)—possibly one of the most universally known philanthropic organizations—provides funding to foster the development of knowledge, nurture individual creativity, strengthen institutions, help improve public policy, and provide information to the public, primarily through support for public interest media. The foundation currently supports four specific programs: the Program on Global Security and Sustainability; the Program on Human and Community Development; the General Program, which supports media and related technologies; and the MacArthur Fellows Program, which awards unrestricted, 5-year fellowships to individuals of exceptional merit in various areas to support their continued creative work. Both the W. K. Kellogg Foundation and the MacArthur Foundation solicit applications for funding programming and research in specific areas and accept unsolicited proposals for programming and research.

Potential and Common Funding Sources in Clinical Program Development

Because there is such a vast array of funding opportunities available from both the government and philanthropic organizations, if you are interested in pursuing funding, you must take the time to become familiar with some of the most common funding sources available for mental health and human services. See Table 8.2 for a listing of common governmental funding

Table 8.2 Governmental Funding Sources for Mental Health and Social Services

Cabinet-Level Agencies	Federal Subagencies	State and Local Agencies
Department of Education	Administration for Children and Families	Community mental health departments
Department of Health and Human Services	Bureau of Justice Programs	Corrections
Department of Justice	Centers for Disease Control and Prevention	Department of Education
Department of Labor	National Institutes of Health	Department of Human/Social Services
Department of Veterans Affairs	National Institute of Mental Health	Health departments
	Office of Juvenile Justice and Delinquency Prevention	Veterans administrations
		Workforce development agencies

sources from the cabinet-level agencies, federal subagencies, and state and local agencies. Please note that the actual names are provided for each of the federal agencies, but state governments vary with regard to the names that are given to agencies; therefore, general names are used to denote some of the specific areas (e.g., corrections).

With regard to potential philanthropic sources of funding, in addition to the foundations provided in Table 8.1, other foundations that provide funding nationally and within specific states to support an array of mental health and human service programs include the following:

- Doris Duke Charitable Foundation
- Ford Foundation
- Kresge Foundation
- McKnight Foundation (Minnesota)
- Robert Wood Johnson Foundation
- William Penn Foundation (Pennsylvania)
- Theodore and Vada Stanley Foundation
- Robert R. McCormick Tribune Foundation (Illinois)

As stated previously, because several foundations were established to address the needs in particular geographic regions that might include a state, several counties within a state, or a city, it is not feasible to identify region-specific foundations here. It is, however, in your best interest to investigate which foundations serve the region in which you wish to work.

Short-Term Versus Long-Term Funding Sources

When moving forward to seek funding for a program or project, a critical issue to explore is the length of the funding cycle needed for the program to operate most effectively. Because funding awards have concrete time limitations, you must know the length of time your program will need to operate in order to realize the intended outcomes (as discussed in Chapter 5 on program design). In addition, the length of funding support may impact your *return on investment* (ROI). ROI simply refers to the benefits of an investment minus the cost of the investment. ROI has particular meaning with regard to new program development in that there are typically start-up costs associated with any new business venture, and in our profession, these most often consist of hiring and training staff. Therefore, the length of funding needed should be a central concern, as it relates to the amount of time required to minimally break even on the costs and expenses incurred to implement the program. Whereas nonprofit organizations are not designed to create profit, breaking even is indeed a necessity, especially since engaging in program development ventures in which more money is spent than received is a likely recipe for a short business life.

Different funding opportunities offer different types of funding, some very short (1 year or less), some moderate (2–3 years), and some long-term (5 years or more). Contracted services—services that are bid on for specific contracts with the government—typically are the longest-term type of funding available. However, some foundations will provide long-term funding by continuously renewing a specific project or program that the foundation is particularly interested in *and* that they feel is an effective investment. The MacArthur Fellows program (aka Genius Grants) is one of the longest-term ongoing grant programs available, providing 5 years of funding to individuals to spend in whatever way they deem most appropriate to continue their work. On the other hand, most programmatic grant funding available from the federal government is awarded for 2- to 3-year periods, some with annual renewable clauses and some without. These moderate cycles also mirror the majority of available foundation funding. Therefore, you must be knowledgeable about not only the length of available funding cycles but, more so, the length of funding needed to fully and most effectively implement your program.

Diversified Funding

Because funds are time-limited, it is often necessary to secure funding from multiple sources. By doing so, the continuation of programming is not so dependent on one funding source and, therefore, not quite so vulnerable to ceasing simply because one source's funding cycle has expired. Diversity of funding is therefore quite common to nonprofit mental health and human service organizations as a means to remain viable and fiscally healthy. In fact, diversification has been found to lead to greater stability (Carroll & Stater, 2008).

Therefore, while it is not uncommon for both small and large organizations to receive funds through government contracts, foundations, individual giving campaigns and other sources (Ezell, 2000), it may be critical to seek revenue diversification. Just as you consider the length of available funding cycles, you will also need to give consideration to attempting to secure funding from more than one source, thus securing mixed funding to support your program. Figure 8.1 provides examples of organizations with nondiversified and diversified funding.

| Figure 8.1 | Nondiversified Versus Diversified Funding |

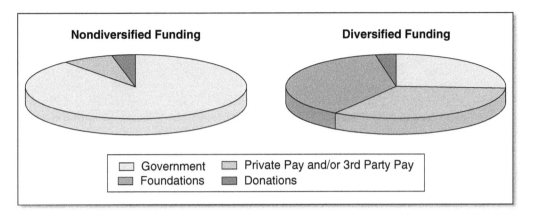

Identifying Potential Funding Sources

More than anything else, identifying potential funding sources requires simply knowing where to look. At the same time, identifying funding sources also requires persistent energy dedicated to investigating what funding is available and when. Fortunately, the development of databases containing numerous funding opportunities and the ability to receive electronic alerts when funding is available from particular sources has made this work much easier. However, whereas technology has streamlined this process, creating a much more efficient workflow related to funding searches, it in no way means that your focused time and attention is no longer needed. You still must dedicate specific time to checking the databases to search and/or cull through alert notices of new funding opportunities in order to identify potential funding sources.

Revisiting the Market Analysis

A first step of exploring potential funding sources requires revisiting the results of the market analysis. This most obvious step should not be overlooked since the market analysis results should inform you specifically about the funding sources that are associated with existing competing programs. Therefore, revisit the market analysis results to identify these funding source(s), and explore these sources to determine if they may be a potential source for your program as well. For instance, as you are seeking funding to support a program on treating depression in postpartum women, examining how other providers of these programs are funded will help you gain this most essential information. By doing this, you not only save quite a bit of time since you already know that these funding sources support programs like the one that you wish to implement, but you are able to benefit—once again—from work that you completed much earlier.

Exploring Funding Sources

After revisiting the results of the market analysis, you need to begin a comprehensive search of funding opportunities. In order to do this, you need access to all or as many funding opportunities as possible, and you have to be able to conduct the most thorough search. There are basically four sources of information pertaining to funding opportunities that include methods that carry a cost and those that are provided at no cost.

Electronic Database Subscriptions for Purchase

Those that carry a cost include subscriptions to comprehensive databases of funding sources. These databases have significantly improved over the past decade as new and better ways to utilize technology have continued to be discovered. In this case, one source/library provides access to information about a number of different funding sources so that you can search for opportunities offered by multiple funding sources in one place. This is no different than research databases available through university libraries in which one provider (e.g., Ebsco) provides access to numerous academic journals. Database subscriptions such as these are available for both governmental agencies and foundations, some that contain only one or the other, and others that contain both. In addition to this type of subscription database, subscriptions can also be purchased for newsletters that compile information and send it to you on a regular basis to alert you to upcoming and existing funding opportunities.

No-Cost Electronic Databases

In addition to the two types of subscriptions that provide extensive information about various funding opportunities, there are also highly effective no-cost sources for some of this information. The federal government hosts the most extensive database of multiple funding sources (available at www.grants.gov). The site contains information about current and future governmental funding opportunities as well as archival information. Likely the most popular site for those currently engaged in or hoping to secure funding from the federal government in the future, this site also has an effective search function so that you can conduct searches at varying levels of detail (e.g., by agency, by keyword). In addition to being a library of governmental funding sources, the site also houses templates and other documents needed to apply for specific funding opportunities and serves as a portal through which to submit applications and monitor the progress of a submission. If you are not already familiar with grants.gov, I encourage you to look into its features.

Public libraries are also a great source for free access to funding directories and other resources. And as libraries are institutions wholly dependent on public dollars, utilizing the public library helps ensure that the extensive resources it offers remain available to us in the future.

Providers' Lists and Electronic Notifications

Finally, there are two other no-cost sources of information for funding opportunities. The first requires that you get on a providers' list so that you receive information about funding opportunities as they are released. The state and local governments, as well as some foundations, typically compile these lists so that information about any new funding opportunities that are being launched can be disseminated as widely as possibly. The other, which is similar, involves registering with potential funding sources to receive electronic notifications—generally to your e-mail—about new funding opportunities.

As you can see, there are multiple sources of information available regarding funding opportunities. The trick, then, becomes ensuring that you are able to take full advantage of this information. To accomplish this, there are several strategies that will assist you in ensuring that you have both the access and the tools to conduct an exhaustive search (see Box 8.1). In addition, the *Resource Directory of Funding Sources* (Table 8.3) provides a comprehensive list of all the funding sources discussed in the chapter, as well as other databases that house multiple funding opportunities.

BOX 8.1

SIX STRATEGIES FOR IDENTIFYING FUNDING OPPORTUNITIES

1. Register with all relevant local and state governmental and foundation funding sources to receive notification of funding opportunities.

2. Utilize electronic settings to receive notification of funding opportunities from web-based resources.

(Continued)

(Continued)

3. Subscribe to relevant funding databases and notification services.

4. Search the web.

5. Network with colleagues to learn about new funding opportunities or new sources of funding information.

6. Make the process of identifying funding opportunities a work priority.

Table 8.3 Resource Directory of Funding Sources

Funding Source	Location	Details
Funding Source Databases		
COS (Community of Science) Database of funding opportunities	www.cos.com	One of the largest subscription-based compendiums of governmental and nongovernmental sources
The Foundation Center	http://foundationcenter.org	Compendium of funding opportunities
Grants, etc.	www.ssw.umich.edu/grantsetc/	Compendium of funding opportunity databases, sponsored by the University of Michigan
United States Government	www.grants.gov	Compendium of governmental funding sources
Philanthropic Foundations		
Annie E. Casey Foundation	www.aecf.org	Child welfare
Aspen Institute	www.aspeninstitute.org	Public policy
Doris Duke Charitable Foundation	www.ddcf.org	Medical research
Ford Foundation	www.fordfoundation.org	Social change and social issues
Bill and Melinda Gates Foundation	www.gatesfoundation.org	Education, poverty

Funding Source	Location	Details
William and Flora Hewlett Foundation	www.hewlett.org	Poverty
Hogg Foundation for Mental Health	www.hogg.utexas.edu	Mental health
Robert Wood Johnson Foundation	www.rwjf.org	Health and health care
W. K. Kellogg Foundation	www.wkkf.org	Child development and social services
John D. and Catherine T. MacArthur Foundation	www.macfound.org	Public policy, human and community development
Kresge Foundation	www.kresge.org	Health, environment, community development, arts and culture, education, and human services
McCormick Foundation	www.mccormickfoundation.org	Children, community development
William Penn Foundation	www.williampennfoundation.org	Children, families, community development
Theodore and Vada Stanley Foundation	47 Richards Ave. Norwalk, CT 06857-0000	Mental health

Evaluating Potential Funding Sources

Whereas you need to know precisely what funding opportunities exist if you are interested in pursuing funding, you also must know how to identify the most viable fit(s)—funding opportunities that are most consistent with your proposed program. This is of particular importance since the time commitment for a grant application can require anywhere from 40 hours to 1 month. As a result of the tremendous amount of time required to complete some applications, it behooves you to narrow down funding opportunities so that you can invest your time in the opportunities that have the greatest likelihood of being awarded. To do this, you have to evaluate the various funding sources so that you can prioritize them as needed. There are several criteria that I believe are quite helpful in sorting this out:

- Philosophical foundations of the funding source
- Funding parameters

- History of funding
- Other pertinent information

Each of these issues will be discussed in detail in the following section.

Philosophical Foundations of Funding Source

At first glance, you might think the philosophical foundations of the funding source really have more to do with the history of the funding source than with how it currently operates its business. However, this would be wrong since the philosophy or guiding principles of a funding source typically relate specifically to the types of projects they fund. As such, these typically reflect the identity of the funding source and communicate to the public who the funding source is and to whom and what it is committed. For philanthropic foundations, the philosophy is often directly related to why the foundation was first conceived—such as to recognize the importance of families in children's lives, as was the case with the Annie E. Casey Foundation—and as such, this information not only holds tremendous historical value but reflects the foundation's core mission. In other cases, foundations may modify their focus while maintaining their basic philosophy. For instance, whereas the W. K. Kellogg Foundation was initially established to fulfill the broad-based mission of "serving humankind," following an examination of the results of many of the projects it funded over the past decade, the foundation's leaders decided to more closely focus their energy on issues related to social class and racial divides.

Other foundations mirror Kellogg in that they retain a broad-based mission while engaging in continuous reevaluation of their funding focus so that they can redirect their energies as needed and as justified to address the most critical and/or emerging issues. Examples of this are the MacArthur Foundation and the Bill and Melinda Gates Foundation. Both of these foundations have modified their focus to different degrees over the past several years and, as a result, have expanded their reach into a variety of social and other critical issues.

Likewise, governmental organizations are not very different from philanthropic foundations, as they, too, have their own philosophical or ideological foundations that drive funding decisions. This is even more relevant today than ever before, particularly as subagencies have evolved to focus on specific issues (e.g., Substance Abuse and Mental Health Services Administration). The shifting focus of governmental organizations, however, is typically directed by research and other external forces, and it is in this manner that shifts in funding are viewed as responsive, changing to address environmental needs. It is also in this manner that governmental funding trends are informed by other factors and that these funding streams inform key issues. For instance, the current focus on reentry issues within the criminal justice system has been informed by research related to the need for comprehensive transition planning for prisoners and, at the same time, has significantly informed decision making about the broader criminal justice system and incarceration. However, these changes have also been initiated by economic factors and the goal of reducing corrections costs by releasing certain groups of prisoners earlier than originally planned—and in this case, philosophy may also be influenced as a result of tough economic challenges.

Because the philosophy of a funding source informs the type and scope of its interests—and to a large degree, its values—it is imperative that you understand this critical aspect of the funding source. If the values of your proposed program are not consistent with the values of the funding source you are pursuing, you likely should not be pursuing support from that source. Conversely, if the values and philosophies are aligned, you may indeed be able to put forward a project that has significant meaning to the funding source and, as a result, receive serious consideration. Therefore, it is highly recommended that for each funding source in which you are interested, adequate time is taken to investigate the current philosophy and focus of potential funding opportunities, the historic funding trends, and the rationale for maintaining that specific philosophy. Doing so will not only ensure that you have a firm understanding of the funding source but also that efficiency guides your search for funding by using this information to either rule in or rule out a potential source.

Funding Parameters

There are several funding requirements or restrictions (i.e., parameters) that may or may not influence your decision making about pursuing a specific funding opportunity. Some of the common features of funding opportunities include

- time limitations related to funding,
- funding floors and ceilings,
- eligibility criteria for applicants,
- collaborative ventures that may be required,
- funding match requirement,
- qualifications of the required project director,
- regular external monitoring of funding, and
- required program evaluation.

The length of time for a funding period is often integral information, especially with regard to the cost/investment that you may need to make in order to implement a new program (as mentioned previously). Funding may be limited to 1, 2, or 3 years and may also require annual renewal. Many multi-year funding opportunities are considered 1-year awards with the possibility of an additional year or more based on availability of funds. This is particularly true with regard to governmental funding since future funding is dependent on the economy and legislative activities and, therefore, subject to change. In addition to issues related to the length of time of funding opportunities, minimum and maximum amounts of funding may also be stipulated. These are termed *floors* (minimum) and *ceilings* (maximum). Whereas ceilings are common for most funding opportunities, ceilings are most common with governmental grant opportunities, since specific amounts of money have been allocated for specific projects. This type of financial information is equally helpful to the length of time for funding, as it assists in the financial planning process. If the ceiling is less than your projected costs to operate the program, you may likely decide against pursuing a particular funding opportunity.

The eligibility criteria for applicants is obviously a key consideration when evaluating potential funding sources since you need to first and foremost know that you (or your organization) are eligible to apply before moving any further in evaluating a potential funding opportunity. Eligibility criteria typically refer to the requirements related to who can apply for a funding opportunity. Eligibility for most governmental funding is limited to organizations, whereas charitable foundations may allow individuals and/or organizations to apply. Funding from the federal government typically includes four major types of eligibility criteria:

1. Funding limited to state or local governmental entities

2. Funding opportunities that are open to state and local governmental entities, federally recognized American Indian or Native Tribes, public or private universities, community-based organizations, and faith-based organizations

3. Funding that is limited to academics or academic institutions

4. Contractual-type funding that is limited to small businesses (e.g., under $1 million, under $5 million)

Following is an example of broad-based eligibility criteria for funding from the federal government:

Eligible applicants are domestic public and private nonprofit enti-
ties. For example, State and local governments, federally recognized
American Indian/Alaska Native Tribes and tribal organizations, urban
Indian organizations, public or private universities and colleges, and
community- and faith-based organizations may apply. (Substance
Abuse and Mental Health Services Administration, 2009, "Additional
Information on Eligibility," para. 1)

The eligibility criteria are typically one of the first items listed on documents for funding opportunities. Because this information is essential to determining if you may or may not pursue specific funding, it behooves you to
locate this information as a first step in evaluating potential funding sources.

Requirements pertaining to the number of applicants for a particular
funding opportunity and the issue of whether collaboration is preferred or
required must also be evaluated. Today, more than ever before, the promotion of collaboration in mental health and social services has become especially popular, and as a result, many funding opportunities require particular
types of collaborative work. When collaborative work is a funding requirement, there are basically two forms:

1. A collaboration between two or more organizations that agree to
   working together in a particular project via a Memorandum of
   Agreement or through a subcontracting arrangement

2. A collaboration in which the applicant (for the funding opportunity)
   stipulates that other organizations will be involved with the project at
   varying levels via letters of support or other relevant documentation

In both of these cases, agreement memoranda and letters of support are
a required part of the application documents that provide confirmation of the
potential collaboration. A recent funding opportunity for comprehensive
community-based substance abuse treatment requires that the applicant (i.e.,
substance abuse treatment provider) has established relationships with both
a mental health provider and a medical provider that will be able to address
other health-related needs of clients. In this case, letters of support specifically
outlining these relationships were required as part of the application process.

Whereas collaboration may be required at different levels in a funding
opportunity, typically, there can be only one identified applicant. This means
that one organization will serve as the applicant organization, and other collaborating organizations will be subcontracted for specific services as relevant to the project. The reason for this is largely that there is one identified
leader of the project and, therefore, one faction to be held accountable.

With regard to evaluating funding opportunities based on collaboration requirements, it is wise to secure the required level of support from potential collaborators prior to moving forward in a grant application since without such, you will not be eligible to apply. In addition, when attempting to engage in a collaborative effort, you must develop effective contractual agreements that clearly spell out the expectations, requirements, financial information, time frames for terminating the relationship, and other key factors that are a part of standard contracts. In addition, very clear protocols and other documentation and reporting requirements must be established between collaborators to ensure that all parties are well prepared to engage in the collaboration.

Some funding opportunities require that the applicant organization dedicate a specific amount of funding to the project. This is typically termed *match funding*. Although the term *match* implies equal contribution, this is generally not the case. When match funding is required, it may be anywhere from 10% to 50%. In some cases, cash matches are required; however, in many cases, match funding can come from other expenses such as supplies, salaries, or other basic charges that may be incurred as a result of the project. When match funding is required, you must examine if there are any specific restrictions, such as not being able to apply rent payments as part of a match.

Match funding is required as a method of demonstrating some degree of sharing the financial costs of the project/program with the funding source and, as such, demonstrating more of a partnership with the funding source. By requiring match funding, the competition for grants will also be more limited since some organizations will be unable to apply based on not being able to provide a match.

Another element of a funding opportunity that should be evaluated is related to the requirements of the project director. The project director may be referred to as the project coordinator, leader, or principal investigator, depending on the type of funding opportunity in question. As stated above with regard to eligibility criteria related to types of organizations and the need for an identified lead organization/applicant organization, most applications also require that a project director is identified. In some cases, there may be specific requirements for project directors, such as that the individual has previous experience with receiving funding, has specific experience with the population targeted in the opportunity, or has specific expertise in the area targeted in the funding opportunity.

Because the project director is viewed as the leader, it is imperative that you identify someone not only who meets any specific requirements but also for whom strong justification can be made to successfully lead the project. As such, a good deal of attention must be paid to evaluating potential funding opportunities to determine if you do have an appropriate project director who will allow you to most effectively compete for the funds since this is such a critical part of how your application is evaluated.

In addition to the significance of a project director, the vast majority of funding opportunities today require data collection and regular performance monitoring. These requirements are often identified in the announcement of the funding opportunity with much more specific information provided at the time an award is made. Because collecting data requires dedication of both individuals and time—as well as software, hardware, and/or other types of data storage and analysis equipment—this is an area that again must be carefully examined to ensure that you are able to fully comply with all data collection and monitoring requirements. In addition, because there are costs associated with data collection, storage, and analysis, these costs must be considered in developing the budget.

Data collection can involve basic issues such as client demographic information or aspects of program implementation, such as the number of counseling sessions provided or the number of clients that successfully completed the program. Because we do—thankfully, I believe—currently live in a data-driven era, data about the project provides integral information to the funding source, often about outputs and outcomes and other performance-related aspects. Therefore, this information is pertinent to the funding source as it reflects the return on its investment while promoting accountability on the part of the funding recipient.

Similar to data collection but more sophisticated is the requirement for a program evaluation that may be a part of some funding opportunities. Program evaluation refers to a comprehensive evaluation of program/project outcomes and may also include a fidelity assessment and a process evaluation. Outcomes, though, are of particular significance to funding sources because these speak directly to their ROI. In addition, outcomes data is tremendously important for future decision making for funding similar programs/projects.

If a funding opportunity requires a program evaluation, you must first ensure that you have someone who is fully capable of carrying out a comprehensive evaluation, including statistical analysis and follow-up. And you must budget for all the costs related to evaluation in the proposal. Additionally, justification regarding your ability to conduct the evaluation will need to be provided in the proposal; so highlighting past experience with evaluation, an established statistician, and an infrastructure conducive to evaluation may serve you well in your application.

History of Funding

In addition to all the various funding parameters listed above and the philosophical foundations of potential funding sources, it is also important to review the history of funding of the potential funding sources as part of your evaluation process. The history of funding refers to the projects and organizations that have previously received funding. These details can provide excellent information about the funding source in terms of what the leaders of the organization value, what other parameters may exist in terms of who has received what type of award, and other trend information that can better inform you about the likelihood of securing funding from the source. Because this information also is reflective of the philosophical foundations of the funding source, you will need to examine if the focus of the funding source has shifted recently to understand just how relevant this information is to your current consideration.

This type of historical information is typically provided on websites of philanthropic organizations. In addition, the information is often available via the Internet for governmental sources and is listed in published documents. Because both philanthropic and governmental funding sources are required to create this information and publish it, it is generally fairly easy to locate.

In reviewing the types of projects and organizations that have received funding in the past, you may learn that the majority of funding awarded did not exceed $100,000 even though the funding ceilings on new opportunities are set at $150,000. You may also learn that faith-based organizations received more funding than other nonprofit organizations and that the project directors more often than not held doctoral degrees. Learning this about the funding source, you may choose to pursue this funding and adjust your application accordingly by not requesting more than $100,000, highlighting other strengths of your organization if it is not faith-based, and considering the involvement of an individual with a doctorate as part of the project team if you do not have an identified project leader with a doctorate. Conversely, like all other information that you use to evaluate the potential fit of a funding source, the history of funding may influence your decision not to pursue a particular source.

Direct Contact With the Funding Source

Another key activity in evaluating a potential funding source and/or opportunity is to initiate direct contact with the funder. This may mean calling, e-mailing, and/or meeting directly with the project coordinator/contract manager to share your interests and abilities and learn more about how your proposal or ideas of future proposals might fit with the intent of the funding opportunity. Cultivating relationships with all potential funding sources should be a top priority when you wish to seek funding from these sources. It is in this way that you may work to prepare the funding source to eventually receive your proposal (Homan, 2004). Indeed, the quality of the relationship that you form with the funding source may be as critical as the quality of the proposal that you submit (Golden, 2001).

In addition, pre-bid sessions may be offered by funders as part of the RFP process so that specific additional information can be provided regarding an opportunity. These can be held on-site or through a webinar or use of other forms of electronic technology. It is essential that you attend these sessions, as details are often provided that may significantly impact your proposal but are not available through other venues.

Other Pertinent Information

In addition to all the aspects identified above, there is other information that may be pertinent to know as you move forward in determining which specific funding opportunities to pursue. Often, other critical information that must be evaluated has unique meaning to the applicant/applicant organization and, therefore, what is most essential is that you fully evaluate each potential funding source to determine which may be the best fit for you. Failing to engage in due diligence in evaluating potential funding sources before pursuing specific funding can result in a significant loss of time, work, and energy—prized possessions in the mental health professions.

Funding Opportunity Evaluation Tool

In order to streamline the process of evaluating potential funding opportunities and to aid in decision making by objectively reviewing multiple sources, the *Funding Opportunity Evaluation Tool* (Figure 8.2) was developed.

Summary

As you can see, securing funding for mental health and social service programs is no easy task and, in fact, is a highly competitive, labor-intensive process. Moreover, because financial support is limited, securing funding must be considered a regular activity of work rather than a special project. This likely ensures that sufficient time is set aside for investigating and

Figure 8.2 Funding Opportunity Evaluation Tool

The Funding Opportunity Evaluation Form was designed as a tool for evaluating potential funding opportunities through evaluation of key characteristics. The first section allows you to capture pertinent information about the funding opportunity, and the second section allows you to evaluate the criteria in order to make decisions. The tool should aid in the decision-making process about which funding opportunities are most worth pursuing.

Funding Opportunity: _____

Funding Source: _____

Key Characteristics	Information
Eligibility status*	
Award amount (annual and total)	
Length of funding	
Match funding requirement and details	
Partner/collaboration details	
Program evaluation requirements	
Other pertinent details	
Evaluation Criteria:	*Respond by using either Yes or No and provide details for each response*
Is there philosophical compatibility?	
Is the program leader effectively justified (i.e., experience and status)?	
Do we have sufficient organizational capability?	
Do we have sufficient data collection capability?	
Does the funding opportunity fit with the organizational mission?	
In addition to meeting the basic eligibility requirements of the funding opportunity, do we have the technical capacity and expertise (i.e., design, implementation, evaluation) to fulfill the requirements?	
Based on potential cost/benefits of proposal development, is proposal development justified?	
Evaluation Criteria:	*Respond by using Strong, Moderate, Weak and provide details for each response*
Rate the overall fit between the funding opportunity and your interests.	
Based on all the criteria, rate the overall strength of the potential bid.	

If you/your organization do not meet the eligibility criteria requirements of the funding opportunity, do not move forward in your evaluation of the opportunity.

pursuing funding—recognizing the significance of pursuing funding alongside managing daily operations since both are ongoing tasks requiring specific attention.

Whereas an extraordinary number of funding opportunities are made available through both philanthropic organizations and the government, knowing where to look and how to thoroughly examine opportunities requires both knowledge and skills. Technology has made the process of exploring funding opportunities not only highly efficient but also highly effective. Searching for funding opportunities, evaluating funding sources, and completing applications for funding can largely be done electronically now. In addition, the federal government has moved to almost exclusive use of electronic technology for all aspects of funding, including management and monitoring of fund awards.

A major aspect of financial planning and management, the process of securing funding for your program can be quite rewarding, both figuratively and literally. Just as it is imperative that program developers possess both the knowledge and skills to competently engage in financial planning and management, they must also be able to effectively understand how funding operates, the climate of public and philanthropic funding, and how to most effectively make decisions regarding which funding opportunities to pursue. By doing so, program developers are much better postured to be successful, not only in securing initial funding but in continuing to secure funding—a key ingredient of sustainability.

CASE ILLUSTRATION

Andy and Amanda had been codirectors of a small foster care program for the past several years and had become all too aware that the majority of their clients were single mothers with children. As a result, their parenting classes—one of the mandatory requirements that must be completed for parents to be reunited with their children—were almost solely filled with females. They were disturbed by their sense that the child welfare system seemed to either overtly or covertly focus on mothers at the expense of neglecting to get fathers involved with their noncustodial children. After doing some research in the area, they found some support for this notion, but more importantly, they came across a specific program model that targeted nonparticipating fathers associated with children in foster care. The model had demonstrated promise as an emerging practice, as preliminary outcome studies showed significantly favorable results.

(Continued)

(Continued)

Energized by this, Amanda suggested they take a stab at implementing a program based on this model. Andy was equally excited about this prospect, especially since, in addition to fulfilling a passion that they shared, it could result in expanding their service array, potentially bringing in a new funding source. And it reflected their mission. Now they just needed to identify potential funding sources.

Through an exhaustive investigation of potential sources, they were able to narrow their search down to four potential funding sources that included the Janet L. Reed Foundation, the Rankovic Forum, the Harrington Foundation, and the state Department of Health and Human Services. Andy reviewed the funding trends over the past 3 years to get a sense of specific projects that each had funded, while Amanda contacted the project managers at each of the philanthropic organizations to discuss their proposed program and determine if the foundation had any interest in supporting it. Amanda discovered that the Rankovic Forum had already dedicated their funding to other specific issues for the next couple of years and, therefore, suggested she check back next year as the upcoming agenda might be prepared by then. After speaking with a representative from the Harrington Foundation, Amanda learned that they were currently not accepting unsolicited proposals and were focusing their attention on large geographic regions such as states, as opposed to smaller regions. However, Amanda was encouraged to continue to check their website for announcements of any new funding competitions in the future. After pitching their program proposal to the children's programming manager from the Reed Foundation, the program manager stated that parenting programs was an area that they were actually beginning to explore and that an RFP was going to be issued in October. She further shared that while the focus of the RFP did not specify mother versus father, several members of the organization had recently been discussing the role of the father in noncustodial parenting, further indicating that proposing a father-focused program might strengthen the proposal.

Amanda shared her news with Andy, and they decided to continue exploring other options while learning even more about the Reed Foundation in hopes of submitting a proposal once the RFP was released in a couple of months. Andy also had set up an electronic notification on a free funding database to ensure that they were notified when funding opportunities in the area became available.

While they were not successful in identifying any other potential funding sources, they received the RFP from the Reed Foundation in October. Using the *Funding Opportunity Evaluation Tool*, Amanda and Andy began rigorously reviewing the RFP. Their findings indicated that the opportunity was indeed a good fit for them, but the data collection requirements were extensive, and they were concerned about their own abilities to effectively manage the data collection process. They currently used the county-administered client information system for their foster care program and used Excel spreadsheets to handle their program data needs.

After discussing the RFP with their staff and with Hank, the executive director, everyone agreed that the opportunity was one they should pursue. Hank stated that the board had been urging him to use some of the company's technology funds to purchase a client information system, but he had been hesitant. Hearing about this new opportunity, he realized that regardless of the outcome of the fatherhood parenting program, it was becoming increasingly clear that having a client information system in place would better posture the organization to pursue other funding opportunities, and it would allow the staff to do more with their existing data.

After receiving the green light, Andy and Amanda got to work on developing the proposal.

RESEARCHING POTENTIAL FUNDING OPPORTUNITIES EXERCISE

In order to get more comfortable with identifying and evaluating potential funding sources, complete the following exercise:

1. Visit www.grants.gov and identify two open (current) funding competitions that might be used to fund the program that you developed in Chapter 6. If your program of interest is school-based, visit the federal or state department of education websites to search for K–12 funding. If you cannot locate funding for your specific type of program in current opportunities, identify two funding opportunities that are somewhat related to your identified treatment issue or population.

2. Explore the Internet and any other sources available to you to identify two philanthropic organizations that provide funding support in your area of interest.

3. Gather the applications for all four of these funding opportunities and, using the *Funding Opportunity Evaluation Tool*, evaluate each one.

4. Explain the results of your evaluation, indicating which, if any, of the funding opportunities appear worth pursuing, which do not, and why.

References

Annie E. Casey Foundation. (n.d.). *Mission and history*. Retrieved September 10, 2010, from http://www.aecf.org/Home/AboutUs/MissionAndHistory.aspx

Carroll, D. A., & Stater, K. J. (2008). Revenue diversification in nonprofit organizations: Does it lead to financial stability? *Journal of Public Administration Research and Theory, 19*, 947–966.

Ezell, M. (2000). Financial management. In R. J. Patti (Ed.), *The handbook of social welfare management* (pp. 377–393). Thousand Oaks, CA: Sage.

Farquhar, C., Lowe, J. I., & Campbell, J. W. (2007). Trends in aging funding and current areas of foundation interest. *Philanthropy and Aging, 31,* 50–53.

Gibelman, M., & Furman, R. (2008). *Navigating human service organizations.* Chicago: Lyceum.

Golden, S. L. (2001). The grant-seeking process. In J. M. Greenfield (Ed.), *The nonprofit handbook: Fundraising* (3rd ed., pp. 666–691). New York: Wiley.

Homan, M. S. (2004). *Promoting community change: Making it happen in the real world.* Belmont, CA: Brooks/Cole.

John D. and Katherine T. MacArthur Foundation. (n.d.). *Overview.* Retrieved September 10, 2010, from http://www.macfound.org/site/c.lkLXJ8MQKrH/b.855245/k.588/About_the_Foundation

Montgomery, M. (2003, September 5). Thank you for advertising, but your needs don't meet my interests [Electronic version]. *Chronicle of Higher Education, 50*(2), B15.

Payne, M., & Applebaum, R. (2008). Local funding of senior services: Good policy or just good politics? *Aging Policy and the States, XXXII*, 81–85.

Singh, J., Illes, J., Lazzeroni, L., & Hallmayer, J. (2009). Trends in U.S. autism research funding. *Journal of Autism Developmental Disorders, 39,* 788–795.

Skillman Foundation. (n.d.). *Always a Rose for Detroit: Rose Skillman.* Retrieved September 10, 2010, from http://www.skillman.org/about-us/history

Substance Abuse and Mental Health Services Administration. (2009). *Offender reentry program.* Retrieved September 10, 2010, from http://www.grants.gov/search/search.do?mode=VIEW&oppId=50070

Vitiello, B., & Wagner, A. (2007). The rapidly expanding field of autism research. *Biological Psychiatry, 61,* 427–428.

W. K. Kellogg Foundation. (2009). *Mission and vision.* Retrieved December 10, 2009, from http://www.wkkf.org/default.aspx?tabid=1163&ItemID=199&NID=344&LanguageID=0

Develop the Financial Management Plan

Learning Objectives

1. Identify key historic issues in financial management that may impact current practices
2. Identify two current trends in financial management of nonprofit social service organizations
3. Differentiate between financial management of nonprofit organizations and for-profit organizations
4. Identify the basic components of an annual program budget
5. Identify the major objectives of an annual report
6. Identify the major objectives of a financial audit
7. Develop a comprehensive annual operating budget

WHOSE JOB IS IT TO MANAGE THE FINANCES?

Bill had been operating a human service organization for the past 4 years, primarily providing an array of services for developmentally disabled adults. The agency had grown significantly over the past 2 years and now had annual revenue of $4.8 million. After presenting the proposed budget that his chief financial officer (CFO) had developed, Bill's board of directors had unanimously approved his program expansion into a clubhouse program (i.e., multipurpose space for clients to gather, recreate, and participate in various structured and nonstructured events).

However, 9 months after successfully implementing the program, Bill learned that his agency was in the red. Even more surprising, Bill found that his agency had been losing money for the past 8 months. Bill immediately met with the CFO to better understand what was going on.

After meeting with his CFO, Bill realized that the projected revenue for the clubhouse program on which the expense budget had originally been based was nowhere near what the agency was collecting in revenue, even though he had been spending all the money initially budgeted to support the program. Bill had always thought of himself as a clinician first, as well as an agency administrator, and felt that his role was to be fully focused on operations and not finances. As a result, he had hired a CFO and two finance staff persons to manage the agency's finances.

However, after realizing that there had been a grave disconnect between what was happening on the operations/expenditures side and what was happening on the revenue side, Eric knew he had to quickly get a handle on his budget. Bill immediately set about learning all he could about the state of his agency's finances and implemented weekly budget meetings to review their financial status. Three weeks later, he realized that he could not afford to retain the clubhouse program given the revenue it had produced thus far and the unlikelihood of its revenue significantly increasing in the future.

Although this was a terribly difficult lesson to learn, Bill was confident that he would never again find himself in this position. He had vowed that from this day forward, he would be completely involved in the finances of his agency, and thus, there would be no more surprises.

CONSIDERING BILL

1. As the organization's leader, what is Bill's responsibility in the financial management of the organization?

2. What responsibility does the CFO have in the agency's financial management?

3. If you were Bill, what specific steps would you take to ensure this type of problem would not occur again?

About This Chapter

This chapter is designed to examine several key financial planning and management issues related to program development. Since it is necessary to first gain a historical perspective and understand current trends in mental health and human service programs related to financial management, this will serve as a starting point. Second, in order to gain an understanding of the distinction between nonprofit and for-profit financial management, we will briefly explore this issue. In addition, we will discuss an integrated approach to discussions and decision making pertaining to program development that directly includes financial aspects and implications.

Next, we will examine types of financial data that include projected revenue and expenditures as well as project-specific budgets and annual program budgets. We will discuss financial reporting mechanisms and time frames, the annual report, and auditing practices toward the end of the chapter to promote increased understanding of the significance of regular reporting and oversight pertaining to financial management. Finally, we will explore the way in which financial planning directly derives from previous steps (i.e., program design, staffing infrastructure), with an exercise at the end of the chapter providing an opportunity for you to develop your own initial budget.

STEP VII: DEVELOP THE FINANCIAL MANAGEMENT PLAN

Finances and Program Development

Despite the most brilliant program design, without clients (i.e., justifiable need), a program cannot be implemented. Similarly, without sound financial management, a program that has been implemented cannot be effectively sustained. Therefore, financial management must be viewed as just as integral to program development efforts as the identification of a viable client population. As a result, the program developer must be equally equipped to effectively engage in comprehensive financial planning as s/he is to engage in asset mapping, community resource development, and all other aspects of program planning.

There are two major areas of finance that are relevant to comprehensive program development—financial planning and management. Financial planning must be conducted as part of initial program planning, whereas financial management is related to program implementation and sustainability. However, because of the interdependent nature of these issues—finances cannot be effectively managed if they have not been effectively planned (as Bill learned in the vignette above)—it is necessary to cover both areas in this chapter.

History and Current Trends

One of the most unfortunate memories that will historically be associated with the new millennium is the behemoth disasters resulting from financial mismanagement and lack of financial oversight. Even though the depression-like era that fully evolved in the United States in 2007 may take center stage in our collective memory for years to come, the public fall of companies such as Enron in the earliest days of the new millennium must not be forgotten—especially since some could argue that what occurred with Enron was simply a symptom of a larger culture of financial negligence in which we so passively allowed ourselves to become entangled, thus setting the stage for what followed.

Rather than spend too much time rehashing such unpleasantness here, what is necessary for this discussion is what we learned from these events of the 21st century—namely, lesson No. 1 from Enron: *Failure to engage in effective accounting and financial management practices and failure to enforce effective oversight of financial management and accounting practices puts everyone at risk, including clients/consumers, employees, and the public, and such negligence can result in harm to all stakeholders and the decimation of the business,* and lesson No. 2 from the banking industry: *Failure to engage in effective accounting and financial management practices, failure to enforce effective oversight of financial management and accounting practices, and failure of the federal government to provide sufficient and effective regulations can result in worldwide financial disasters of a proportion never before witnessed.*

We would likely be hard-pressed to identify any more-significant historical events related to financial management. And the far-reaching impact of these events may remain yet to be seen since they so recently occurred. However, even as the conditions were being created that eventually led to these financial disasters, trends related to financial management in the nonprofit human service industry were beginning to change. In fact, three major trends that have gained increasing traction over the past several years are

1. heightened scrutiny and accountability of finances,

2. the use of turnaround planning, and

3. changing attitudes about financial knowledge.

Heightened Scrutiny and Accountability

Myriad changes have affected the human services industry over the past 2 decades, such as changes in governmental funding patterns, greater emphasis on more localized management of funds, and significant losses in the stock market that have not only affected philanthropic organizations' funding but have had a far-reaching effect on literally all funding sources. Each of these, in addition to the well-publicized financial catastrophes discussed above, has led to increased scrutiny and accountability of nonprofit financial management. In nonprofit human service organizations, "accountability is rooted in how organizations spend the money entrusted to them" (Gibelman & Furman, 2008, p. 49).

One of the drivers of this increased scrutiny was the new legislation that was passed in 2002, the Sarbanes-Oxley Act. This legislation was specifically put in place as a result of the financial negligence that came to light during the past several years and, as such, was designed to create increased accountability of finances. With the passage of Sarbanes-Oxley, public attention initially focused on board members of for-profit companies; however, public attention is now shifting to increased scrutiny of nonprofit organizations, including human service organizations and charitable organizations (Grunewald, 2007). As a result of increased scrutiny, the manner in which nonprofits handle their money is a primary focus of various constituencies (e.g., funders, board members, politicians) that now hold management of these organizations far more accountable than ever before (Katz, 2005).

Turnaround Planning

Related to the significant changes that the human service industry has faced in recent years, particularly with regard to the tremendous shrinkage in available funding, an inordinate number of organizations have been unable to remain in business. In some instances, the reduction in the number of human service organizations was a natural and necessary response to shrinking funds—since the pieces of pie are limited and, therefore, can feed only so many—and as a result, it has become an issue of survival of the fittest. However, most organizations have not been able to survive simply by resting on their past successes. Rather, in order to remain in business, many have had to engage in various degrees of turnaround planning—incorporating responsive and, at times, radical changes to their business model in order to redefine the business and continue to compete. In many cases, this has meant diversification. For some, diversification has meant expanding the service array to include community-based services in organizations that had traditionally provided only residential treatment programs; for others, it has meant pursuing funding from new and different sources, such as the federal government and large national foundations, in addition to state and local governmental funding sources.

The majority of nonprofit human service organizations typically engage in less formal types of turnaround planning, utilizing key administrators and, in some cases, forming internal committees to think through potential operational changes. However, with increased frequency, nonprofit human service and mental health organization leaders have sought financial and management advice from turnaround firms—once the bastion of the for-profit world (Katz, 2005). This trend constitutes another recent significant change in financial management of mental health and human service organizations.

Changing Attitudes About Financial Knowledge

Further connected to these other trends are the changing attitudes regarding financial knowledge within human service organizations and, namely, ideas about who should hold such knowledge. Whereas, traditionally, the chief financial officer and other finance staff were looked to for their expertise in all things financial, it is now widely understood that while there still must be those who have significant expertise within the organization, this does not exclude the necessity for managers and administrators to possess a strong working knowledge of finance. In fact, because the program administrator is ultimately responsible for the program operations, s/he must be knowledgeable about each and every aspect of operations, including finance.

Precisely because much of the funding for mental health and human services derives from governmental, foundational, or philanthropic funding, program developers are stewards of the resources of others (Lewis, Packard, & Lewis, 2007). This is a tremendous responsibility and one that requires the ability to effectively manage these resources in a manner that allows for the greatest amount of good to be achieved. As a result, it is now widely accepted that effective financial management and accountability are key responsibilities held by program developers.

Historic events and current trends have dramatically changed financial planning and management in the mental health and human service industry in recent years. As a result, today more than ever before, program developers must be keenly aware, knowledgeable, and skillful regarding financial planning and management.

Financial Planning

Financial planning refers to the financial design process that is directly related to program design in the program development process. Initial financial planning derives directly from the program design and is based on the type and scope of services that will be provided and the staffing infrastructure that will be in place. Initial financial planning is composed of projections—projected expenditures that are expected to be incurred as a result of implementing the program. In addition, initial financial planning is equally based on projections of expected revenues that will be received as a result of program implementation. Because of the significant implications related to projections of expenses and revenues, it is imperative that these projections be as accurate as possible in predicting actual expenses and revenues. In addition, cost-containment practices and effective monitoring must be in place to protect against over-expenditures, and appropriate billing and highly effective collection practices must exist to ensure that all revenues are received. In fact, the ongoing ability of a human service agency to operate efficiently in a constantly changing environment is dependent on how well the organization's finances are managed (Kettner, Moroney, & Martin, 2008).

With regard to financial planning for mental health and human service programs, two key issues must be considered:

1. The financial management–related differences between nonprofit and for-profit organizations

2. Utilizing an integrated approach to financial planning

Both of these have specific significance for comprehensive program development, and so each will be discussed in depth.

Financial Management for Nonprofit Organizations Versus For-Profit Organizations

Within the mental health and human services, a large portion of organizations are nonprofit. This is not to say that for-profit corporations do not also provide mental health and human services, but because the field is indeed composed of a significant number of nonprofit organizations, it is necessary to fully understand the characteristics that make these organizations unique.

The fundamental difference between for-profit organizations and nonprofit organizations is aptly conveyed in each title: for-profit versus nonprofit. Simply put, for-profit organizations operate in order to make money by selling some good or service, whereas nonprofit organizations function to use the money provided to them by third parties (e.g., government, charitable organizations, individuals) to carry out specific services to other individuals and/or groups. Although the manner in which each acquires funds is vastly different, the amount of revenue generated may be similarly meaningful to both for-profit and nonprofit organizations. Indeed, for-profit companies often seek to make as much money as possible, typically basing profit directly on what the market will bear and resulting in increased salaries, equipment, facilities, and—for publicly traded companies—increased value to stockholders. Similarly, nonprofit organizations are also often concerned with increasing the amount of revenue that is generated by the organization since this often translates into a broader organizational staffing infrastructure, more equipment, and other items needed to directly support operations. As a result, the key difference between for-profit and nonprofit human service organizations is not related to the amount of revenue produced—or desired—by the organizations but, rather, how the revenue that is generated can be spent. Whereas leaders of for-profit organizations typically enjoy a high degree of freedom and autonomy in decision making about how money can be spent—albeit, with oversight from the board of directors when applicable—leaders of nonprofit organizations have limited autonomy in decision making about expenditures. This is precisely because, from a financial perspective, nonprofit organizations are primarily concerned with justifying all revenue *through* expenditures, thus demonstrating that funds generated were utilized to directly and indirectly deliver the services for which they were initially provided.

In addition to this fundamental difference between for-profit and nonprofit organizations, there are also characteristics specifically related to nonprofit organizations. According to Horejsi and Garthwait (2004), attributes of a nonprofit human service organization include

- operating legally under the control of a board of directors whose members are empowered to act on behalf of the organization and represent the interests of the clients served;
- being created or chartered to serve some facet of the common good;
- being held publicly accountable for all its activities;

- being specifically empowered to hire individuals that will carry out the mission of the organization and provide and support its services and programs;
- being empowered to engage in fundraising to support the mission of the organization and to support its services and programs; and
- being restricted by the Internal Revenue Service (IRS) and many state statutes from participating in political activities, including lobbying and promoting political candidates.

Additionally, Carver (2006) offers three other characteristics of non-profit organizations specific to financial management, which include

- being exempt from certain taxes,
- typically receiving a large portion of revenue from other organizations and from donations rather than for the direct sale of a product, and
- having no place for profit in their accounting systems.

Each of these characteristics distinguishes nonprofit organizations to some degree from their for-profit counterparts. And as a result of these unique features related to financial management of nonprofit organizations, it is essential that most, if not all, stakeholders minimally possess a basic understanding of financial management. Moreover, it is imperative that most, if not all, employees possess a basic understanding of financial management, while program developers, administrators, managers, and supervisors are equipped with an even deeper knowledge of this aspect.

Integrated Approach to Financial Management

It is because of this need for program leaders and program developers to possess an effective amount of finance-related knowledge that an integrated approach must be used in initial financial planning and management. What I mean by an integrated approach is that the program developer must initially be able to demonstrate her/his strong working knowledge of finance through leading the development of a comprehensive budget. By doing this, the developer conveys that s/he understands the integral relationship between finances and services, staffing, and other aspects of the program and, thus, is able to integrate each of the various components of the program into a whole. *Integrated* also then means that discussions about the program are inclusive or integrated—addressing both operations and finances, not simply one aspect versus the other. While it is important to have an expert (i.e., finance manager) both review and provide input to the initial budget, this responsibility should never be shifted directly to the finance leader in lieu of the program developer's involvement. This is because mental health professionals can fully understand the programs that they are operating only when they understand how those programs are financially managed (Lewis et al., 2007).

Unfortunately, some organizations continue to operate in this compartmentalized fashion, ceding full responsibility for the initial budget development to the finance leader. As a result, organizational leaders and program staff often struggle to understand financial decision making simply because they are somewhat ignorant about this crucial aspect of programming.

By utilizing an integrated approach, the program developer is able to gain a much greater vantage point for fully understanding the full program operations and, thus, is better equipped to deal with any challenges that might arise. Whereas this initially occurs at the point of program development and development of the initial budget, the program's financial issues must be incorporated into all dialogue related to program implementation and evaluation. As a result, it is necessary that all post-implementation program review processes include review and discussion related to the financial aspects of the program as integral to the program operations. These discussions must be led by program leaders and staff to ensure that an integrated approach to discussions and decision making continues to be inculcated at all levels of the program. Indeed, this serves to promote a keen understanding and appreciation of the interdependent relationship between program operations and finances and, ultimately, to increase the collective knowledge of the program/organization.

Types of Financial Data

There are two primary types of financial data used in accounting and financial decision making in the nonprofit mental health and human service industry—expenditures and revenue. As you know, quite an intimate relationship exists between these two types of data, since one refers to what goes out (expenditures) and the other to what comes in (revenue).

Projected Expenditures

Whereas expenditures will differ somewhat based on the specific type of programming being provided, there are several basic expenditures that the majority of programs incur:

- Staff salaries
- Staff benefits
- Insurance
- Office space
- Office equipment
- Office supplies
- Transportation

As you would likely imagine, staffing costs frequently constitute the largest expense. This is particularly significant to mental health and human service, since programs are primarily composed of interventions directly provided by individual staff members. In fact, without individual staff, interventions or services cannot be rendered. The various salary amounts and the sum of expenses per salary are based on the scope of the program and the necessary staffing infrastructure. For example, because residential (i.e., inpatient) programs are much more complex than most community-based programs and because they require 24-hour staffing, the range of personnel and associated salaries in residential programs may be quite expansive. To highlight this, Table 9.1 illustrates a comparison of staffing for an inpatient substance abuse treatment center for adolescents and an outpatient substance abuse treatment center for adolescents. Both programs serve up to 24 clients at a time.

As you can see, the staffing structures of these two programs are quite different, although each is designed to treat adolescent substance abuse and

Table 9.1	Salary Structure and Range Comparison: Inpatient Versus Outpatient Substance Abuse Treatment Programs

Inpatient Program	Outpatient Program
Program director (1)	Program director (1)
Treatment staff supervisors (3)	Counselors (2)
Counselors (3)	Case managers (2)
Case managers (3)	
Treatment staff (18)	
Medical director (1, contractual)	
Psychiatrist (1, contractual)	

each serves the same number of clients. The intensity of residential treatment, not to mention other costs associated with supporting the primary needs of individuals (e.g., housing, food, hygiene) on a daily basis, contributes to the vast budgetary differences inherently based on program type.

In the above example of the residential program, all the staff members are full-time salaried employees—with the exception of the medical director and psychiatrist, both of whom are contractually paid. With salaried employees, as well as with some part-time employees, come employee benefits. Benefits primarily refer to employer contributions to employee health and possibly life insurance programs and typically cost an employer approximately 30% of the employee's salary. Therefore, for an employee with a salary of $32,000, the employer may pay up to $9,600 in employee benefits.

In addition to employee health insurance benefits, employers in mental health and human service programs also must carry insurance for their business. Typically, this includes insurance on the buildings/facilities and professional liability insurance for any malpractice lawsuits.

Office space, equipment, and supplies compose another large group of expenses and, again, vary depending on the type and scope of programming provided. Minimally, one office space is needed to house the administrative functions of the program and to provide space in which the clinicians and other staff work. The office space itself refers to the work space that is either purchased or rented and that houses the program operations. Whereas outpatient or community-based programs may have one office space/location, residential programs may have both the inpatient facility that serves as the office space for all the direct care workers (e.g., clinicians, case managers, treatment staff, physicians) as well as an additional administrative office housing administrative support staff (e.g., finance, human resources). This schema may be particularly relevant if the organization is operating multiple residential facilities.

Office equipment generally refers to the basic furnishings and equipment necessary to conduct business. Items such as desks, chairs, and tables compose basic furnishings, while computers, copiers, printers, telephones, and fax machines are some of the equipment needed. Paper, pens, calendars, highlighters, and staplers are some such basic office supplies.

Transportation is another typical expense incurred by mental health and social service programs. Transportation costs may result from mileage reimbursement to employees who conduct home visits or other business involving transportation to or from off-site meetings, conferences, and other professional or administrative duties involving transportation. The federal and state governments provide guidance for mileage reimbursement, as each publishes its annual mileage rate paid to employees or subcontractors.

For a basic reference point, over the past several years, mileage rates have ranged from $0.38 to $0.52 per mile.

Determining Salary Ranges and Other Expenses

Just like all the other components of comprehensive program development, determining expense allocations must be guided by research and due diligence. Salary ranges should be determined based on both national and local market analysis data. Often, salary data is compiled by various professional associations (e.g., Child Welfare League of America) as well as the government, and as a result, you simply need to review all the pertinent data and use it to guide the salary range development process. In addition, because many human service organizations affiliate with colleagues in local consortiums, it is not uncommon for both informal and formal dialogue about salaries to emerge, particularly for a specific position (e.g., therapist). Also, because salary information is often disclosed in job postings, a review of job postings from similar organizations in your region should also be examined. Unfortunately, some program administrators learn about the salary ranges offered by competitors by witnessing a continuous exodus of their own employees to their competitors' somewhat *greener* pastures.

The point here is that information about salaries is available; therefore, the program developer/manager must simply ensure that the information is effectively used in determining salary ranges. Salary ranges are typically guided by competition; therefore, in order to remain competitive, you often must ensure that you can offer a competitive wage. This is not to say that salary is necessarily the most compelling feature of a position for potential employees, but it is to say that, by and large, salary matters to many individuals—particularly when there are significant differences in salary between employers for the same work. Because salaries are collectively influenced—by the various competing organizations—salary ranges typically are created based on the market, and not only what the market can bear but also what the market wishes to bear. In terms of what the market wishes to bear, contractors of services either directly or indirectly impact salaries. For instance, contracts and grants may be awarded based on projected salary ranges for various positions, and conversely, contracts and grant funding may not be awarded if the funding source deems the projected salary ranges inappropriate. In other cases, and particularly with governmental contracts, salary ranges may be pre-established by the contractor.

The work of gathering and analyzing salary data can and should be done in concert with a human resources staff person—but not solely by the human resources person. No different than other aspects of financial management, mental health professionals must understand the entire scope of their programs—not simply the clinical components—and doing so requires active involvement in all aspects. In addition, whereas the initial salary ranges must be established prior to setting program implementation, comprehensive review of salary ranges must be regularly conducted to ensure that you remain competitive.

Because salary is only one form of employee compensation, determining other aspects that together compose the total compensation package must also be guided by market research. These aspects include, but are not limited to, insurance, time off, mileage reimbursement, professional development, and other benefits.

Finally, research must also guide decision making about all other expenses, including office space, equipment, and other supplies. By first ensuring that all costs are justified, then regularly reviewing the markets for each type of expenditure and conducting effective cost-benefit analyses, you can be confident that your expenditures are not only well justified but also cost-effective.

Projected Revenue

To reiterate, the projected revenue is the amount of money you hope to collect as a result of service provisions. Typically, there are three types of revenue streams in human service programming—governmental funding; foundation funding; and individual, fee-for-service payments. In addition, nonprofit organizations can receive funding through charitable giving. Each of these funding sources was discussed in detail in the previous chapter. However, for the sake of this discussion, what is important to note is the manner in which the funding is provided. Whereas some contracts with both governmental and nongovernmental organizations are based on providing a lump-sum payment, others provide payment based on a per diem schema (e.g., per client, per day). Precisely how the reimbursement occurs is particularly significant since this information is crucial to projecting and managing expenses. To get a sense of the differences in revenue based on program type and funding type, see Tables 9.2a and 9.2b.

The per diem rate for residential programming is obviously much greater than that for community-based programming, since the residential per diem payment supports 24-hour staffing as well as housing, food, clothing, and other necessities of daily living. In contrast, the per diem rate for community-based treatment supports clinical staff and supervision. With regard to Table 9.2b, both programs are residentially based and have a capacity of 30 youth. The first is paid a per diem rate based on the days in

Table 9.2a	Per Diem Revenue Comparisons Between Different Program Types

Program Type	Residential treatment program for adolescent sex offenders	Community-based treatment program for adolescent sex offenders
Payment Type	$304 per diem rate	$38 per diem rate

Table 9.2b	Different Payment Type Comparisons Between Identical Programs

Program Type	Residential treatment program for adolescent sex offenders	Residential treatment program for adolescent sex offenders
Payment Type	$304 per diem rate	$312,000 annual lump-sum payment

which the youth are physically placed in the facility. As a result of this payment schema, the program is paid based on the number of beds filled by clients. Conversely, any time that a bed is not filled, the program does not receive payment. To counter this issue, contractual agreements for payment may specify a lump sum to be paid on an annual basis (or some other regular time period), therefore paying the program independent of the number of clients placed in the program at a given time. Both payment schemas have merit; both also come with their own advantages and disadvantages. In short, per diem payment may work best when programs are able to operate at full capacity and/or are flexible enough to regulate expenditures effectively based on client numbers. On the other hand, a lump sum payment schema may work best for programs that are not always able to operate at full capacity so that the payment can be spread out based on the number of clients in treatment at a given time. Regardless of type of program and manner in which payment is made, how the funding is managed is by far the most critical issue facing the financial livelihood of a program. This only reinforces the need for program developers, leaders, and all stakeholders to possess specific and deep knowledge of financial management.

Budgets

Because projected expenditures and projected revenue are the two key ingredients needed to develop a budget, once this information is available, the initial budget can be developed. As such, the budget allows you to view all the projected financial data and, more significantly, provides day-to-day guidance for financial management. Just as an effective logic model provides a road map for program implementation, an effective budget provides a road map for financial management. Moreover, "a budget must be seen as the concrete documentation of the planning process, bringing ideals into reality" (Lewis et al., 2007, p. 12). As such, budgets must never be thought of as static documents that serve a purpose in initial planning and are then left to be revisited in a year or more; rather, budgets should be integrated into day-to-day operations and, as such, can be fully utilized as a critical operational tool.

There are several types of budgets, including project-specific budgets, annual operating budgets, and multiyear budgets. Each is discussed below.

Project-Specific Budget

Project-specific budgets are typically created for mental health or human service projects that are time-specific. I use the term *project-specific* to denote that these are contained and finite with a clear start-and-stop funding cycle. For instance, funding may be provided to develop and implement a prevention program to address depression in adolescents. As such, a specific amount of funding has been made available; specific performance objectives have been established; and specific time frames for development, implementation, and evaluation of the project have been identified. These types of funding opportunities are project-based since there are clear stop-and-start time frames and it is understood that there is no plan for continuation of funding. As such, project-based budgeting is based on completing the agreed-to project and achieving the established outcomes. Table 9.3 provides an illustration of a project-based budget for a depression prevention project.

The project budget illustrates several items worth further discussion, first of which is staffing and salaries. As you can see, the budget provides for one full-time employee (FTE) who will be fully dedicated to the program. Because this particular project consists of a prevention program that involves individual assessment, a group-based psychoeducational curriculum, and 6-month follow-up telephone contact, only one primary staff person is needed. However, in addition to the full-time clinician, two other core components of the program require additional staffing: data collection activities and evaluation. Both of these jobs require limited time and will result in tangible outcomes. It should be noted here that in this project, the data collection is being conducted by someone other than the clinician to ensure objectivity in the data collection process—an important ethical consideration

Table 9.3 Project-Specific Budget Sample

Description	Calculation	Total Expenditure
Salaries		
Prevention clinician (1)	$34,500	$34,500
Data collection	$38,000 (0.10 FTE)	$3,800
Data evaluation (statistician)	$2,500	$2,500
Materials and supplies		
Transportation	$5.20 per client (160 clients)	$832
Building space	——————————————	In-kind donation
Paper	$0.04 (1,920 sheets)	$76.80
Binding	$2 (160 booklets)	$320
Assessment instruments	$453.20 (kit) $234.30 (additional tests = 160)	$687.50
Telephone (follow-up)	$2 (160)	$320
Salaries subtotal		*$40,800*
Supplies subtotal		*$2,236.30*
Project total		$43,036.30
Total funding request		**$43,036.30**

in research. Because the organization has an employee in another program who can perform the duty of data collection, the project funding will be used to support the amount of the employee's salary dedicated to the project, which in this case is 10%. This type of schema has benefits to both the project and the organization. The project benefits from someone already engaged in the organization's larger mission and, thus, someone who is likely competent and committed to the work. At the same time, the organization benefits from being able to offer a different type of work to an employee—most of whom are strongly attracted to a work life full of variety and, thus, have chosen a career in the mental health profession. On the other hand, the organization does not currently employ a clinician with the degree of statistical knowledge needed to evaluate the project. To provide this service, a set dollar amount is dedicated to supporting specific data analyses and report development (based on market research). By budgeting in this manner, the program developer is able to identify the specific *deliverables* required for payment to which both s/he and the statistician can agree. This type of work is particularly suited for contractual hiring because it is specialized and is associated with concrete outcomes.

The supplies needed to operate the program include assessment instruments, paper, and binding, for which specific costs have been identified. In addition to supplies, the budget includes funding for client transportation to and from the prevention workshops. To determine this projected cost, an analysis of the distance between the majority of clients and the office site was calculated and an average was computed. Telephone calls were also included in the budget, which account primarily for the follow-up data collection process. Finally, because the organization has existing office space that can be used for this project, the organization is providing use of this space as an *in-kind donation*. Whereas some funding opportunities specifically require a match from the applicant, others do not. This particular project did not require a match, but because space was needed for the project and was provided at no cost by the organization, this was reflected in the budget without a specified cost.

The total budget is $43,036.30, which also is the total request of funding (i.e., revenue). This is typical of project-based funding in that the requested revenue is often for a lump sum, and then the lump sum total is used to calculate the expenditures. Finally, because of the relatively small financial costs associated with the project and the need for resources from an existing program/organization (e.g., data collection staff, building), this project budget also illustrates why projects often complement an organization's core business, rather than constituting the primary operations.

Annual Operating Budget

Because project-based funding is typically short-term, human service organizations may engage in projects sporadically while focusing core business around continuous and renewable types of programming. Often, this means that funding is specified for a particular amount of time (typically 3 years or more), at the end of which, funding may be renewed. This type of ongoing programming is often based on contractual agreements or awards that have been granted by a contractor; however, it could also be based on the development of fee-for-service programming. For instance, you could receive a contract to provide family-focused treatment to women with HIV and their children. Or you could operate an outpatient clinic to treat adults with a variety of mental health challenges for which you receive third-party reimbursement from insurance companies or accept cash from clients. Regardless of the type of programming, from a financial perspective, receiving long-term funding for various types of programming requires the development of an annual operating budget. Similar to a project-based budget, an annual operating budget allows you to identify the projected expenditures and revenues over a 1-year time frame and provides ongoing financial guidance to program administrators and staff. Different than most project-based funding, funding for ongoing programs may be structured as a per diem or lump-sum payment (as discussed earlier), and therefore, this must be taken into consideration in the development of the budget. Table 9.4 provides an illustration of an annual operating budget.

Table 9.4 illustrates a fairly comprehensive annual operating budget for a residential program. Several elements require further explanation to increase understanding of the budget development process. The budget uses a line-item format, with each line indicating one category of the budget (Raggio, 2004); however, it is based on the budget for one program—not an entire organization. This particular example deals with a residential program that is funded through a state contract. The pay structure is based on a per diem cost paid per client, per day that the client is residing in the program. In residential programs, a full per diem is typically paid only when the individual remains in the program overnight, meaning that if a client enters the program in the morning and is discharged in the evening before spending the night, the organization is not eligible for full payment. Partial payment may be made in this case, but full payment typically is not. Along these same lines, the day that a client is discharged (exits) the program is typically not considered a billable day, but rather the last full billable day would be the preceding day in which the client spent the night in the home/facility. This has significant implications for budgeting and is also why residential programs refer to the number of beds filled in financial discussions.

The total amount of money available through the contract is $573,780 which is based on the residential program operating at full capacity (six clients) for the entire year. In order to account for times that the program may not be at capacity, a more conservative projection of revenue that the program can expect to receive is used (80% or $459,024), which is based on occupancy rates in comparable local programs that typically run between 80% to 86%. The purpose of this conservative projection is to ensure that the expenses that are contained in the budget are realistically based on what the program will receive in revenue. Eighty percent is determined not only to be a more accurate financial projection but also to possibly provide an

Table 9.4	Annual Operating Budget Sample: Small Group Home for Individuals With Dementia of the Alzheimer's Type

Revenue Type	Revenue	Unit	Total
State contract	$459,024	$262 per diem (80% occupancy)	$459,024
Donations	$9,500		$9,500
Total revenue			**$468,524**

Expense Type	Expense	Unit	Total
Personnel costs			
Administrator	$25,000	0.50 FTE	$25,000
Program manager	$42,000	1 FTE	$42,000
Case manager	$30,000	1 FTE	$30,000
Treatment technicians	$23,000	7 FTEs	$161,000
Nurse	$26,000	0.50 FTE	$26,000
Psychiatrist	$28,080	208 hrs @ $135	$28,080
Fringe benefits	$34,000	—	$34,000
Payroll tax	$32,000	—	$32,000
Professional liability insurance	$12,000	—	$12,000
Personnel subtotal			**$390,080**
Supplies and other			
Utilities	$6,100		$6,100
Groceries	$7,800		$7,800
Vehicle	$25,000		$25,000
Transportation	$3,276	7,800 miles @ $0.42	$3,276
Vehicle and home insurance	$4,800		$4,800
Vehicle maintenance	$2,000		$2,000
Office supplies	$3,000		$3,000
Telephone	$1,900		$1,900
Computers	$700	2	$1,400
Home maintenance	$1,000		$1,000
Household supplies	$2,400		$2,400
Furnishings	$16,000		$16,000
Supplies Subtotal			**$74,676**
Grand Total			**$464,756**

additional protection against overspending—both of which are essential to effective financial planning and management.

The budget is formatted so that revenue projections are at the top followed by a separate area for projected expenditures. In addition to the revenue that will come directly from the contract, it is also anticipated that approximately $9,500 will be donated to the program through fundraising activities. The estimate is conservative at $9,500 and is based solely on anticipated cash donations (not donation of supplies or other tangibles). Program leaders have a targeted first-year fundraising goal of $15,000, but because the program is new and therefore not well known to community members, $9,500 was projected in the budget as the minimum amount anticipated. Whereas the revenues in this sample are solely based on one contract and cash donations, other programs may receive revenue from multiple sources. In addition, the payment levels may differ. What is most critical is that in developing the annual operating budget, all potential sources and levels of revenue are identified and sound projections of the actual revenue anticipated for collection are made.

In the expense area of the operating budget, multiple items have been identified. First, all the staff positions that support the program are listed. In this section, you will see an expense, unit, and total, which each provide more detailed information about each line item on the budget. The administrator is listed as a half-time position (0.50 FTE), with FTE used to denote full-time employment status. Because there is a full-time program manager in place, this program is structured in a manner that allows for administrative oversight at a part-time level. In addition to the full-time program manager, there are eight other full-time employees that include one case manager and seven treatment technicians. The case manager handles all the resource coordination and overall case management activities, while the treatment technicians compose the direct care staff that provides 24-hour care and support to the clients. Because 11 of the employees assigned to the program are either part- or full-time staff persons, payroll taxes and fringe benefits for these employees must also be included in the expenses. Finally, a part-time nurse is dedicated to the program (0.50 FTE), and a psychiatrist is used by the program on a contractual basis. Because of the limited and highly specific work performed by the psychiatrist—psychiatric evaluation, medication monitoring, medical consultation—it is most appropriate from both a logistical as well as financial perspective to engage the psychiatrist as an independent contractor. A total amount of funding is specified in the contract, which reflects an average of 4 hours per week that is paid only upon completion of specific work. This type of employment relationship allows for the provision of specific work and promotes increased accountability—consistent with the specialized nature of the work. Finally, and also related to staff expenses, professional liability insurance serves to protect the organization against malpractice.

Each of the other expenses details the various costs associated with operating a residential program in which you must provide for the day-to-day support of individuals. All cost projections are annualized and include direct care supports, such as groceries, utilities, and transportation; program-related expenses, such as office supplies and computers; and joint expenses (client and staff), such as the telephone.

Also highlighted in this budget, staffing expenses far outweigh non-personnel-related expenses at a rate of more than five times more (as discussed previously). Finally, the small gap between revenue and expenses is important to note. Because the projected annual operating budget must be based on the most accurate projections of both revenue and expenses, there should be a very small gap between expenses and revenues, with more revenue anticipated than expenses. This is because as a nonprofit operation, the financial objective is to have a balanced budget that demonstrates that all funds are dedicated directly to the program's operations.

Multiyear Operating Budgets

Directly related to annual operating budgets, multiyear operating budgets are generally created for long-term programming. The development of multiyear budgets allows you to consider any financial changes that may be planned from one year to the next (e.g., increased capacity) as well as increases in funding that may occur from one year to the next (or conversely, decreases in the budget). Multiyear budgets are typically developed for a 3-year period. Multiyear budgets contain the same information as annual operating budgets but with multiple years included, as well as all revenue and expense projections associated with each year. In addition to the benefit that multiyear budgets provide to long-term financial management, these types of budgets can also be particularly helpful in spreading costs over time for large purchases, such as a client information system or a building.

Each of the three types of budgets is used for specific purposes, and as such, each has unique and similar value. It is imperative that program developers be familiar with all three and that program developers/mental health professionals possess the necessary knowledge and skills to develop program budgets.

Financial Management

The development of a sound initial budget sets the stage for effective financial management to begin; however, it in no way ensures it. In fact, as you have seen above, initial financial planning is largely based on the identification of cost allocations that can most effectively support the program or project while remaining within the anticipated revenue to be received. In addition, it is based on the ability to make the most accurate initial revenue and expense projections. Subsequently, sound financial management is predicated on internal monitoring and reporting processes, public reporting, and external oversight.

Internal Monitoring and Reporting Processes

Budget management (aka financial management of the program) is the responsibility of the program administrator, and as such, the program administrator (i.e., leader, manager, supervisor) must ensure that mechanisms are created that enable close monitoring to occur. Whereas individual programs and/or organizations may have either minimal standards in place or quite elaborate systems, all program administrators should minimally have several standards in place to aid in managing the budget. Each of these standards is illustrated in Table 9.5, the *Program Administrator's Financial Management Aid Checklist*. The checklist can be used as a tool to ensure that the necessary standards are in place.

Whereas at this point the importance of financial management knowledge should be well appreciated, a bit of further elaboration on some of the items identified in Table 9.5 might be helpful. As you can see, monitoring of expenditures and revenues is the most critical aspect of financial management. Program administrators must concern themselves equally with financial management of their programs as they do with the clinical operations, since these are interdependent activities. Ensuring that ad hoc monitoring and review of expenditures occurs—meaning a quick review of expenditures immediately following purchase and a comparison of the actual with the projected expenditure—allows you to maintain an ongoing eye on the budget, thus, allowing you to take action when necessary and avoid any long-term buildup of financial issues that may present challenges more difficult to overcome. This type of monitoring is simply absorbed into the day-to-day activities of the manager and is an informal process. On a monthly basis, all the financial activities of the previous month should be reviewed with a comparison of actual versus projected revenues and expenses. Any gaps that are identified between the two should require the development

Table 9.5 Program Administrator's Financial Management Aid Checklist

Financial Management Aid	Status
Knowledge of financial planning and management	
Mechanism by which to ensure that all staff are trained in financial management	
Development of a program/organizational culture that promotes a keen understanding of financial management and the integral role it plays in programming	
Immediate and direct knowledge of all expenditures and the rationale for the expenditures	
Ad hoc comparisons of actual expenditures with projected expenditures and an established plan to compensate for any over-expenditures within the shortest time frame possible	
Monthly review of all revenues and expenses and comparison to projections	
Accounting protocols that include immediate and complete follow-up for all uncollected revenues within 30 days of billing	
Brief monthly review and reporting of expenditures and revenues that includes plans to compensate for any over-expenditures and/or collect any unpaid revenues during the following month	
Comprehensive formal quarterly reporting that includes all elements of operations (e.g., program implementation and outcomes, staffing and training, budget and financial management)	
Mechanisms in place to make any necessary adjustments to the budget as a result of significant changes to revenue or expenditures	

and institution of a plan to resolve them during the following month. Similar to ad hoc daily monitoring, this will help ensure that financial issues can be quickly identified and resolved.

On a more formal basis, quarterly reports should be developed that provide for a comprehensive review of the program's finances as part of a more comprehensive program review. This type of formal and comprehensive review allows for increased understanding of the essential role that financial management plays in overall program implementation and allows for broad-based discussion about the comprehensive program operations. Whereas the development of a written report provides the program administrator the necessary opportunity for a thorough review, how this information is communicated both to staff and to superiors for additional oversight and monitoring is equally important. In addition to the dissemination of a written report, the information should be verbally communicated and discussed with staff through staff meetings or other communication forums. In addition, a venue should exist in which the report can be presented to superiors for dialogue, oversight, and engagement in any additional planning that might be needed to tackle any financial management issues. The same format should be used on an annual basis, simply providing for a review of the previous year rather than the previous quarter.

Each of the items identified in Table 9.5 accounts for internal practices that together promote sound financial management. The use of these protocols may work to create an environment in which the role of finance remains central to program operations and that contains mechanisms by which to effectively monitor finances and quickly resolve any issues so that long-term program sustainability is not jeopardized.

The Role of the Board in Financial Management and Oversight

Because the board of directors plays a primary role in governance of the organization, a key part of this oversight is related to the financial management of the organization. Not only are boards responsible for approving the policies of the organization, they also "share collective responsibility for the fiscal and programmatic aspects of the organization's performance" (Gibelman & Furman, 2008, p. 75). As such, boards should participate in the approval of all budgets. This may not be the case in many organizations, but with increased scrutiny on the financial management of organizations, board members should heed the current climate and become much more effectively involved in financial decision making, particularly since they can indeed be held accountable.

Since the inception of the Sarbanes-Oxley Act, board members have no choice but to become much more involved in the ongoing oversight of their organizations. Sarbanes-Oxley is guided by fiscal transparency. As such, organizations that are mandated to comply with the law require that the chief executive officer and the chief financial officer certify that the organization's financial statements are accurate (Grunewald, 2007), thus, this is an area that the board is responsible for overseeing. Whereas board members may have previously played a more minor role within certain human service organizations, in the 21st century, such passivity is no longer possible. Boards must ensure that the organization does indeed have the necessary controls in place for effective financial management and that its role provides for essential oversight that can stand the test of fiscal transparency.

Public Reporting

Whereas internal monitoring and review ensures that the program can be effectively managed from a financial perspective, public reporting allows for public disclosure of financial activities—a requirement for all nonprofit organizations and publicly held companies. There are two primary methods used for public reporting or public disclosure of finances of nonprofit social service organizations. These include the annual report that is issued to stakeholders and the tax return that is submitted to the IRS and is available for public inspection. For nonprofit organizations, the tax form that must be filed with the IRS is the 990.

Annual Report

The annual report is a written document that is published on an annual basis to reflect financial and other relevant organizational information (e.g., types of programs, board of directors, donors). Whereas annual reports often provide a venue for marketing and disseminating information about the organization's programs, clients, and staff, the annual report ultimately provides a mechanism for disclosing financial information to the organization's stakeholders. As such, financial reporting can serve both as a coordinating and monitoring function (Mayers, 2004). Annual reports are typically available in both print and electronic format and often provide straightforward yet comprehensive information about programs and organizations.

Tax Return Documents

As stated earlier, nonprofit mental health and human service organizations are exempted from payment of specific taxes and are thus given the designation of tax exemption. Because of this tax-exemption designation, these organizations are required to submit specific information to the IRS, and the organizations must make specific information available for public inspection. The following information from the IRS website (www.irs.gov) further explains the rules for public disclosure:

> An exempt organization must make available for public inspection and copying its annual return. . . . Returns must be available for a three-year period beginning with the due date of the return (including any extension of time for filing). (IRS, 2010)

External Oversight

Both the annual report and the public disclosure rules related to the tax returns of nonprofit social service organizations provide for public disclosure of the organization's finances. However, other mechanisms provide for external oversight of the organization's financial management: regular auditing and state and federal tax filing, review, and possible audits.

Regularly Scheduled Auditing

For external oversight of financial activities, organizations hire independent auditors for broad-based regular monitoring. Typically, auditors review financial transactions on a regular basis (e.g., quarterly, semiannually), requesting further information and follow-up and, ultimately, certifying that the financial records have been independently reviewed. "The audit is typically conducted by an independent public accounting firm that applies appropriate industry accounting standards" (Gibelman & Furman, 2008, p. 65). The audit can be anxiety-producing for program developers, administrators, and finance staff, but if an effective financial management system is in place, major surprises should be greatly reduced (Lewis et al., 2007). More significantly, external auditing protects the organization against financial negligence or other troublesome issues while providing an added layer of financial review that ultimately can further inform the organization's operations.

In addition to contributing to sound fiscal policy, regular audit reports are also often required by funding sources both as a regulatory process and when applying for new and/or continued funding. Also, audit reports may be required by accrediting bodies as part of the comprehensive accreditation review process.

Tax Return Process

Just as we all must file personal taxes on a regular basis, so must all businesses file taxes. With regard to nonprofit mental health and human service organizations, there are specific tax forms that must be filed. By requiring this information, the federal government provides another layer of oversight and review for the organization. Further, the government has the ability to require further information or explanation, penalize the organization, or take other action against the organization as a result of lack of payment, falsification of information, or other problems with notification, filing, or payment of taxes.

As you can see, financial management is a complex process consisting of multiple layers, each with its own attendant nuances. From internal monitoring and reporting to public reporting and external oversight, each aspect has its own unique yet overlapping role to play in the financial management process of the organization.

Revenue Diversification and Financial Stability

In the previous chapter, we discussed the importance of revenue diversification with regard to program sustainability; however, the role that revenue diversification may play in the broader organizational stability is even more significant. Revenue diversification simply refers to receiving funding from multiple sources and, as such, may offer financial protection to an organization—when diversification exists, the loss of funding from one source does not necessarily equal a total loss of organizational funding. And because the climate in mental health and human services in the 21st century continues to be highly volatile, the protection organizations have may indicate which ones will not only survive but thrive.

A modest body of research has been conducted on revenue diversification and nonprofit organizations, with more recent findings consistently indicating a positive relationship between diversification of revenue sources and financial stability (Carroll & Stater, 2008; Frumkin & Keating, 2002; Greenlee, 2002; Greenlee & Trussel, 2000; Keating, Fischer, Gordon, & Greenlee, 2005). Frumkin and Keating identified revenue diversification as a specific strategy to minimize financial volatility. Illustrating similar results, Greenlee and Trussel and Greenlee found that revenue diversification reduced the likelihood that an organization would experience a net loss over several years or decrease its program expenses, both indicating the long-term stability associated with revenue diversification. Keating et al. examined the opposite of revenue diversification by evaluating the effects of revenue concentration and found that such concentration leads to a significant decline in revenue and much greater risk to the sustainability of the organization.

Finally, in one of the largest studies to date, Carroll and Stater (2008) examined financial records of 294,543 public charities between 1991 and 2003 to better understand the relationship between revenue diversification and nonprofit organizations. In short, the findings revealed that revenue diversification promoted organizational sustainability and reduced financial volatility and that, conversely, organizations relying primarily on contributions experienced much greater instability. Interestingly, they also found that larger, more growth-oriented nonprofit organizations experienced much less volatility and that nonprofits located in urban areas had more stable revenue over time, highlighting the notions that both size and place matter.

Therefore, there must be concerted efforts made to ensure that financial planning and management emphasize revenue diversification and continuous monitoring of the comprehensive revenue portfolio.

Developing the Budget

Equipped with both the knowledge and skills needed for initial financial planning and financial management, you must take the first step and develop the program budget. As with all other components of the comprehensive program development model, the step involving budget development is directly informed by previous steps. However, differing from other steps of the planning process, developing the initial budget also requires some knowledge of anticipated revenue, thus creating the need to be informed by previous steps as well as subsequent steps in the planning process.

The degree of knowledge pertaining to projected revenue that can be used to develop your initial budget will vary based on the type of program you are proposing and the manner in which you are seeking funding. For instance, in some program development efforts, the amount of available funding will be known to you at the point of budget development. This is particularly true if you are bidding on a contract offered by a local, state, or federal governmental agency; philanthropic organization; or other contracting agency. It may also be the case if you are applying for a project or program through a grant process in which the amount of available funding has been specified. Often in this case, funding parameters are provided that consist of *floors* (i.e., lowest level of funding available) and *ceilings* (i.e., highest level of funding available). Whereas these provide broad guidance for budget development, it is up to you to identify the revenue target that will be used to support expense projections. If you are proposing a new program in which a specific call for proposals has not been issued, and you intend to pitch the program to foundations and/or other funding organizations, you should base your funding request on existing levels of funding supporting similar programs. Thus, the results of the market analysis will be particularly useful in determining costs and the subsequent funding request. So what all this means is that in order to develop the initial budget, you must have a sound understanding of what level of funding support may be available for your program.

Once you have gained the necessary information regarding potential available funding, you are able to use this information as the parameters to develop the expense portion of the budget. Depending on the nature of funding support that you are seeking, you will develop either a project budget or an annual operating budget. In addition to an annual budget, funding sources may also require that you submit a multiyear budget.

Revisiting the Logic Model and the Staffing Infrastructure

Equipped with this knowledge of potential available revenue, developing the budget then requires specific work on the expense portion. Three specific data sets that you previously compiled are needed to inform the expense budget:

1. The logic model, outlining the program's core components (e.g., interventions, services)

2. The staffing infrastructure

3. The results of the market analysis

The staffing infrastructure is used specifically to determine costs associated with the necessary staff positions, inform the number of each type of position, and assign the status of each position (e.g., part-time). The results of the market analysis should also be revisited here, particularly with regard to staff pay. As such, it is helpful to use information regarding potential competitor pay to inform your staffing pay structure, just as it is necessary to fully understand the staffing qualification levels of competitors for use in establishing your own.

Expenses related to other aspects of the program should be informed by the logic model to ensure that all costs associated with the program's implementation are effectively reflected in the expense budget. Again, this is guided by the notion that the budget is simply an illustration of the clinical program in financial terms. Clinical supplies such as assessment tools and workbooks, office supplies and equipment, and accreditation fees are all items that may be included in the "Supplies and Materials" section of the budget, but again, each expense must be directly related to the program. Moreover, each expense must be thoroughly justified as critical to program implementation (e.g., intake assessment instruments) or program sustainability (e.g., program evaluation materials, accreditation fees).

Once you have identified all necessary expenses and have computed total expenditures, you are able to revisit and complete the revenue portion of the budget. At this point, you will either be able to use the total expenses to identify the total revenue needed to fully support your program, knowing that you may need to pursue more than one funding source if your expense needs far outweigh the available revenue, or use the gap in expense/revenue projections to revise the expense budget. This type of interplay or back-and-forth movement between the revenue and expense portion of the budget is common and is an integral part of developing the initial budget. In addition to the numerous learning benefits associated with the challenges of lining up revenue and expense predictions, this process may result in the knowledge that you simply cannot afford to engage in certain programming because the gap between available revenue and the projected expenses is far too big.

It is also during this time of initial budget development that you should work directly with a finance specialist, either through independent consultation or through the organization, if you are part of a larger organization with finance staff. Whereas it is essential that program developers and administrators possess thorough knowledge of financial planning and management, it is also necessary that individuals with specialized financial knowledge and experience be utilized to provide input to the initial budget. This simply ensures that you begin with the most effective initial budget through expert review, consultation, and input.

Summary

Financial planning and financial management are indeed essential to comprehensive program development. Engaging in initial budget development allows for a much deeper understanding of the fundamental relationship that exists between funding and programming and, as such, provides the necessary context to fully appreciate not only the cost of programming but the need for advocacy to maintain and/or increase funding of specific treatment and/or services. This is knowledge not easily come by, but once you are equipped, the relationship between what you do and how you are able to do it can be significantly enhanced. Particularly in the mental health and human services, the interdependent, at times frighteningly tenuous relationship between funding and programming is one that is both exciting and nail-bitingly frustrating. However, as clinicians and program developers, it is our duty to be not only well informed but competent in all aspects of program development, including finance, so that we can effectively lend our voice to pivotal discussions regarding funding and finances.

Unfortunately, I still hear clinicians stating, "This is too businesslike—I am a clinician." This is highly unfortunate for those speaking it, but more so, this is unfortunate for us and for those whom we wish to serve. When clinicians fail to recognize that mental health and human services are indeed a business, they put our collective work in jeopardy and run the risk of neglecting the individuals that they wish to treat and/or serve. In order for any business to be successful, it must be well planned and effectively managed, and financial planning and financial management are critical to achieving this. Therefore, rather than viewing financial management as a burden, we should view it as an essential component of our livelihood.

Moreover, the inability of any professional to successfully manage a program and/or organization may have significant implications on the industry as a whole, since financial support is almost solely provided by public and/or philanthropic funding. Indeed, if we cannot prove that we can effectively handle the funding that has been entrusted to us, future funding may not be available to us. Knowing this, it is my hope that the last time I heard a clinician disregard the need for business knowledge and skills was, indeed, the last time.

CASE ILLUSTRATION

Kathy and Judy recently were awarded a contract to provide vocational assessment and employment placement services to individuals recently displaced from the workforce. Because they had invested the necessary amount of time and effort in the development of the budget, they were confident that the program could be effectively implemented within the projected cost parameters. But they wanted to ensure that they had appropriate mechanisms in place to continuously monitor the program's finances. In addition, since they realized how important it was that they had developed the budget—thus, allowing them to better understand all the aspects of the new program—they wanted to involve the program staff in the ongoing financial monitoring process. They knew that by doing so, they would ensure that those most involved in the program were able to also be engaged in this most essential aspect of the program's operations.

To accomplish this, they devised a plan that outlined the methods by which the two of them, the staff, and the relevant stakeholders could continuously examine and monitor the finances. The methods involved the following:

- A weekly report of service activity indicating all clients served, types of services provided, and billed amounts to be compiled by the Finance Department and distributed to all program staff
- A biweekly report of outstanding payments to be compiled by the Finance Department and distributed to all program staff
- A biweekly budget report indicating all expenditures and revenue to date to be compiled by the Finance staff and distributed to all program staff
- Weekly staff meetings facilitated by Judy and Kathy in which all the financial reports would be discussed as part of the overall program progress updates and ongoing program planning efforts
- Time set aside during the staff meetings to develop strategies for any adjustments that had to be made based on where the program's finances were in relation to the budget and assignments of specific program staff to work directly with the Finance staff to recoup any unpaid overdue bills
- Purposefully integrating the program's finances into other both informal and formal dialogue with program staff

- The adoption of a comprehensive quarterly report format that tied finances directly to all other aspects of program operations, compiled collaboratively by various members of the staff and presented to the rest of the staff on a quarterly basis as well as to the board of directors
- Monthly meetings between the CFO and Kathy and Judy to review and discuss the program's finances
- A requirement for Judy and Kathy, in concert with the CFO and the CEO, to file a formal Financial Management Correction Plan with the board any time the net balance of the budget fell below 5%

By setting each of these activities in place, Kathy and Judy felt confident that the financial management of the program would be conducted in the most transparent manner. In addition, by involving all program staff, they hoped that they would be taking an active step toward improving the financial knowledge base of their staff, thus promoting staff development while offering further protection to the program's operations. Finally, they believed that these activities would promote significant accountability for the two of them, the program staff and administrators, and the board—further ensuring fiscal integrity and ongoing fiscal health.

PROGRAM BUDGET EXERCISE

To consolidate all that you have learned about financial planning, develop your own program budget. To do so, complete the following steps:

1. Using the proposed program and organizational staffing structure that you developed previously, develop the expense portion of an annual operating budget.

2. Use the expense portion of the *Annual Operating Budget Sample* provided in Table 9.4 as a guide to formatting your budget.

3. In the expense budget, identify all staff positions with the following information: number of each position, employment status (e.g., full-time), pay, payroll taxes, fringe benefits, and any other staff-related costs.

4. Identify all the supplies, materials, and other expenses associated with the program.

5. Subtotal the "Staff" and "Supplies and Materials" expense sections and provide a grand total.

6. Develop a brief summary (three pages or less) justifying each of the costs associated with the program.

References

Carroll, D. A., & Stater, K. J. (2008). Revenue diversification in nonprofit organizations: Does it lead to financial stability? *Journal of Public Administration
Research and Theory, 19,* 947–966.

Carver, J. (2006). *Boards that make a difference: A new design for leadership in
nonprofit and public organizations* (3rd ed.). San Francisco: Jossey-Bass.

Frumkin, P., & Keating, E. (2002). *The risks and rewards of nonprofit revenue concentration* (Working Paper). Cambridge, MA: Hauser Center for Nonprofit
Organizations.

Gibelman, M., & Furman, R. (2008). *Navigating human service organizations.* Chicago:
Lyceum.

Greenlee, J. (2002). Revisiting the prediction of financial vulnerability. *Nonprofit
Management and Leadership, 13,* 17–31.

Greenlee, J., & Trussell, J. (2000). Estimating the financial vulnerability of charitable
organizations. *Nonprofit Management and Leadership, 11,* 199–210.

Grunewald, D. (2007). The Sarbanes-Oxley Act will change the governance of nonprofit organizations. *Journal of Business Ethics, 80,* 399–401.

Horejsi, C. R., & Garthwait, C. L. (2004). *The social work practicum: A guide and
workbook for students* (3rd ed.). Boston: Allyn & Bacon.

Internal Revenue Service. (2010). *Exempt organizations: Documents subject to
public disclosure.* Retrieved September 13, 2010, from http://www.irs.gov/
charities/article/0,,id=135008,00.html

Katz, R. D. (2005). The not-for-profit sector: No longer about just raising funds.
Journal of Private Equity, 8, 110–113.

Keating, E., Fischer, M., Gordon, T., & Greenlee, J. (2005). *Assessing financial
vulnerability in the nonprofit sector* (Working Paper No. 27). Cambridge, MA:
Hauser Center for Nonprofit Organizations.

Kettner, P. M., Moroney, R. M., & Martin, L. L. (2008). *Designing and managing
programs: An effectiveness-based approach.* Thousand Oaks, CA: Sage.

Lewis, J. A., Packard, T. R., & Lewis, M. D. (2007). *Management of human service
programs* (4th ed.). Belmont, CA: Thomson Learning.

Mayers, R. S. (2004). *Financial management for nonprofit human service agencies*
(2nd ed.). Springfield, IL: Charles C. Thomas.

Raggio, D. (2004). *Fostering career paths to independence: Model proposal.*
Unpublished manuscript, San Diego State University.

Develop the Proposal

Learning Objectives

1. Discuss methods that can be used to justify professional and/or organizational capability

2. Explain the differences between a grant writer and a program developer

3. Identify three skills of proposal writing

4. Discuss the role of collaboration with partners and or other providers in proposal development

5. Discuss the purpose of including letters of support in proposals

6. Explain how each of the preceding steps of the comprehensive program development model relates to proposal development

HOW DIFFICULT CAN THIS BE?

Dan had been the director of mental health and substance abuse treatment at a large nonprofit outpatient clinic for the past 4 years; over the past 2 years, revenue had declined by 10%. Because of this decline in revenue, Dan was interested in looking for new business and possibly branching out into a new area. With the recent legislative changes that had created an onslaught of casinos in the area and with new state monies allocated to gambling addiction prevention and treatment, Dan was particularly interested in exploring funding for the treatment of gambling addiction, even though this was not an area in which he or anyone in his office specialized.

When a Request for Proposal (RFP) was issued by the state for a gambling addiction treatment program, Dan was immediately interested in pursuing it. Because Dan's clinic worked directly with insurance companies and individuals who privately paid, no one in the clinic had experience developing a proposal. Dan did not think this was necessarily a barrier, and in fact, he thought, *How difficult could it be?*—especially since the proposal was not due for 3 weeks, and Joe knew he could probably take care of it much quicker than that. Rather than make more of it than need be, Dan decided to finish up with some other projects he had been working on and take care of the proposal the following week.

When Dan started working on the proposal, he was surprised at the level of detail that was required. The proposal requirements included a review of literature on gambling addiction treatment, the use of an evidence-based model to treat gambling addiction, and identification of staff with appropriate credentials to provide the treatment. Although Dan felt as though he was in over his head, he had already told his president and staff that he was going to take care of this proposal—not to mention the fact that he had also assured them that it would be a "piece of cake."

Because Dan still had his own clients to see and supervision sessions to facilitate, in addition to his other administrative duties, he spent the next 10 days working late into the night trying to learn all he could about gambling addiction. He was able to piece together a literature review and a basic program design. Since he did not know anyone who specialized in gambling addiction, he put together a basic organizational chart, stating that clinicians with specific experience in gambling addiction would be hired once the program received funding. The day before the proposal was due, Dan was exhausted. Although he realized the proposal was weak, he was determined to see it through; so he quickly read the submission instructions and took another glance at the proposal requirements. Staring him in the face was the requirement for a budget narrative report, detailing each budget item. Dan thought, *How did I miss this?* Then his eyes landed on another requirement that he had missed: three letters of support! Dan thought he could probably knock out the budget narrative that day, but how in the world would he get three letters of support by the next day? Plus, he questioned whether he was even comfortable asking anyone to write a letter with such short notice. Dan decided he would go ahead and submit the proposal without the letters of support and claim ignorance if asked about them—after all, how much bearing could they have on the proposal? The county needed someone to provide the treatment, and he was willing to do it. Dan was excited when he received a letter back from the county a week later, and he quickly opened it. The letter indicated that his proposal would not be reviewed since it had failed to meet the basic requirements outlined in the RFP, which included a list of key staff persons and their credentials and three letters of support.

CONSIDERING DAN

1. What mistakes did Dan make, and how could he have avoided them?

2. What did this failed project cost Joe and his clinic, both in terms of concrete costs and other costs?

3. What advice would you give Dan about developing a proposal in the future?

About This Chapter

This chapter is specifically dedicated to the proposal development process and the various factors that are related to this all-important step. Just as was the case with Steps VI and VII, the order of Steps VII and VIII should not necessarily be viewed as fixed since in some cases, Step VII (Develop the Financial Management Plan) may be completed after developing the proposal. As such, the sequence in which these steps occur may differ for each new project, depending on how you move forward in the program development process. But this step does presume that Step VI (Identify and Evaluate Potential Funding Sources) is complete and, therefore, picks up from the point when a viable funding opportunity has been identified.

Since proposal writing has become a relatively big business associated with the human services field—with numerous how-to books written on the subject, a regular flurry of grant-writing workshops offered across the country, and an endless number of grant writers available for hire—the intent of this chapter is not to provide a *how-to* on proposal development. Rather, this chapter is designed to investigate the proposal development process to increase your knowledge about all that developing the proposal entails.

This investigation begins with an examination of several considerations of proposal development, including time needed in proposal development, the depth of material required in a proposal, the importance of justifying professional and/or organizational capability to effectively implement the proposed project or program, the role of collaboration in proposal development, and the purpose of and need for letters of support.

Following this discussion, we will explore several major aspects of proposal development, including the use of grant writers versus program developers in proposal development, planning the work of proposal development, skills of proposal writing, the use of internal reviewers, and other considerations in proposal development. Finally, a case illustration will reinforce the chapter's key points.

STEP VIII: DEVELOP THE PROPOSAL

Developing the Proposal

Have you ever heard this? "This opportunity looks perfect for us—we can do this!" or "If they were able to get funding for that, we certainly can." How about this one? "How could we not have been selected?" or "I cannot believe they did not find our program worthy of funding." Unfortunately, these are all common exhortations in the world of funding for the human services. Too often, the process of securing funding for mental health and human service programs is underestimated, and as a result, individuals often believe that doing so does not present too difficult a challenge. As a result of underestimating the rigor involved in the proposal process, applicants may become quite upset when they are not awarded funding—as Dan learned. As Dan also learned, you must follow the guidelines of a proposal if you are interested in having it reviewed. Indeed, one of the major reasons behind rejection of proposals is simply failure to follow the instructions (New, 2001).

Engaging in due diligence with regard to exploring and identifying the most appropriate funding opportunities to pursue ensures that, minimally, you will be investing your time wisely when you do decide to apply for funding. But these are only the initial steps, whereas actually developing the proposal for funding is the final step toward potentially securing funding. When you are interested in pursuing funding for program development and/or research activities, there are several issues that require serious consideration: the time required to develop a proposal, the depth of material needed for the proposal, justification of professional and/or organizational capability to effectively implement a program, the role of collaboration in proposal development, and letters of support.

Time Considerations in Proposal Development

Developing a grant proposal for a mental health or human service program or project is a time-consuming process that requires a tremendous amount of work. Whereas the precise extent of a grant proposal is often dictated by the specific funding source, I would estimate that many medium- to large-scale proposals (i.e., awards of $100,000 per year or more) may require anywhere from 1 to 6 months (Devine, 2009) and from 40 to 100 hours to complete. For most of us, that means that we must plan for at least 1 month of our work year to be dedicated to proposal development. And this is typically spread over a greater amount of time, since often only a portion of our workload can be dedicated to grant writing because of our other regular duties. Indeed, when I have the luxury of spending 8 hours a week on a grant proposal, I am happiest, because I know that I should be able to steadily complete it in about 4 weeks. Having said this, please note that these are simply broad time parameters since there is so much variation in the types of proposals required for specific funding opportunities.

In addition, the specific type of funding opportunity often dictates the time frame involved in completion of a proposal. In fact, there are basically three types of funding opportunity specific to time frames for accepting applications:

1. Open application periods, which are most common to funding opportunities from philanthropic organizations

2. Continuous funding opportunities with annual submission deadlines, which are common in clinical research grants and also tied to specific continuously funded areas of interest of philanthropic organizations

3. Funding opportunities with specific submission deadlines, which may be released one time only or on an annual basis for more than 1 year

Many funding opportunities offered by the county, state, and federal governments to mental health and human service programs fall into this third category, with very specific submission deadlines. Unfortunately, it is not uncommon for there to be a time frame of 6 weeks or less from the time a funding opportunity is announced to the time applications are due. This often means that the application must be completed quickly and also reinforces viewing proposal development as part of one's regular workload. Particularly in the case of very short time frames for completion of applications, proposal development must temporarily become *the* work priority— an easier pill to swallow if these activities are already considered part of your regular activities.

Of course, developing grant proposals often requires the input of more than one person and, therefore, it is not only the time of the individual leading the proposal development that is of issue but the time of everyone who is involved in the process. And because of the complex nature of some proposals, more than one person is needed to plan and carry out the writing (Homan, 2004). The issue of time is probably one of the most surprising aspects to first-time proposal developers. This may be particularly true for those of us who have been conditioned to think, "It has a 30-page limit, so it couldn't possibly require too much time or be too difficult—I have written longer papers in school for just one minor assignment." Indeed, page limits can seem like a positive aspect insofar as they should reflect the degree of time required; however, the old adage about *quality not quantity* fits well here. Similar to any effective research paper, in developing a sophisticated piece of writing, the amount of words and pages is not necessarily an accurate reflection of the depth of the material. Therefore, appreciation for the complexity involved in most grant proposals and the need for sufficient time to do an adequate job is crucial.

Depth of the Proposal

Another aspect that often surprises first-time proposal developers is the fact that page limits may refer to the narrative portion of the proposal and not to other required documents. Often, other documents may need to be developed to be submitted with the proposal. These additional documents may include

- budgets,
- biographical sketches of key program staff,
- job descriptions,
- organizational charts,
- project timelines, and
- logic models.

These documents often are attachments to the narrative, and each may require a good deal of time to develop. In addition, existing documents about the applicant organization and proposed project staff may need to be gathered to be included as part of the appendix. These may include such items as

- resumes,
- past financial statements,
- verification of business status,
- certifications,
- professional and/or program licensure,
- verification of accreditation status, and
- other existing documents.

Finally, documents from potential collaborators, supporters, and/or other authorizing agents may need to be requested and provided with the proposal. These may include

- letters of support,
- memoranda of understanding or agreement indicating collaborative partners, and
- approval by authorizing agencies or general support for the program/ project.

These documents can require a great deal of time and energy since they are predicated on not only existing but supportive relationships with other organizations. Therefore, if these relationships are not already in place, it may prove a barrier to meeting this requirement based on the time frame in which the proposal must be developed.

To better illustrate the amount of material that may be required in a proposal, what follows is an example of a funding opportunity for mental health and substance abuse services, authorized by the Department of Health and Human Services, Substance Abuse and Mental Health Services Administration (SAMHSA; 2009):

- Application format requirements
- Application face page
- Table of contents
- PHS 5161-1 HHS checklist
- Budget
- Budget justification
- Staffing plan/personnel requirements
- Assurances
- Certifications

- Project abstract
- Program narrative
- Program-specific forms (e.g., logic model, organizational chart)
- Attachments

As you can see, the application requires far more than a narrative of the program, and in fact, the narrative is simply listed as one of the required documents for this proposal.

In addition to the various documents that are needed for a comprehensive proposal, funders may specify program-specific requirements that must be met, some of which are very focused. For instance, see the following excerpt from the funding opportunity discussed above:

> Applicants for this funding opportunity are expected to (1) describe the target population and its need for mental health/substance abuse services; (2) present a service delivery plan that demonstrates responsiveness to the identified needs of the target population; and (3) present a sound business plan that links the goals and objectives from the service delivery plan to the budget. . . . The populations served by these programs are medically underserved populations in urban and rural areas; migratory and seasonal agricultural workers and their families; homeless people, including children and families; and residents of publicly-subsidized housing. (SAMHSA, 2009)

As you can see, this snapshot of some of the requirements provides a great deal of essential information critical to proposal development. As such, the funding source has communicated pertinent information about the opportunity to the applicant, including the

- defined target population,
- need for applicants to provide evidence of the target population's needs for services,
- requirement that applicants produce a sound program model to effectively address the needs of the target population, and
- requirement that applicants develop a comprehensive budget that directly relates to program implementation.

Although this information may have been communicated very concisely, you can see just how detailed it is. Essentially, you should usually be able to review this type of snapshot—common to funding opportunities—and gain a firm understanding of the specific funding opportunity.

After viewing both of the requirement sections of this funding opportunity, you should note that all the requirements have already been covered in this text, including identifying and justifying a target population, providing evidence of need, designing a program model and implementation plan, determining staffing structure and requirements, setting a budget that is tied directly to program implementation and outcomes, and providing budget justification. This further reinforces the effectiveness and relevance of the comprehensive program development model presented in this text and again reflects the need for this type of systematic approach to this work.

In their discussion of the merits of a proposal, Lewis, Packard, and Lewis (2007) identify several questions that may be useful in evaluating a proposal:

- How well does the applicant demonstrate that there is a real need for the proposed project?
- How clear and attainable are the project's objectives?
- Does the proposal spell out a plan of action that suits project goals and objectives?
- Is the program model supported by research and best practices?
- Is the applying agency likely to be able to carry out the proposed project and meet the specified goals within the suggested time frame?
- Is the budget clearly thought out and appropriate for the scope of the project?
- Are plans for evaluation and dissemination well documented, feasible, and appropriate?

If you understand the amount of material needed in most grant proposals, it is much easier to appreciate the amount of time and work required to complete this process. At this point, though, I do want to remind you that this discussion of developing grant proposals solely pertains to program/project-based and clinical research-based grants—consistent with the focus of the book. Because other types of funding exist for equipment and other non-program/project/research grants and because the process for applying for such funds is much different (i.e., much less rigorous), it is important to clarify the difference here so that you fully understand the type of grant proposals to which this chapter (and book) is referring.

The development of program/project grant proposals is indeed a tremendous undertaking, particularly with regard to time considerations and the volume of work involved. In addition to these two key considerations, applicants must consider if they have both the organizational and professional/individual capability needed to justify that they are capable of successfully implementing a proposed program.

Justifying Professional and Organizational Capability

A key requirement of most funding opportunities is that justification is provided as to the capability of both the organization and a lead individual/ other staff to carry out the intended project. In terms of organizational capability, this is typically provided by official documents that verify an organization's corporate status; board of directors; fiscal health and banking status; administrative staffing structure; licensure and/or other relevant credentials; accreditation status; facility; hardware, software, Internet, and other communication and electronic capabilities; and other relevant aspects of the business. For each of these factors, you may be required to provide evidence of the organization's functional status as an eligible entity and one that has the organizational capabilities to implement the proposed project based on previous business experience.

Whereas official documents provide justification of organizational capability, other types of evidence are needed to prove that the applicant has an individual capable of carrying out the proposed project. This individual is usually referred to as the project director or principal investigator and is an essential requirement of most funding opportunities. While organizational capability is a prerequisite to apply for funding, identifying an individual who is fully capable of leading the project is equally necessary. Again, depending on the type of funding opportunity you are pursuing, the requirements of the project leader will vary.

Funding sources are understandably concerned that their funds are awarded to applicants that present the least risk—or put more positively, to applicants that seem the most likely to effectively utilize the funds. This seems perfectly reasonable since, to a funding source, every award is a financial investment; therefore, officials of the funding agency are most concerned with yielding the greatest return from each investment. One of the criteria by which the funding agency attempts to evaluate this is based on the experience and credentials of the project leader and other key members of the program/project staff. In fact, for specific types of clinically based and research proposals, reviewers may look specifically at the expertise and publication record of the applicant and any other key individuals who are a part of the project team (Kessel, 2006), whereas for other program- and project-based proposals, reviewers will be most interested in the relevant work experience of the applicants. While a sound program design is a necessity for a successful proposal, demonstrating expertise is a crucial part of selling your proposal; therefore, having both the right project leader and also experienced team members may greatly improve your proposal (Zlowodzki, Jonsson, Kregor, & Bhandari, 2007).

This means that applicants must provide evidence that the project team does indeed have sufficient knowledge and skills to effectively coordinate and implement the proposed project. Evidence of this can be provided in several ways, which may include any and all of the following, depending on the funding opportunity:

- The project leader's résumé documenting academic and professional credentials and relevant experience
- A biographical sketch documenting additional and more detailed relevant knowledge, skills, and experience
- A record of scholarly publishing in the relevant area
- Documentation of experience with past funding opportunities

Each of these may provide justification that the project team has specific knowledge and skills and, possibly, expertise in the identified area—precisely what funders wish to know.

However, in addition to establishing the capabilities of the professionals involved in the proposed program, funders are also interested in knowing that the organization is appropriately structured to effectively implement the program. A number of factors typically are reviewed to establish organizational capability, such as the length of time in business, organizational licensure and/or certifications, accreditation, and funding history. Recall the list of attachments provided, as many of these were already cited, and thus, documents such as these are often required to provide evidence that the organization is capable of carrying out the proposed plan. One other specific and highly common requirement that speaks to organizational capability is the letters of support from peer organizations, other contractors, or other key officials.

Letters of Support

Often, three or more letters of support are required with submission of a proposal. The purpose of the letters of support is to provide additional evidence that the organization and/or the program staff are qualified for the proposal. Therefore, letters of support should be requested from those that are in a position to provide such information. Other contractors with whom the organization is currently doing or has done business are often the most relevant source to provide letters since they have firsthand knowledge of the organization/staff performance. In addition, peer agencies with whom your organization has worked collaboratively form a second group whose letters of support may be particularly meaningful since they, too, are in a position to directly attest to your organization's past performance. When collaboration with other organizations has not occurred, peer organizations may still prove valuable in providing a letter of support; however, a stronger level of support can be provided by those that have direct knowledge of your past performance.

The letter of support is typically used to provide another level of evidence of the program team and/or organization's ability to successfully implement the proposal, hence such should be the primary objective of the letter. Other information that provides further context to the letter of support is also helpful, such as

- length of time the support writer has worked with/known you or your organization,
- existing and/or past focus of the business relationship, and
- specific reasons why the writer believes you/your organization is uniquely qualified for the project.

Whereas letters of support from colleagues at peer organizations are especially helpful, acquiring them and letters from contractors may at times prove challenging. This is often the case when peer organizations and/or contractors are pursuing the same funding opportunity as you; thus, they are competing against you and likely not interested in supporting you in the competition. In addition, when two or more organizations that a funder contracts are pursuing the same opportunity, the contractor may be comfortable supporting only one or may simply decide not to support either. As a result, obtaining letters of support can indeed come with its own set of challenges. But being in a position to even request such a letter is primarily based on having established effective business relationships with contractors, peer organizations, and other key resources. This again highlights the purpose of identifying and engaging community resources (previously discussed in Chapter 7) and building and preserving these relationships (Chapter 13).

Collaboration

As discussed previously, collaboration in new program development efforts is more common in the 21st century than ever before (Donahue, Lanzara, & Felton, 2006). In fact, foundations and government agencies look favorably on collaborative efforts (Klein, 2000; Quick & New, 2000), and today, some funding opportunities are specifically limited to collaborative efforts. Engaging in collaborative efforts may strengthen a proposal—especially when, through collaboration, essential resources can be shared, thus increasing organizational capability and justification. However, when developing a proposal for a collaborative effort, it is imperative that the relationship between the two or more organizations be clearly defined during the proposal development step, if not before. This includes but is not limited to establishing the following:

- The applicant/lead organization
- Work expectations for each organization
- Time frames for delivery of specific activities and specific deliverables
- Communication expectations
- Payment expectations

To discuss each briefly, most funding sources require that one organization and individual be assigned the role of applicant for the funding opportunity, taking responsibility as both the primary contact person and the individual and organization ultimately responsible for effectively utilizing the funding provided. As a result, the applicant organization is the direct payee of the funder (i.e., fiduciary), and thus, any collaborating partners become subcontractors of the applicant organization. Therefore, because collaborating organizations are embarking on a joint business venture, it behooves the organizations to clearly identify the role that each will play, specifying the work activities to be performed by each as well as the time frames in which certain activities will be accomplished and any deliverables, such as reports, data, and other documentation, will be completed. The role and work expectations are directly tied to payment. In addition, expectations about communication should be outlined to establish types (e.g., telephone, e-mail, meetings) and frequency of communication. A formal contract should be drafted to articulate all these expectations and to also address issues related to dissolving the relationship. However, the contract is typically maintained between the collaborating organizations, while a Memorandum of Understanding/Agreement is the document that is prepared and signed for submission with the proposal. The Memo of Understanding/Agreement is usually required by the funding agency to provide evidence of the collaboration and captures the basic primary aspects of the contract. The Memo of Understanding/Agreement does not include all the details contained in the contract that are particularly necessary to establish the business relationship between the collaborating organizations but, rather, includes the basic facts of the relationship.

In addition to clearly defining the roles and expectations of collaborating organizations, collaborative organizations often wish to either jointly develop the proposal and/or provide significant input to the proposal. Like all collaborative development projects, working together on a grant proposal requires negotiation of roles, consensus building, and solid interpersonal skills in order to develop the best product that reflects shared ownership. Fortunately, these are skills that most counselors and other mental health professionals naturally possess.

Each of these issues—time considerations, depth of material needed, justifying professional/organizational capability, letters of support, and collaboration—must be given considerable thought when developing a proposal. Each of the issues may have specific ramifications for the proposal development process and, ultimately, for the proposal outcome; therefore, it is essential that each is given attention before and during the proposal development process.

Major Aspects of Proposal Development

In addition to the factors outlined above, there are also a great many aspects of proposal development that should be examined. In particular, there are four that I would like to specifically discuss here, because they are more universal in nature than others. These are

1. the use of grant writers or program developers,

2. planning for the work of proposal development,

3. the skills needed in proposal writing, and

4. the use of internal reviewers.

To begin this discussion, let's first tackle the issue of using external grant writers versus internal program developers to develop the grant proposal.

Internal Versus External Grant Writers/Proposal Developers

Because I am using the term *grant writer* here, I do want to again clarify that I am speaking solely about grant writing for program/project development and not for fundraising or other charitable giving activities—an important distinction to make. Particularly with the number of grant-writing workshops and consultation services available today, organizations may struggle with deciding whether they should hire a grant writer to develop their proposal or write their proposals independently—with valid reasons for doing both.

As such, reasons for hiring a grant writer may include, but are not necessarily limited to,

- not having an employee on staff that might be capable of developing a proposal,
- not being able to allow an existing staff person to take time away from other duties in order to develop a proposal,
- wishing to utilize someone with prior experience in successfully securing funding in hopes of increasing the organization's chance of securing grant funding, and
- utilizing a grant writer for assistance in developing initial proposals so that existing employees can begin to learn to develop their own proposals.

As you can see, organizations may decide to hire a grant writer for various reasons. In addition, some organizations may choose to contract with a grant writer for specific projects or on a part- or full-time basis. Organizations that employ a grant writer part- or full-time may also decide to contract a grant writer for a specific project, especially if it involves new territory for the organization or the organization's leaders feel that a grant writer's services may be especially needed for a certain proposal.

However, whereas hiring a grant writer often makes sense for an organization, today's program developers/mental health professionals should know how to develop their own proposals. Just as mental health professionals must be competent at developing their own budgets, managing the finances of their program, developing job descriptions, and hiring staff, proposal development skills compose another essential aspect of the 21st-century mental health professional. This does not mean that external grant writers cannot be used to provide additional support and guidance, particularly as one is learning to become effective in proposal development, but it does mean that external grant writers should not be used *instead of* program developers but in addition to, as needed.

This is especially true since, unlike finance and human resource personnel that are specially credentialed and needed to serve a core function within an organization, there are no specific credentials for grant writers. Rather, grant-writing skills are learned and, therefore, can be acquired by anyone and particularly by mental health professionals. In addition, someone's success in securing past funding for a specific type of program does not necessarily translate into success in securing grants in other areas or in the future. Consider the major aspects of a proposal that were examined earlier—depth of material, justification of personal and organizational capability, letters of support, and collaboration. None of these major aspects of a proposal has to do with writing skills but, rather, with having specific structure and knowledge in place that can be utilized to make an effective argument. Therefore, while an external grant writer may be able to provide the narrative of a proposal, s/he can only do so based on work that has already been done or is being accomplished by the organization and, as such, is not creating but rather stating what the organization has done/plans to do.

In addition, hiring a grant writer may mean that an organization will miss an opportunity for organizational engagement. This is because when someone outside the organization is hired to perform work that will ultimately be done within the organization, the initial opportunity to engage staff in the project may be lost. This is no different than any time that someone external is brought in to perform specific work or to do something that is part of the organization. Therefore, unless organizational leaders are purposeful in their efforts to involve key staff in the grant-writing process, it is unlikely that the staff will feel engaged in or connected to the project. Unfortunately, this lack of engagement at the proposal development stage can result in a lack of engagement in the project if and when it's funded.

Finally, whereas for some organizations, hiring an external grant writer is simply a question of economics—*Can we afford to hire this person or not?*—for others, it is a question of hedging the bet and trying to minimize risk—ensuring that you hire the best person for the job and achieve the right outcome. Both of these can come with significant financial risk to the organization since most organizations have to pay for grant-writing services regardless of the success or lack thereof of the proposal being funded. While this is perfectly understandable, it does raise the issue of using a pay structure that can both reduce financial risk to the organization and reward positive outcomes. For instance, organizations that do wish to hire a grant writer should consider a two-tier pay structure: a minimum amount down for proposal development and submission and a second payout if the proposal is funded. By doing this, organizations would be in a position to negotiate their financial risk—an issue made more critical today within the climate of shrinking dollars.

For each of these reasons and more, it makes most sense to view grant writing/proposal writing as simply a component of comprehensive program development and not as an activity to be done solely by individuals external to the organization. By doing so, mental health professionals are able to expand their repertoire and learn to effectively articulate the reasons that their programs should be funded—an essential part of program development.

Interestingly, just as securing funding is essential to the survival of mental health and human service providers, it is often equally important to researchers. As a result and in order to ensure that young researchers are equipped with the ability to develop their own proposals, colleges (Blair, Cline, & Bowen, 2007) and professional associations (Kessel, 2006) have provided specific instruction in this area. In fact, Jacksonville State University developed three new courses for its undergraduate biology students to increase knowledge and skills related to developing effective research designs and proposals. And Kessel, writing for the American College of Chest Physicians, not only provides a highly useful article about grant writing across disciplines but also includes some simple tips for grant writers, such as

- check out the websites of grant-making agencies for tips,
- have your proposal reviewed before submission, and
- attempt to participate on the review panel of a funding agency to learn more about the evaluation process.

By taking these extra steps, professions outside mental health are reinforcing the necessity of grant-writing skills for their colleagues—a necessity that mental health professions share. Therefore, we must have the same expectations for ourselves and ensure that we, too, have mechanisms in place by which to teach grant-writing skills.

Planning for the Work

Because developing a proposal is often such a tremendous undertaking, effective planning is crucial to successful proposal development. This is particularly necessary given the aggressive deadlines associated with many funding opportunities. First and foremost, long before you prepare to develop an application for funding, you must garner support from administrators and other organizational leaders. This will ensure (1) that you do not waste any time pursuing something that you may not be able to complete after an initial investment of time and energy, (2) that you have the necessary resources to effectively complete the proposal, and (3) that you are able to devote sufficient time to completing the proposal.

Once you have received support for the project, there are several logistical aspects of planning that must be considered. Because developing a proposal often requires the input of other individuals—in addition to the program developer—it is necessary to treat the proposal development process as you would any type of time-limited project. This typically means ensuring that everyone with a need to know understands the expectations for the proposal development project and that concrete plans are in place to see the process to completion. Often, this minimally involves the following steps:

- Identify all the individuals that will need to be involved in the proposal development, including internal reviewers and professionals from collaborating organizations.
- Hold an initial meeting to discuss the proposal, develop a plan for completion, and clarify the roles that each individual will have in the proposal development process.
- Schedule time to complete the proposal based on the proposal deadline.
- Schedule an update (if needed) and final meeting with all the involved individuals to review progress and finalize the proposal.

Skills of Proposal Writing

Specific skills are needed for successful proposal writing. These include both priority skills that are based on comprehensive program development and secondary skills that are needed to complete the proposal. Priority skills refer to the activities that have been previously completed in the program development model, including the following:

- Ability to develop a rationale for the program/project through identifying a need and target population
- Ability to establish a research basis for program design to effectively address the needs
- Ability to identify and incorporate multicultural aspects in program design
- Ability to design an effective clinical program
- Ability to design a staffing and organizational structure to effectively implement the program
- Ability to plan an effective budget that directly ties program interventions to outcomes
- Ability to design an evaluation program that effectively assesses the program

Each of these skills directly corresponds with a previous step already covered in the text, with the exception of Step X (Evaluate the Program), which is covered in Chapter 12. See Table 10.1 for an illustration of this connection.

Table 10.1 Priority Skills and Corresponding Program Development Steps

Priority Skills of Proposal Development	Program Development Steps
Ability to develop a rationale for the program/project through identifying a need and target population	Step I: Establish the Need for Programming
Ability to establish a research basis for program design to effectively address the needs	Step II: Establish a Research Basis for Program Design
Ability to consider multicultural aspects in program design	Step IIa: Address Cultural Identity Issues in Program Design
Ability to design an effective clinical program	Step III: Design the Clinical Program
Ability to design a staffing and organizational structure to effectively implement the program	Step IV: Develop the Staffing Infrastructure
Ability to develop an effective budget that directly ties program interventions to outcomes	Step VII: Develop the Financial Management Plan
Ability to design an evaluation program that effectively assesses the program outcomes	Step X: Evaluate the Program

As you can see, the priority skills are simply the basic skills that program developers must possess. Therefore, mental health professionals who possess these skills will find that they already have the most critical skills needed to develop a successful grant proposal. You will note that none of these skills refers to *writing* but, rather, to *possessing* a sophisticated level of knowledge and skills.

Secondary skills refer to additional skills needed for successful proposal development. Unlike the priority skills listed above, secondary skills refer to writing and other logistical aspects of proposal development that include such issues as articulation, flow of ideas, organizing the proposal, and compliance with proposal requirements (see Box 10.1).

BOX 10.1

SECONDARY SKILLS FOR WRITING A SUCCESSFUL PROPOSAL

- Review all application instructions thoroughly to gain a firm understanding of content and submission requirements.
- Determine if any presubmission steps are required prior to application submission, and complete these steps.
- Write in an articulate and concise manner.
- Ensure that there is an effective flow of ideas that is directional, beginning with justification for the project, then the project description, and then the project outcomes.
- Communicate a firm understanding of what the funding source is looking for—speak the language of the funding source, as applicable.
- Develop all required tools and other documents.
- Collect and compile other required documents.
- After completing the application, conduct a thorough review to ensure that you have completed all required documents.
- Read the entire proposal packet personally in order to critically evaluate it, paying special attention to the following: thoroughness in responding to all content requirements, soundness of proposal, flow of information throughout the proposal, and justification for budget and plan given the identified scope of problem/identified needs.

In addition, successful grant writing requires significant preparation and deep knowledge about not only the proposed program but what other research or programs have previously been funded and how to speak directly to the grant maker's interests (Devine, 2009). Finally, the use of a team approach to grant writing may prove successful to the proposal development process (Miller, 2008). In addition to scholarly articles, books, and tips from professional associations, there are several web-based resources that may be helpful to the proposal development process (see Box 10.2).

BOX 10.2

WEB RESOURCES FOR PROPOSAL WRITING

Action Without Borders: www.idealist.org

The Foundation Center: http://foundationcenter.org

The Grantsmanship Center: www.tgci.com

U.S. Environmental Protection Agency: www.epa.gov/ogd/recipient/tips.htm

However, whereas these websites may provide useful broad-based suggestions about grant writing, they should not be used in place of all suggestions and guidance provided by the funding agency. In fact, many funding agencies provide both general and specific tips, suggestions, and strategies to improve your proposal, and therefore, obtaining all the available information and guidance from the funding agency itself is essential to the success of a proposal.

Internal Reviewers

In addition to the overwhelming amount of work involved in developing a proposal, there are also significant stakes involved as a result of the initial investment of time and work and the degree of risk/potential business outcomes at play. As a result, every attempt should be made to ensure that you have developed the best proposal possible. Having completed due diligence throughout the process is essential, just as is reviewing the proposal personally and checking and double-checking that all the requirements have been met. But another set of eyes—or two—should also thoroughly review the entire proposal to ensure that it is strong. Reviewers should particularly be those individuals who possess the necessary objectivity to effectively evaluate the proposal. In fact, critiques by colleagues can be particularly helpful in evaluating the content of the proposal and the effectiveness of the argument (Hegyvary, 2005). These critiques are completed by internal reviewers—individuals who did not participate in the proposal development and who are not a part of the funding agency's review team and, therefore, are able to be highly objective. Internal reviewers may be from within your organization or outside it, depending on who is accessible to you. It is obviously ideal to utilize someone external to your organization as a reviewer if you can; however, this is not always possible, especially today, given the competitive environment in which mental health and human service organizations operate—indeed, some program developers are afraid of sharing too much information with competitors.

Regardless of who is identified as an internal reviewer, what is most important is that the individual(s) is familiar with grant proposals and has reviewed the particular funding opportunity so that s/he has a firm understanding of the purpose of the funding opportunity and the requirements of the proposal. The review should focus on three key areas:

1. The content of the proposal, including the strength of the entire argument (e.g., identified need, program design, budget)

2. The writing

3. Compliance with the funding opportunity requirements

Because the proposal will be reviewed by a team of reviewers upon submission, this type of internal review may serve as a preliminary, comprehensive review resulting in valuable feedback about the proposal and its merits that can be used to further strengthen the proposal. Often, internal reviews may identify thoughts or arguments that have not been articulated clearly enough, grammatical issues, or lack of substantial evidence to support claims—each of which, once corrected, is understandably helpful in improving the proposal. In addition, using internal reviewers can help prepare you for the official review process.

Other Considerations in Proposal Development

There are two other considerations in proposal development that deserve special attention here:

1. Experience as a reviewer

2. Specific attention to budget requests

While it is critically important that you fully understand the funding source—its history, philosophy, and major goals—prior to pursuing a funding opportunity to ensure that you fully understand the rationale and broader context of the funding opportunity, it is wise to also have deep knowledge of the review process. To this end, it is recommended that you apply to become a reviewer for grant proposals for the sources with whom you most likely will be applying. However, if you cannot review for a funding source that is particularly relevant to you, seek out other review opportunities, since it is the experience of reviewing itself that is most valuable. By participating as a reviewer, you are able to gain firsthand knowledge of the review process, learning precisely how proposals are evaluated, if there are particular issues that tend to resonate with the funders, and what a successful proposal looks like. As you can imagine, this experience can be invaluable to you as you develop your own proposal.

The findings from a study examining the personal perspectives of scientists who served as reviewers for the National Science Foundation further highlight some reasons why reviewing may be pivotal as a professional endeavor (Porter, 2005). After examining the primary motivational factors influencing reviewers to engage in the review process, the findings included four main reasons (Porter, 2005):

1. A desire to learn the ropes about the review process in order to improve their own proposal development skills

2. A strong obligation to serve the professional community

3. A desire to remain current and relevant in their own work through learning about the work of others

4. Additional opportunity for professional networking

Each of these issues can also easily be applied to explain why mental health professionals should participate in the review process.

The second issue has to do with paying specific attention to the budget. Aside from ensuring that the budget is commensurate with the plan and the identified needs and that all expenditures are justified, specific attention must be paid to ensuring that the budget accurately reflects the needs of the proposal. To this end, budgets typically should not contain items such as computers, office space, and other items that are regular expenses of the organization but, rather, specialized items that are specifically needed to implement the program/project. As Devine (2009) summarizes,

> Budgets are often very specific and include salaries for personnel, equipment, supplies, travel to the field site, travel to meetings to present results, and educational support, as allowed. Each aspect of the budget must be sufficiently justified to ensure accountability to the grant makers; time frames must be included. Justifying the proportion and duration of each individual's time is critical. (p. 584)

In addition, projected expenditures for program evaluation and other such specialized activities must be competitive and limited to fair pricing. In simple terms, all expenses must be fully justified, and budgets cannot contain any fluff—either in budgeted items or projected costs. Some funding sources provide specific guidelines to ensure these restrictions, such as prohibiting certain expenditures (e.g., hardware, rent) and limiting expenditures for specific activities, such as program evaluation. In fact, it is common today in federal grant opportunities to limit program evaluation activities to no more than 20% of the total cost requested in the proposal.

Summary

As you well know by now, available funding for mental health and human service programs is highly limited and, as a result, extremely competitive. Therefore, successfully acquiring funding is no easy task but, rather, one that is quite challenging and predicated on effective research skills, creativity, and the ability to establish sound justification for both the proposal and the professional skills, knowledge, and organizational infrastructure needed to implement the proposal. In addition, grant proposals require support from the applicant organization and input from other individuals and, therefore, are rarely completed independently. It is precisely because of each of these issues and the necessary unique skills that program developers are best suited to lead the grant proposal process.

Although developing the actual proposal does require a significant amount of skill and attention to detail, the proposal itself has already been built for those who have completed Steps II through VII of the comprehensive program development model. Doing so means that all the essential building blocks of a grant proposal have been assembled, and the job of the program developer then focuses on consolidating all the work into the most effective proposal and presenting a clear argument for funding. It is in this manner that the task of developing the grant application allows the program developer to integrate all the program development steps—allowing for the sum of work to come together into a coherent, effective, and highly justifiable plan.

CASE ILLUSTRATION

Maya had been working in the schools with kids who had various types of learning disorders and their families. The program was a collaborative effort between the human service agency for which Maya worked and the local school district. During the past year, Maya had become more and more disturbed by what appeared to be an increase in youth violence, including new gang activity. As a result of her increasing concern, Maya had spent the past several months systematically gathering information and designing a prevention and treatment program to prevent and combat the issue. She began by investigating whether what she thought was a problem/need (i.e., youth violence) really was. To this end, she conducted a comprehensive needs assessment, asset map, and market analysis and found that a need did exist—not only had there been a 36% increase in youth violence over the past 2 years, but there was no formal programming currently in place to address the issue from either a preventive or treatment aspect.

Maya then began an exhaustive review of the research and other literature to begin learning the most effective strategies for addressing the issue. From this, she was able to design a community-based prevention program as well as a treatment program that would involve caregivers and teachers and that would be delivered in the schools and community, with specific reinforcement provided in the home by the caregivers. Having previously discussed this potential need for new programming with her supervisors and administrators, Maya was able to then work directly with her agency's human resources and finance departments in order to collaboratively design an effective staffing infrastructure and an operating budget for both programs. Whereas Maya led the development of both the staffing infrastructure and the projected budget, she was able to gain valuable input from the finance and human resources administrators, particularly in regard to developing job descriptions and pay scales.

Realizing she could get more accomplished if she shared the work, Maya spoke with Sofia, one of her colleagues, to see if she was interested in working on the project. Sofia was interested, noting her shared passion for this type of program. Both Sofia and Maya began exploring funding opportunities, and each set aside 20 minutes each week to explore two free websites dedicated to philanthropic and federal funding opportunity notifications. In addition, the administrators at their organization were looking out for any related funding opportunities from the state or local government. After identifying a specific charitable organization that had funded youth programs in the past and that currently was focused on children and youth programs, Sofia and Maya developed a letter of inquiry briefly outlining the program proposals. Because this particular funding source accepted only letters of inquiry, they followed the instructions provided and submitted such a letter in hopes of being invited to submit a full proposal.

A week later, Maya and Sofia received an announcement for a funding opportunity for youth violence prevention programming. The state's Department of Human Services issued a Request for Proposal (RFP) for violence prevention programs in their target community. The terms of the RFP included $130,000 annually for a period of 3 years to fund evidence-based programming. In addition, proposed interventions were required to utilize a multisystemic approach and were expected to be provided for at least 6 months.

(Continued)

(Continued)

Although Maya had viewed the RFP just 3 days after it was issued, the application deadline was less than 3 weeks away. They quickly got to work divvying up the assignments and scheduled an initial meeting with a fellow clinician, case manager, administrator, and representatives from the information technology, finance, and human resources departments to review the RFP. Together, the group developed a plan for completing the proposal that included the finance representative gathering all the required corporate documentation and information, the information technology representative developing a draft response to the application sections regarding computer and communication technology, and the fellow clinician gathering the required letters of support from the schools and community organizations. Because Maya had previously developed relationships with the local schools and two community organizations providing youth programming, the letters simply solidified the relationships that she had already worked to establish as part of program implementation. Maya and Sofia would lead the development of the application—largely using the proposal that Maya had already developed—gaining input from others, as needed. In addition, the administrator agreed to serve as an internal reviewer, and Sofia and Maya were also able to get one of their former colleagues, who was practicing out of state, to agree to be a second reviewer.

Once they sat down to complete the application, they were relieved and happy to see that a multisystemic approach was required, since Maya had learned from reviewing the literature that multisystemic approaches had been proven effective in preventing youth violence. This reinforced the thoroughness of her work on the literature review and subsequent program design. The only aspect of the application that they struggled with was justifying professional capability to effectively carry out the program through an individual with expertise since there was not someone in the organization with specific expertise in youth violence prevention. To deal with this, Sofia and Maya decided to argue from the point of view of organizational capability via rich experience with youth and family treatment coupled with strong ties to the schools and specific community organizations, one of which did specialize in violence prevention. Because Maya had already developed a comprehensive proposal, completing the application simply involved tailoring the proposal to the requirements, compiling required tools and other documents and collecting other documentation.

Maya and Sofia and the rest of their team were able to meet their self-imposed deadline of completing the application 6 days before it was due so that both Sofia and Maya could fully review the proposal and then have it reviewed by both the administrator and out-of-state colleague. Following the reviews, Maya and Sofia made final changes, and the proposal was submitted the day before the deadline.

Postscript

Six weeks later, Sofia and Maya received notice from the charitable organization to which they had submitted the letter of inquiry that they would not be invited to submit a full proposal. Citing economic challenges, the philanthropic organization informed them that they would not be pursuing any new ventures until the following year but that they could resubmit another letter of inquiry at that time. They were disappointed about this, particularly because they thought they had identified a solid match to fund one or both of their programs.

Maya and Sofia were not upset for too long, though. Two months later, they received notification that they had been awarded the state contract for youth violence prevention programming. Maya and Sofia were promoted to program director and supervisor, respectively, and they began preparing for program implementation. They—and organizational leaders—felt that gaining this experience in violence prevention would well position their organization to pursue youth violence treatment programming in the future; so they decided to dedicate their energies to the newly awarded contract and shelve the treatment program with an eye toward possibly pursuing funding for it in the near future.

References

Blair, B. G., Cline, G. R., & Bowen, W. R. (2007). NSF-style peer review for teaching: Undergraduate grant-writing. *American Biology Teacher, 69,* 34–37.

Devine, E. B. (2009). The art of obtaining grants. *American Journal of Health-System Pharmacists, 66,* 580–587.

Donahue, S. A., Lanzara, C. B., & Felton, C. J. (2006). Project Liberty: New York's crisis counseling program created in the aftermath of September 11, 2001. *Psychiatric Services, 57,* 1253–1258.

Hegyvary, S. T. (2005). Writing that matters. *Journal of Nursing Scholarship, 37,* 193–194.

Homan, M. S. (2004). *Promoting community change: Making it happen in the real world.* Belmont, CA: Brooks/Cole.

Kessel, D. (2006). Writing successful grant applications for preclinical studies. *Chest, 130,* 296–298.

Klein, K. (2000). *Fundraising for the long haul.* Berkeley, CA: Chardon.

Lewis, J. A., Packard, T. R., & Lewis, M. D. (2007). *Management of human service programs* (4th ed.). Belmont, CA: Thomson Learning.

Miller, P. W. (2008). *Grant writing: Strategies for developing winning proposals* (2nd ed.). Munster, IN: Patrick W. Miller & Associates.

New, C. (2001). Grants from the government. In J. M. Greenfield (Ed.), *The non-profit handbook: Fundraising* (3rd ed., pp. 692–712). New York: Wiley.

Porter, R. (2005). What do grant reviewers really want, anyway? *Journal of Research Administration, 36,* 47–55.

Quick, J. A., & New, C. C. (2000). *Grant winner's toolkit: Project management and evaluation.* New York: Wiley.

Substance Abuse and Mental Health Services Administration. (2008). *Service expansion in mental health/substance abuse.* Retrieved September 13, 2010, from https://grants.hrsa.gov/webExternal/FundingOppDetails.asp?FundingCycleId=2E31CDA0-5DE6-4AB4-8F89-2CFF50A4A978&ViewMode=EU&GoBack=&PrintMode=&OnlineAvailabilityFlag=&pageNumber=&version=&NC=&Popup=

Zlowodzki, M., Jonsson, A., Kregor, P. J., & Bhandari, M. (2007). How to write a grant proposal. *Indian Journal of Orthopaedics, 41,* 23–26.

PART II

PROGRAM IMPLEMENTATION AND SUSTAINABILITY

Implement the Program

Learning Objectives

1. Identify specific issues that should be addressed with the funding source at the beginning of the relationship

2. Identify the three documents related to the proposal that must be reviewed to ensure effective implementation

3. Discuss the roles of information systems, quality assurance, and contract compliance in program management

I MUST HAVE MISSED THAT

Kyra had just received notification that the proposal she and her colleagues had developed had been funded. Their project involved facilitating a training curriculum for foster care and adoption workers across the state, using an existing curriculum. Because Kyra and two of her clinicians had developed the proposal, they felt comfortable that they had a firm grasp on the project's expectations; so they briefly reviewed the contract they had just received, had it signed by the agency's president, and sent it back to the contractor. Then they got to work planning for implementing the project. Knowing that they were required to deliver the trainings across the entire state, they mapped out a 1-year plan, identifying each of the locations to which they needed to deliver the training. In addition, they used a *Gantt chart* to identify each of the major activities needed for implementation, as well as time frames and the individuals responsible for each activity. Feeling as though they had a firm plan in place, they began implementation, finalizing the training schedule by coordinating with representatives from each of the organizations that would receive the training, preparing for training facilitation, and getting on the road to begin training.

Kyra and her co-trainers were excited by the initial responses of the training participants—the participants often telling them that they had enjoyed the training and commenting on the trainers' ability to connect with the audience. In addition, Kyra and her team found that they really enjoyed facilitating the training—even more than they had thought they would—and they liked the added bonus of getting out and meeting others across the state who worked in the child welfare field.

After training about one-third of their assigned population and spending approximately 6 months delivering the training across the state, Kyra received a call from the contract manager. The contract manager stated that she had still not received any of the training evaluations from the organizations that had been trained, although she knew from the monthly progress reports Kyra had submitted that they had in fact trained several organizations in multiple locations. Not quite knowing how to respond since she did not recall any type of evaluation requirement, Kyra asked the contract manager for more information about the evaluations. The contract manager stated that standardized evaluation tools had been developed for the training program and were available through the contract manager's office. She further stated that it was Kyra's responsibility as the trainer to distribute the evaluation form to all training recipients, along with instructions regarding electronic submission of the evaluation, following each completed training curriculum. Since the contract manager had never heard from Kyra, she assumed that Kyra had obtained the evaluation form from someone else in the funder's office.

Kyra was aghast—she was not aware of the evaluation and had not provided it to any of the training recipients, and she could only admit her oversight to the contract manager. The contract manager encouraged Kyra to review her contract so that she did fully understand all its requirements. She then let Kyra know that she would have to speak to her supervisor to determine how they would handle this initial failure to comply with the contractual expectations and would get back to Kyra within a week.

CONSIDERING KYRA

1. How could Kyra have avoided this?

2. If you were Kyra, what might you propose to rectify this situation?

3. If Kyra is permitted to continue the contract, what advice would you give her to effectively move forward in her relationship with the contract manager?

About This Chapter

This chapter focuses specifically on program implementation—the step that follows successfully securing funding. This step in the comprehensive program development model follows developing the proposal and precedes program evaluation; however, as you know, implementation activities and initial evaluation activities are originally developed in Step III (Design the Clinical Program). As a result, this chapter is specifically connected to Step III, as well as Steps X (Evaluate the Program) and XIII (Develop an Information-Sharing Plan), again illustrating the interconnectedness of the model. Therefore, specific components of the program evaluation, such as process evaluation, fidelity assessment, and outcomes evaluation, are not fully examined here but, rather, in the following chapter, and whereas quality assurance methods and contract compliance issues are initially explored here, the significance of this type of data collection is specifically discussed in Chapter 15.

This chapter explores two major areas—program implementation and program management, which begins during initial implementation. In terms of program implementation, we will explore key issues that must be attended to during this time. These issues include establishing a relationship with the funding source, reviewing and implementing the grant/contract, and attending to the specific aspects of the program implementation process, including the implementation of various evaluation and monitoring activities. In addition, critical aspects of program management are examined, with specific attention paid to four major areas: leadership and administrative oversight, the use of information systems, quality assurance planning and mechanisms, and contract compliance.

STEP IX: IMPLEMENT THE PROGRAM

Fully Implementing the Program

After investing a great deal of time, energy, and hard work into the development of a clinical program, the greatest reward is seeing it come to fruition—and this is possible only after funding support has been awarded. Indeed, receiving notification that your proposal for a new program/project has been selected for funding validates all the work that went into developing the proposal—from the exhaustive needs assessment process to the comprehensive literature review to putting the finishing touches on the program design. But as validating as such an award is, it also comes with a great deal of new work and a much longer time commitment. In fact, whereas the preplanning and planning phases may have taken up a year or so and possibly up to 5% of your overall time during the year, the implementation phase most often requires 80% to 100% of your time (as well as the time of other key staff), typically for the next 1 to 5 years.

Implementation signals a far more significant and steady commitment to the program/project and, as such, means that the program will likely become the primary focus of the program developer/mental health professional's energies. Further, there are dramatically different stakes involved in implementation versus proposal development, since funding was awarded on the basis of the funder's trust and a belief in the success of the project. As a result, the program developer must prove worthy of the funding but also must appreciate that the success of the program implementation has significant implications on future potential to garner funding. To be certain, how well a program developer is able to implement a program and effectively use the funds provided is critical not only to the relationship between the developer and the funder but also to the program developer's future ability to attract new funding.

Establishing the Relationship With the Funding Source

The first step in program implementation is formally establishing the relationship with the funding source. In many cases, a relationship with the fund/contract manager will already have been formed—and should have already been formed—since cultivating relationships with potential funders is a critical aspect of pursuing funding (as discussed in Chapter 8). However, once funded, the relationship with the funder moves from being an informal one without contractual expectations to a formal business relationship and, therefore, must be treated as such.

On receipt of the notification of funding award, the program developer should immediately contact the funding source to acknowledge the award and personally extend gratitude. Depending on the funding source, there may be specific requirements regarding acceptance that may be both formal and informal. For instance, federal grants typically require formal acceptance of funding as well as the completion of initial setup activities. State and local governmental grants and philanthropic organizations may also require formal acceptance of funding, whereas others may initially require only a simple acknowledgment. In most—if not all—cases, instructions regarding acceptance and beginning implementation are provided in the initial notification letter, and these instructions must be followed.

Regardless of the requirements regarding acceptance of the funding award, the issue remains that the relationship between the program developer and the funding source is a particularly important one. Since clinicians are in the business of building effective relationships, this should not constitute too much of a challenge. As such, using the same skills that make clinicians effective can allow program developers to quickly establish a good working relationship with the contract manager. The type and scope of the relationship between the contract manager and the program developer will vary based on the particular funding source, just as the types of required acceptance activities do. Some relationships will require formal regular written reporting and frequent verbal communication and, thus, are characterized by frequent contact and close working relationships, whereas others may require minimal communication. Because it is the program developer's responsibility to comply with all the requirements and preferences of the funding source, it is important to find out exactly the type of relationship required and/or desired by the contract manager as part of establishing the relationship.

Interestingly, the type of relationship and reporting requirements may not be remotely correlated with the type of funding awarded or the amount of funding but, rather, are typically a reflection of the funding source itself. In fact, a $25,000 award from a corporation's community giving program may come with much more rigorous reporting requirements and require a greater level of involvement than a $300,000 award from the federal government. This again underscores why it is imperative that the program developer finds out exactly what type of relationship is required and/or desired by the funding source and then complies fully with this, careful to avoid attempts to prejudge the scope of the relationship. Since any person and/or organization that receives external funding is a steward—trusted to carry out the mission and/or objectives of the funding source and all its constituents—the relationship between the program developer and the contract manager forms the basis for this type of *stewardship*.

Review of the Grant/Contract

Following acceptance of the award and as you are beginning to establish the relationship with the funding source, you must thoroughly review the grant/contract. This is of particular significance since it may have been a year or more since the proposal was actually developed. If you are anything like me, much of what you developed even a short time ago may not be easily recalled today; thus, a thorough review of the original proposal and all the accompanying documentation must occur. Failing to conduct a thorough review may put you in Kyra's shoes—a third of the way into the project and overlooking a critical requirement.

There are three basic components that must be reviewed:

1. The initial application requirements

2. The initial proposal

3. Any changes or modifications to the original requirements or documents

I have found the initial application requirements and initial notice of the funding competition to be among the most important documents to review, because it is in these documents that the rationale, objectives, and other aspects related to the intent of the funding are set forth. As such, this information can be quite rich in outlining the priorities of the funding source and can provide a unique window into the thinking behind the funding source leaders. Because funding recipients are most often evaluated based on the degree to which they can carry out the agenda of the funding source, as well as its more subtle ideological aspects, it is imperative that the recipient understand precisely what that agenda is so as to ensure that all aspects of the project reflect this—not simply the interventions themselves. As such, you must keep in mind that one of your jobs in carrying out the program is to help the funding source be successful (Porter, 2005). For instance, a Request for Proposals (RFP) to provide mental health treatment for returning veterans may include a narrative about the importance of family involvement in the treatment process and reducing isolation. Whereas the funding recipient was successful in designing a treatment program that effectively addressed both of these issues, as evidenced by the award, it is equally necessary that other aspects of the program, including clinical decision making, are guided by these priorities; thus, clinical decision making would need to reflect family involvement. By attending to this, you are able to fulfill both the content and the substance of the funding source's expectations.

Reviewing the initial proposal that was developed in response to the RFP is also of critical importance, since this document outlines precisely what the program developer has agreed to do in terms of implementation and delivery of services. The proposal is a legal document insofar as it provides the initial agreement that the program developer has stipulated with the funding source. Moreover, funding was awarded based on what was outlined in the proposal. As a result, any changes or diversions from the proposal must receive preauthorization by the funding source so as to avoid a potential *breach of contract*—failure to conform to the contractual requirements.

Finally, it is not uncommon for changes or modifications to be made to the initial requirements of the funding source. These changes may occur as part of the review process in which the funding agent may request specific changes to your original proposal or request that you provide further explanation for part of the proposal—both of which can result in modifications to the proposal. As a result, any modifications to the original proposal and/or requirements of the funding source must be reviewed thoroughly, since these will replace parts of your initial proposal.

For each of these, a thorough reading must be conducted to ensure full understanding of the intent and requirements of the funding source and precisely what was promised by the applicant/funding recipient. Bear in mind that it is solely the responsibility of the funding recipient to comply with all requirements of the funding grant/contract. Therefore, this process must be wholly initiated by the funding recipient/program developer with a commitment to thoroughness, lest something of significance be missed in implementing the program.

To ensure that all individuals who will be working in the program/project are fully informed as to the program requirements, all relevant documentation should be shared with all key staff. In addition, an orientation should be held to further discuss the requirements and other aspects of the project and to answer any questions regarding the documentation. This should allow for all involved individuals to gain a thorough sense of the project/program. Moreover, these initial review activities can reinforce the significance of being awarded funding and the stewardship it brings—for which all key staff are accountable.

Program Implementation Monitoring

Once everyone has had an opportunity to get acquainted or reacquainted with the project/program through reviewing the official documents and orientation, program implementation is ready to begin. At this point, documentation from the original proposal is essential, especially with regard to planning and design tools such as timelines, Gantt charts, and logic models. Whereas there are multiple aspects of implementation that must be carefully considered and coordinated, each is directed at ensuring the most effective implementation process. Effective, in this sense, means that the program/project is implemented as originally designed (i.e., promised).

In order to ensure this is the case, the implementation must not only be closely guided by the program developer but also be evaluated throughout the implementation process. This type of evaluation is considered a *process evaluation* and focuses on assessing all aspects of the program by comparing the implementation of various activities with the information stipulated in the proposal and other requirements of the funding source. Activities assessed include the time frames in which staff are hired, trained, and begin work; the number and type of staff employed in each of the roles; the recruitment of clients; orientation; and delivery of each of the interventions and supporting activities, to name a few.

Whereas the existing planning tools are essential to effectively guide the implementation process, depending on the scope of the project/program, you may need to develop additional tools for use in implementation and assessing the implementation process. Because process evaluation is one of the types of evaluation that compose a comprehensive program evaluation, it is discussed indepth in the following chapter. At this point, we will focus primarily on methods by which to monitor the implementation process.

Implementation Update meetings are especially helpful in both guiding and assessing the implementation process. For most programs/projects, I recommend that these meetings be held weekly during the first 2 months of implementation and then reduced to biweekly and monthly, as necessary. I say this because the first 2 months of any program/project can be the most challenging and harried time in a program's life cycle. It is not difficult to imagine why this is the case, since during this time, there are competing pressures to finalize the development of any program manuals, policies, or other relevant documents; finalize and coordinate the program evaluation; train and orient new staff; orient clients; engage in public relations and/or marketing efforts to communicate the new program to the public; and attend to a multitude of other activities that all must be done in order to fully implement the program. Because of the chaotic nature of this time period, open and constant communication is a necessity to ensure that nothing is missed, questions are answered, and continuous guidance is provided throughout the process. By creating a venue for this type of communication via weekly *Implementation Update* meetings, you are able to provide the necessary nurturing and monitoring needed to ensure successful implementation. And since achieving a successful program is no easy task, by spending the time up front to guide the implementation process, you are much better suited to attain long-term success for the project.

Program Management

Just as effective implementation is essential to the success of a program, effective management is critical to the sustainability of a program. Sound management begins with fully understanding and appreciating the objectives of a program and possessing a keen understanding of the program's meaning that can be effectively conveyed to clients, staff, and the public— all of which should be revealed through a review of the initial program documentation. Because management comes with a need for leadership, managers must be excellent communicators, able to convey not only the program's purpose but the reason why the purpose is so important to multiple groups.

However, in addition to providing leadership and guidance to the program throughout its life cycle, there are many other aspects of program management. Indeed, management of mental health and human service programs is also composed of the various activities of planning, designing, staffing, budgeting, supervising, monitoring, and evaluating (Lewis, Packard, & Lewis, 2007)—each of which is discussed throughout this text as part of the comprehensive program development process.

Program management is big—in both size and scope, often varying depending on the type of individuals serving as managers and the culture of the organizational and external environment in which they manage. Whereas individuals are needed to manage—thus, the job classification called *managers*—management is not the exclusive domain of individuals with the title of manager/supervisor/administrator. In fact, every staff person connected to a program typically engages in some form of program management. This is because program management includes paying attention to all the details that compose a program, working to ensure that everything is executed as planned, discussing issues and challenges, working collaboratively, collecting and reporting various data, and making changes as warranted, all with the shared goal of program success.

In this context, management refers to a series of processes that is shared by all key stakeholders and is highly collaborative, with input and monitoring occurring at multiple levels (Gibelman & Furman, 2008). As such, these management processes are designed to

- guide, inspire, and motivate;
- monitor and assess;
- correct or resolve problems and/or threats; and
- improve and lead to the attainment of success.

For the sake of this discussion, there are four key areas on which I want to focus, as each relates to program management: leadership and administrative oversight, information systems, quality assurance planning, and contract compliance. These four areas are integral, as each constitutes a specific management system that can effectively guide implementation.

Leadership and Administrative Oversight

"Management is about human beings. Its task is to make people capable of joint performance, to make their strengths effective and their weaknesses irrelevant" (Drucker, 2001, p. 10). As only Peter F. Drucker could, he sums up management concisely and brilliantly. I liken this characterization of management to the aspects of leadership and administrative oversight that are essential parts of program management. The program director/manager is primarily responsible for the program/project, overseeing day-to-day operations, serving as the chief program administrator, and engaging in multiple levels of decision making pertinent to the program, among other tasks. However, leaders of the organization and key administrators, such as human resource and finance executives, provide another layer of oversight to the program. As such, organizational executives are charged with broad-based responsibility for all the company's programs and operations and, therefore, indirectly provide leadership and engage in various types of oversight activities.

Most significantly, an organizational leader directly supervises the program director, ensuring that the director can effectively and successfully implement and sustain her/his program—thus, highlighting the director's strengths while, ideally, teaching the director how to be an effective manager. In addition, organizational leaders and administrators must closely observe and monitor the program's operations, reviewing various types of data (e.g., staffing reports, finance reports, client vacancy rates) and discussing findings and ongoing plans with the program director and/or other program leaders, as well as requiring modifications and/or action plans to correct any deficiencies. In this regard, the organizational leaders and administrators provide a critical layer of management to the program, ultimately designed to ensure the program's success.

Information Systems

Information systems basically refer to forms and types of data collection and storage that allow for maintaining and analyzing various types of information. Today, it is difficult to imagine information systems without immediately thinking of computer technology. Indeed, computers have exponentially changed every aspect of the way that we work and live and, for many, are simply a common part of work and life. And because of the technological advances that have been made, funding source requirements for data collection and data reporting have changed dramatically over the past decade (Kettner, Moroney, & Martin, 2008). As a result, electronic technology is the most common means today to ultimately store and analyze data. However, the sophistication level of technology at a given agency may vary greatly based on financial disparities between organizations that dictate precisely what an organization can afford. Thankfully, relatively inexpensive hardware and software are now available that allow agencies to computerize many of their critical activities (Kettner et al., 2008). Basic spreadsheet programs such as Microsoft Excel and database programs such as Microsoft Access can be used with relative ease and little expense. And through charitable giving programs that provide reduced or no-cost technology to nonprofit organizations, acquiring technology is easier today than ever before in the mental health and human services. For instance, consider the impact that TechSoup Global—an essential technology resource in our field—has made in increasing access to technology for nonprofit organizations over just the past several years.

TECHSOUP GLOBAL

TechSoup Global is one of the most comprehensive technology resources for nongovernmental organizations in the world. Working with corporate donors, including Microsoft, Adobe, Cisco, and Symantec, TechSoup provides nongovernmental organizations, nonprofits, libraries, and community-based organizations with the latest professional hardware, software, and services they need. These information and communication technology donations are available alongside educational content such as articles, webinars, and nonprofit technology community forums. As of June 2009, TechSoup Global has served more than 101,000 organizations, distributed more than 4.9 million technology donations, and enabled nonprofit recipients to save more than $1.4 billion in information technology expenses (TechSoup Global, 2001–2009).

Since we now have such a variety of information systems available, program developers and managers must determine which types of data should be collected through which types of methods. In addition, they must specify precisely how the data will be used. In the mental health and human services industry, multiple types of electronic information systems are available that range in scope and degree of sophistication and functionality. There are electronic information systems designed specifically for accounting and other financial practices, systems designed to support human resource functions such as staff records and benefits, and systems designed to manage client information. Whereas these types of single-focused electronic systems have been developed as stand-alone systems (e.g., accounting), there are also now a host of *integrated electronic systems* that have been developed specifically for the mental health and human service industry. These systems are integrated in the sense that each of the major functions—accounting, human resource management, and client information management—is contained in one electronic information system.

Since the beginning of the new millennium, a host of integrated systems has hit the market, creating quite a wide selection from which organizations can choose. However, the cost of both integrated and function-specific electronic systems varies tremendously and can be cost-prohibitive for many organizations. Because nonprofit organizations typically do not receive specific funding to support such expenses as technology and rent/property, agencies must utilize other funds or create other mechanisms by which to support these critical components of the organizational infrastructure.

Further complicating the financial implications related to purchasing an integrated or stand-alone information system is the fact that payment for these systems is often an ongoing factor. This means that when making these purchases, you must be able to financially plan for 10 to 20 years to ensure the appropriate level of funding support will continue to be available for the system that you wish to use. To give you a sense of the costs that are involved, I recently shopped for a Client Information System (CIS) for a $50 million+ revenue nonprofit agency with approximately 400 users (revenue and users are noted here since costs of systems may be based on one or both). All four of the systems reviewed required both initial setup fees as well as annual maintenance fees. After annualizing the costs of each over 10 years, these products ranged from $40,000 to $130,000—meaning each year, the organization would have to be able to financially support this payment level. To give you another illustration of these costs, these products were projected to cost anywhere from $400,000 to $1.3 million over a 10-year period. This is not to say that all CIS systems require annual maintenance fees, but when they do, thoughtful financial planning must guide purchase decision making. I should add that much less expensive CIS systems are available; however, purchasing a comprehensive client information system for most presents a considerable expense that must be appreciated and thoroughly examined.

In order to address this, due diligence must be conducted to determine precisely what need the organization has and examine the extent of the financial ramifications to ensure effective decision making in this area. Whereas the financial status of an organization will largely dictate the type of information system an organization will be able to purchase, there are a number of questions that should be asked to guide the purchase. First and foremost, everyone involved in the decision-making process must acknowledge that information systems were developed to make work more efficient and effective. At the same time, information systems can be used by individuals and organizations in a manner that produces wasted time and energy and, in effect, creates unnecessary costs to organizations—precisely what information systems are designed to combat! Indeed, I have witnessed many an organization purchase an information system and invest more than 3 years of multiple staff persons' time in modifying it to fit the perceived needs of the organization, just to abandon the system without ever fully implementing it. As a result, the organization is left where it started—only, now with an exorbitant amount of money lost, on both technology and staff time. Therefore, this most fundamental aspect of information systems must be understood prior to engaging in decision making about the potential type of system needed. There must be an understanding that if data is to be captured in an electronic system, the capture must be justified—meaning there must be a plan to use the data following its capture. As such, "every form, procedure, measure, data collection task, and data summary should be created in direct response to a particular need of the agency" (Lewis et al., 2007, p. 197).

Simply by spending the time to evaluate each desired data element and determine if each can be effectively justified for capture, program administrators are able to ensure that all the data they are capturing is necessary. This is not only essential to running an effective and efficient operation, but it is also necessary to convincing and motivating the individuals that are charged with collecting the data. Rare is the individual who wishes to engage in a futile act, and staff persons that collect data are certainly no exception. In fact, because data collection is not typically viewed as an exciting or necessarily meaningful act, it is that much more critical that those collecting data fully understand the rationale for their work. In order to guide the process of determining what types of data should be captured—and are thus justified—the *Data Element Evaluation Tool* was developed (see Table 11.1).

To illustrate the use of the *Data Element Evaluation Tool*, Table 11.2 provides an example of a partially completed evaluation for an independent living program for developmentally disabled adults.

Table 11.1 Data Element Evaluation Tool

The *Data Element Evaluation Tool* is intended for use in initial planning for data collection activities. For each identified data element to be captured, identify the purpose and explain how the data will be used. By doing so, you should be able to effectively vet the data collection process, ensuring that only data that is specifically needed is captured.

Data Element	Purpose of Data	Explanation as to How Data Will Be Used

Table 11.2 Sample Data Element Evaluation Tool

Data Element	Purpose of Data	Explanation as to How Data Will Be Used
Client date of birth	Determines age at various points of intervention	Client demographic reporting
Date of initial intake intervention	Quality assurance indicator	Assessing quality assurance; reporting contract compliance
Date of discharge from program	Calculates number of days of intervention; used to determine 6-month follow-up	Program evaluation; annual report of program
Completion of program status	Contract compliance issue related to number of clients that successfully completed program	Program evaluation; annual report of program; reporting contract compliance

By using this or a similar tool, you can identify desired data elements—which you need to do anyway when preparing to use an information system—justify the reason for needing to collect the data, and explain precisely how the data will be used. While this work may seem tedious, ensuring that all data captured has a specific purpose may result in saving staff and the organization an inordinate amount of time and money that may otherwise have been used to collect unnecessary data. As such, engaging in this work up front may indeed reduce future work.

Quality Assurance Planning

Historically associated with the medical field and emphasized by accreditation bodies, quality assurance has become a basic feature of mental health and human service programming. Just as it sounds, quality assurance is concerned with ensuring quality and seeks to achieve this through ongoing assessment. By utilizing quality assurance, mental health professionals are able to continuously assess the extent to which a program meets identified standards (Royse, Thyer, Padgett, & Logan, 2006). However, unlike outcomes assessment, quality assurance focuses on process issues and activities that reflect the operations of the program. Because of this unique emphasis on processes, quality assurance can indeed be a highly useful component of a comprehensive program/organizational evaluation (Lewis et al., 2007), since it complements other types of assessment.

Quality assurance processes derive from clearly defined policies and procedures that initially guide program implementation. Therefore, planning for quality must begin during the program design phase, with much thought initially given to how each of the program operations will function and how and when each activity will be implemented. Therefore, programs that have been carefully planned and well documented with great attention to detail are highly amenable to quality assurance monitoring. As a result, program developers can ensure that clients receive quality service from the moment the program begins (Hutchins, Frances, & Saggers, 2009) and throughout the entire life of the program.

Quality assurance–related aspects may include

- the time frame in which a client received a physical examination,
- the completion of a comprehensive intake evaluation, or
- the development of an initial treatment plan that reflects a person-centered planning philosophy.

From a psychiatric perspective, quality assurance may include monitoring such treatment aspects as drug selection, changes in drug prescriptions, and compliance with prescription treatment guidelines (Pyrkosch, Psych, & Linden, 2007). By monitoring these activities, program developers and other mental health professionals are able to assess the degree to which quality is maintained throughout implementation.

Whereas some quality assurance aspects are self-determined by the program developer and other key mental health professionals, other aspects may be externally established by accrediting bodies, funders, or other governing bodies. It is because various stakeholders have an investment in the program that clients, board members, staff, and funding sources each should and usually do have input in determining precisely what constitutes quality (Kettner et al., 2008). For instance, issues such as the occurrence of an initial treatment team meeting within the first 3 days of a client's admission and a 6-month follow-up with clients post-discharge may be primary program components chosen by program leaders for quality monitoring, whereas the development of an initial treatment plan within the first 30 days of a client's treatment may be required by the funding agency. Both of these may then be included in the quality assurance plan.

Quality assurance is another area in which, for obvious reasons, it is not quantity but quality that matters. In this sense, the number of quality assurance aspects that are monitored does not necessarily reflect the sophistication level of a quality assurance program, but it is important that each aspect being monitored has substance. Any activity that is being monitored for quality assurance purposes should be deemed a quality indicator. Quality indicators refer to the fact that the activity/aspect being monitored is a reflection of the program's quality. In this regard, the occurrence of the initial treatment team meeting within the first week of a client's admission is indicative of a high level of program responsiveness to client needs and, therefore, constitutes a quality indicator. Similarly, the composition of a multidisciplinary treatment team is also reflective of quality, in that the input of multiple professional perspectives will likely impact the treatment planning process. However, the time of day that the meeting occurred or the number of individuals participating in the treatment team meeting would not constitute quality, as neither is substantive.

For the most part, quality assurance indicators are goals, since they identify a target to be attained. As a result, they should be developed as goal statements that specify both the desired threshold as well as the method by which it will be assessed/measured. Box 11.1 provides a sample of quality assurance indicators developed for a foster care program. It is important to note that, consistent with the nature of quality management, some quality assurance indicators are intended to change over time, illustrating continuous improvement. For instance, once the foster care program staff have reached and sustained the target goal of 470 days or less for permanency (Item 8), the indicator may be revised to 450 days or less, since this type of activity refers specifically to working more diligently on reducing the time children are in the foster care system.

BOX 11.1

SAMPLE QUALITY ASSURANCE
INDICATORS FOR A FOSTER CARE PROGRAM

1. Eighty percent of all foster parents will report that staff members return their calls within 48 hours.

   Measurement: Annual Foster Parent Survey item

2. A team approach to service delivery will be used 100% of the time that includes birth parents, staff, foster parents, and other significant persons and will demonstrate evidence of this approach in the Service Plan and/or Wraparound meeting notes.

   Measurement: Quarterly supervisory case record audits

3. Visitation between birth parents and children in foster care will be arranged within the first 14 days for 100% of families unless contraindicated by the court, and evidence of visitation arrangements will be documented in the Service Plan.

   Measurement: Quarterly supervisory case record audits

4. Foster care workers will have a private, face-to-face visit with all assigned foster children within the first 3 days of placement, and documentation of this will be recorded in the case file in the Initial Service Plan and/or Foster Home Visit record.

   Measurement: Quarterly supervisory case record audits

5. Welcome Packs will be distributed to all birth parents during the first 5 days that their children are in care and will contain information regarding the legal system, foster care, foster homes, foster parents, their rights, and other relevant information in order to provide an orientation to foster care.

   Measurement: Quarterly supervisory case record audits

6. The time between intake completion and case manager assignment will be 4 days or less.

   Measurement: Quarterly supervisory case record audits

7. A mean average number of days in care will be 171 days or less for family reunification cases.

   Measurement: Year-end discharge data analysis

8. Permanency (family reunification or availability for adoption) will be achieved within 470 days or less in order to reduce days in care for children and families.

   Measurement: Year-end discharge data analysis

The degree to which a program/organization establishes a system of quality assurance can vary dramatically; however, it is essential that all programs institute some type of quality assurance program. In fact, it is highly unlikely in this day and age that a program lacking a quality assurance plan will be able to remain in business long, since quality assurance has become an embedded feature in our business and part of standard practice. Without quality assurance monitoring, program developers and leaders have no real sense of how well they are succeeding—or not succeeding—in regard to compliance with various standards of practice.

Because data is a primary ingredient of quality assurance, electronic technology often plays an instrumental role in data storage, management, and analysis. Indeed, the use of an electronic spreadsheet program or a database is critical to maximizing the quality assurance program.

Because quality is predicated on a clear understanding by the program staff of precisely what constitutes quality and a commitment to quality, procedures and plans that allow for ongoing data collection, monitoring, and reporting must be established (Gibelman & Furman, 2008). At the most basic level, a quality assurance system may consist of a brief checklist that captures major quality indicators and that can be easily used by program staff to monitor quality assurance activities twice per year or in some other specified time frame. More sophisticated efforts may involve the development of a quality assurance committee composed of various levels of staff that are charged with both leading and overseeing the quality assurance program. The committee may conduct monthly monitoring, develop quarterly update reports, and engage in annual quality assurance planning. Regardless of the type of quality assurance program that is instituted, a culture of quality must be created within the program/organization in order to most effectively support quality assurance efforts. First and foremost, creating a culture of quality requires a commitment to quality by all staff. This means that every individual staff person has an appreciation of quality assurance, recognizes the significance of the quality indicators, and views quality assurance as pivotal to overall program success. This obviously requires program leaders who can effectively communicate this to staff. More significantly, though, this requires program leaders who view quality assurance as an opportunity for learning and professional development and not a cause for punishment. Therefore, failures to attain quality are viewed as opportunities to learn more about a specific aspect, to dissect what may have gone wrong, to review all its connected parts, and to rethink the aspect/process and perhaps make modifications. Such a culture can exist only when there is open and frequent communication about quality, with constant reinforcement of its significance through regular sharing of results and modifications to the program.

Contract Compliance

Not wholly separate from quality assurance, contract compliance refers specifically to compliance with activities that are required by the contractor/funder. These activities or aspects may be process-oriented and constitute areas that are a part of a quality assurance program, or they may be outcome-oriented and consist of a critical part of an outcomes evaluation. Because contractors/funders are most interested in ensuring that their investment was wisely made, the promulgation and monitoring of specific standards promotes accountability amongst the programs that they have funded and allows funders to be aware of exactly how successful these programs are in this regard.

Examples of contract compliance for an outpatient gambling addiction program may consist of items such as

- a comprehensive intake interview and evaluation conducted within 24 hours of program admission,
- 80% of clients successfully completing the program,
- 100% of clients having an identified sponsor, or
- 80% of clients refraining from gambling 6 months post-discharge.

As you can see, there are both process and outcome issues that may be part of the contractor's compliance requirements. As you can also see, contract compliance issues, just like quality indicators, may be directly related to program outcomes and, therefore, may also be incorporated into the outcomes evaluation.

Because contract compliance issues are not voluntarily selected but rather delineated by the funder, these aspects are nonnegotiable; therefore, continued funding may be dependent on the program's ability to achieve them. Moreover, these must be regularly monitored in accordance with the time frame established by the funder. Therefore, these items should automatically be included in the quality assurance program so that they are embedded in the program's quality assurance plan. Furthermore, if the contractor's monitoring time frames are more frequent and rigorous than those established by program staff, the contractor's time frames should be adopted and used to guide the other aspects of the quality assurance program. This is all done in the spirit of ensuring that the bar is set high enough for us to continuously strive to reach it.

Summary

As you can see, the program implementation process requires attention to multiple details and a great deal of planning and organization; however, effective implementation is largely aided by the work accomplished in the program design phase. As a result, comprehensive and thorough program planning that took place in earlier steps can lead directly to efficient and effective program implementation—once again reinforcing that time and effort invested up front should never be underestimated.

There are two main aspects to program implementation that include fully implementing the program and specific components of program management. The initial implementation involves attention to such details as (1) establishing the relationship with the funding source/contract manager, (2) conducting a thorough review of the grant/contract, and (3) developing a program implementation plan and mechanisms by which to monitor and evaluate the implementation. In terms of program management as related to implementation, the key issues of (1) program leadership and administrative oversight, (2) information systems, (3) quality assurance planning, and (4) contract compliance must each be given appropriate attention.

By attending to each of these areas, the initial program implementation should proceed smoothly. And since so much of the work that has brought you to this point is at stake in the initial implementation, this level of attention to detail is precisely what is needed at this step.

CASE ILLUSTRATION

Lisa and Ann received notification that their proposal for a family-based autism treatment program had been selected to receive funding. After an ample celebration of lattés and muffins, they sat down to fully review the award notification letter and the attached instructions. Per the instructions, they logged into the funder's website to officially accept the award and to consent to following the specific guidelines outlined in the instructions. They then contacted the contract manager who had been assigned to their project. After personally thanking the contract manager, Lisa asked if she would prefer that they check in by phone each month with a verbal update to keep her abreast of their progress between the required 6-month written reports. The contract manager agreed that monthly telephone calls would be effective and that, other than that, Ann and Lisa should feel free to contact her if they ran into a problem or had a question. She also stated that if there were no problems or questions, she did not need more frequent or alternate communication than the monthly phone calls.

After hanging up, Ann and Lisa felt that they had successfully begun to establish a relationship with the contract manager and that they had established a solid plan for keeping her updated throughout the project. Excited to move forward, Ann then coordinated a meeting for all the staff that would be involved with the program. This meeting provided an opportunity for Lisa and Ann to review all the major aspects of the project, including the rationale behind the funding. Lisa highlighted the objectives of the project from the original RFP, and Ann explained the major aspects of the proposal. Ann also shared the award notification letter with all the staff, emphasizing that the funders were particularly pleased with the commitment to family and community building that had been reflected in their proposal.

After answering questions about the program and gaining confirmation that everyone fully understood, Lisa reviewed the implementation plan with the group. She and Ann were glad they had taken the extra time when writing the proposal to develop detailed timelines and project maps to guide implementation. Assignments were made to ensure that someone was responsible for each part of the implementation, including such activities as finalizing staff hiring, recruiting clients, and developing the quality assurance plan.

Because the first clients would need to be served within the next 52 days, Ann reinforced the need for diligent work to the group. And in order to provide additional guidance to everyone during implementation, she established a weekly *Program Implementation Update Meeting* schedule. The update meetings would provide a forum to update progress, answer any questions, and monitor the implementation process.

Ann took on the task of updating the existing client information system to capture specific information for the autism program, some of which was required by the funder and some of which Ann and Lisa determined should be captured. These updates required adding new fields to the database and establishing new linkages between certain data fields. Ann worked directly with Gerri, the information systems administrator, to finalize these changes and prepare the electronic system for the new program.

While Ann devoted time to updating the technology, Lisa worked with Alli, one of the new program supervisors, on developing the initial quality assurance plan. To begin this process, they culled the contract compliance issues and performance standards that were identified in the award documents from the funder. They then incorporated the quality indicators that Lisa and Ann had stipulated in the proposal. Whereas these two data sets provided comprehensive quality indicators, Lisa wanted to ensure that they were not missing anything essential. After reviewing national accreditation standards for children's mental health programs, Alli identified two more critical quality assurance aspects related to individual educational planning and family-based decision making. At the same time, Lisa noted the need for documenting review of the state and federal Mental Health Codes with clients and families as an essential quality issue. They then asked for input from the staff regarding other specific aspects of quality that they wished to monitor. Following several hours of work and lots of input, Alli, Lisa, and Ann took a step back to review the initial draft of the quality assurance plan. Having done so, they felt that they had a solid plan in place and were anxious to present the draft to the group at the upcoming update meeting. Once the plan was finalized with the staff, they would set up the monitoring systems to begin tracking quality and would plan to share the quality assurance plan with the contract manager during their first monthly telephone call.

References

Drucker, P. F. (2001). *The essential Drucker*. New York: HarperCollins.

Gibelman, M., & Furman, R. (2008). *Navigating human service organizations*. Chicago: Lyceum.

Hutchins, T., Frances, T., & Saggers, S. (2009). Australian indigenous perspectives on quality assurance in children's services. *Australasian Journal of Early Childhood, 34*(1), 56–60.

Kettner, P. M., Moroney, R. M., & Martin, L. L. (2008). *Designing and managing programs: An effectiveness-based approach*. Thousand Oaks, CA: Sage.

Lewis, J. A., Packard, T. R., & Lewis, M. D. (2007). *Management of human service programs* (4th ed.). Belmont, CA: Thomson Learning.

Porter, R. (2005). What do grant reviewers really want, anyway? *Journal of Research Administration, 36,* 47–55.

Pyrkosch, L., Psych, D., & Linden, M. (2007). Why do psychiatrists select or switch an antipsychotic? *Psychiatric Times, 24*(4), 42–46.

Royse, D., Thyer, B., Padgett, D., & Logan, T. (2006). *Program evaluation: An introduction* (4th ed.). Belmont, CA: Thomson/Brooks Cole.

TechSoup Global. (2001–2009). *About TechSoup*. Retrieved September 13, 2010, from http://home.techsoup.org/pages/about.aspx

Evaluate the Program

Learning Objectives

1. Differentiate between treatment fidelity assessment, process evaluation, and outcomes evaluation

2. Discuss the significance of research design in program evaluation

3. Provide an example of a quasi-experimental design used in an outcomes evaluation

4. Explain the concept of a *culture of evaluation* and identify at least three methods by which to promote this

5. Identify three costs and three benefits of evaluation

IMPLEMENTING THE *STOP THE VIOLENCE* PROGRAM

After being directly approached by one of her funders/contractors to design a new program for female batterers, Nikki immediately began examining the research in this area. She located a relatively new program model, *Stop the Violence*, which had been implemented in a similar geographic region and had initially achieved successful program outcomes. The program had been evaluated twice, both times by the program developer. Because of the rigor involved (i.e., experimental design) in both of the reviews, the evaluations were considered highly effective, and as such, the program had an established evidence basis.

Encouraged by what she had learned through reading about the program, Nikki contacted the *Stop the Violence* program developer directly, and they talked at length about the program and her hope for implementing the program in her region. The program developer was excited to hear of this interest and agreed to send Nikki additional material about the program. Nikki then communicated back with her funding/contracting agency to let them know that she had identified an evidence-based model and was ready to implement it. Together, they agreed on an implementation date.

After hiring new staff and transitioning existing staff into new positions in the program, Nikki met with the group to review the program. Nikki provided a thorough orientation to the group and spent a considerable amount of time discussing the various aspects of the program, attempting to ensure that the program model was implemented correctly. Nikki also discussed the program evaluation that would begin at implementation to assess the program's success in their region and with their specific client population.

A couple of weeks into the implementation, with 14 clients enrolled in the program, Nikki was called away by her supervisor to address some challenges that were occurring in the agency's independent living program. While Nikki tried to check in on a semiregular basis with her *Stop the Violence* staff, she found this more and more difficult as she became more absorbed in trying to resolve problems in the independent living program.

After being away from the *Stop the Violence* program for 7 months, Nikki was anxious to get back to it and examine the preliminary program outcomes. After reviewing the program evaluation data, Nikki was surprised to see that the program outcome rates were far below the outcomes that the original program had achieved. Nikki met with the program supervisor to talk more indepth about this issue. Through the course of their conversations, the supervisor shared with Nikki that she and the staff had made several modifications to the program that seemed necessary given their client population. The most significant modification involved eliminating group therapy as the primary modality and replacing it with individual therapy. The program supervisor explained to Nikki that this seemed a better option since staff had complained that it was logistically too difficult to get all the clients to a group session. Learning of this and other program modifications that had been made, Nikki quickly called a staff meeting so that she could speak with everyone involved in the program.

Nikki informed the staff that she had made a critical error by not fully educating each of them on the importance of implementing the treatment model in accordance with its original design. She further stated that she had failed to teach the staff about the significant relationships that exist between program design, implementation, and evaluation. She explained that because the *Stop the Violence* model had not been implemented consistent with the original design, similar successful outcomes would likely not be achieved and the initial evaluation data had limited relevance. Rather than wasting any further time, Nikki was able to chalk this unfortunate incident up to an important learning experience for all, and she and the staff quickly turned their attention to thoroughly reviewing every aspect of the original program model, learning specifically about treatment fidelity, process evaluation, and outcomes evaluation—with Nikki ensuring that all her staff were well educated about each. They then immediately set a date for another program implementation and a new program evaluation that would begin simultaneously.

CONSIDERING NIKKI

1. Identify the various steps that Nikki could have taken to prevent this from happening in the first place.

2. What, if any, relevance might the initial evaluation data that Nikki's staff collected have?

3. What is Nikki's responsibility to the clients that received this modified treatment—and what should she do to address this?

4. If you were Nikki, how and what would you communicate to the funder/contract manager?

About This Chapter

This chapter is dedicated to program evaluation and the three major components that compose a comprehensive program evaluation—fidelity assessment, process evaluation, and outcomes evaluation. This step of the model is directly related to Step III (Design the Clinical Program), as it is based on the logic model that was previously developed, as well as the outcomes assessment tools that were initially identified, and utilizes these in finalizing and implementing the formal evaluation. In addition, because evaluation activities—especially fidelity and process evaluation—focus specifically on aspects related to implementation, these evaluation activities must begin concurrently with program implementation (Step IX).

To begin this exploration of program evaluation, we must start with revisiting the program design. Then, we will examine fidelity assessment, process evaluation, and outcomes evaluation. Next, we will discuss the development of the program evaluation plan, giving special attention to measuring program outcomes, selecting outcomes tools, and establishing time frames. This will be followed by a discussion of the various considerations in evaluation, including the costs and benefits associated with evaluation and the importance of creating an evaluation-friendly environment. The chapter will conclude with an exercise to further illuminate the costs and benefits related to evaluation and a case illustration to highlight the major issues discussed throughout the chapter.

STEP X: EVALUATE THE PROGRAM

Evaluation

Each of the steps (i.e., components) of the comprehensive program development model has a specific value and plays a specific role, and without attending to each, the full benefits of the model cannot be realized. This is because the components are interdependent—relying on one another to build toward the overarching goal of designing, implementing, and sustaining a program that is successful in addressing the mental health or human service needs of its consumers. No better example of the interdependent nature of these relationships can be found than that of the relationship between program design and program evaluation. Measuring the effectiveness of a program design requires a program evaluation, and an effective program evaluation requires planning for the evaluation at the point of program implementation. Therefore, without one, the other is severely limited.

An emphasis on program evaluation has continued to gain strength over the past several decades as a means by which private and public organizations can work toward quality and efficiency (Stufflebeam, 2000). Because evaluation allows you to measure and assess various elements of design, process, and impact or outcomes, it is critical to sustainability. This is truer in the 21st century than ever before, since accountability and evidence-based practices are standard protocol in program development today. Indeed, few funding sources will support programs and/or projects without an established evidence basis, and in addition, programs/projects that cannot achieve their intended outcomes may be short-lived. At the same time, an evidence-based program design does not guarantee that the program outcomes will be automatically attained or that the program will be implemented in the same manner as the original design. Moreover, an evidence-based design does not imply that the results of an evaluation are necessarily valid, since the validity is dependent on the degree to which evidence-based methods are replicated in subsequent implementations.

> In any evaluation, it is important to address not only whether the intervention worked but also whether the implementation of the intervention was sufficient to permit a good test. The problem is compounded when a weak implementation is accompanied by a weak process evaluation. Then when the program yields null results, there is no way to determine whether the negative findings were due to poor implementation of the program, poor implementation of the evaluation, or poor program theory. (Orwin, 2000, p. 309)

Nikki was able to take her mishap in stride, not only taking responsibility for the mistakes that were made but turning the mistakes into an opportunity to teach her staff about the significance of such concepts as fidelity, process evaluation, and outcomes evaluation. Few would deny that this type of learning is often the richest kind—attained through our own actions, our own mistakes, and allowing for a redo in order to get it right. Unfortunately, though, this type of mistake can be extraordinarily costly—not only in staff time and other expenses incurred in the initial and subsequent implementations but, more significantly, in the costs to the clients who did not receive adequate treatment. This last cost is the one that matters the most, and it is the primary reason that mental health professionals must be knowledgeable and fully competent in evaluation methods.

Revisiting the Program Design

Any type of program-related evaluation must begin with the program design. This is because the program design is the essential driver needed to guide the evaluation. For instance, you cannot assess the degree to which a program model was implemented in accordance with the original design if you are uncertain of the original design and have not accounted fully for the design in the assessment procedures. The same is true for an evaluation of the processes involved in implementation—if you do not know what steps should be involved, you will not have anything meaningful to measure the implementation process against. Finally, if an outcomes evaluation is not constructed based on the program design, while you may be able to identify outcomes, you will have limited information as to the specific interventions that may have led to those outcomes—and failures to achieve outcomes.

To better understand this, consider the logic model discussed in Chapter 5. Recall the purpose of the logic model in providing a graphical representation of the program that, in short, identifies

- the need or problem to be addressed,
- the interventions and services designed to address the need, and
- the short- and long-term outcomes of the program.

All this information is needed to guide the program evaluation process. And as a result, the logic model is not only an essential program design tool but also an essential evaluation tool. In fact, the logic model and other design tools and components of program design contain information necessary to program assessment and evaluation efforts so that all program assessment and/or evaluation planning efforts actually begin during the initial program design process.

There are three major types of evaluation relevant to clinical programs:

1. Fidelity assessment

2. Process evaluation

3. Outcomes evaluation

These are all highly interdependent (as Nikki illustrated in the case vignette above)—work in one area will undoubtedly impact work in another. In addition, each is distinct—serving a specific purpose. Therefore, program developers and other mental health professionals must not only understand the various types of evaluation methods, but they must be able to distinguish between them.

Types of Evaluation

Fidelity Assessment

"Intervention fidelity means that the intervention was conducted as planned" (Horner, Rew, & Torres, 2006, p. 80) or indicates the degree to which the integrity of a program's original design is maintained when the program is being implemented. Fidelity assessment is concerned with ensuring that the original intent of the design is maintained and that each design component has been adhered to throughout the implementation process. Moreover,

> treatment fidelity is defined as the strategies that monitor and enhance the accuracy and consistency of an intervention to ensure it is implemented as planned and that each component is delivered in a comparable manner to all participants/clients. (Smith, Daunic, & Taylor, 2007, p. 121)

Whereas fidelity assessment is highly useful when assessing newly designed treatment models that have not yet been evaluated, it is imperative in assessing treatment models that have previously been evaluated to ensure that the treatment was implemented as designed.

Fidelity assessment is critical to determining the efficacy and effectiveness of any treatment practice (Smith et al., 2007), and as such, fidelity assessment can be viewed as a part of process evaluation; however, whereas process evaluation assesses the entire implementation process and related aspects, fidelity assessment specifically focuses on adherence to the original treatment design.

Because fidelity assessment is a relatively new concept in mental health and human services, the Treatment Fidelity Workgroup of the National Institutes of Health Behavior Change Consortium was created to advance understanding and knowledge of treatment fidelity as well as methodology and measurement of fidelity (Bellg et al., 2004). The Workgroup developed a conceptual framework for understanding treatment fidelity and set forth guidelines and recommendations that cover the five major areas of fidelity:

- Design
- Training
- Delivery
- Receipt
- Enactment

Each of these areas is considered pertinent to maintaining treatment fidelity, and as such, great attention must be paid to each prior to and during treatment implementation. *Design* focuses on each of the specific elements of program design to ensure that there is complete understanding of the design and the original design is kept intact during implementation. *Training* focuses on various issues related to preparing staff for program implementation and various characteristics that might influence fidelity, such as competency and theoretical orientation. The recommendations that were made in the area of training related to such issues as hiring for the appropriate qualifications and developing training and other supports to ensure treatment fidelity. *Delivery* focuses on the implementation process itself and methods for monitoring implementation to ensure that the interventions were delivered as intended. The *Receipt* category refers to the degree to which treatment recipients understand the treatment interventions and anticipated outcomes. Finally, *Enactment* refers to treatment outcomes and the ability of recipients to enact the skills acquired from the intervention.

These categories are not mutually exclusive. Inattention to one category could compromise the internal validity of the study despite adherence to the other categories. For example, without assessing provider skill acquisition and maintenance, it cannot be determined if nonsignificant results are due to an ineffective intervention or to a lack of attention to the training issues (Borelli et al., 2005).

To move the conceptual framework into practice, Borelli et al. (2005) developed the *Treatment Fidelity Assessment Checklist* (see Box 12.1). The assessment evaluates fidelity in each of the five categories and was derived directly from the conceptual framework of fidelity.

BOX 12.1

TREATMENT FIDELITY ASSESSMENT CHECKLIST

Treatment Design

Provided information about the treatment dose in the intervention condition

Provided information about the treatment dose in the comparison condition

Mention of provider credentials

Mention of theoretical model or clinical guidelines on which the intervention is based

Training Providers

Description of how providers were trained

Standardized provider training

Measured provider skill acquisition post-training

Described how provider skills are maintained over time

Delivery of Treatment

Included method to ensure that the content of the intervention was being delivered as specified

Included method to ensure that the dose of the intervention was being delivered as specified

Included method to assess if the provider actually adhered to the intervention plan

Assessed nonspecific treatment effects

Used treatment manual

Receipt of Treatment

Assessed subject comprehension of the intervention during the intervention period

Included a strategy to improve subject comprehension of the intervention above and beyond what is included in the intervention

Assessed subject's ability to perform the intervention skills during the intervention period

Included a strategy to improve subject performance of the intervention skills during the intervention period

Enactment of Treatment Skills

Assessed subject performance of the intervention skills assessed in settings in which the intervention might be applied

Assessed strategy to improve subject performance of the intervention in the setting in which the intervention might be applied

The *Treatment Fidelity Assessment Checklist* may prove a useful guide to developing a fidelity assessment for use with a broad range of treatment interventions and, as such, is a welcome addition to an assessment toolbox.

In terms of the actual use of fidelity assessment in evaluating specific programs, efforts have been made in an attempt to quantify and guide fidelity assessment of different types of treatment interventions that have included family grief therapy (Chan, O'Neill, McKenzie, Love, & Kissane, 2004), the Wraparound Model of community-focused programming for youth and their families (Bruns, Burchard, Suter, Leverentz-Brady, & Force, 2004), serious emotional disorders in children (Epstein et al., 2003), and a cognitive-behavioral approach to relapse prevention in individuals with psychosis (Alvarez-Jiminez et al., 2008). Let's take a closer look at two of these fidelity assessments, in which two very different tools were developed—the Wraparound Model and the cognitive-behavioral approach for relapse prevention. In the first, attempts have been made to evaluate fidelity of the nationally used Wraparound Model. To this end, the Wraparound Fidelity Index was developed (Bruns et al., 2004), and initial reports found this tool to be useful in assessing the model—a model that has been used across the country over the past 2 decades.

The second fidelity assessment tool may be of even greater interest to mental health professionals because it was designed to focus specifically on the therapeutic process (Alvarez-Jiminez et al., 2008). This tool, the Relapse Prevention Therapy-Fidelity Scale, was designed to assess the major therapeutic components, which included assessment/engagement, agenda, psychoeducation, early warning signs, cognitive-behavioral interventions, and review/termination as well as the use of general therapeutic factors. The tool allowed the evaluators to drill down to the micro level of the therapeutic process to evaluate the degree to which treatment fidelity was maintained. This type of micro-level tool may have specific promise as efforts toward treatment fidelity assessment continue to grow and varying levels of fidelity are explored.

Fidelity is critical for many reasons, chief among them being the relationship between fidelity and the use of evidence-based practices. In our 21st-century climate that emphasizes the use of evidence-based practices and increased accountability in mental health treatment, the concept of fidelity is critical. This is because evidence-based practices are predicated on previous evaluations that have found the practices to be effective and, thus, evidence-based. Therefore, individuals wishing to adopt evidence-based practices must do so in a manner that replicates the original implementation of the treatment and maintains the integrity of the practices. Failure to do so would imply that evidence-based practices have not been adopted.

The fact that we currently emphasize the use of evidence-based practices without a parallel emphasis on fidelity assessment should cause concern, since without assessing for fidelity, there is no evidence that the integrity of the program/model has been maintained. In fact, only 27% of the practice research conducted on youth with emotional and/or behavioral disorders reported treatment fidelity data (Mooney, Epstein, Reid, & Nelson, 2003). Interestingly, Borelli et al. (2005) used the *Treatment Fidelity Assessment Checklist* to evaluate treatment fidelity in articles in five journals and found that only 27% of the 342 studies reviewed had assessed if the treatment was delivered as specified. So while recent discussions of treatment fidelity assessment have gained prominence, the act of conducting treatment fidelity assessments has yet to become part of the common protocol of program development—much to my dismay.

However, if we continue in the future to examine treatment fidelity as a critical issue of program development, we should hopefully begin to see an increase in fidelity assessment as well. Moreover, the process of assessing for treatment fidelity may draw attention to the need for clearly delineated program design that is conducive to effective fidelity assessment. This additional outcome may indeed move the area of program development forward as greater attention to detail is provided in the initial program design. In the case of multisystemic therapy, the Office of Juvenile Justice and Delinquency Prevention has put forth funding to specifically promote the successful dissemination of the treatment model (Schoenwald, Henggeler, Brondino, & Rowland, 2000). This is not an uncommon occurrence, since often, the relationship between research and funding is a symbiotic one—with research agendas being driven by funding priorities and vice versa. So it is hoped that with this specific funding made available to promote treatment fidelity, there will indeed be an increased focus on the implications of treatment fidelity in comprehensive program development.

Process Evaluation

Whereas treatment fidelity focuses intensively on adherence to program design, process evaluation focuses on the broader aspects related to the implementation process. I should point out that process evaluation has been referred to by other names, such as *monitoring* and *implementation evaluation,* and in some cases, fidelity assessment has been referred to as process evaluation (Kettner, Moroney, & Martin, 2008). To effectively differentiate these three constructs—fidelity, process implementation, and outcomes evaluation—I will be referring to each independently.

Basically, a process evaluation sets out to accomplish the following:

- Describe the program's implementation process
- Assess whether the services were delivered to the intended recipients (Orwin, 2000)

- Provide descriptive information about the type and quantity of program activities
- Provide information about program outcomes relative to program costs
- Assess if programs have been implemented as expected (Lewis, Packard, & Lewis, 2007)

Whereas fidelity assessment provides essential information specifically related to maintaining the integrity of a clinical model, process evaluation has a much broader scope—thus, it provides several other benefits. For one, process evaluation allows program administrators an opportunity to critically evaluate the number and type of resources dedicated to a particular program. Resources such as staff, travel, training, and other such expenses attributed to a program can be examined. As such, administrators and managers can better understand the relationship between program interventions, resources, and outcomes. Because of this focus, administrators may be better equipped to think about program development efforts not only in terms of effectiveness but also in terms of efficiency (Lewis et al., 2007).

In addition to evaluating resource allocation, process evaluations also allow for immediate feedback, since this type of evaluation assesses activities as they are being implemented (i.e., in process). As a result, you are able to obtain immediate feedback about many aspects of the implementation, some of which are crucial to ongoing planning efforts. For instance, a process evaluation assesses such areas as client type, number of clients served, and time frames in which clients were served. This type of information can inform you not only if the *target population* is being served (i.e., client type) but also if the intended number of clients are being served within the expected time frames. Equipped with such information, program staff are able to make necessary adjustments quickly, particularly if increased recruitment activities are needed. This information also can be used to prompt program staff to engage in more thorough planning efforts to address any challenges detected during implementation. In addition, this type of information is often required by funding sources, thereby reflecting another concrete purpose of conducting a process evaluation.

Technically speaking, the types of issues examined in a process evaluation are varied and often determined by the program design, staff, and the evaluator/evaluation team based on specific data needs. Whereas evaluating data related to the target population—such as the number of clients served and the time frames in which they were served—is a typical part of a process evaluation, the number of interventions and the scope of services provided to each client and changes in assigned clinicians and/or other support staff may also provide meaningful information. By collecting this type of information, you are able to monitor specific aspects of the program—ensuring that identified targets are met and reviewing essential data. This type of monitoring (Lewis et al., 2007)—another feature of a process evaluation—can provide additional benefits needed to effectively manage the program and, as such, is often related to quality assurance.

Kettner et al. (2008, p. 256) sum up some of the major questions answered through a process evaluation:

- What proportion of the community need is the program meeting?
- Are only eligible target-group clients being served?
- Are subgeographical areas and subgroups being served in appropriate numbers?
- What products and services are being provided and in what amounts?
- What results are being achieved in terms of outputs and outcomes?

Additional questions that may be used to guide a process evaluation include the following:

- Are the expected number of staff involved in the program?
- Are the expected types and levels of resources being dedicated to the program?
- Are the services being provided in the expected location(s)?
- Are the expected number of services being provided?
- Is the service being provided in the expected time frames?
- Were there any changes in staffing throughout the implementation process?
- What factors may have influenced the implementation process?

The answers to each of these questions can provide important information to promote increased understanding of the implementation process. Moreover, this information is essential to outcomes evaluation since any nuances of program implementation may significantly impact the program outcomes and, therefore, need to be fully considered.

Outcomes Evaluation

Unlike fidelity assessment and process evaluations, outcomes evaluations focus on the results or the effect of the interventions on the clients. Outcomes evaluations—also confusingly referred to as *program evaluations*—provide the most important information to mental health professionals—that is, the impact that their work has had on the individuals served. Whereas process evaluations rely on clearly defined objectives that are activity-based (e.g., number of sessions) in order to conduct the evaluation, outcomes evaluation relies on impact objectives (Lewis et al., 2007). This clearly differentiates these two types of evaluation. In addition, outcomes evaluation is a hypothesis-testing activity (Kettner et al., 2008)—the results of which indicate if the desired impact has been achieved.

In order to be effectively evaluated, outcomes must be observable, measureable, and developed in behavioral terms. "If objectives are clearly written, criteria and standards for success can be developed in relation to them" (Lewis et al., 2007, p. 234). In the mental health and human services industries, there are typically three major categories into which program outcomes fall:

1. Knowledge-based outcomes

2. Affectively based outcomes

3. Behaviorally based outcomes

Knowledge-based outcomes are used to evaluate changes in a client's knowledge as a result of an intervention. Alternatively, affectively based outcomes are concerned with assessing changes in a client's affect or emotional state that may be impacted by treatment, while behaviorally based outcomes focus on changes in behavior resulting from therapeutic interventions. Table 12.1 provides examples of short-term/intermediate and program completion outcomes for each of the three categories.

As you can see in the examples provided, each of the outcomes is written in measureable and observable terms, with the exception of the self-reported outcome related to self-esteem. This is because of the inherent difficulty in trying to quantify the construct of self-esteem. As a result, self-report may be used as a means for the client to indicate change in self-esteem. Whereas this type of evaluation method is not ideal, at times, it may prove the best of what is available, depending on the types of outcomes being measured. In addition to the self-report measure used, the examples also illustrate various other types of outcome measurements that include pre/post-test scores of a standardized instrument (e.g., Beck Depression Inventory) and concrete measures (e.g., independent living). The selection of outcome measures should be guided by identifying the most relevant and effective tool/activity given the outcome. Finally, the examples illustrate outcome thresholds or targets. This, too, is highly significant and must be based on previous rates of success with the interventions/program—when the

Table 12.1 Examples of Outcome Types

Outcome Category	Example
Knowledge-based outcomes	At the end of the sixth week of treatment, 90% of clients will be able to identify their cycle of addiction.
	At program completion, 80% of clients will be able to identify three community resources that they can access for domestic violence services.
Affectively based outcomes	At the end of the eighth week of treatment, 80% of clients will report improved self-esteem.
	At program completion, 80% of clients will have experienced a decrease in depressive symptoms as measured by pre/post-test scores of the Beck Depression Inventory.
Behaviorally based outcomes	At the end of the eighth week of services, 80% of clients will be employed or enrolled in an academic or vocational training program.
	At program completion, 95% of clients will be living independently.

interventions and/or program are not being piloted for the first time—or with success rates from alternative interventions. As such, target areas are guided by data and existing evidence that indicate expected results.

For instance, when implementing a newly designed program for young women with bulimia nervosa, the targeted outcome threshold should be based on previous outcome studies so that if outcomes of full recovery at 1 year post-treatment have ranged from 76% to 92% with a mean of 85%, the targeted outcome for the same goal should be set at 85%. By doing this, you are able to evaluate your program outcomes in relation to other previously reported outcomes, ensuring that you are indeed setting the bar high enough to achieve results previously attained.

Loesch (2001) most effectively sums up outcomes evaluation as a process that is

1. used for making reasonable determinations about program efforts, efficiency, effectiveness, and adequacy;

2. based on systematic data collection and analysis;

3. designed for uses in external accountability and internal program management and future planning; and

4. focused on acceptability, awareness, availability, comprehensiveness, accessibility, integration, continuity, and cost.

Because outcomes evaluation has grown into a distinct field on its own, referring to specialized skill sets and often large-scale evaluations that may include multiple states and regions, it is important to differentiate between the scale levels of outcomes evaluations. Depending on the work that you do, you may be involved with large-scale program evaluation; however, most mental health and human service practitioners engage in small-scale, localized program development efforts. As such, these small-scale outcomes evaluations are considered micro-evaluations—a type of action research geared toward monitoring and improving a particular program or service (Astramovich & Coker, 2007).

The United Way's Outcome Measurement Resource Center contains a broad array of books, tools, and other resources to aid in outcomes evaluation. To review their offerings, visit www.liveunited.org/outcomes.

Developing the Outcomes Evaluation Plan

As is true of all evaluation efforts, the outcomes evaluation is a complex process and, as such, requires significant planning. In addition to conducting all the preparatory work needed to effectively support the evaluation process, there are three major areas that compose the planning process:

1. Determining the evaluation design
2. Selecting the assessment instruments
3. Establishing the evaluation time frames

Outcomes Evaluation Design

Similar to fidelity assessment and process evaluation, outcome evaluations are highly complex and require a tremendous amount of planning, effort, and attention to detail. Outcome evaluations are the driving force behind the development of evidence-based practices. Indeed, without an effective program evaluation, an evidence basis cannot be established. As a result, the highest degree of scientific rigor is required in order to most effectively evaluate outcomes. To this end, randomized clinical trials (RCTs) have become the gold standard for the efficacy of outcome evaluations. This is because of the potential of RCTs to maximize internal validity (i.e., attribute outcomes directly to the treatment rather than other causes; Del Boca & Darkes, 2007). The significance of the interdependent relationship shared by fidelity assessment, process evaluation, and outcomes evaluation is further underlined by the requirement of RCTs, because RCTs are dependent on treatment fidelity as well as an effective process evaluation.

Whereas RCTs are indeed the gold standard, experimental designs that use a control group (i.e., withhold treatment) are not always feasible in practice settings for ethical as well as logistical reasons. As a result, program developers must be well versed in various types of program evaluation design to ensure that the most effective and ethically sound evaluation is used. Although there are multiple types of design that can be used, I would like to focus briefly on quasi-experimental design, since it may account for the most rigorous type of design, given the inherent challenges of research in practice settings.

One of the most commonly used types of quasi-experimental design in mental health and human services is the pre/post-test design. In the pre/post-test design, clients can be randomly assigned or deliberately assigned to either one of two treatments or to a treatment or control group (i.e., no treatment is provided). But again, because of ethical reasons prohibiting the withholding of treatment to those in need, pre/post-test design in practice settings typically involves assigning clients to one of two treatments—an evaluation design that is increasingly common today (Heppner, Wampold, & Kivlighan, 2008).

A pre/post-test design allows you to examine pretest differences, a critical aspect when comparing unequivalent groups. In comparison to a post-test–only design, the pre/post-test design is stronger and more interpretable because of this (Heppner et al., 2008). However, it should be noted that a threat to this type of design is related to potential problems with external validity that can occur as a result of pretest sensitization—the pretest itself creates a difference between the two groups. However, most agree that this is minor, and the benefits of the design outweigh this risk (Heppner et al., 2008; Kazdin, 2003).

The aspect of random selection should be briefly discussed, particularly as it can significantly impact the integrity of the pre/post-test design. In order to maximize the strength of research findings, the two treatment groups being evaluated should be equal. Such equality among treatment participants is referred to as between-groups design—meaning that the groups are equal prior to treatment. By ensuring this, you are able to more easily attribute post-treatment differences to the treatment. Accounting for between-groups equality requires random selection of participants to one of the two or more groups. Random selection, or randomization, means that participants have been assigned without bias. Random selection can be accomplished in several ways, such as assignment to one of the two groups based on order of program admission—Client 1 is assigned to Treatment 1, Client 2 to Treatment 2, Client 3 to Treatment 1, Client 4 to Treatment 2, and so on. In this type of randomization, all odd-number admissions are assigned to Treatment 1, while all even-number admissions are assigned to Treatment 2. While quite straightforward, this type of randomization requires that clients enter in a sequential manner and that the sequence of client admission is tracked. This may not be feasible in some practice settings, particularly when clients are admitted en masse. To address this issue, the old and trusted hat trick may serve better. You can simply place the names of all clients in a hat, and use the order in which names are pulled to assign the clients to one of the two treatment groups (i.e., first name pulled is assigned to Treatment 1, second name to Treatment 2, third name to Treatment 1, etc.). As with every aspect of research design, the issue of random selection must be given adequate attention in order to further strengthen your overall design.

While basic research design composes one part of an evaluation program, the other area that must be given thoughtful attention is that of research methods; however, such a discussion is outside the scope of this text. A number of quantitative and qualitative research methods may be used in program evaluation as relevant to the study design, and a good resource for use in designing the program evaluation is Heppner et al.'s (2008) *Research Design in Counseling*.

Whereas little can replace firm knowledge of research design, attention to specific issues related to design may provide basic guidance for planning the research design (see Box 12.2).

BOX 12.2

BASIC GUIDE TO DETERMINING THE RESEARCH DESIGN

- Consult your profession's ethical standards related to research.
- Review each of the potential types of research design to identify the most rigorous design that can be implemented within the practice setting.
- Seek out more and new knowledge as needed to increase your own competency level with regard to research design and analysis.
- Consult with experts in research design and statistical analysis as needed.
- Involve staff and other stakeholders in the design selection process to promote early engagement in the research.

Most importantly, before embarking on any research design project, ensure that you have a comprehensive grasp of research design and methods. This often requires revisiting research methods coursework, pursuing new coursework, attending training and workshops focused on research design and methods, and utilizing the vast array of texts and tools available to you in this area. Failure to do so will almost certainly threaten your ability to effectively evaluate your program's outcomes. It is often at this stage that we get to finally put to practice in the real world what we have learned only conceptually or through academic assignments. As a result, this should be viewed as an exciting opportunity to grow. Therefore, regardless of any previous struggles that you may have experienced with research design and/or methods, applying research in practice often signifies the opening of a window that has not been opened before. So rather than facing it with discomfort or fear, pursue it with zest and perseverance, and once you have thoroughly engaged in it, the stimulation and sense of accomplishment will reinforce how truly rewarding the process of learning is.

Selecting Assessment Tools

The research design will guide the selection of assessment instruments. This is particularly true if you have selected a pre/post-test design, since assessment instruments that assess change over time are needed rather than assessment instruments that have been developed to assess issues that are static or not prone to change. For instance, there are assessment instruments that evaluate potential risk based on events that occurred at a particular time in a person's life, such as the age at which an individual committed his/her first crime or when an individual was physically abused. The results of this type of assessment will not change over time; therefore, the assessment is intended to be used just one time to gain specific information. However, other assessment instruments are developed precisely to evaluate change over time and, therefore, are designed to be given multiple times. Examples of these types of outcomes include mental health functioning, recidivism, sobriety, and employment. These types of outcomes lend themselves to evaluation through a pre/post-test research design, whereas the former (i.e., static outcomes) do not.

Selecting both the most effective and the most relevant assessment tools for an outcomes evaluation requires quite a bit of work and investigation; however, much of this work should have been completed during the program design stage (discussed in Chapter 5). At this step, then, it means revisiting the program design in order to review previously selected assessment instruments and determine if additional instruments are needed. There are several guidance factors that should be considered in the selection of assessment instruments:

- Use assessment instruments only with established psychometric properties.
- Use assessment instruments only for their intended purpose and in the manner in which they have been found to be effective.
- Ensure a thorough understanding of the strengths and limitations of assessment instruments.
- Review the qualifications level needed to administer a test, and ensure that individuals charged with test administration have the required qualifications.
- Ensure a firm understanding of the ethical standards that guide the use of assessment instruments.
- Use assessment instruments for the purpose of treatment planning and improving treatment and services, not for denying or limiting services that would otherwise be provided.
- Ensure a firm understanding of the role that testing conditions play in test performance, work to promote optimal testing conditions, and include a discussion of testing conditions and potential impact on test scores in the testing summary.
- Gather and maintain assessment data, as you do all client information, in a confidential manner, and protect it in accordance with all relevant state and federal laws.
- Practice additional compliance as required for all research protocols, policies, and laws when using assessment data for research purposes (e.g., outcomes/program evaluation).
- Gain consent and/or authorization, when required, from the oversight organization with indirect responsibility for the client, in addition to gaining consent from clients and/or other authorized individuals (in the case of minors and vulnerable adults).
- Conduct all research in accordance with laws regarding the protection of human subjects and with authorization and oversight by an institutional review board.

In addition, a valuable resource regarding the use of tests is *Responsibilities of Users of Standardized Tests*, promulgated by the Association for Assessment in Counseling (2003). The publication provides broad-based guidance in seven key areas:

1. Qualifications of test users

2. Technical knowledge

3. Test selection

4. Test administration

5. Test scoring

6. Administering test results

7. Communicating test results

The publication is available at no cost through the association's website (www.theaaceonline.com).

Establishing Evaluation Time Frames

Conducting any type of evaluation is always a lengthy process—and understandably so, given all that is involved. This is why planning for the evaluation is such a critical aspect. Part of this planning process requires the establishment of evaluation time frames. Essentially, these are the time frames in which the actual evaluation will be conducted. For instance, a basic research design may include one pretest and one post-test that will be given at program admission and then at program discharge, respectively. However, there are multiple other time frames that may be used based on the research design, some of which allow you to evaluate progress during the treatment process and others that allow you to evaluate long-term treatment gains. Table 12.2 provides examples of time frames for conducting assessment activities based on the research design.

Table 12.2 Evaluation Time Frame Samples

Design Type	Admission	6 Months Post-Admission	Discharge	6 Months Post-Discharge	1 Year Post-Discharge	2 Years Post-Discharge
Basic pre/post-test	X		X			
Pretest, intermediate, and post-test	X	X	X			
Pre/post-test, short- and long-term follow-up	X		X	X	X	
Pre/post-test and long-term follow-up	X		X		X	X

In addition to identifying time frames for conducting specific assessment activities, "developing a timeline to facilitate the collection of data for the development, maintenance, and revision of the program evaluation plan is recommended" (Gard, Flannigan, & Cluskey, 2004, p. 177). Again, I cannot stress enough the use of specific planning tools to help organize the planning process. Whereas timelines are often essential, Gantt charts and project maps may also prove indispensable not only in managing your time but also in communicating plans to others.

Comprehensive Evaluation Planning

Whereas a large part of this chapter has been devoted to outcomes evaluation and its various aspects, mental health professionals should be engaging in comprehensive evaluation that includes all three types of evaluation discussed above—fidelity assessment, process evaluation, and outcomes evaluation. This is because each has specific relevance and, therefore, is conducted for specific purposes. Indeed, comprehensive evaluation planning should include the use of multiple types of evaluation and should be used to guide long-term evaluation activities.

When engaging in comprehensive program evaluation, several issues must be attended to that include, but are not limited to, the following:

- Identify specifically what is being evaluated and why and how the evaluation results will be disseminated and used to inform treatment and services.
- Engage all stakeholders in the evaluation process early in order to sustain engagement throughout the evaluation process.
- Provide orientation and training to all evaluation participants to promote knowledge and understanding of evaluation procedures, rationale, and methods.
- Establish a comprehensive evaluation plan with identified evaluation types and time frames as part of initial program planning.

In addition to promoting effective program management, engaging in comprehensive evaluation planning ensures that the evaluation processes are well organized and are a pivotal part of program development.

Considerations in Evaluation

As mentioned earlier, evaluation can be one of the most rewarding endeavors in which you engage, particularly as viewed from a program management perspective. In order to fully consider all that is involved and related to evaluation efforts, there are three key areas that I would like to highlight:

1. Evaluation as a tool for organizational sustainability

2. Costs and benefits of evaluation

3. Creating a culture of evaluation

Evaluation as a Tool for Organizational Sustainability

Evaluation is a tool—a tool that is used by professionals in order to gain critical information. In the case of process and outcomes evaluations, data is collected and analyzed to determine the efficiency, effectiveness, and impact of programs and services (Boulmetis & Dutwin, 2005). As such, evaluation demonstrates accountability—the accountability of a provider of services to the recipient/client, to the funder or contractor of services, to the public, to the profession to which the provider belongs, and to the industry in which the provider is working. It is this accountability that may allow the provider to continue providing services—just as, conversely, a lack of accountability may result in the discontinuation of practice.

Because the appropriate and effective use of evidence-based practices guides the mental health and human service fields today, evaluation is no longer an optional activity for those who are so moved but a required activity that must be incorporated into all aspects of practice. Indeed, when called on to provide evidence of program or intervention effectiveness, mental health professionals can effectively draw on information gathered from the evaluations that they have instituted (Astramovich & Coker, 2007). As such, evaluation is a tool—a tool necessary for the long-term sustainability of the service, program, organization, and counseling and other mental health professions.

The Costs and Benefits of Evaluation

As any good manager knows, never embark on any new endeavor without conducting a thorough cost-benefit analysis. Otherwise, you may find that your investment far outweighs your return, that what you received was far from what you originally hoped, or any number of other unfortunate surprises. There are multiple potential costs and benefits related to engaging in evaluation efforts. I use the term *potential* since, ultimately, the outcomes will dictate actual costs and benefits. Table 12.3 provides a sample of some of the costs and benefits typically associated with evaluation efforts.

| Table 12.3 | Sample of Potential Costs and Benefits of Engaging in Evaluation Efforts |

Costs	Benefits
Staff/personnel time and energy	Increased staff/personnel engagement to work/program/organization
Economic costs in staff time and/or purchasing the work of outside consultants	Professional development of staff; increased knowledge and competencies
	Professional satisfaction related to increased understanding of the effects of work
	Client trust related to organizational accountability
	Contractor/funder trust related to organizational accountability
	Increased business
	Long-term sustainability of service, program, organization

The point here, although rather obvious, is that the benefits resulting from engaging in evaluation efforts should always greatly outweigh the costs. And while only few costs and benefits are economic and can be easily quantified, the benefits to the professionals involved in evaluation efforts are priceless. This is of particular significance in a profession that does not naturally receive immediate feedback about the impact of our work. Unlike the car salesperson who gains immediate feedback about her/his selling ability based on the act of completing a car sale or the senator who witnesses the passage of a bill that s/he authored, many mental health professionals rarely gain substantial feedback about their work unless an evaluation has been conducted. It is in this regard, then, that evaluations provide significant and meaningful information about our work. Even when anticipated outcomes have not been attained, evaluation data usually provides other significant information and is useful for service/treatment improvement efforts and, as such, provides essential input to our work.

Creating a Culture of Evaluation

The environment in which an evaluation is conducted plays a major role in any evaluation process. This is due to many reasons, not least of which is the very intent of evaluation—to assess or evaluate how one is doing. And in this case, it means evaluating the work of mental health professionals. For many of us—regardless of how otherwise healthy we might be—the notion of having our work evaluated has a tendency to make us a bit uneasy. It is because of this that the climate created within practice environments is key to effectively supporting evaluation efforts.

Creating a culture or climate for evaluation requires close attention to several details and adequate preparation of the work environment. Murray (2005) identifies two of these issues:

1. Encouraging an atmosphere of openness and trust throughout the evaluation process

2. Including all relevant stakeholders throughout the evaluation process

In addition, all stakeholders must understand the purpose of the evaluation and how the results will be used. Often, uncertainty about how results will be used can cause the greatest anxiety to stakeholders in an evaluation process. Therefore, an environment must be created in which continuous improvement is the overarching goal—and the philosophy that there is no failure, only room for improvement, is used to guide the process. It is only in this type of environment that evaluation can be viewed as a necessary and positive experience, regardless of the results. However, this also means that evaluation results cannot be used for punitive measures, since such measures are counterproductive to creating a healthy evaluation environment.

The following activities should also be used to promote a culture of evaluation:

- Before starting the evaluation process, identify where you would like it to lead and all that will result from the evaluation.
- Openly and frequently discuss the relationship between evaluation and accountability and long-term sustainability.
- Incorporate progress updates into existing forums so that evaluation information and activities are consistently shared among stakeholders as part of the ongoing communication cycle.
- Share various types of results with stakeholders frequently to keep the evaluation process alive.
- Explain precisely how each set of evaluation results will be used, and then provide ongoing updates regarding their use.
- Celebrate evaluation processes as a core part of work life.

Summary

Evaluation is an integral part of comprehensive program development and one that is specifically connected to program design and program implementation. The significance of evaluation has grown steadily over the past several decades and today is viewed as standard practice in mental health and human services. Moreover, the significance of the various types of evaluation has also continued to grow as our understanding of the influence of treatment fidelity and process implementation on evaluation has developed. While there is still room for growth in broad-based acknowledgment about the role that fidelity and process implementation play in comprehensive program evaluation, today there are signs that this knowledge will only continue to evolve. As such, fidelity and process implementation may soon reach the same level of significance as outcomes evaluation holds today.

The manner in which mental health professionals perceive evaluation as a core part of program development and thereby embed evaluation activities throughout programs and organizations is largely indicative of their commitment not only to quality and accountability but to long-term sustainability. Whereas there continues to be a need to bring in external evaluation experts to handle evaluation activities on behalf of the organization, evaluation knowledge and skills are essential skills of all mental health professionals. As a result, there is increased understanding of the link between program design, implementation, and evaluation and a much more intimate relationship between the treatment provider and the treatment. This is not only a basic right of accountability to which all consumers are entitled but also what consumers most prefer—a closer relationship between the product and the seller to ensure that the seller is intrinsically aware of all that the treatment and/or service is and is not able to provide.

CASE ILLUSTRATION

Alana and Ava had been cofacilitating a treatment program for adults with panic disorder and agoraphobia for the past year and a half. Their interventions consisted of individual and group therapy using cognitive-behavioral interventions. Whereas cognitive-behavioral interventions had been found to be effective in addressing panic disorder, Ava and Alana knew that they needed to evaluate their approach to determine if it was indeed evidence-based, and they also needed to explore existing evidence-based models. Adding a sense of urgency to this, Alana and Ava were increasingly being recognized as specialists in their community for treating panic disorder, and therefore, they were anxious to ensure that they were providing the best treatment they could to their clients.

After reviewing the research, Ava discovered a treatment approach that was evidence-based and shared the details with Alana. The approach had been rigorously evaluated with strong outcomes over multiple evaluations—reinforcing their excitement to implement the approach with their clients. Alana got a hold of all the details of the model, examining all the components and how each was implemented so that she and Ava could implement it as designed, thus retaining the model's fidelity. At the same time, Ava designed the evaluation components, including a fidelity assessment, process implementation, and outcomes evaluation.

The outcomes that would be measured were determined based on the research about expected outcomes for panic disorder and the results of previous outcomes evaluations. The assessment tools were identified based on the research as well as on the previous outcomes evaluations.

Because they wanted to evaluate their existing program as well, Alana and Ava decided to use a quasi-experimental design to evaluate their existing treatment approach against the evidence-based model. They would do this through randomly assigning clients into one or the other of the treatments, evaluating treatment outcomes during treatment, at discharge, and at 6 months post-discharge. Neither Ava nor Alana had conducted a formal evaluation before, so they consulted with an evaluator for guidance in finalizing the evaluation design, thus learning how to design and conduct the evaluation. They then developed informed consent forms for their clients and obtained approval through the agency's human subjects committee to conduct the study.

Ava and Alana developed a timeline to guide the evaluation, including the implementation date for the new treatment model, which was also the date that the evaluations would begin for both the existing and the new model. Following implementation, Alana and Ava met to review the initial fidelity and process evaluation data and were pleased to note that they had implemented the evidence-based model as designed. After 4 months, they had their initial outcomes data set, which did in fact illustrate significant differences between the two treatment groups, with clients who had received the evidence-based treatment showing greater improvements (i.e., fewer panic symptoms and less frequent episodes) than those clients who had received their existing treatment. Whereas Ava and Alana realized that these short-term outcomes may not translate into long-term outcomes, they were anxious to learn what the long-term outcomes would be.

Soon enough, they witnessed the first four groups complete treatment and had enough data to analyze the post-treatment outcomes. The post-treatment outcomes

(Continued)

(Continued)

also revealed significant differences between the two treatment groups, with the clients who had received the evidence-based treatment continuing to show even greater improvements (i.e., less panic symptoms and less frequent episodes) than those clients who had received the existing treatment. In addition, Ava and Alana's existing treatment did not produce significant positive outcomes in comparison with the evidence-based model, and the findings did not indicate any significant change for this group.

Because both the fidelity assessment and process implementation assessment results indicated that Alana and Ava had implemented the treatments as originally designed and intended and they had effectively conducted the evaluations, they were confident that the results of the outcomes evaluation were valid. Unfortunately, the outcomes did not provide evidence that the treatment approach that they had been using was effective, and therefore, they planned to immediately stop using it. In its place, they would continue to use the evidence-based treatment model that they had now become comfortable using and, more importantly, that had yielded significant positive outcomes for their clients. Being guided in this decision making by the evaluation data, Ava and Alana were excited about their newly adopted treatment approach, their outcomes, and the continuation of their evaluation program—which would continue to inform and guide their practice well into the future.

COST-BENEFIT ANALYSIS EXERCISE

Using the table below and beginning where I left off in Table 12.3, take some time to identify additional costs and benefits of evaluation. Share and compare results with others to gain a better sense of the varied costs and benefits resulting from evaluation activities.

Costs	Benefits

References

Alvarez-Jiminez, M., Wade, D., Cotton, S., Gee, D., Pearce, T., Crisp, K., et al. (2008). Enhancing treatment fidelity in psychotherapy research: Novel approach to measure the components of cognitive behavioral therapy for relapse prevention in first-episode psychosis. *Royal Australian and New Zealand College of Psychiatrists, 42,* 1013–1020.

Association for Assessment in Counseling. (2003). *Responsibilities of users of standardized tests* (3rd ed.). Alexandria, VA: Author.

Astramovich, R. L., & Coker, J. K. (2007). Program evaluation: The accountability bridge model for counselors. *Journal of Counseling and Development, 85,* 162–172.

Bellg, A. J., Borelli, B., Resnick, B., Hecht, J., Minicucci, D. S., Ory, M., et al. (2004). Enhancing treatment fidelity in health behavior change studies: Best practices and recommendations from the NIH Behavior Change Consortium. *Health Psychology, 23,* 443–451.

Borelli, B., Sepinwall, D., Ernst, D., Bellg, A. J., Czajkowski, S., Breger, R., et al. (2005). A new tool to assess treatment fidelity and evaluation of treatment across 10 years of health behavior research. *Journal of Consulting and Clinical Psychology, 73,* 852–860.

Boulmetis, J., & Dutwin, P. (2005). *The ABCs of evaluation: Timeless techniques for program and project managers* (2nd ed.). San Francisco: Jossey-Bass.

Bruns, E. J., Burchard, J. D., Suter, J. C., Leverentz-Brady, K., & Force, M. M. (2004). Assessing fidelity to a community-based treatment for youth: The Wraparound Fidelity Index. *Journal of Emotional and Behavioral Disorders, 12,* 79–89.

Chan, E. K. H., O'Neill, I., McKenzie, M., Love, A., & Kissane, D. W. (2004). What works for therapists conducting family meetings: Treatment integrity in family-focused grief therapy during palliative care and bereavement. *Journal of Pain and Symptom Management, 27,* 502–512.

Del Boca, F. K., & Darkes, J. (2007). Enhancing the validity and utility of randomized clinical trials in addictions treatment research: Treatment implementation and research design. *Addiction, 102,* 1047–1056.

Epstein, M. H., Nordness, P. D., Kutash, K., Duchnowski, A., Schrepf, S., Benner, G. J., et al. (2003). Assessing the wraparound process during family planning meetings. *Journal of Behavioral Health Services and Research, 30,* 352–362.

Gard, C. L., Flannigan, P. N., & Cluskey, M. (2004). Program evaluation: An ongoing systematic process. *Nursing Education Perspectives, 25,* 176–179.

Heppner, P. P., Wampold, B. E., & Kivlighan, D. M. (2008). *Research design in counseling* (3rd ed.). Pacific Grove, CA: Brooks/Cole.

Horner, S., Rew, L., & Torres, R. (2006). Enhancing intervention fidelity: A means of strengthening study impact. *Journal of Specialists in Pediatric Nursing, 11,* 80–89.

Kazdin, A. E. (2003). *Research design in clinical psychology* (4th ed.). Boston: Allyn & Bacon.

Kettner, P. M., Moroney, R. M., & Martin, L. L. (2008). *Designing and managing programs: An effectiveness-based approach.* Thousand Oaks, CA: Sage.

Lewis, J. A., Packard, T. R., & Lewis, M. D. (2007). *Management of human service programs* (4th ed.). Belmont, CA: Thomson Learning.

Loesch, L. C. (2001). Counseling program evaluation: Inside and outside the box. In D. C. Locke, J. E. Myers, & E. L. Herr (Eds.), *The handbook of counseling* (pp. 513–525). Thousand Oaks, CA: Sage.

Mooney, P., Epstein, M., Reid, R., & Nelson, J. R. (2003). Status and trends in academic intervention research for students with emotional disturbance. *Remedial and Special Education, 24,* 273–287.

Murray, V. (2005). Evaluating the effectiveness of nonprofit organizations. In R. Herman & Associates (Eds.), *The Jossey-Bass handbook of nonprofit leadership and management* (2nd ed., pp. 345–370). San Francisco: Jossey-Bass.

Orwin, R. G. (2000). Assessing program fidelity in substance abuse health services research. *Addiction, 95,* 309–327.

Schoenwald, S. K., Henggeler, S. W., Brondino, M. J., & Rowland, M. D. (2000). Multistemic therapy: Monitoring treatment fidelity. *Family Process, 39,* 83–103.

Smith, S. W., Daunic, A. P., & Taylor, G. G. (2007). Treatment fidelity in applied educational research: Expanding the adoption and application of measures to ensure evidence-based practice. *Education and Treatment of Children, 30,* 121–134.

Stufflebeam, D. L. (2000). Foundational models for 21st-century program evaluation. In D. L. Stufflebeam, G. F. Madaus, & T. Kellaghan (Eds.), *Evaluation models: Viewpoints on educational and human services evaluation* (2nd ed., pp. 33–96). Boston: Kluwer Academic.

CHAPTER 13

Build and Preserve Community Resources

Learning Objectives

1. Differentiate between coalitions, partners, and support agents

2. Identify at least two direct benefits and two indirect benefits resulting from relationships with partners and/or support agents

3. Identify four strategies to preserve relationships with community resources

4. Explain what is meant by creating a culture of collaboration

WHY WON'T YOU HELP ME?

When Joe was developing a proposal for a community-based gang violence prevention grant, he reached out to a program leader who had been doing youth violence prevention work in the schools in a nearby region. Joe had spent several hours with the program director, Nicole, learning about her work, and she freely shared her experiences, particularly emphasizing the interventions and scope of the program. Because Nicole worked directly for the public school system, she was not eligible to apply for the same grant, which was limited to nonprofit human service organizations. So after having developed this initial relationship, Joe asked if she would be willing to provide him with a letter of support reinforcing the need for additional gang violence prevention programs. Joe also reminded Nicole that he saw her as an integral ally and hoped to continue and strengthen their relationship, especially if his proposal was funded. Nicole provided Joe with a letter of support indicating that she, as a representative of the school, did indeed believe there was a need for more gang violence prevention in the region and that she believed that Joe and his organization were uniquely postured to deliver the services in the community. Joe thanked Nicole for the letter, promising to let her know the outcome and to stay in touch.

Ten months later, Joe's proposal was awarded funding, and he quickly went to work finalizing the program, hiring and training staff, and beginning the implementation process. A year later, Joe ran into Nicole at a state conference on bullying and other forms of youth violence. Not having spoken to her since he had received her letter of support and submitted his proposal, Joe told Nicole that his proposal had been funded and that he had been working on the program for more than a year. Nicole congratulated him, and after a brief conversation, Joe promised to stay in touch and told her that he was hoping they might be able to collaborate on future projects.

Eight months before funding for Joe's project was scheduled to end, he had identified a new funding opportunity focused on broader issues of youth violence prevention and decided it was worth going after. The proposal required letters of support from at least two organizations. While Joe felt a bit uncomfortable calling Nicole for another letter of support since he had not spoken to her since the conference, he had not developed any new relationships with professionals that might be able to provide relevant letters of support. So Joe called Nicole, letting her know how his program was going and then sharing with her details of the new proposal he was working on, emphasizing how he believed this program could really strengthen the work that they had both been doing in violence prevention. Before hanging up, Joe asked Nicole if she would provide him with a letter of support that he could include in the proposal. Nicole asked Joe how he believed she and her program might benefit from this new funding opportunity, and Joe again stressed that he believed that the region itself would benefit because of an expanded service continuum of youth violence prevention programming. Nicole agreed that the broader the continuum of available services, the greater potential they all had to make a difference in their efforts to reduce youth violence, but she said that she would have to check with her superintendant to determine if the school could provide another letter of support. Nicole called Joe back a week later to let him know that the school administrators had decided that they would not provide a letter of support because they did not believe they were familiar enough with Joe's work to do so. After a good deal of work, Joe was able to obtain one letter of support from a local organization working in juvenile justice; however, without the letter from the school, he did not have the required two letters of support needed as part of the application. As a result, Joe was unable to pursue the funding opportunity.

CONSIDERING JOE

1. What was Joe's first mistake in how he handled his relationship with Nicole and why?

2. Should Joe now try to redevelop his relationship with Nicole? Why or why not?

3. If you were Joe, what steps would you take to ensure that you continue to build and preserve relationships with community resources?

About This Chapter

Because of the critical role that meaningful and long-term business relationships play in the mental health and human services today, this chapter is dedicated to preserving relationships with community resources. Whereas Chapter 7 introduced the notion of identifying and engaging community resources, this chapter focuses on preserving those relationships once they have been established.

To fully explore the issue of preserving relationships with community resources, we will examine several aspects. To begin, we will discuss the different types of relationships, which include coalitions, partnerships, and support agents. This will be followed by an examination of both direct and indirect benefits potentially resulting from these relationships. Next, we will review methods by which to preserve relationships. These methods include engaging in regular communication and enhancing relationships through specific means. The chapter concludes with a case illustration that highlights the central concepts explored in the chapter and several questions for reflection and discussion focusing on collaboration and its role in mental health and human services today.

STEP XI: BUILD AND PRESERVE COMMUNITY RESOURCES

Significance of Community Resources in Program Sustainability

Unfortunately, the example Joe and Nicole provide is not all that uncommon in the human services, illustrating the importance of not only engaging community supports but, more significantly, maintaining those relationships. Whereas Joe effectively developed an initial relationship with a highly relevant community resource via Nicole, he failed to appreciate the importance of preserving that relationship. As a result, the benefits that he received from the relationship were short-lived.

Few mental health and human service organizations today can exist in isolation but, rather, must actively engage with the larger community of providers and other resources in order to sustain their business. This means that the onus is on each provider to initiate and nurture a variety of relationships with other supports. In fact, now more than ever before, collaboration in programming is often the preferred mode of service delivery, yet collaboration is available only to those who have established relationships with potential collaborators. Being aware of the current emphasis on collaboration in programming and being able to adapt your business to it means that you are able to effectively manage the environment in which you work. This type of environmental management results from monitoring the trends in the environment and being critically aware of changes that impact the way in which business is done at the local, state, national, and at times, global levels (Lewis, Packard, & Lewis, 2007)—a key characteristic of an effective program administrator. In this manner, program developers and administrators must constantly be tuned in to the greater context in which they work, lest they be unprepared to move with the rapidly changing tide.

Collaboration is becoming increasingly the norm rather than the exception in mental health and human services for a multitude of reasons, including sharing resources between organizations. However, interagency collaboration has also been viewed as a promising managerial approach and one that not only allows for sharing resources between agencies but also for more effective use of society's resources (Entwistle & Martin, 2005). In addition, collaboration may lead to improved quality and/or reduced costs, thus enhancing the organizations that participate in collaborative efforts (Nylen, 2007).

The types of collaborative relationships that exist among human service and mental health providers can vary considerably. Collaboration may be very informal, consisting of ongoing communication among individuals around particular areas of interest (Nylen, 2007), or it can be much more structured, with regularly scheduled communication and the development of more concrete relationships (Gittell & Weiss, 2004; Hill & Lynn, 2003). As a result, different types of collaboration not only have distinct features, but they also may offer different benefits to their participants. However, each collaboration constitutes a business relationship since each is built and focused on the business of the organization and/or the broader field in which the organization operates.

To begin to examine the significance of relationships with other community providers and resources, three prominent types of business relationships are explored: coalitions, partnerships, and support agents. Each of these relationships represents some form of collaborative effort in varying degrees, and thus, collaboration is what binds them; however, each is different and, as a result, may offer a different set of benefits as well as challenges.

Coalitions

Because of the ever-shrinking dollars available to address social and mental health issues, coalition building has become an increasing necessity in the human services. As discussed in Chapter 7, the term *coalition* refers to "a group of organizations working together for a common purpose" (Lewis, Lewis, Daniels, & D'Andrea, 2003, p. 238). Because of the unifying nature involved in trying to address a specific problem, organizations may become empowered and emboldened to work collectively toward solutions. This can be quite pragmatic since coalitions are often created when one group realizes that it does not have the power to effectively tackle an issue alone and, therefore, needs to join forces with others in order to expand its power base (Homan, 2004). However, even though initial participation in a coalition is often highly inspiring and may propel newfound motivation in work, a primary challenge of coalitions is related to their staying power. Like any collective endeavor, when participants cease to perceive a benefit, they are no longer motivated to continue in the coalition. Therefore, whereas building a coalition often proves to be exciting work initially, preserving coalitions can be quite challenging. As a result, preserving coalitions requires appreciation of the inherent challenges and perseverance needed for sustainability.

Coalitions in the mental health and human services typically emerge as organizations coalesce around shared work and interests. Whereas coalitions emerge for similar reasons, they may differ quite a bit in terms of the formality of their structure, the reach of the coalition, the number and type of participants, and other factors that can significantly impact their ability to be sustained. Informal grassroots-level coalitions are typically initiated by one or two community organizations. Often, motivation to develop a coalition may be based on an interest in developing a community support network, and the coalition may not have well-defined objectives or goals.

Other coalitions may be initiated in a more formal manner, with financial dues/contributions provided by participants to support a leader and other aspects of the coalition's work. This type of coalition often has a specific organizational structure in place. In addition to the organizational structure of a coalition, coalitions can be developed at various levels—local, regional, state, national, or international. In this regard, coalitions often vary in the type of activities they pursue and the degree of reach they desire. For instance, local coalitions are most invested in seeking change at the local level, motivated by the need to directly and immediately impact a locality. For instance, a group of foster care providers in a region may come together to address the need for foster homes for teens, or two providers working with individuals with dementia may work together to increase local support services for dementia. Conversely, national coalitions are most directed toward change at the national level, motivated by a need for large-scale change that can ultimately impact regional and local environs. For instance, a national coalition may be formed to increase both recognition and funding for substance abuse treatment or to demand that equal funding be provided for the treatment of autism as is given to research on autism. Neither of these types of coalitions is superior to the other; they each simply occur at different levels.

The number of participating organizations that compose a coalition may vary widely as well and may be directly related to the specific work or geographic structure of the coalition (e.g., local, statewide). Finally, the primary objectives of the coalitions may vary greatly, as some coalitions may evolve to address a particular broad issue such as mental health while others may be much more specifically focused on the treatment of an issue such as bipolar disorder. Each of these myriad factors may significantly impact the coalition's sustainability, and therefore, each must be given attention in order to preserve coalitions. I should also note here that the exception to the issue of preserving coalitions is the rare occurrence of coalitions that are developed to tackle a specific short-term issue. In these cases, coalitions are initiated as temporary structures that serve a specific purpose and, therefore, are not intended as long-term support networks. However, even in these instances when the work of a coalition is meant to be time-limited, it is not uncommon for the coalition to morph into new work, thereby becoming a more permanent endeavor—especially when the coalition has developed effective cohesion and, therefore, has a need to continue working collaboratively.

The boxes below provide examples of three existing coalitions. The first (Box 13.1) is based on a very new, locally developed coalition focusing on a specific zip code in a region. This coalition reflects a grassroots effort at the most local level. The second (Box 13.2) is a national coalition of child welfare and mental health organizations that is much more reflective of a business and a professional association. The third (Box 13.3) is a regional coalition developed in a completely inclusive manner that has accomplished significant change through local collaborative work.

BOX 13.1

MID-CENTER COALITION: THE 55555 ZIP CODE

The Mid-Center Coalition is a group of nine organizations providing mental health, human services, and educational services in a 4-square-mile radius. Mid-Center was formed at the initiation of one of the local mental health providers in an effort to focus the collective efforts of the organizations on exploring new ways to garner funding and ensure that the region, a large urban area in the Midwest, had a sufficient community support network in place. The extreme economic conditions facing the region—one of the poorest in the nation—was another driving force in the initial development of Mid-Center.

An administrator from the mental health organization chairs the meetings, but there is no formal leadership in place as of this writing. Mid-Center is open to all organizations providing mental health and human services in the region, and all are encouraged to participate. The group has continued to hold quarterly meetings since its inception 1 year ago. To date, the meetings have largely focused on brainstorming possible endeavors that the coalition may be interested in pursuing. No

(Continued)

(Continued)

formal action has yet been taken to pursue any new venture as a group; however, the creation of Mid-Center marks the first forum in which community organizations have come together voluntarily to work collaboratively.

To date, Mid-Center has established a membership directory and is examining how the group might work with another local group that is planning to provide free services in the community. In addition, two of the participating organizations have begun a collaborative business relationship, and other participating members have provided letters of support to three member organizations as they each have pursued new funding opportunities on behalf of their respective organizations.

BOX 13.2

THE ALLIANCE FOR CHILDREN AND FAMILIES

The Alliance for Children and Families (2009) was formed in 1998 as a result of a merger of Family Service America and the National Association of Homes and Services for Children. Today, the Alliance provides services to nonprofit child, family, and economic empowerment organizations. In fulfillment of the Alliance's vision of a healthy society and strong communities, the organization is dedicated to strengthening America's nonprofit sector and using advocacy to assure continued independence (Alliance for Children and Families, 2009).

The Alliance has an extensive and sophisticated organizational structure led by a chief executive officer and consisting of seven administrative support departments, several project-specific departments, and two administrative office locations and employing more than 60 paid staff members. The Alliance is supported through annual membership dues of participating organizations, donations, and other funding.

The services provided to member organizations range from public policy and advocacy at the national level; publications, which include a journal, magazine, and newsletters; alerts regarding funding opportunities; consultation and evaluation services; conferences and training institutes; and a job posting board.

In 2010, more than 360 organizations in the United States and Canada were members of the Alliance.

BOX 13.3

THE HAVERHILL VIOLENCE COALITION

The Haverhill Violence Coalition has been in existence since 2001 and was developed in response to research conducted in the region on abuse during pregnancy. Haverhill is supported by federal funding and is composed of more than 30 agencies and institutions that meet monthly (Hawkins et al., 2008).

Haverhill's mission involves bringing together individuals interested in addressing all forms of violence and coordinating services for those experiencing or witnessing violence in the community.

Haverhill has a formal governance structure in place, including leadership and bylaws designed and supported by the membership.

Since its inception, Haverhill has successfully created new programs to address violence in homes, schools, and communities and has designed interventions for children witnessing violence. In addition, Haverhill has garnered funding support from a variety of sources to forward its mission.

Haverhill works collaboratively with the community, holding open meetings in which its efforts are evaluated by community members and community members provide input to Haverhill's ongoing agenda. After more than 8 years of making a significant impact in the region and garnering widespread support, Haverhill is well positioned to continue its important work addressing the various dimensions of violence in the community.

As you can see, these examples represent three very different types of coalitions. The Mid-Center Coalition is quite limited in its organizational structure and has yet to engage in any specific planning efforts that might result in tangible action; however, the development of Mid-Center has served to bring organizations in a local community together and, as such, has resulted in the development of a semiformal community support network in which community organizations work together in a variety of manners. One collaborative partnership has been formed as a result of Mid-Center's existence, and organizations have lent formal support to one another as they pursued funding for new programming. Based on the types of new relationships that have been formed by members of some of the participating organizations, these relationships may be well postured to become long-term. However, without specific efforts to keep participating organizations engaged in Mid-Center, the coalition itself may not be able to continue. Mid-Center provides an example of a coalition in its initial stages of development; however, Mid-Center's challenge will be for its participants to continue to promote its growth by adopting a formalized, action-oriented approach.

Conversely, the Alliance for Children and Families has a long history, is well established, and operates with both an extensive staffing infrastructure and an ambitious and comprehensive agenda. In this regard, it appears to be a well-oiled machine designed to attract new members while continuously acting to maintain relationships with existing members by offering new and seemingly meaningful benefits. We cannot forget that the Alliance is a professional membership association first and foremost; however, it is included because it shares some of the critical features of a coalition (e.g., works toward collective goals, sets the stage for enhanced relationships among professionals). In addition, the Alliance is included because it highlights the distinct differences related to finances in coalitions. In comparison with regional or local coalitions that have no membership fees, the Alliance's membership fees and other available funding further differentiate it. Of course, the actual benefits of membership in the Alliance may not be easily deciphered and may vary from one member agency to another, but as long as members do perceive benefits from their relationship with the Alliance, this coalition is likely to sustain.

Whereas the Mid-Center Coalition and the Alliance for Children and Families highlight two very different types of coalition in terms of organizational structure and organizational reach, the Haverhill Violence Coalition arguably provides an ideal example of a regional, community-based coalition. Developed in response to an evidence-based need, open to all interested individuals possessing a shared commitment to addressing the issue of violence, and operated fully by the membership, for the membership, and for the community, the work of Haverhill showcases the outcomes of orchestrated community-action planning. In addition, Haverhill reflects all that can be accomplished when effective organization takes place at the local level to address local needs and how sustainability can be achieved through self-evaluation, organizational flexibility, and long-term planning.

To illustrate the perseverance required in preserving coalitions, after realizing that members were losing interest in Haverhill, they decided to bring in an expert to formalize the organization and redefine the mission and vision. As a result, Haverhill has firmly established itself as a force in the community and, more significantly, has demonstrated the significance of preserving community relations.

Preserving Coalitions

All the participants must share an appreciation of the many factors that can threaten the sustainability of a coalition as a prerequisite for actively working to preserve the coalition. By promoting a culture in which members of the coalition can actively work to maintain it, a climate of engagement can be inherently developed and harnessed for the survival of the coalition. In addition, because the membership of a coalition is subject to change over time, both in terms of organizations represented and the individuals representing specific organizations, it is imperative that ideological commitments be continuously renewed. In this regard, incentives may serve a particular role in maintaining more senior members of the coalition and may, in fact, enhance their commitment (Roberts-DeGennaro, 2001).

In an attempt to better understand what leads to a coalition's success, Mizrahi and Rosenthal (2001) surveyed 40 coalitions. Six of the major factors that the coalition members reported contributing to their success are

1. competent leadership,

2. ownership and shared responsibility,

3. commitment to the coalition's work and to coalition unity,

4. equal decision making,

5. achievement of short-term accomplishments, and

6. mutual respect and trust among members.

Whereas each of these factors represents a feature of a successful coalition, each could easily be applied to the effectiveness of the group therapy process (e.g., effective leadership, shared responsibility, respect, trust, visible outcomes). This is because some of the factors that make the group therapy process so successful are transferrable to many types of group processes. Moreover, what is most evident here is the importance of leadership and structure, unity, and achievement of outcomes—essential to gaining success as a coalition.

It would stand to reason that the factors that contribute to a successful coalition are also paramount to preserving the coalition. So in addition to the factors identified above, seven strategies are recommended to preserve coalitions (see Box 13.4). Whereas this list is in no way conclusive, one of the most important lessons to take away from this is that preserving coalitions must be well planned—it does not simply happen but, rather, is strategically accomplished and requires ongoing determination.

BOX 13.4

STRATEGIES TO PRESERVE COALITIONS

1. Adopt a formal leadership structure to guide the coalition's work and provide continuity to the coalition (Lewis et al., 2003; Roberts-DeGennaro, 2001).

2. Engage in long-term planning (Lewis et al., 2003) and strategic planning with ongoing reviews and assessments of the coalition's work.

3. Work to maintain long-term strategic effectiveness (Tefft, 1987).

4. Regularly evaluate the degree to which participants benefit from the work of the coalition, and use the findings to inform subsequent reengagement efforts.

5. Maintain open communication.

6. Work to develop a flexible culture that allows for the coalition to change and grow over time in order to be sustained.

7. Continue to collectively modify the mission and objectives of the coalition.

Whereas there is no guarantee that any type of coalition can be sustained long-term, you can be certain that without conscientious and continuous efforts to preserve the relationships that compose the coalition, it will indeed be short-lived. It is not uncommon for you/your organization to establish other business relationships with coalition members outside the coalition, and therefore, coalitions often provide opportunities for other types of relationship building. Further, some organizations may not belong to a coalition yet may have established formal and informal relationships with other professionals/organizations that serve a distinct purpose. Two of the most common types of these other business relationships in mental health and human services are partnerships and support agents.

Partnerships

In basic terms, partnerships imply that both organizations benefit from the specific relationship. Partnerships often are established to serve a variety of purposes—from large-scale partnerships in which two or more organizations merge, creating a new collective organization, to a schema in which two organizations come together to jointly administer a specific program/project. In addition, a partnership may result from the subcontracting of one organization by another to provide specific services that are part of a larger service array. Table 13.1 illustrates examples of some common partnerships in mental health and human services today.

Similar to coalitions, partnerships may be temporary or long-term. For instance, a partnership composed of the merging of two human service organizations is in most cases a long-term partnership, whereas partnerships that emerge to jointly administer a time-limited funded project are often short-term. As a result, the degree of interaction and investment of partners may vary quite a bit. In addition, the scope of the partnership may shift over time, beginning as a contractor-subcontractor relationship and then developing into a joint venture.

Preserving Partnerships

Partnerships typically represent the strongest type of relationship between community organizations, particularly because each of the parties involved receives concrete and mutually satisfying benefits. As a result, there naturally is a high degree of interaction and sharing among the partners; however, even though frequent communication and sharing may be occurring, partnerships require the same attention to preserving the relationship as do coalitions. In fact, because of the intense type of relationship that partnerships imply, even greater efforts must be made to preserve the partnership. Therefore, in addition to the seven strategies listed in Box 13.4, in order to preserve partnerships, the members of the partnership

Table 13.1 Common Partnerships in Mental Health and Human Services

Project-based partnership	Two or more organizations work collaboratively on a given time-limited project
Joint program administration partnership	Two or more organizations work collaboratively in the administration of a program
Administrative services partnership	Two or more organizations share administrative services—for instance, with one providing finance services in exchange for human resource services
System administration partnership	Two or more organizations work collaboratively in the administration of a system of care, such as adult mental health services
Merger-based partnership	Two or more organizations merge, with each retaining some degree of autonomy, while sharing resources and engaging in collaboration

must also pay attention to other issues such as power sharing and roles of the partners. Indeed, business partnerships are built on a power-sharing/responsibility-sharing relationship, and as a result, the partnership must be continuously evaluated to ensure that equality in both areas continues to exist, lest the partnership itself begin to diminish. This can be helped along not only by maintaining open communication but also by adopting transparency with the members of the partnership. Because partners are akin to colleagues working in the same organization, transparency is needed to move toward shared goals. In addition, transparency contributes to a healthy environment that may effectively prohibit one partner gaining more power than another and, as such, serves to maintain an effective balance of power.

Whereas concerted efforts to ensure appropriate power sharing are needed to preserve partnerships, the roles that each partner plays in the relationship also must be given a good deal of attention. Roles are directly impacted by and directly impact the power-sharing schema that is an inherent part of a partnership. In order to preserve partnerships, the roles that each partner/organization will play must be clearly articulated and mutually agreed on, if not mutually designed. Throughout the partnership, the roles must be continuously evaluated and efforts made to immediately address any issues or conflicts related to roles. This type of ongoing evaluation is another form of transparency that ultimately should serve to strengthen the partnership by ensuring that all partners remain continuously engaged.

According to Cohen, Linker, and Stutts (2006), effective partnerships and other collaborations require the adoption of specific attitudes and behaviors in order to be successful and sustainable:

- Avoid adopting an *us versus them* mentality.
- Formalize roles.
- Develop partnership language.
- Take a long-term view of the collaboration.
- Allocate sufficient resources.
- Consider co-location of services (partners provide different services in one location).
- Require accountability of the partners.

It is believed that by adopting this type of cognitive framework of partnership and collaboration, a culture of shared responsibility and collective work can be gained. This culture is pivotal to the sustainability of partnerships, since without it, the continued engagement of partners is threatened. Partnerships, like coalitions, are subject to change over time, and in simple terms, long-term preservation of the relationship requires communication, evaluation, and negotiation.

Support Agents

Support agents are not partners that mutually share in specific work but rather professionals/organizations that support the work of you/your organization in some tangible manner and typically receive some benefit from doing so. For instance, in the vignette provided at the beginning of the chapter, Nicole initially was a support agent for Joe, teaching him about her business and providing him with a letter of support to assist him in garnering funding for his own program. Joe was not, however, a support agent for Nicole, as ultimately she did not receive any benefits from the relationship. And as a result of the one-sided nature of this particular relationship, it was unable to be sustained or preserved.

Support agents may consist of professionals providing the same type of services as you do (i.e., competitors), those providing different services to the same population as you, or those possessing some other relationship to your work. In addition, a funding source may be a support agent, particularly when the funding agent is pleased with your work. Regardless of the type of support agent, these individuals and their organizations have a particular investment in you/the success of your work/your organization and, therefore, are willing to support it. Most often, this is because doing so provides some type of direct or indirect benefit to them as well. For instance, an organization providing community-based services to victims of domestic violence may support your efforts to establish a shelter for child survivors of domestic violence because they believe not only that more services for this population are needed to ensure the most effective treatment of the issue but that, ultimately, more attention given to the issue and more services available will be beneficial to their business as well. Another example of a support agent is a philanthropic or advocacy organization dedicated to addressing the same needs that your program/organization seeks to address. This type of support agent may provide you with funding or a voice in new and different venues to continue to draw attention to the issue. Finally, support agents may participate on the same coalition and, as a result, engage periodically or continuously as supports to one another in fulfillment of their collective agenda.

Preserving Relationships With Support Agents

Regardless of the nature of the relationship that exists among support agents, preserving the relationship requires specific effort; however, unlike coalitions and partnerships, the degree and type of effort needed differs. Because support agent relationships are the simplest and most straightforward of the three business relationships discussed here, preserving these relationships is equally straightforward. As such, the following strategies may serve to effectively preserve the relationship:

- Maintaining open communication that ensures that each participant understands the type of support provided
- Ensuring a mutual understanding of perceived benefits of support
- Engaging in ongoing evaluation of the relationship and commitment to quickly address and/or resolve any challenges in the relationship
- Maintaining a mutual understanding of and agreement to the parameters of the relationship

Relationships with support agents may by nature be especially time-limited, unlike coalitions and partnerships, particularly if they evolve to address a specific time-limited issue (e.g., passing specific legislation, garnering funding). Therefore, a clear understanding of the parameters of the relationship must be understood by all participants as well as the fact that gaps in participants' interactions with one another do not necessarily indicate the dissolution of the relationship. Support agent relationships are not always constant but, rather, are utilized when and as needed; therefore, a lack of constant contact does not pose a threat to the relationship.

The Power of Community Support

In today's human service arena, most professionals/organizations find that they are involved in all three types of business relationships—coalitions, partnerships, and relationships with a variety of support agents—at varying times or simultaneously. It is in this manner that this unique type of work is not conducted in isolation but, rather, within a larger helping network of community support—a support network that works collaboratively toward shared, over-arching goals and objectives with each organization filling a specific role in the network. Because of the various business relationships that mental health and human service providers develop with community resources, each type of relationship can contribute to a broad community support network. It is when this happens—when a community support network is formed—that communities may be effectively empowered to address their inherent challenges.

The relationships shared among mental health and human service professionals/organizations is central to the work that organizations do in addressing social and mental health issues. In addition, these relationships provide a great many direct and indirect benefits to the participants and, as such, must be preserved.

Direct and Indirect Benefits of Relationships With Community Resources

Recall that Chapter 7 discussed the primary benefits of engaging with community resources, which included

- augmenting the existing service array,
- building an advocacy coalition,
- garnering additional and/or new funding,
- promoting long-term sustainability planning, and
- strengthening communities from within by recognizing and utilizing existing resources.

Each of these is extremely significant to the long-term health and survival of a mental health or human service organization and, moreover, to the success of the work that is carried out by these organizations. However, in addition to these primary reasons for initially developing these relationships, there are several other direct and indirect benefits that may arise from preserving these relationships.

Direct Benefits

Direct benefits refer to the direct and tangible benefits that organizations receive as a result of preserving relationships with community resources. In addition to augmenting the existing service array, building an advocacy coalition, and promoting long-term sustainability (listed above), two other direct benefits worthy of discussion here are

- exchanging and/or sharing organizational resources and
- impacting public policy.

Exchanging or Sharing Organizational Resources. As a result of relationships with community resources, organizations may explore and act on sharing and/or exchanging a variety of resources. Resources might include basic supplies, technology (e.g., client information system), support services (e.g., finance management, training, research and evaluation), staff/ personnel, or knowledge. For some organizations, sharing resources may be the only option available due to lack of finances, whereas some startup organizations may find that sharing resources with an established organization provides a form of mentoring—learning about specific aspects of the business from more seasoned professionals.

Another motivating factor for sharing resources today is related to our current economic climate. As funding continues to shrink and organizations are challenged with how to continue doing what they are doing for less, sharing resources may be a necessary tool for survival. This is particularly true in the 21st century as we continue to witness an unprecedented number of human service organizations merging with other organizations, being fully acquired by another organization, or folding altogether. By proactively working to determine new cost-saving measures built on various types of resource sharing, organizations that wish to remain fully independent may be able to do so.

The issue of cost is typically one of the most compelling reasons to share resources, especially when it allows an organization to have something that it otherwise may not be able to (e.g., building space, information system). In addition, because most mental health and human service organizations have specific and, at times, multiple specialties, exchanging one set of knowledge for another can be mutually beneficial. For instance, after collaborating on a number of projects together and while involved in a formalized partnership, two organizations with which I have closely worked realized that the other had specialized knowledge of specific clinical assessment tools. Rather than purchase training for staff from a training company or other venue, the program managers from each of the companies decided to exchange training with each other. By doing so, staff from both organizations gained new knowledge and skills, but in addition, this exchange opened the door for other types of sharing and worked to further preserve the relationship between the two organizations.

Impacting Public Policy. In addition to sharing organizational resources, another significant direct benefit of preserving relationships with community resources involves impacting public policy at the local, state, or national level. By working collaboratively with other community resources/ organizations, organizations may be better postured to impact public policy. Because some public policy can either threaten or support mental health and human service programming, it is imperative that program developers and leaders remain keenly aware of any proposed changes to public policy so that they may be prepared to take action, if necessary. Indeed, public agencies are more apt to respond to political versus economic arguments (Heintze & Bretschneider, 2000), and focusing on the political environment may serve advocacy efforts well.

An example of the power of community partnerships in influencing public policy is reflected in the work of the Mission Neighborhood Resource Center (Wenger, Leadbetter, Guzman, & Kral, 2007). A local coalition of mental health and substance abuse providers and housing, public health, and other community organizations in San Francisco was created based on their shared commitment to supporting individuals in transition (i.e., homeless individuals). In 2004, when a new policy was proposed to close multiple homeless shelters in the region, coalition members came together to resist and argue against this policy, using their collective strength. As a result, the revised policy included reopening shelters, enhancing shelter budgets, and creating a new immigrant housing development. This type of grassroots coalition developing in response to a specific threat really highlights the power of a unified front, which was created quite quickly by a group of committed individuals, largely driven by their passion for a shared cause.

Indirect Benefits

Unlike direct benefits, indirect benefits refer to the intangible benefits derived from preserving relationships with community resources— benefits that do not directly impact the organization but that are important nonetheless. Strengthening communities from within (discussed in Chapter 7) is one such indirect benefit. In addition, indirect benefits resulting from relationships with community resources may include

- professional development of staff through collaborative learning experiences,
- informal mentoring,
- professional networking and expanding the list of potential future business partners, and
- providing access to new and different business opportunities.

In her discussion on the impact of community partnerships for older adults, Bailey (2009) further concludes that such partnerships significantly change communities by

- promoting region-wide thinking that stretches beyond *turf* and *silos*,
- creating and piloting new best practices as part of continued efforts to address emerging needs and to work toward continuous improvement,
- changing relationships between stakeholders that foster collaborative work and develop new programming options, and
- advancing coordinated problem solving and action that can be replicated in other regions.

Whereas indirect benefits do not provide an immediate or concrete impact on organizations, they may in fact lead to direct benefits of considerable significance. However, more importantly—and consistent with Bailey's (2009) last point—engaging in and preserving relationships with other community resources contributes to the greater good, further advancing the central mission of mental health and human service work. As such, it benefits all those who have committed their lives to this work.

Summary

Whereas historically, it has been the case that mental health and human service organizations could function independently—working in silos and protecting their turf, as Bailey (2009) puts it—this is no longer the case. In order to work in this industry in the 21st century, professionals must not only be open to collaborative efforts but must participate fully to some degree in collaborative efforts with other professionals. Such collaborations may be composed of many types of arrangements, including coalitions, partnerships, and support agents.

As with most relationships, the types of collaborative relationships that professionals participate in may change and grow over time, with some engaging simultaneously in each type of collaboration with different entities as well as multiple relationships with one entity (e.g., partnership and support agent). Ideally, through engaging in these relationships, many direct and indirect benefits are given to the individuals and to the participating organization. But none of this can be taken for granted, since all relationships require commitment, determination, and effective work to be sustained. And particularly because of the significance that these relationships have in human service and mental health organizations today, it is imperative that program developers and leaders work diligently to preserve them in order for their own businesses to continue to grow and develop. Moreover, only by participating as part of a broader network can the collective energies of many be fully achieved and, thus, can the community at large effectively benefit.

CASE ILLUSTRATION

Nyree had been successfully managing her transitional housing and comprehensive care program for runaway gay youth for the past 4 years. She had just received notice that she had been awarded a new 3-year contract to expand her service array to include mentoring. Nyree's existing program provided an array of services, including counseling, family and support building, academic coordination and support, vocational exploration and support, and activities to support permanent living conditions; however, she had no previous experience operating a mentoring program. Because of this, she had approached one of her colleagues, John, at a peer organization. John had been managing a substance abuse prevention and mentoring program for teens for more than 6 years, and Nyree and he had become acquainted through the Coalition for Teens, which Nyree had initiated the year before.

After various interactions with leaders and workers from several community organizations and schools since the inception of her program, Nyree realized that a forum was needed by which the various groups working on teen issues could come together, pool their resources, and begin to explore collaborative and comprehensive efforts to further their shared mission, thus the Coalition for Teens was born.

When Nyree discovered the Request for Proposal (RFP) on the mentoring program, she immediately thought of John and contacted him to discuss a partnership in the proposed project. As a result of this partnership, the contract for the mentoring program was awarded to Nyree.

After discussing the award and enjoying a celebratory coffee, Nyree and John got to work on planning for program implementation, revisiting what they had originally designed and planned in the proposal. They had developed the administrative structure for the program, which included comanagement of the program and both organizations having specific staff dedicated to the program. In addition, the program would be operated through Nyree's shelter program with staff from John's organization having offices there. Nyree and John believed that by integrating the two organizations in this way, they could promote the most effective type of collaboration.

John suggested that he and Nyree meet weekly with their staff involved in the mentoring program during the first 3 months and then determine if they should continue with weekly meetings or move to biweekly meetings during the remainder of the program. They agreed that this type of frequent meeting schedule would ensure continuous sharing of information. In addition, they agreed to commit to working fully as partners and to continuously assessing how well they were functioning as a partnership. Finally, they committed to maintaining open communication and transparency and to making their ongoing communication, including regular meetings, a priority.

During the second year of the mentoring program, John found an announcement for a new RFP for teen vocational training and career planning programming.

(Continued)

(Continued)

He immediately shared this with Nyree and proposed that they submit an application to pursue the project as another collaborative effort. Nyree agreed that since their initial partnership was so successful, they should continue their efforts and work to further increase the array of services provided by each of their organizations—and more importantly, to attempt to increase the continuum of services available to the teens in their region. John secured letters of support from two of the members of the coalition, which was still going strong and had recently elected its first president and vice president. Nyree received a third letter of support from another coalition member—a woman with whom Nyree had recently worked while providing testimony about the need for more funds for children's mental health services.

Several years later, as Nyree looked back on all that had transpired, she realized that relationships with other community providers had been essential to her work in a great many ways and that without them, she may not have been able to keep her program alive. Moreover, she realized that as she worked to preserve these relationships, the connections between each became stronger or led in some new direction. As a result, she had grown her continuum of programming—and organization—considerably. She had also experienced two successful partnerships in new business endeavors and had recently signed on to a partnership with a new community organization serving kids 7 to 12 years of age that had experienced the loss of a parent/caregiver. In addition to all the benefits that Nyree and her organization had received as a result of her ability to not only engage in but preserve relationships with community resources, the coalition that she had originally established had accomplished a great deal.

In addition to connecting each of the providers with one another, seven partnerships had evolved from the coalition, several organizations shared resources with one another, and three had developed a new business that they collaboratively oversaw. The coalition had worked together to successfully pass new hate crime legislation that included bullying based on sexual orientation and legislation to increase funding for alternative education and vocational training programs for teenagers that may not succeed in traditional high school programs. Finally, the coalition had pursued and received funding as a collective group to develop an awareness and educational curriculum for teachers, law enforcement, and others working with teens. The training focused on issues such as adolescent and teen development, sexual orientation, communication, family and supports, and independence, among other areas, and was designed to promote more effective and broader social support networks for the region's teen population. All in all, Nyree was quite happy with all that had been accomplished, and when she examines her community today, she realizes just how much it has been enhanced as a result of the broad support network that now exists.

REFLECTION AND DISCUSSION QUESTIONS

Take some time to reflect on the following questions about collaboration and its role in work.

1. What does the concept of collaboration mean to you?

2. How and in what ways has your thinking about collaborative work been influenced, either positively or negatively?

3. What do you believe poses threats to collaborative efforts?

4. Even though collaboration is so prominent in today's mental health and human service industry, do you believe this is a fad or do you believe that collaboration will continue well into the future?

5. What types of collaborative efforts have you witnessed in human services and mental health? What were the strengths and the deficits of these efforts? If you could have participated directly in the collaboration, what changes would you make and why?

6. In what ways do you foresee collaborating in your work and why?

References

Alliance for Children and Families. (2009). *About the Alliance*. Retrieved February 10, 2010, from http://www.alliance1.org

Bailey, P. A. (2009). Community partnerships for older adults. *Journal of the American Society on Aging, 33*, 79–81.

Cohen, R., Linker, J. A., & Stutts, L. (2006). Working together: Lessons learned from school, family, and community collaborations. *Psychology in the Schools, 43,* 419–428.

Entwistle, T., & Martin, S. (2005). From competition to collaboration in public service delivery: A new agenda for research. *Public Administration, 83,* 233–242.

Gittell, J. H., & Weiss, L. (2004). Coordination networks within and across organizations: A multilevel framework. *Journal of Management Studies, 41*, 127–153.

Hawkins, J. W., Pearce, C. W., Windell, K. W., Connors, M. L., Ireland, C., Thompson, D. E., et al. (2008). Creating a community coalition to address violence. *Issues in Mental Health Nursing, 29*, 755–765.

Heintze, T., & Bretschneider, S. (2000). Information technology and restructuring in public organizations: Does adoption of information technology affect organizational structures, communications, and decision making? *Journal of Public Administration Research and Theory, 10,* 801–830.

Hill, C. J., & Lynn, L. E. (2003). Producing human services: Why do agencies collaborate? *Public Management Review, 5,* 68–81.

Homan, M. S. (2004). *Promoting community change: Making it happen in the real world.* Belmont, CA: Brooks/Cole.

Lewis, J. A., Lewis, M. D., Daniels, J. A., & D'Andrea, M. J. (2003). *Community counseling: Empowerment strategies for a diverse society* (3rd ed.). Pacific Grove, CA: Brooks/Cole.

Lewis, J. A., Packard, T. R., & Lewis, M. D. (2007). *Management of human service programs* (4th ed.). Belmont, CA: Thomson Learning.

Mizrahi, T., & Rosenthal, B. B. (2001). Complexities of coalition building: Leaders successes: Strategies, struggles, and solutions. *Social Work, 46,* 63–78.

Nylen, U. (2007). Interagency collaboration in human services: Impact of formalization and intensity of effectiveness. *Public Administration, 85,* 143–166.

Roberts-DeGennaro, M. (2001). Conceptual framework of coalitions in an organizational context. In J. E. Tropman, J. L. Erlich, & J. Rothman (Eds.), *Tactics and techniques of community intervention* (pp. 130–140). Belmont, CA: Wadsworth/ Thomson Learning.

Tefft, B. (1987). Advocacy coalitions as a vehicle for mental health system reform. In E. M. Bennett (Ed.), *Social intervention: Theory and practice* (pp. 155–185). Lewiston, NY: Edwin Mellen.

Wenger, L. D., Leadbetter, J., Guzman, L., & Kral, A. (2007). The making of a homeless center for homeless people in San Francisco's Mission District: A community collaboration. *Health and Social Work, 32,* 309–314.

CHAPTER **14**

Develop an
Advocacy Plan

Learning Objectives

1. Differentiate between the four levels of advocacy

2. Identify two strategies to be used at each level of advocacy

3. Describe an advocacy orientation

4. Differentiate an advocacy coalition from another coalition in which you may participate on behalf of your program

5. Identify the relationship between advocacy efforts and long-term sustainability of your program

6. Develop your own advocacy plan

YES, I'M MAD, BUT WHAT ELSE CAN I POSSIBLY DO?

Tracey had been operating an outreach center for homeless and impoverished seniors for the past 2 years. She had recently added onsite Narcotics Anonymous and Alcoholics Anonymous meetings and a senior support group to further enhance her service array, which also included a warming center, two meals per day, medical exams, and basic care. Occasionally, Tracey would learn that one of her clients had been charged with indecent exposure for urinating in public. Because the city did not have any public restrooms, the homeless population did not always have access to restrooms. The situation was worsened by the fact that most of the shelters and warming centers had limited hours. Each time Tracey heard about one of her clients being charged in this way, she became enraged. Finally, on hearing the news that yet another client had been charged with indecent exposure, she immediately contacted Danielle, one of the prosecuting attorneys that typically handled these charges, to express her concern. Danielle stated that there was little she could do, as the law was the law.

Before Tracey could spend any more time on this issue, a crisis occurred at the outreach center that required her complete attention. As a result, she forgot about this issue until it was raised again. Several months later, one of her clients was arrested as a result of receiving his third indecent exposure charge. According to the recently passed sex offender registration and community notification laws in the state, three or more indecent exposure charges required registration as a sex offender, and therefore, her client not only received jail time but was also now required to regularly notify the public of his whereabouts.

On hearing this, Tracey was even more outraged, and this time, she went directly to Danielle's office. Tracey argued that it was the responsibility of the region to provide public facilities to its residents and that by not doing so, the region and state stood to be punished, not her clients. She went on to share her utter disbelief that because the region could not effectively accommodate its residents, one of its most marginalized groups was being further marginalized through unnecessary legal action. Danielle replied that she understood Tracey's frustration and that she shared it, particularly because of the unintended consequences that the sex offender registration legislation was causing. Danielle stated that the legislation was designed to promote safer communities through closer monitoring of individuals who had sexually offended—not to classify and punish homeless individuals who did not have access to bathroom facilities. But again, Danielle noted that she had to follow the law as written and that the situation could be changed only through legislative action. After further discussing this problem as a social justice issue, Danielle again agreed with Tracey but noted that she could not do anything about it.

Tracey left feeling that she had at least shared her concerns with Danielle, and she thought briefly about how she might raise awareness of this issue in an effort to change it so that her clients were no longer caught in the middle. Unfortunately, Tracey's good intentions to rectify this issue did not last long. She realized that she was only one person and likely could not do much to change something so big—especially since statewide legislation was involved. Rather than devote any more time to thinking about the issue, Tracey turned her attention to her other duties when she got back to the outreach center—and she quickly realized that she already had enough to keep her busy.

CONSIDERING TRACEY

1. Do you believe that Tracey advocated for her clients? Why or why not?

2. What did Tracey mean when she referred to the issue of charging homeless individuals with a sex offense for publicly urinating as a social justice issue?

3. What do you believe Tracey's responsibility is in this matter? Danielle's responsibility?

4. As a busy mental health professional like Tracey, how are you supposed to get involved in advocacy while still attending to all your other duties?

5. If you were Tracey, what would you have done differently, if anything?

About This Chapter

This chapter focuses on a topic of specific significance to the mental health and human service industry—advocacy. Whereas advocacy has historically had a firm foundation in the mental health professions, as mental health professionals have continued to grow and develop a more sophisticated understanding of social justice, we have experienced a renewed sense of precisely what advocacy means. This is because advocacy and social justice are highly interrelated, and typically, efforts in advocacy on behalf of clients and communities are directly related to social justice. Therefore, advocacy—as well as social justice—plays a significant role in comprehensive program development and particularly in sustaining programs and organizations.

To frame this discussion of advocacy, we will first explore the history and significance of advocacy in mental health professions. We will follow this with an examination of the four levels of advocacy, which include the individual, community, public, and professional. Next, we will discuss various types of advocacy strategies, including individual empowerment, community-level, public arena, legislative-level, and professional. In order to further clarify the relationship that advocacy efforts have with one another, we will discuss this specifically. We will follow this with an examination of the concept of an advocacy orientation and its significance to work in the mental health professions. And in order to explore how to put an advocacy orientation into action, we will discuss the development and use of an Advocacy Plan. Finally, in order to clarify the major points of the chapter, a case illustration is provided, followed by an advocacy plan exercise.

STEP XII: DEVELOP AN ADVOCACY PLAN

Advocacy in Clinical Program Development

Advocacy is an innate part of clinical program development, since without some form of advocacy, clinical or human service programs would never come to fruition. In fact, think of a program with which you are familiar and then consider how it came to be. What you will likely find is that at the root of every clinical program is a voice—a voice demanding that a particular need be addressed, demanding attention to a specific population, demanding funding to support treatment or services, demanding to be heard, and demanding action. Without one such voice, the job that you currently hold or wish to hold in the future would likely not exist.

Unfortunately, Tracey was unable to effectively use her voice, and as a result, she was unable to prompt any change. This does not mean that all advocacy results in change, but it does mean that advocacy requires perseverance and focused efforts and not simply walking away after only a minimal investment toward change. Indeed, if the voices that helped create all that we enjoy in mental health and human services had not persevered, we would likely not have this incredibly rich field of practice. To better understand the role of advocacy in mental health and human services in the 21st century, it is necessary to both briefly review the history and examine the significance of advocacy today.

History and Significance

Advocacy is innately related to clinical professions and, as such, has been the driving force behind mental health and human services programming since the inception of the field. Regardless of the specific discipline—counseling, psychology, or social work—advocacy has been the impetus behind the evolution of that discipline as well as an essential role of the clinician. In their discussion of the history of advocacy in counseling, Toporek, Lewis, and Crethar (2009) provide a succinct summary:

> Through the years that the profession has existed, there have always been career and employment counselors who fought against racism and sexism in the workplace, family counselors who brought hidden violence and abuse into the open, school counselors who sought to eliminate school-based barriers to learning, and community counselors who participated in social action on behalf of their clients. As long as there have been counselors, there have been counselor-advocates. (p. 260)

In the 21st century, social justice advocacy has taken center stage, particularly in the counseling profession, as counselors have renewed their vows and invested new energies into calling the profession to action in implementing advocacy strategies and interventions (Bemak & Chung, 2005; Stone & Dahir, 2006; Toporek, Gerstein, Fouad, Roysircar, & Israel, 2006). Much of this renewed focus on social justice advocacy has stemmed from increased recognition of existing inequities and the responsibility of clinicians to more adequately address the various forms of oppression that often present significant challenges to the individuals being served (Lee, 2007). As a result of systemic oppression and other inequities, clinicians must be not only committed to advocacy but able to effectively advocate on behalf of others in order to dismantle barriers and promote justice wherever injustice prevails.

In fact, according to Lewis and Bradley (2000),

> Advocacy is an important aspect of every counselor's role. Regardless of the particular setting in which he or she works, each counselor is confronted again and again with issues that cannot be resolved simply through change within the individual. All too often, negative aspects of the environment impinge on a client's well-being, intensifying personal problems or creating obstacles to growth. When such situations arise, effective counselors speak up! (p. 3)

While advocacy is an innate part of our professional history, the role of advocacy has been much more specifically illuminated in the 21st century.

This is particularly evident in the promulgation of the American Counseling Association (ACA) Advocacy Competencies (Lewis, Arnold, House, & Toporek, 2002). Whereas the model provides a graphical representation of the three levels of advocacy competencies of the client/student, the school/community, and the public arena, as well as the major domains of advocacy needed at each level, the 43 specific competencies that compose the model are articulated in the advocacy competencies. The ACA Advocacy Competencies are provided on the ACA website: www.counseling.org/publications.

The Advocacy Competencies serve a similar function to the Multicultural Competencies (Arredondo et al., 1996) endorsed by the Association for Multicultural Counseling and Development. This is because both sets of competencies highlight the significance that these two areas (i.e., cultural competence and advocacy) have in the counseling profession and both provide comprehensive guidance to counselors and other mental health professionals in these areas by articulating specific practice competencies.

The Advocacy Competencies were endorsed by the ACA Governing Council in 2003, and through this endorsement, the ACA "acknowledges that oppression and systemic barriers interfere with clients' health and well-being and may even be the cause of their distress" (Toporek et al., 2009, p. 265). Moreover, the development of the Advocacy Competencies demonstrates the commitment of professional counselors to acknowledging and further understanding the role of advocacy in counseling.

Levels of Advocacy

As you will see in viewing the ACA Advocacy Competencies, they identify three levels toward which advocacy efforts can be directed: client/student, school/community, and the public arena. These competencies illustrate the need for mental health clinicians to engage in advocacy at multiple levels, because a different set of challenges is often present at different levels. For instance, at the client level, the clinician must engage in such advocacy as ensuring that the client receives the social security disability benefits to which s/he is entitled, while at the sociopolitical level, the clinician must advocate for such issues as state legislation for mental health parity. In addition to the three levels identified by Lewis et al. (2002), I would add a level of advocacy for the professional arena. This level of professional advocacy is often necessary to further the profession itself (i.e., counseling, psychology, social work) and, therefore, will also be discussed here.

Individual/Client

Advocacy at the individual level constitutes the most direct type of advocacy—connecting the client to the clinician and engaging in specific action to most expediently resolve an unmet need. Individual/client needs often are recognized by clinicians or other service providers during the course of treatment and may include such concrete needs as heat or other less concrete needs such as access to an entitlement, such as social security disability. In these situations, the clinician focuses on assessing the need for direct intervention, identifying allies, and implementing an action plan (Toporek et al., 2009).

Often, these needs may be shared among several clients with whom a clinician is working. This is particularly true when clinicians work with a specific subpopulation that may be treated unjustly or oppressed in a similar manner. For instance, the inequities faced by some students of color and students from low-income families indicate the need for clinicians to strategically address various environmental factors that are barriers to personal/social, academic, and career development (Ratts & Hutchins, 2009). As a result of continued exposure to this, clinicians may be much better prepared to specifically assess and address these issues. However, regardless of the number of individuals with an unmet need that a clinician recognizes, an unmet need for one individual typically implies an unmet need for other individuals. As a result, whereas clinicians must first address the needs of those whom they directly serve, the unmet needs of clients often reflect the unmet needs of the broader community. Therefore, while advocacy efforts must first be directed toward the individual, the advocacy needs of the individual often indicate the need for much broader advocacy at the community and public arena levels. As such, individual advocacy can often serve as an initial assessment and roadmap for advocacy efforts—providing essential information about widespread needs and guiding efforts to address such needs on a larger landscape.

Community

Community-level advocacy refers to advocacy that is directed at a broader population, such as a community, neighborhood, or school. Whereas individual-level advocacy focuses on the individual, community-level advocacy shifts to the needs of a group. As stated above, individual-level advocacy may move into community-level advocacy, particularly as one becomes aware that specific unmet needs go beyond one person and impact an entire group. The needs of groups may be the same as those noted in individuals (e.g., concrete needs, entitlements), and they often indicate the need for systemic or broad-based change in order to be effectively addressed. For instance, for some years, I worked with teenage girls who were living in community-based residential placements while they were involved in the child welfare system. These young ladies had been removed from their parents/caregivers due to abuse and/or neglect. As residents of new communities, these teens were often delayed admission to school and experienced delays in receiving Individualized Educational Plans to aid in academic placement and coordination of necessary supports. After having witnessed this occurrence more than once, it was clear that this type of discrimination was not simply happening to an individual but to a group of individuals. Moreover, it was clear that this type of discrimination was systemically generated by the school (i.e., the system). To address this, community-level advocacy was needed that would specifically target system change at the school level.

Public

Public-level advocacy goes beyond individual and group advocacy, impacting multiple and large groups across vast regions. Public-level advocacy is indicated when sociopolitical change is needed to address broad-based issues, and the objective of public-level advocacy is to impact public policy and influence legislation (Lewis et al., 2002). To accomplish this, increased public awareness is needed. Needs identified in individuals or in groups may indeed be needs that reach well beyond both individuals and groups and are much bigger than both, reflecting the need for public-level advocacy. For instance, as I learned, the discrimination that I witnessed against teens did not simply reflect the children in my region but, rather, reflected a widespread issue related to discriminatory practices leveled at child welfare–involved individuals. This meant that I had to engage in advocacy at both the individual and community levels in order to effectively care for my clients, but my efforts could not stop there; public-level advocacy was also needed to ensure that public policy was in place to protect these kids and families from further oppression.

Arguably, one of the most well-known public-level advocacy needs of the 21st century is mental health parity. Mental health parity, in the simplest terms, is pay and treatment access for mental health needs equal to those provided for physical health needs. And this has been an ongoing public-level advocacy issue for mental health professionals for several years. As a result, clinicians across the nation have worked tirelessly and collectively to raise public awareness and to influence legislation. Whereas these efforts have been successful at the national level with the passage of federal legislation, continued public-level advocacy is needed to address this issue at the state level.

Professional

Professional-level advocacy differs from individual, community, and public-level advocacy in that professional-level efforts are not geared toward directly impacting an individual but, rather, the professionals that belong to a clinical discipline. This does not mean that individuals/consumers do not benefit from some of these efforts, nor does it mean that these efforts are not related to other levels of advocacy; rather, it means that the intent centers on forwarding the profession. For instance, whereas mental health parity represents a public-level advocacy need, multiple mental health disciplines ranging from counseling to psychiatry have advocated for inclusion as mental health providers within this legislation.

Advocacy Strategies

Whereas advocacy is conducted at multiple levels—client, community, public, and professional—there are basically six types of advocacy strategies that can be used. As conceptualized in the ACA Advocacy Competencies (Lewis et al., 2002), these include individual advocacy and empowerment, community collaboration and systems-level advocacy, and public information and social-political advocacy that are targeted at the specific level (i.e., individual, community, public arena). Advocacy on behalf of the profession is most often related to other advocacy efforts; therefore, new strategies are not necessarily utilized, but rely on similar strategies. These strategies most often include collaboration, public information/awareness-raising activities, and social-political advocacy. As discussed above, there is often overlap among advocacy efforts—with advocacy beginning at one level and then moving to another. This is often the case since smaller-scale advocacy (e.g., individual, community-level) may serve as the catalyst for larger-scale advocacy efforts (e.g., public-level).

Because advocacy needs go well beyond the purview of mental health professionals, advocacy lessons can be taught by many. In fact, the advocacy work of Alice Waters (Box 14.1) provides an effective illustration of how advocacy efforts may move from one level to the next.

BOX 14.1

ADVOCACY LESSONS FROM A CHEF

Alice Waters, the renowned chef and mastermind behind *Chez Panisse* restaurant in Berkeley, initially recognized the need for people to be intimately connected with their food—understanding its source, caring for it, and ultimately, bringing it to the table. As a result, the food she serves is a result of close relationships she has formed with farmers and gardeners who practice humane and organic farming and who are completely connected to their land.

Taking her philosophy outside the restaurant, Alice realized that a school serving kids in a poor neighborhood lacked any type of kitchen and nutritional food options but had a microwave oven available for cooking pizzas and burgers. As a result, the kids had absolutely no connection to the food they were eating (not to mention no access to healthy foods). To address this need, she met directly with the principal and then went to the school board to advocate that the school grow its own garden. Successful in her advocacy efforts, "she would create a garden at Martin Luther King, where the children—about a thousand of them in the sixth, seventh, and eighth grades—could learn to plant, cultivate, harvest, cook, and serve food that they grew themselves" (McNamee, 2007, p. 259). She called this The Edible Garden, and although it took some time to bring to fruition, through her staunch determination, perseverance, and undiluted energy, the garden did come to be. While the idea of school gardens did not originate with Alice Waters—school gardens were common in the 19th century—Alice Waters did reenergize this movement, which has long since received significant attention.

The Edible Garden was a monumental success, but Alice knew that large-scale change required large-scale intervention; therefore, Alice took her advocacy efforts to a broader platform with her *Rethinking School Lunch* campaign. One of the results of this was the successful change that she initiated from steam-table cafeteria food to freshly cooked, seasonal local foods at the American Academy in Rome.

Through her school and community advocacy efforts, Alice Waters—one woman— was able to accomplish a great deal in changing how we think about food and our relationships with food, as well as working to ensure that all people have equal access to healthy foods and, most importantly, that individuals and communities are empowered to be self-sufficient and hold the tools to create sustainable food sources.

Individual Empowerment and Individual Advocacy Strategies

When dealing with individual-level advocacy needs, individual/self-empowerment strategies are often used. Self-empowerment is consistent with the basic ideology of mental health professions today and initially evolved from behavioral theory in that mental health professionals strive to help individuals learn to help themselves. Because self-empowerment is taught, empowerment strategies must begin with an assessment to determine if the individual possesses the skills to successfully advocate on her/his behalf (Ratts & Hutchins, 2009). Empowerment strategies may include identifying individual strengths and resources, collaborating with others in advocacy efforts, and developing an advocacy plan (Lewis et al., 2002).

Individual/self-empowerment is necessary when individuals have been marginalized in some way and, as such, require advocacy. However, rather than speaking on behalf of the individual, empowerment strategies are used to teach individuals how to effectively speak on their own behalf. Self-empowerment is obviously very powerful, as it enables oppressed individuals to speak out and to take action, directly responding to the issue without a liaison or middleman. Moreover, once empowered, individuals may continue to recognize other forms of oppression and utilize their skills to effectively deal with new situations as they arise.

Whereas self-advocacy can be extremely powerful, it is often not enough to effect change either sufficiently or quickly enough when an unmet need exists, and as a result, advocacy on behalf of the individual is also needed. Advocacy on behalf of the individual means that the clinician must be the voice of the individual, call attention to the issue, and work to address the need. Individual advocacy skills include such activities as negotiating relevant services on behalf of individuals and helping individuals gain access to needed resources (Lewis et al., 2002).

For clinicians working with individuals who have been marginalized for any reason (e.g., socioeconomic status, criminal history, sexual orientation, race, age, mental health status, ethnicity), advocacy typically composes a core part of the work. As such, clinicians often find themselves working on behalf of their clients to remove barriers, navigate through complicated bureaucratic processes, and coordinate access to needed services. Just as self-empowerment strategies must be taught to individual clients, clinicians must learn advocacy skills so that they can most effectively speak on behalf of their clients. However, similar to self-empowerment, once learned, advocacy skills used on behalf of another have the potential to improve with use, thereby continuously enhancing the power of the clinician as advocate—a force to be reckoned with.

Community or System-Level Advocacy Strategies

Because community-level or group needs often reflect systemic problems, different types of advocacy strategies are necessary. System-level needs often are deeply embedded in a system and, as such, may require paradigmatic or ideological shifts in order to be effectively remedied. For instance, in the case of educational placement of kids in the child welfare system that I referenced earlier, practices were put in place by some schools to prohibit timely placements of these kids, thereby treating them differently from other residents in the community. Whereas these practices may have originated as a method for effective school management and not as a discriminatory practice, the fact is that they evolved into a discriminatory practice and, therefore, needed to be removed.

In order to advocate at this level, awareness-raising activities are often the first step. By gathering data pertaining to the issue (Lewis et al., 2002), clinicians are in a position to increase awareness and knowledge of the issue for community members and those in positions of power who can effectively resolve the issue. By engaging in various discussions with various factions, clinicians may be able to illuminate the problem and engage others in their efforts to resolve the issue. In fact, it is this type of dialogue with others that usually is the catalyst for the development of advocacy coalitions. This is especially true since clinicians and other professionals who work on behalf of others or who share similar values related to helping are often drawn to one another and are naturally situated as allies.

Advocacy coalitions are similar to other coalitions (as discussed in Chapter 13), as they are formed as a result of shared interests and seek progress through collective efforts and collective strength. Advocacy coalitions can be extremely powerful, particularly because advocacy work is driven by passion—passion for a specific issue—and as such, the collective energy built by passion can be not only contagious but tremendously powerful. Advocacy coalitions at the community level may focus on such issues as increasing home health services or developing nonpunitive measures to support children with behavioral challenges. The work of advocacy coalitions centers on a specific issue, set of issues, or population, organizing individuals and groups together in advocacy work.

> Organizational actors in an advocacy coalition often serve as members of policy-making boards and monitor legislation or policy decisions. They can organize public education workshops or campaigns to gain support for specific issues, such as a workshop to educate the community on the proposed allocation of federal block grant funds. Their community education work can increase public attention to an issue by the use of various forms of the mass media. This public attention can put pressure on elected decision-makers to be more responsive to the needs of their constituents. Through

coalescing around these advocacy efforts, a bond is created between the member organizations, as they seek to maximize their supply of scarce resources. (Roberts-DeGennaro, 2001, p. 137)

While we often think of community-level advocacy work involving a fight against a system, sometimes the *system* that must be fought is made of individual community members, and as mental health professionals, we sometimes find ourselves on different sides of the aisle. For instance, consider the dramatic changes in inpatient mental health care that were marked by the deinstitutionalization of psychiatric facilities that began in the 1970s and the subsequent dismantling and significant reductions in residential options and hospital stays that have continued to this day. Throughout this time, mental health professionals have often found themselves working to get their neighbors and local residents to support community living for individuals with severe mental illness and/or developmental disabilities while at the same time advocating for hospitalization stays when warranted as the most effective form of treatment.

Another example of this type of dual-directional advocacy has resulted from the more recent sex offender legislation—most specifically, the community notification and sex offender registration legislation. Whereas many mental health professionals and legal professionals have argued for this legislation and its objective of promoting safer communities, others have argued that the legislation is far too punitive and, in some cases, constitutes a civil rights violation. As a result, mental health professionals have again found themselves on competing sides, often trying to balance effective treatment with community safety and upholding individual civil rights.

Community-level advocacy is often complex for the very reason that systemic change is usually deeply rooted and, therefore, challenging to change. At the same time, it is because of the type of significant change that can ultimately be achieved that community-level advocacy is often so necessary and the use of advocacy coalitions is so highly effective.

Public Arena–Level and Legislative Advocacy Strategies

Whereas community-level advocacy focuses on systemic issues at a regional level, public arena advocacy needs often result from systemic needs at a governmental or national level. As such, the stakes are even greater, since at this level, advocacy efforts are designed for sweeping change that will impact a significant population. Advocacy at every level is a professional responsibility of mental health professionals, and from an ethical perspective, advocacy work at the public arena level requires mental health professionals to assume an advocacy role that is focused on affecting public opinion, public policy, and legislation (ACA, 2005).

There are multiple strategies that can be used in public arena advocacy efforts that include media communication, working with alliances/coalitions, and lobbying (Lee & Rodgers, 2009). However, all advocacy efforts begin with basic awareness-raising efforts—arguably the toughest step in advocacy.

Raising awareness of an issue often requires an extraordinary amount of work and an enormous degree of perseverance aimed at getting the message out. Because of the vast complexities of individuals, a message that is effectively heard by one may not be heard by another, and as a result, the advocate must be constantly committed to finding the right message to reach the most individuals. This can be quite acrobatic as advocates reshape their message, attempt to reposition it in a slightly different manner, deliver it through a variety of means with various and changing platforms, and use different tactics that can speak to specific groups. As a result, advocates must be dedicated to continuing to move the issue forward, constantly engaging in a *try, try again* philosophy. And at times, advocates must use radical methods in order to be heard.

Florynce Kennedy is an excellent example of this. In 1969 New York, during a meeting on abortion law reform, only one woman was called to testify—the one woman being a nun whose views were clearly anti-abortion/pro-life. Incensed about the legislation and the absence of individuals with varying perspectives invited to discuss this critical issue, Kennedy spoke out against compromising on abortion reforms rather than repealing the abortion law altogether. Trying to get the attention of the all-male committee about the dangers that illegal abortions cause women, she cheerfully interjected, "Listen, why don't we shoot a New York state legislator for every woman who dies from an abortion?" (Steinem, 1969/1995). Regardless of where one stands on the issue of abortion, it is clear that Kennedy was determined to be heard and was not willing to stop trying to raise awareness of the issue, moved more by the issue she was fighting for than those whom she might offend along the way. It is in this way that her example reflects the base of advocacy, or the *soul* of advocacy—the intense need and relentless nature of the advocate to push forward.

In efforts to raise awareness, the media may prove to be a most effective outlet, particularly due to its potential reach. A variety of media outlets, including print media, television, and the Internet, may provide powerful tools by which to inform the public about the need for advocacy and change (Lee & Rodgers, 2009). Especially today, with the technology that is currently available and the access such technology gives to so many, advocates are wise to utilize these tools in their efforts. In addition to disseminating information through various media channels, advocates may engage in editorial writing and staging public demonstrations as other creative ways by which to use the media to raise public awareness about an issue.

Collaboration and the development of advocacy coalitions become even more necessary at the public level than at the community level since the scale of systemic change needed is that much greater. Moreover, it is important that advocates collaborate with not only a broad and diverse group of individuals but also with individuals with specific power to effect change at this level. In fact, specific qualities in co-collaborators, such as political credibility, social influence, leadership skills, financial influence, competence, authority, and diverse cultural perspectives, may contribute significantly to the achievement of collective goals (Lee & Rodgers, 2009).

In addition to raising public awareness through the use of media and collaboration and the use of advocacy coalitions, lobbying provides another effective strategy for advocating at the governmental level. Lobbying policymakers and legislators is almost always a crucial component of efforts to effect public policy change, since much too often, public policy is at the root of advocacy issues in mental health and human services.

To illuminate this, consider Hill's (2008) concise discussion on the gaps in research and public policy. In the unpacking of various issues, Hill identifies three major shortcomings in public policy that specifically contribute to disproportionate racial and ethnic representation in the child welfare system: (a) an overemphasis on child removal, (b) limited services to caregivers, and (c) inadequate funding to regions interested in reducing this disproportionality. He then further emphasizes the relationship between public policy and needs by pointing out significant gaps in government spending that are based in ideology rather than evidence, noting that the federal government spends approximately $8 billion on child welfare services (e.g., foster care, adoption), while only $1 billion is spent on family preservation or reunification services (U.S. Government Accountability Office, 2007).

To effect change in public policy, effective legislative advocacy is essential. Letter-writing campaigns, telephone calls, and participating in town hall meetings and other forums provide various means of direct communication with legislators. Moreover, establishing public forums in which legislators are invited to exchange dialogue provides another means by which to influence legislation and public policy. Finally, hiring a lobbyist to represent the advocacy needs of a group or coalition may be essential to effecting change at the national level.

Professional Advocacy Strategies

Whereas advocacy for a profession is substantively different from advocacy for an individual or group, there often is overlap between the two. The example of mental health parity provided earlier illustrates this. To provide another example of this, consider advocacy efforts aimed at achieving an effective scope of mental health services in the schools. While one aspect of these advocacy efforts may be directed at increasing access to comprehensive mental health care for school-aged children and teens, another aspect may be directed at ensuring that there is adequate representation among treatment professionals to support this level of care (e.g., school counselors, school psychologists, school social workers). As a result, mental health professionals must focus their advocacy efforts both on addressing the treatment issues of the client group and on their own professional discipline.

Because advocacy needs are not vastly different from client-focused needs to profession-focused needs, strategies needed to advocate on behalf of the profession are the same as those used to advocate on behalf of individuals and groups. As such, the use of different strategies is based on the level at which advocacy is occurring, with a need for broad-based approaches to effect public or legislative change and more grassroots efforts to confront community-level change.

Advocacy for the profession is predicated on engagement in one's profession and a healthy professional identity. As such, professionals are connected through the affiliations of others and understand the significance of collective identity and collective work. The major forum for such collective work is the professional association. Because advocacy work on behalf of the profession requires such collective work, all mental health professionals must demonstrate their responsibility to advocacy through participation in professional associations (e.g., ACA, American Psychological Association, National Association of Social Workers). Moreover, without maximum participation at the local, state, and national levels, progress and change are that much more challenging for the profession.

Advocacy and Long-Term Sustainability

Whereas advocacy is a primary responsibility of all mental health clinicians since it centers on the needs of the individual or group, it also is essential to the long-term sustainability of mental health and human service programs. The major objectives of advocacy efforts are to treat and/or serve unmet needs, remove barriers, increase access, and promote equity through increasing awareness and effecting change. Without such efforts, the vast needs of individuals would remain unrecognized, and as such, the very purpose of our work would not be highly visible or valued. Therefore, while advocacy efforts are designed to ensure access and equity in treatment, without a strong commitment from mental health professionals to continuously participate in advocacy efforts, the business that is mental health and human services is not only threatened but may not be sustained over time. Indeed, far too many well-designed and essential mental health programs have failed because the professionals operating them failed to fully understand the need for ongoing advocacy and the significance of their voices in effecting change.

Think about it this way: Today, the government has a deficit of more than $12 trillion (*I so wish this were only hypothetical*) and must create a balanced budget. This means that money that was previously allocated elsewhere must now be diverted to begin paying down this debt, which means that all existing expenditures are vulnerable to significant reduction or elimination.

Significant portions of governmental spending support an astounding array of mental health and human service programs and also specifically target marginalized individuals. However, significant portions also support defense, medicine, wildlife, and the arts, to name just a few. The decisions that lawmakers have to make are obviously difficult, since in these types of financial decision-making processes, mental health needs can be pitted against ecology and medicine. But these decisions are not made in isolation, and lawmakers are simply representatives of their respective constituents; therefore, each faction has an opportunity to voice its concerns and to push its cause to the forefront in order to protect it. Unfortunately, not all voices are used—and the only voices that are never heard are those that are never used. As a result, the dollars that end up being protected typically are associated with the strongest faction of advocates—individuals who not only have the skills to advocate but also exercise the perseverance to continue communicating their message.

Advocacy Orientation

Like all competencies, advocacy requires awareness, knowledge, and skills. However, advocacy also requires a specific orientation—an *advocacy orientation*. An advocacy orientation implies that one not only is capable of speaking up, taking action, and seeing something to completion but also is highly sensitive to potential advocacy needs and able to be assertive whenever and with whomever necessary. This type of orientation does not usually come naturally but, rather, is developed over time and honed through practice. However, it also requires mental health professionals to be in touch or completely connected to the environments in which they work and live—to be fully present so that they are able to recognize disparities and other needs. This type of presence is akin to Martin's (2000) third ear. As he so eloquently describes, therapists must not only possess the ability to listen to what is said or the type of emotion being expressed, but they must be able to identify what the client is not saying and the affect that is beneath the surface—thus, using their third ear. It is in this way that the presence or intense connection necessary to an advocacy orientation is best understood.

While mental health professionals work to develop greater sensitivity and presence with regard to identifying advocacy needs, basic assertiveness training can serve as an effective preparatory activity. Learning how to speak up, how to deliver the message, and how to modify the message to increase its potential to be heard are skills that must be acquired and require a great deal of attention. As I stated earlier, advocacy is akin to acrobatics, since the advocate must constantly move and bend to deliver the most effective message to the various recipients.

One of the exercises that I have my students complete to practice advocacy is the *60-second sell* to advocate for funding of their particular program or service. A traditional business practice, developing this type of pitch forces the students to reduce their argument down to its bare essentials and to adorn the argument with whatever they believe necessary to make it most effective. While this can create quite a challenge for many, it serves four primary purposes: It focuses the message, focuses the messenger, promotes a powerful connection between the message and the messenger, and provides an opportunity for the student to be assertive and engage in advocacy.

Developing an Advocacy Plan

Because advocacy is such an essential part of the work of mental health professionals, it must be given specific and sufficient attention on an ongoing basis. As such, advocacy work must be treated as a proactive activity— purposely and consistently initiated by the mental health professional. Without such a proactive approach, mental health professionals often find themselves in the unfortunate position of being on the defensive, quickly trying to articulate a response and taking time away from other pressing matters because of a failure to make time for advocacy efforts.

The development of an advocacy plan can assist in ensuring that advocacy efforts are cemented into practice and that this work becomes an essential part of one's professional life. Whereas the specific types of advocacy involvement you and your colleagues engage in on behalf of your clients will vary based on the needs of your population and the level of advocacy needed, what is essential is that you are postured to engage in advocacy efforts as needed. To do this, the following minimal roles and/or activities should be assigned and put into place:

- Advocacy training for all staff, with a specific focus on advocacy levels, strategies, and responsibilities of mental health professionals (content training)
- Assertiveness training/advanced advocacy training for all staff (skills training)
- Advocacy as an ongoing staff meeting topic to build advocacy into the program/organizational culture
- Community-level advocacy liaison—an individual responsible for identifying and leading efforts at the community level
- Coalition liaison—an individual responsible for representing the program/organization in existing coalitions or leading the development of a new coalition to address key issues with other community partners
- Legislative liaison—an individual responsible for identifying and leading advocacy efforts at the governmental level

By structuring the program/organization in this way, advocacy is inculcated as a core value of staff and the program/organization is postured to effectively deal with advocacy issues as they arise. Thus, an advocacy orientation is achieved at the organizational level, allowing the organization to maintain a proactive stance in its advocacy efforts.

Summary

Advocacy is a critical function of the mental health professional's work and one that requires close attention from the program developer. Engaging in effective advocacy requires not only awareness, knowledge, and skills that reflect competence in advocacy but also diligence, long-term commitment, and an innate ability to remain attentive to needs as they arise. The various levels of advocacy—client, community, public, and professional—each correspond with specific strategies for effective implementation, as well as sharing overlapping strategies. This is largely because needs typically exist on multiple levels, and therefore, advocacy work must be completed on multiple levels.

Advocacy work is rarely carried out in isolation since most needs are rarely limited to one individual. However, the power of one voice—one advocate—cannot be underestimated, as we are ultimately responsible for only our own actions. And as such, we must all appreciate not only the power of our own voice but the responsibility we have to use it whenever and wherever it is needed. This is the commitment that we all share in our continuous efforts toward equity and justice for all whom we serve and all who are marginalized.

CASE ILLUSTRATION

After having individually met with more than 60 of her students during the first 2 months of school for guidance and academic planning, Terri, a middle school counselor, realized that grief and loss appeared to be a prominent theme in her students' young lives. Terri met with her colleagues and administrators to discuss her concerns. After sharing her concerns, she stated that she needed to learn more to determine what was going on. To this end, Terri said that she needed to gain a more objective understanding of the issue through formal assessment in order to determine if grief and loss was indeed a clinical issue that required more systematic action on the part of the school.

Initially, her colleagues argued that their students seemed to present with so many challenges, including family violence and substance use, and they felt the school's primary role was to educate the students. Further, they felt they should try to help students deal with any severe clinical problems through outside referrals. Whereas Terri had heard this type of rhetoric before, she vigorously defended her stance that the school's role was to support the entire student and that failure to attend to a student's emotional issues may indeed prohibit academic success or maximal development.

After further discussion and perseverance, Terri won support from her colleagues to further assess the problem. She got to work designing a brief survey tool that was distributed to all the school's students and parents/caregivers. After collecting all the surveys, Terri was pleased that 57% of the surveys had been completed. Analyzing the data, Terri found that grief and loss due to recent separation from loved ones, home, and friends, and death of loved ones was something with which more than 62% of the students were dealing. Terri immediately took her findings to her colleagues and administrators, arguing that they quickly needed to develop and institute services to address grief and loss among the students and also provide specialized training for school personnel to more effectively support students experiencing grief and/or loss. While Terri still encountered fierce opposition from several colleagues and administrators, the principal decided to permit her time to design a comprehensive program to address the issue. However, whereas he would allow her some time during the workday to work on the new program development, there would be no funding available to support it. Appreciating her responsibility as a counselor to provide the most effective treatment and services to her clients, Terri knew that additional funding was not what was needed but, rather, hard work and commitment. This was especially true as the interventions that appeared to be most needed (based on the literature review) were ones that could easily be integrated into the workday simply by modifying schedules.

Two years later, Terri's program, *Tomorrows,* consists of support training for parents, teachers, and administrators to recognize and effectively respond to adolescents experiencing grief and loss; curricular changes that promote sensitivity and awareness about grief and loss; an ongoing therapeutic group open to all students in need of group-based clinical intervention; and a psychoeducational approach to increase awareness and knowledge of grief and loss among students. Today, as a result of achieving successful program outcomes, Terri's program continues to operate in her school and has been implemented in two other schools in the region—both of which are currently being evaluated to assess if they are able to achieve the same outcomes that Terri was able to achieve in her school during the program's first 2 years.

Terri has received accolades from her colleagues and administrators and has been officially recognized for her work by the regional school board. Most significantly, she has made a difference in the lives of children and families by redefining the role of the school counselor and the integral role that schools play in caring for the whole child— all with no additional funding but, rather, embedded into the school's programming.

ADVOCACY PLANNING EXERCISE

Using the target population identified earlier in your program design, consider the following questions:

1. What potential or existing advocacy needs currently exist among the population?

2. For each potential or existing advocacy need, identify the related level(s) at which advocacy efforts are needed.

3. Identify the various types of advocacy strategies you would use to address the needs, including the anticipated outcome of each.

4. Develop an initial advocacy plan for your program, identifying how you would structure the staff and activities around advocacy issues.

References

American Counseling Association. (2005). *ACA code of ethics.* Alexandria, VA: Author.

Arredondo, P., Toporek, M. S., Brown, S., Jones, J., Locke, D. C., Sanchez, J., et al. (1996). *Operationalization of the multicultural counseling competencies.* Alexandria, VA: Association for Multicultural Counseling and Development.

Bemak, F., & Chung, R. C. Y. (2005). Advocacy as a critical role for urban school counselors: Working toward equity and social justice. *Professional School Counseling, 8,* 196–202.

Hill, R. B. (2008). Gaps in research and public policy. *Child Welfare, 87,* 359–367.

Lee, C. C. (2007). *Counseling for social justice* (2nd ed.). Alexandria, VA: American Counseling Association.

Lee, C. C., & Rodgers, R. A. (2009). Counselor advocacy: Affecting systemic change in the public arena. *Journal of Counseling and Development, 87,* 284–287.

Lewis, J. A., Arnold, M. S., House, R., & Toporek, R. L. (2002). *ACA advocacy competencies.* Retrieved September 13, 2010, from http://counseling .org/Resources/Competencies/Advocacy_Competencies.pdf

Lewis, J., & Bradley, L. J. (2000). Introduction. In J. Lewis & L. J. Bradley (Eds.), *Advocacy in counseling: Counselors, clients, and community* (pp. 3–4). Greensboro, NC: Caps.

Martin, D. G. (2000). *Counseling and therapy skills* (2nd ed.). Prospect Heights, IL: Waveland.

McNamee, T. (2007). *Alice Waters and Chez Panisse: The romantic, impractical, often eccentric, ultimately brilliant making of a food revolution.* New York: Penguin Press.

Ratts, M. J., & Hutchins, A. M. (2009). ACA advocacy competencies: Social justice advocacy at the client/student level. *Journal of Counseling and Development, 87,* 269–275.

Roberts-DeGennaro, M. (2001). Conceptual framework of coalitions in an organizational framework. In J. E. Tropman, J. L. Erlich, & J. Rothman (Eds.), *Tactics and techniques of community intervention.* Belmont, CA: Thomson Learning.

Steinem, G. (1995). The city politic: A nice place to live for revolutionaries. In C. Heilbrun, *Education of a woman: The life of Gloria Steinem* (p. 168). New York: Ballantine. (Reprinted from *New York Magazine,* pp. 8–9, March 10, 1969)

Stone, C. B., & Dahir, C. A. (2006). *The transformed school counselor.* Boston: Lahaska.

Toporek, R., Gerstein, L., Fouad, N., Roysircar, G., & Israel, T. (Eds.). (2006). *Handbook for social justice in counseling psychology: Leadership, vision, and action.* Thousand Oaks, CA: Sage.

Toporek, R. L., Lewis, J. A., & Crethar, H. C. (2009). Promoting systemic change through the ACA advocacy competencies. *Journal of Counseling and Development, 87,* 260–268.

U.S. Government Accountability Office. (2007, July). *African American children in foster care* (GAO-07-816). Washington, DC: U.S. Government Printing Office.

Develop an Information-Sharing Plan

Learning Objectives

1. Identify three costs and three benefits related to information sharing of program data

2. Identify four primary types of data and the purpose of collecting and analyzing each

3. Differentiate between process and outcome data

4. Discuss the importance of assigning responsibility for data collection, analysis, and reporting, and identify who should be responsible and why

5. Discuss the significance of data reporting methods, including responsibilities, time frames, methods, and recipients

6. Develop a comprehensive data-reporting plan

BUT THE PROGRAM IS EFFECTIVE

On Tuesday afternoon, Reggie received a call from his contract manager telling him that his contract for mentoring at-risk youth would not be renewed next year because funding for children's services had been reallocated. The contract manager went on to explain that the county was facing budget cuts and, therefore, had to make decisions about which programs to continue funding. While these decisions were difficult to make, they were based on identifying the most essential programs and those that had produced strong outcomes. Unfortunately, the mentoring programs were not viewed as essential nor was there evidence of their success.

When Reggie heard this, he was flabbergasted. He explained to the contract manager that he had been conducting a program evaluation since his program's inception 2 ½ years ago and that the outcomes were extremely positive. He quickly shared with her some of the highlights of his program:

- Teens who had been successfully matched with mentors: 342
- Percentage of mentees who graduated high school compared with the region's 67% graduation rate: 94%
- Percentage of the mentees who pursued college: 68%
- Of the 32% who did not pursue college, percentage who pursued vocational training or were employed: 25%
- Percentage of the mentees who were either living at home or living independently: 92%
- Percentage of the mentees who had been involved in criminal activities post-mentoring services: less than 5%
- Percentage of the mentees who had experienced substance abuse problems: 6%; less than 3% required treatment
- Percentage of mentees and parents/caregivers who identified having had a mentor as one of the most important aspects of their teenage years: 94% and 98%, respectively
- Total cost per youth: $302 (compared with the $1,680–$6,440 costs related to much more intensive case management services and comprehensive community-based programs for court-involved youth—precisely what Reggie's program was designed to prevent being needed)

After quickly reviewing these outcomes with the contract manager, Reggie promised to send her the full set of evaluation data and the summary report. He told her that he had been planning to send her the report and evaluation results once he had 3 full years of data and said he was sorry that he had held onto the information.

The contract manager shared her surprise with Reggie, stating that she wished she had known sooner about the program's success, since it very well could have meant that the funds for mentoring programs would not have been cut. However, legislative action had already been taken, so the funding decisions were final. She did encourage Reggie to make the evaluation findings available and told him that they may still prove fruitful in the next funding cycle's decision-making process.

CONSIDERING REGGIE

1. What did Reggie do right, and what mistakes did he make?

2. If you were Reggie, what would you do next?

3. What practices should Reggie put in place to ensure that relevant program information is shared with all who have a need to know on an ongoing basis?

About This Chapter

This chapter's focus is the significance of data, the critical information that data provides about all aspects of a program and organization, and most importantly, the invaluable need for comprehensive information sharing. We will examine both indirect and direct benefits of information sharing. In addition, we will explore the various types of data that are collected as part of comprehensive program development, including outcomes data, process evaluation data, human resource data, financial data, compliance and quality improvement data, and other pertinent data. We will explore the questions related to whom information should be shared with and why, as well as how frequently and through what medium information should be communicated. To guide comprehensive data collection and to illustrate the importance of examining all the program data in order to understand the total program operations, the *Quarterly/Annual Comprehensive Data Report Tool* is provided. The chapter concludes with a case illustration to further reinforce the content of the chapter, followed by a data report plan exercise and questions for reflection and discussion.

STEP XIII: DEVELOP AN INFORMATION-SHARING PLAN

Significance of Information Sharing

Seemingly, Reggie did everything right. At the implementation of a new program (i.e., mentoring), he designed and implemented a comprehensive process evaluation and a comprehensive outcome evaluation. He methodically collected and analyzed the data and, as a result, was intimately aware of the significant details of his program and the impact that it had made. However, he made one unforgiving mistake: He failed to share the data that he had collected and analyzed with all the people who had a need to know. As a result, his highly successful program would cease to operate.

While Reggie's example illustrates one of the toughest lessons about the business of which program development is a part, it is unfortunately not uncommon. As mental health and human service professionals have continued to become much more concerned with evaluation methods and other data collection activities, there continues to be a lag in following through once data has been collected. This can create obvious challenges, particularly since any data that is collected but not used should not have been collected in the first place, since it incurred a cost without producing a benefit.

There are many other important lessons that Reggie's vignette illustrates (see Box 15.1).

BOX 15.1

LESSONS FROM REGGIE

- Comprehensive program evaluation must be conducted at the start of any new program.
- Outcome data is essential and, therefore, must be collected.
- Output data, such as cost-effectiveness, is essential and, therefore, must be collected.
- Program data must be shared frequently and regularly with all stakeholders.
- Collecting and analyzing data without sharing it with stakeholders may have devastating results.
- Collecting and analyzing data and not sharing the results may have the same effect as if no data had been collected or analyzed.
- Conducting various types of evaluation and sharing the findings with stakeholders may have a direct effect on your program's sustainability.

Whereas each of these lessons is significant, the more critical issue related to information sharing has to do with why data is collected in the first place. A large part of this answer is provided in previous chapters in the discussions related to program design, implementation, and evaluation and assessment. However, in addition to implementation and evaluation data, other data must be collected, such as client demographic data and financial data. Through comprehensive data collection and analysis, mental health professionals are empowered—empowered to better understand and manage their program. The notion that *information is power* can be clearly illuminated in program development efforts, particularly as the more knowledgeable the program developer is about the program, the easier it is to articulate the program to others. Conversely, without detailed information about the ongoing operations of the program, it's more challenging both to communicate the program to others and to garner support for the program. Because the operations provided by human service organizations depend on people (Gibelman & Furman, 2008), the central role that ongoing communication, including information sharing and data sharing, plays in supporting a program's operations is critical.

More importantly, without effective means by which to communicate the work that mental health professionals provide and the impact that this work makes, mental health care itself is at risk. Morris et al. (2010) speak about this global issue from an Irish perspective:

> As with all areas of health care in Ireland and internationally, the health information deficit in the mental health services serves to impede the decisions of policymakers, health care workers, patients, and their families. It is imperative that mental health information becomes more accessible, useful, and comprehensible so that a culture of information gathering and use can be fostered both internationally and in Ireland. This information can then provide the evidence required for the provision of high-quality health care. (p. 360)

Direct and Indirect Benefits

In addition to what is listed above, there are numerous other benefits—both direct and indirect—that may result from sharing information related to program operations and outcomes with stakeholders. Indirect benefits refer to benefits that may not produce a direct result but that produce some impact, whereas direct benefits are those whose effect is concrete. For instance, by sharing information about program operations with staff, employees may have an increased level of engagement with the program/organization. This level of engagement may not be quantifiable, but it may mean that some employees choose to remain at the organization even when other more lucrative opportunities arise. Because you may not be aware of this impact, particularly since you may not have had any idea that someone was considering leaving, the impact is indirect—yet still significant. Alternatively, the sum effect of employee engagement may produce the direct benefit of employee retention, especially since employee retention results in decreased expenditures associated with hiring. This benefit can be tremendous, as any effective program developer and human resources manager can tell you exactly what it costs to *replace* an entry-level professional employee (e.g., case manager, therapist), which may range from $6,000 to $12,000. Thus, reducing unwanted employee turnover is an objective of most managers, because replacing an employee creates additional and often unnecessary expense to the organization that cannot be recouped. The costs are largely attributed to such administrative work as processing new applicants, hiring-related activities, coordination of employee benefits, and new employee orientation and training, among others. Considering these unnecessary costs, it is not difficult to see the benefit of staff retention.

Box 15.2 provides a snapshot of other indirect and direct benefits related to information sharing.

BOX 15.2

INDIRECT AND DIRECT BENEFITS
RELATED TO INFORMATION SHARING

Indirect Benefits

- Increased ownership in the program/organization among employees, resulting from increased knowledge of shared responsibilities
- Creation of a culture of transparency and shared commitment
- More flexible workforce that can more easily adapt to changes when needed as a result of being consistently informed

Direct Benefits

- More productive and effective workforce as a result of increased knowledge of the business
- Problems and deficits able to be quickly identified and resolved so that program/organization is continuously improving
- More competitive program and organization as a result of increased productivity and effectiveness
- Increased business and growth opportunities
- Program/organizational sustainability

Types of Data

There are multiple types of data that mental health and human service professionals collect as part of the program management process. Indeed, at times, some mental health professionals claim that they are more data collectors than mental health professionals—with responsibilities of collecting intake information and administering and collecting assessment data, treatment planning data, quality assurance data, contract compliance data, and so on. However, the issue is not one of data collector versus mental health professional but, rather, of mental health professional whose role very much involves data collection and management. Data is pertinent to our ability to effectively assess and treat clients, manage staff and other resources, manage programs and organizations, and continue to enjoy our livelihood. Or put even more succinctly, "Data collection is the *sine qua non* of effectiveness-based program planning" (Kettner, Moroney, & Martin, 2008, p. 19). Data collection and management, therefore, must be both respected and appreciated—not as an added job but as one of the most integral parts of our job. Once this has occurred, the power that information holds can be fully unleashed.

While there is an enormous amount of data that may be collected, the primary reason for collecting the data has to do with gaining knowledge about all aspects of the program. However, all data that is collected must be fully justified. And as Gard, Flannigan, and Cluskey (2004, p. 176) remind us, the four questions that should guide the data collection process are as follows:

1. What do we want to know?

2. Why do we want to know it?

3. What should we measure?

4. How should we measure it?

Knowing that all data that is collected has a specific use is essential. Often, the most essential data is collected for a process or outcome evaluation, human resource management, financial management, or contract compliance and quality improvement activities. While these data sets can be reviewed independently, they also must be thoroughly reviewed concurrently, thus forming a complete picture of the program. By doing so, a critical understanding of how each of the data sets interacts with the others can be achieved. Each of these various types of data sets is discussed next.

Process Evaluation Data

As discussed in Chapter 12, a comprehensive process evaluation allows you to assess the myriad aspects of a program throughout its implementation. Depending on the type and scope of the process evaluation, a variety of data can be collected that includes client demographic and other descriptive characteristics and program outputs such as number and type of interventions provided, treatment length, and number and qualifications of staff providing treatment. In addition, coverage and equity data can be collected to provide specific information about who is being served and who is not being served.

Demographic and descriptive data can be highly useful in gaining increased understanding and knowledge of your client population and, therefore, must also be collected and analyzed. This data has multiple uses, including as part of a process evaluation in identifying the target population and needs, increasing knowledge about program outcomes as related to client subpopulations and specific characteristics, advocacy efforts, and pursuing funding opportunities. Indeed, possessing specific and comprehensive knowledge about client populations is essential to effective program management. Box 15.3 provides a sample of possible types of demographic information that may be collected and reported.

BOX 15.3

SAMPLE OF DEMOGRAPHIC DATA CHARACTERISTICS FOR A TRANSITIONAL HOUSING PROGRAM

- Age
- Gender
- Race
- Ethnicity
- Language
- Dependent children (ages, gender, and special needs)
- Intimate partner status
- Special needs
- Academic history
- Employment history
- History of homelessness
- Family, friends, and other supports

Demographic data provides rich information; however, it is often in collecting this type of data that mental health professionals run into trouble. Much too often, data is collected that is not needed—data that is not going to be used for a specific purpose. This goes back to the issue that no data should be collected that does not have a specifically identified use, because otherwise, you risk doing a disservice to those whom you are serving as well as wasting time and money. For instance, each of the data elements in Box 15.3 must serve a specific purpose, to justify why it is being collected. And in this case, each data element does serve a purpose, as illustrated in Table 15.1.

Table 15.1 Data Elements and Rationale

Data Element	Rationale/Purpose of Data Collection
Age	Increases knowledge of target population and need based on age
Race	Increases knowledge of target population and need based on race; provides additional knowledge of population when considered with ethnicity
Ethnicity	Increases knowledge of target population and need based on ethnicity; provides additional knowledge of population when considered with race
Language	Increases knowledge of target population and need based on primary language; used to determine if other supports are needed to effectively communicate with client
Dependent children (ages, gender, and special needs)	Increases knowledge of target population and need based on children who are also in need of housing and care
Intimate partner status	Increases knowledge of target population and need based on intimate partner who may also be in need of housing and care; supports treatment and service planning; aids in identifying possible client support(s) to be utilized in treatment
Special needs	Identifies any special needs (e.g., mental disability, physical disability) that may require accommodations and/or may make one eligible for entitlements and other supports
Academic history	Increases knowledge of target population; supports services and treatment planning focused on academics

(Continued)

Table 15.1 (Continued)

Data Element	Rationale/Purpose of Data Collection
Employment history	Increases knowledge of target population; supports services and treatment planning focused on vocational development and employment
History of homelessness	Increases knowledge of target population; increases knowledge of the homeless experience; uses past intervention experiences in service and treatment planning to avoid service and treatment failure
Family, friends, and other supports	Supports treatment and service planning; aids in identifying possible client supports to be utilized in treatment

In addition to the specific purposes listed above, client demographic and descriptive data also can be used to learn specifically about program coverage and program equity—significant information for program developers, communities, and funding sources.

> Coverage data provide feedback on the extent to which a program is a) meeting the community need and b) reaching its target population. Monitored during program implementation, coverage data can be used not only to determine the extent to which the target group is being reached but also to ensure that individuals ineligible for the program are not served. (Kettner et al., 2008, p. 258)

Similarly, equity data provides feedback on the various subgroups within a region to identify what, if any, disparities exist in regard to who is being served.

> Unless a program is targeted at a specific subgroup of a community, all other things being equal, geographical subareas and subgroups should be served by a program in roughly the same proportion as their composition in the community. Equity data can be used to ensure adequate coverage of subgeographical areas and subgroups during implementation or at the end of a program to document that a program is or is not reaching some geographical subarea or subgroup. Utilized in a performance measurement approach, coverage data provides stakeholders with information about the distribution of outputs, quality outputs, and outcomes across subgeographical areas and subgroups. (Kettner et al., 2008, pp. 258–259)

In addition to client demographic and descriptive data, various types of information are collected specifically for the process evaluation to provide comprehensive information related to program implementation and operations and to promote further knowledge of outcomes. Several of the types of data that are collected as part of a process evaluation are reviewed in Chapter 12; so please refer back to that chapter if needed. Briefly, information about the implementation process itself is collected, including the number of resources (e.g., staff, money) allocated to the program, location of service delivery, and unexpected occurrences, to name a few.

To reiterate, fidelity assessment may be included in the process evaluation in order to specifically assess the degree to which a treatment is delivered as intended. The five major areas of fidelity are treatment design, training, treatment, receipt of treatment, and treatment skill enactment (Borelli et al., 2005), and each requires specific data to be collected and analyzed. Treatment design data may include number and type of interventions and theoretical basis of treatment, while training may include the content and methods used to prepare staff to deliver the treatment and staff credentials. Treatment delivery data may include the number and type of interventions actually delivered, the time frame in which treatment was delivered, and the credentials of the individual(s) delivering the treatment. Other specific data that may be collected and analyzed in a fidelity assessment were also discussed in Chapter 12; so again, please refer back for a more comprehensive discussion of data types involved in a fidelity assessment.

Because of the unique power that process evaluation data holds—including demographic and fidelity assessment data—sharing this information with stakeholders is critical. Client demographic data can be particularly useful not only in increasing knowledge of your particular target population or region but also in informing the broader field about client needs and characteristics. Therefore, this information is of great value to staff, funding agents, and other professionals. In addition, this data is pivotal to ongoing program planning efforts. For instance, program modifications may need to be made to a program that was originally designed for adolescents but that currently has a majority client population of older teens, since there are often significant developmental differences between the two groups. Likewise, a subpopulation of clients may not speak English, and therefore, specific program modifications and additional supports will be required to effectively serve this group. In addition, information about the type and scope of resources, such as staff credentials, administrative oversight, and adjunctive services, is essential not only to fully understanding all the aspects that contribute to the program's success but also to understanding all that must be in place to effectively support the program. This information has specific relevance to planning, managing, and sustaining programs and is directly related to the program's finances.

Because treatment fidelity data speaks directly to the design of a particular treatment, sharing information about the degree to which fidelity has been maintained throughout implementation is critical for program staff. As such, this information provides direct feedback about their performance as well as about the success or failure of the program developer in planning for retaining treatment fidelity. In addition, this information is critical to clients as part of the informed consent process and as consumers of services with a right to know that they did receive what they were told they would receive. Moreover, this information is significant to funders, as it speaks to accountability and treatment design. Finally, this information is essential to other professionals and stakeholders in continued efforts to better understand treatment design and to understand the relationship between design, implementation, and outcomes.

Outcomes Evaluation Data

The types of data collected in the outcomes evaluation are specific to the program's objectives and, therefore, are unique to a program. However, there are also often common outcomes relevant to different types of programs. For instance, a treatment program for juvenile sex offenders and a second-chance academic program for young adults (i.e., a high school diploma program for young adults) may share the outcome of academic success. Whereas both programs may share an outcome related to academic success, the outcomes for juvenile sex offenders may also include recidivism (i.e., reoffending), improved family functioning, and increased independence.

Outcomes are generated directly from the program design. For instance, family therapy and the development of a family support network are designed to improve family functioning and, therefore, must be evaluated to determine if the interventions did indeed lead to the anticipated outcomes. This interdependent nature between design, implementation, and evaluation is essential to understanding the complexity of programs and program development efforts, and therefore, highlighting these relationships in discussions of outcomes is helpful in increasing knowledge of the program's efforts.

In addition, because outcomes reflect a program's success, they are critical to all stakeholders, including clients, staff, funding agents, community members, legislators, and professionals in the field. Staff are particularly interested in outcomes since they reflect another measure of their performance and, as such, provide another integral link to what they do and why they do it—a critical benefit to us all while working with individuals. However, whereas it is necessary and healthy for any organization to continuously evaluate outcomes, caution must be exercised in the degree to which outcomes are directly associated with employee performance. Indeed, the employee is a vehicle by which an intervention is delivered, and therefore, rarely is it the employee who failed but, rather, the intervention that failed.

Funding sources and legislators are specifically interested in outcomes since this information is pertinent to decisions about continued and future funding. Community members are interested in outcomes, since they also have a particular interest in what works and what doesn't. After all, as taxpayers, community members provide primary support for nonprofit services. Finally, other mental health professionals have a vested interest in the continued development of knowledge and understanding not only related to what works but why it works so that efforts can continue to develop and implement the most effective types of services and treatment.

Continuous collecting, analyzing, and reporting of outcomes must occur to ensure that all stakeholders are well informed about outcomes. Without doing so, the dilemma that Reggie faced may become a reality for other mental health professionals—regardless of just how good the work they are doing is.

Human Resources Data

Human resources data includes all data pertaining to staff (i.e., personnel). This includes but is not limited to such data as illustrated in Box 15.4.

BOX 15.4

EXAMPLES OF HUMAN RESOURCES DATA

- Hiring
- Job descriptions
- Performance reviews
- Educational records
- Medical information
- Salary information
- Insurance
- Company-sponsored retirement plan information
- Tax information

(Continued)

(Continued)

- Citizenship information
- Staff vacancies (unfilled positions)
- Training completed by staff
- Staff credentials
- Retention
- Separation
- Disciplinary action
- Staff challenges/problems
- Staff commendations/rewards

Sample of Human Resources Data

Human resource professionals maintain various documents and data pertaining to staff and are responsible for each staff member's personnel file to ensure that confidential information remains confidential. The types of data that are private and, therefore, must be maintained in a confidential manner include medical and other personal information, salary, tax and citizenship information, and disciplinary action. Whereas this data is relevant to program managers/administrators, specific personal information is not relevant to program staff, and it is not permissible to disclose such information to staff who do not have a justified need to know. However, data related to staff that can be reported in aggregate and that is not considered confidential is highly useful to program developers/clinicians and all program staff, as it relates to program operations.

This data, including staff vacancies, hiring, credentials, job descriptions, and training activity, is often most valuable to program managers and staff when examined as trend data—for instance, you might examine staff training needs versus training completion on a quarterly basis to strategize methods to address training needs. Or you may evaluate staff retention to determine what trends might exist related to when staff end their employment and the reasons why they choose to do so.

By collecting and analyzing data related to staff, program managers are equipped with pertinent information about their staffing infrastructure. For example, if employee exit interview results indicate that 76% of staff voluntarily terminated their employment last year due to either not feeling connected to the program/organization or due to the lack of professional development activities the organization offered, this essential information can be used in staff retention efforts. However, this data is meaningful to all staff—not simply the manager/supervisors—particularly because sharing this type of information among staff and involving staff in retention efforts may serve to engage staff. As a result, the method by which future retention efforts are developed may in fact be a critical retention tool.

Financial Data

Financial data comprise all the program's finances—costs and revenue. Data such as employee salaries, office space, furniture, supplies, administrative support services, and the contract rate(s) are all essential financial data. Financial data is pertinent to program planning, management, and sustainability and, as a result, must be collected and analyzed frequently. Effective program developers and managers are keenly aware of the financial aspects of their program(s) and maintain close attention to financial details. Basic information that all mental health professionals should know is the per client cost of a program. This is typically gathered as part of the process evaluation (Byford et al., 2007) and provides essential information for increasing economic knowledge of the program. A basic method for computing this cost is to divide the number of clients served by the total cost of the contract amount or revenue produced. For instance, if the total contract amount for a mentoring program is $100,000 and you serve 260 youth, the cost per client is $384.62. This means that the cost of mentoring services per youth is approximately $384.62. Knowing this most basic economic information is critical to fully understanding a program and understanding the financial needs related to specific interventions. It has particular significance to maintaining funding, pursuing new funding, and advocacy efforts. Moreover, employees and other professionals are interested in this since it provides another critical perspective of programming and the financial aspects of interventions.

By frequently sharing financial information, employees are able to feel more closely connected to the business that is their work—and, at least from my perspective, one of the most important businesses conducted on earth. That is precisely why it is so important that we protect it, and one form of protection is to demonstrate respect for our business by increasing the knowledge of all stakeholders about the business. Moreover, frequently sharing financial information with employees promotes transparency and contributes to a more engaged workforce.

Two other groups with whom financial information has specific ramifications are community members and funders. In fact, sharing financial information with community members in concert with information about program outcomes may also be particularly helpful in garnering more financial support through donations and other means. In addition, sharing financial information with funding sources not only is required but also provides critical information that is useful in ongoing contract negotiations and decisions about releasing new funds.

Compliance and Quality Improvement Data

Compliance data refers to compliance with requirements of contracting organizations, accrediting bodies, licensing organizations, other oversight organizations, or self-imposed requirements. Compliance data often includes both outcome data and other types of data. For instance, contracting organizations are specifically interested in a program's effectiveness in treating clients; however, they are often equally interested in the credentials of staff and the availability of services. Box 15.5 provides a sample of contract compliance data.

BOX 15.5

SAMPLE OF CONTRACT COMPLIANCE DATA

- Acceptance rate of all referred clients
- Length of time from initial referral to program admission
- Number of clients served annually
- Percentage of clients successfully treated in accordance with preestablished success criteria
- Percentage of clinicians with a master's degree or above in major mental health discipline and licensure as a mental health therapist
- Percentage of clients discharged prematurely

Compliance data often overlaps with process evaluation data, because contractors have a vested interest in ensuring that programs/models are implemented as designed. Because contract compliance data reflects the degree to which goals or targets are met, contractors or other oversight organizations dictate the required target thresholds. For some issues, such as the percentage of qualified therapists, there is no tolerance for noncompliance, meaning the required compliance rate is 100%; for other areas, compliance may be set at less than 100% or at a specific number. For instance, the percentage of clients discharged prematurely (without completing the program) may be set at 85%, the expected length of time between referral and program admission may not exceed 48 hours for any client, and there may be a requirement to serve a minimum of 160 clients per year.

Contract compliance data has obvious implications. Failure to comply with performance expectations may result in the cancellation or nonrenewal of a contract. Therefore, collecting, analyzing, and sharing this data with all program stakeholders is critical to the program's sustainability.

Quality improvement data is required by accrediting bodies and is often a standard part of organizational practices and, thereby, self-imposed by organizations. Quality improvement speaks to the specific areas in which improvement is sought and the improvement goals. While it is a standard part of business operations today, quality improvement originated in Japan (Senge, 2006) in the 1940s. Unlike contract compliance goals that are predetermined by contractors or other oversight organizations, quality improvement goals often evolve organically from data analysis findings. For instance, if exit interview data indicated that staff chose to leave the organization due to lack of engagement, a quality improvement goal might be developed to address this specific issue. The goal, such as *95% of staff will be engaged with the program within 6 months of employment as measured by the Employee Engagement Scale* (hypothetical standardized assessment instrument—with sound psychometric properties, of course), is developed by program staff with specific strategies by which to attain it. Through the collection and analysis of various program data, staff are able to quickly identify areas in need of improvement and can then develop means by which to address these areas.

The structure surrounding quality goals may vary considerably from organization to organization, with some organizations using quality improvement committees to lead quality improvement efforts and others requiring a specified number of quality goals in key areas (e.g., client satisfaction, community relations). However, what is of greatest import is not how quality improvement efforts occur but, rather, that they occur and that their purpose is fully understood by all stakeholders. This is because of what quality improvement efforts reflect—a commitment to quality and continuous improvement.

Whereas contractors and/or accrediting bodies often require reporting of both contract compliance data and quality improvement data—even when not required—it is wise to share this data with oversight organizations since it reflects the program/organization's dedication to quality. Equally important is that this data is shared frequently and with all staff. Contract compliance and quality improvement data are byproducts of the work of staff, and therefore, all staff must have open and continuous access to this data. By ensuring that this occurs, staff are able to better understand the critical issues that compose their program and are able to more effectively participate in ongoing improvement efforts.

Other Pertinent Data

In addition to the five major areas just discussed, there are other types of data that must be collected and shared with various groups. Other client data, such as satisfaction with services, is not only required by several accrediting bodies and/or contractors but particularly meaningful to program staff and necessary for program improvement efforts. Employee information, such as employee satisfaction, engagement, and retention each provide pivotal data for use in continuous improvement efforts. In addition, organizational structures and decision-making processes are pertinent areas to both employees and funders, since they directly impact efficiency and effectiveness and provide additional guidance to employees.

Whereas there are lots of other types of data that are pertinent to collect, analyze, and share with others, you must be guided by the premise of collecting and analyzing the right data and sharing that data as frequently as needed with all who need to receive it. By doing this, data collection and information sharing can be highly efficient and can contribute to the overall effectiveness of the program operations.

Data Reporting

WE'RE DOING WHAT?

At a recent fundraising event hosted by a nonprofit agency, one of the agency's board members was speaking with Kyle, one of the agency clinicians. The board member shared his excitement about the new contract on which the program director (Kyle's supervisor) was bidding and discussing how, if awarded, the contract could result in a significant expansion of services for the agency. Kyle smiled and agreed about the positive prospects the new contract could bring and then delicately extricated himself from the conversation, going in search of one of his program colleagues. On finding a fellow clinician, he recounted the conversation he had had with the board member, stating that he had no idea that his supervisor was pursuing a new contract. Kyle's colleague was not aware of this either. Flummoxed by the apparent lack of information they both had about their program, they agreed they would need to follow up with their supervisor in the morning.

Have you ever experienced this type of awkward situation? Someone knows something about your program/agency that you should know as well, and after hearing this information from another source, you feel uncomfortable and not wholly aware of why you weren't informed. Unfortunately, this happens all too often and typically not because there is a motive to withhold information; rather, in the absence of any type of information-sharing structure, information is not properly or effectively shared. In other words, there must be a method to your madness, and this is particularly true where information sharing is concerned.

This can be easily accomplished by putting a specific structure in place to ensure that information is effectively shared. By doing this, the extensive work accomplished in the data collection and analysis process can be fully realized. In terms of developing a basic structure to promote effective sharing of information, each of the following aspects of data reporting should be established:

- The individual(s) responsible for reporting the data
- The time frames in which data will be reported
- The means by which data will be reported
- The recipients who will receive the various types of data

Each of these issues is discussed below.

Responsibilities for Data Reporting

Assigning responsibilities is a prerequisite for accountability—in any business or other endeavor. Therefore, the starting point for effective information sharing lies first and foremost in identifying who is responsible for reporting what type of data/information. Because there are often various types of data (as described above), there may be various individuals assigned to reporting specific types of data to different groups. For instance, clinicians might report program outcomes to the program staff, whereas the chief financial officer might report the program's financial status to the board of directors. However, as I have emphasized throughout this text, program developers/mental health professionals must have comprehensive knowledge about the programs with which they are involved. And there is no better indicator of the degree of knowledge a program developer has about her/his program than her/his ability to report on the various data related to the program. During those times when program developers are not directly reporting program data, they must be fully aware of the data and its implications.

Along these same lines, all program staff should be knowledgeable about the various aspects of their programs—regardless of the degree to which they directly interact with specific data. This is because information does often translate into power, and thus, by being empowered to report on various data, the staff person is gaining new knowledge and is given an opportunity to develop new skills related to reporting data. Therefore, data reporting must not be simply the role of one person (e.g., program developer/director) but a role shared by many and one in which assignments change related to the type of data reported by the specific staff person. By spreading out responsibilities for data reporting among all staff persons, program managers may in fact engage more staff with the program and the organization while providing specific opportunities for professional development. Table 15.2 provides an example of how the small staff of a gambling prevention program for teens shares data reporting responsibilities.

The five staff persons illustrated in Table 15.2 compose the entire program staff: Kimberly (program manager), LaShawn, Rhonda, Dorothy, and Roma (prevention specialists). Each staff person is responsible for regularly leading the collection, analysis, and reporting of their assigned data to the rest of the program staff for a year at a time. By using this type of schema for sharing data-reporting responsibilities, Kimberly is able to ensure that each of her staff members is highly knowledgeable about the major aspects of the program. Regardless of the manner in which data reporting responsibilities are assigned, the primary objective is that responsibilities are shared among program and organizational staff to ensure that everyone who is a part of the program is knowledgeable about the various aspects of the program.

Table 15.2 Data Reporting Assignments

Year	Process Evaluation Data	Financial Data	Outcome Data	Quality Assurance Data	Staff Retention and Hiring Data
1	LaShawn	Kimberly	Roma	Rhonda	Dorothy
2	Dorothy	Rhonda	LaShawn	Kimberly	Roma
3	Roma	Dorothy	Rhonda	LaShawn	Kimberly

Reporting Time Frames

Establishing time frames for reporting data can be as important to ensuring that information is shared as is assigning responsibility for data reporting. As you witnessed by Reggie's example, his program may have continued if short-term and frequent time frames for reporting had been established.

Time frames provide another necessary level of structure to the information-sharing process and another level of reinforcement for accountability. Whereas data about each major area of a program should minimally be shared on a quarterly basis with all program staff, specific types of data may need to be shared much more frequently, depending on the data type and special circumstances. For instance, if program revenue that is paid on a fee-for-service basis has fallen below the annual projected revenue, resulting in the possibility of reducing a staff position unless the revenue improves quickly, revenue data may require analysis and reporting on a weekly basis. On the other hand, it may not be appropriate to report on outcome goals more frequently than each quarter, because the limited number of outcomes occurring on a weekly or biweekly basis may not reflect aggregate outcome data and will, therefore, skew the actual outcomes picture as a result of focusing on a few outcomes rather than the total outcomes.

Methods for Data Reporting

Once decisions about who is responsible for reporting specific data are made and the time frames within which data will be reported have been established, the methods by which data will be reported must be identified. The methods for reporting specific types of data may be varied based on the recipients, and multiple methods may be used to communicate the same data. Methods for reporting data include but are not limited to

- verbal communication in meetings or other group forums,
- presentations of data in meetings or other group forums,
- comprehensive written reports,
- written snapshots of data (i.e., data briefs),
- electronic snapshots of data posted on the Intranet,
- annual reports, and
- website postings.

Methods should be selected based on effectiveness to reach the intended recipients and the rationale for sharing the specific data. For instance, verbal communication of data in biweekly staff meetings may be a highly effective method for ensuring that critical information is frequently shared with program staff. However, quarterly board of directors meetings may require both a formal presentation of data as well as an accompanying report to ensure that the information is effectively communicated and that the information provided is thorough enough to allow for effective governance.

Because effective communication is critical to information sharing, methods for reporting data should be continuously evaluated to ensure that they are working. Simply because the development of a presentation involves quite a bit of work and contains significant information, that does not automatically translate into the information being effectively communicated. Gathering the input of recipients about preferences of communication methods, engaging in follow-up dialogue to discuss information shared, and engaging in more rigorous evaluation of the effectiveness of information sharing can be helpful in ongoing efforts to ensure productive information sharing.

Data Recipients

Finally, the various groups of individuals who will receive the data must be identified—the data recipients. Technically, data recipients are all stakeholders. This includes but is not limited to program staff, clients, administrators, contractors, accrediting bodies, the governing board, and the public. Each of these groups has a need to know specific program information, and as such, program developers have an obligation to regularly share data with each group. Further, for some groups, there are specific requirements about what data must be reported, how often it must be reported, and in what format it must be reported. For instance, written reports on contract compliance data might be required on a semiannual basis by contractors. Alternatively, while specific requirements may not exist regarding information sharing with program staff, best practices may indicate that specific program data is shared on a weekly basis to ensure a well-informed workforce.

The basic rule of thumb regarding who should receive program information is that anyone who has a need to know should know, and they should know as soon as possible. This will ensure that what happened to Kyle does not happen to other clinicians or program staff—that is, learning about a possible significant change in the program from a board member.

As you can see, all these aspects of data reporting are interconnected—responsibilities for data reporting, time frames, methods, and recipients. By thoroughly considering each, program managers posture themselves to effectively share information and data with their stakeholders. The next section provides specific examples and tools to aid in accomplishing this.

Data Protections and Safeguards

Because the bulk of data collected by mental health professionals is related to those whom we serve, our first obligation is to protect the privacy of our clients and to ensure that information about them is maintained in a confidential manner. There are several state and federal laws that set forth rules on this—most notably, HIPAA (1996) and HITECH (2009), which provide strict guidance for the collection, storage, protection, and use of health-related information, with strong protections for the privacy of individuals' health information (Mai et al., 2007). In addition, federal guidelines regarding the protection of substance use information—42 CFR Part 2—confidentiality of alcohol and drug abuse records, and federal and state therapist patient confidentiality laws provide specific guidance. If you are not wholly familiar with the federal laws regarding client/patient protected health information, this is an area with which you will need to become quite familiar.

All data collection must be conducted in accordance with legal statutes and with all necessary protections in place. In addition, all research activities must be conducted with necessary oversight procedures in place, including authorization and ongoing monitoring from an institutional review board/human subjects committee. Organizations must have comprehensive policies and procedures in place specifically dealing with client confidentiality, data storage and maintenance, data sharing, and reporting through release and disclosure. Organizations also must ensure that required hardware and other electronic safeguards are in place to protect electronic data.

Just as both state and federal laws and other guidance regarding client confidentiality have changed dramatically over the past several years, with continued changes in electronic technology and continued development of knowledge related to data collection and protection, change will likely continue to occur. It is essential that mental health professionals maintain current knowledge regarding the rules that govern the collection, use, and storage of confidential information to ensure appropriate guidance in this area.

Developing the Data Reporting Plan

As discussed earlier, without a solid framework to structure data reporting and information sharing, it is likely that pertinent information will not be shared with those who have a need to know or that information will not be shared in a timely fashion. Therefore, structure is needed to guide these activities. The *Annual Data Reporting Plan* in Table 15.3 provides an example of how to structure data reporting by addressing each of the four key aspects (i.e., responsibility, time frame, methods, recipients). Please note as you review Table 15.3 that the time frames and methods are intended as a

Table 15.3 Annual Data Reporting Plan

Data Type	Responsibility	Time Frame	Method(s)	Recipients
Client demographics and/or trend data	Program staff with rotating roles; program manager	Biweekly—staff; quarterly—administrators; annually—contractors; other oversight organizations as required	Verbal communication in staff meetings; presentation; written report—contractors and other oversight organizations	Program staff; administrators; contractors and other oversight organizations
Process/program implementation data	Program staff with rotating roles; program manager	Biweekly—staff; semiannually—contractors and administrators	Verbal communication in staff meetings; presentation; process evaluation report	Program staff; contractors; administrators
Outcomes	Program staff with rotating roles; program manager	Monthly or quarterly—program staff; quarterly—administrators and contractors; all stakeholders	Written report; annual report	Program staff; contractors; administrators; all stakeholders (including public)
Contract compliance and quality improvement	Program staff with rotating roles; program manager	Quarterly	Written report	Program staff; contractors; administrators
Financial	Program staff with rotating roles; program manager; chief financial officer	Quarterly—program staff, administrators; annually—all stakeholders	Written report; annual report	Program staff; administrators; all stakeholders
Program evaluation data	Program staff with rotating roles; program manager	Quarterly	Written report; presentation; peer-reviewed journal	All stakeholders and broader profession

Human resources data	Program staff with rotating roles; program manager	Quarterly	Written report	Program staff; administrators
Client satisfaction and other client survey data	Program staff with rotating roles	Annually	Written report	Clients; program staff; administrators; contractors; stakeholders
Annual report	Collaborative effort between program staff and administrators	Annually	Comprehensive written publication mailed and available electronically	All stakeholders

guide only—contractors, organizational policies, and other oversight organizations may require more stringent reporting time frames and methods.

Whereas the *Annual Data Reporting Plan* illustrates the broad data types that should be shared, there are numerous details that are needed to guide this type of data collection, analysis, and reporting. The *Quarterly/Annual Comprehensive Data Report Tool* (Box 15.6) was developed precisely to guide and provide essential structure to the data collection, analysis, and reporting process.

BOX 15.6

QUARTERLY/ANNUAL COMPREHENSIVE DATA REPORT TOOL

Program:

Data reporting time frame:

Reporter:

1. Clients served

a. Total number served during report period:

b. Total program capacity:

(Continued)

(Continued)

c. Is program capacity limited by contract?

d. If unlimited, what is your target goal for number of clients for the year?

e. How does current number of clients compare with last quarter or last year?

f. If reporting quarterly data, how does this quarter's data compare with the same quarter 1 year ago?

g. What types of trends in client numbers exist?

h. Provide evidence for item g trends:

i. Reasons/explanations for client population trends:

j. Projected number of clients to be served next quarter:

2. Clients discharged/released/no longer in program

a. Provide the definition of successful termination for your program:

b. Number of successful terminations during report period:

c. Percentage of total terminations that were successful:

d. Number of unsuccessful terminations during report period:

e. Percentage of total terminations that were unsuccessful:

f. Reasons for unsuccessful terminations:

g. Please state how those numbers compare with last quarter/last year data:

h. If reporting quarterly data, how does this quarter's termination data compare with the same quarter 1 year ago?

i. Any trends identified in terminations (e.g., increase in unsuccessful terminations due to truancy during the summer):

j. Any program plans, enhancements, or changes that you made as a result of the successful or unsuccessful discharge data:

3. Contract compliance

a. What percentage of contract compliance items were you in full (100%) compliance with this reporting period?

b. Please state each of the specific contract compliance items that were not in full compliance during report period:

c. How does the percentage of contract compliance results compare with last quarter/ last year?

d. If reporting quarterly data, how does the percentage of contract compliance results compare with the same quarter 1 year ago?

e. Please state any program plans to address any contract compliance challenges:

4. Assessments

a. What standardized assessment instruments, if any, are used within your program?

b. How are the results used in individual treatment planning?

c. If you provide an assessment at entry and at termination, please discuss the differences/similarities in scores:

d. Please discuss your aggregate program assessment data for report period:

e. If applicable, please discuss how you have used the aggregate assessment data to make program changes:

5. Quality improvement status

a. Please report on the results of each program outcome goal:

b. Please discuss how you have used the results of your quality improvement data:

c. Please discuss how your quality improvement activities have been used in program changes and program development:

d. Please discuss the frequency with which your program's quality plan changes and why:

e. How often is quality improvement data reviewed with staff?

f. Please state the methods that you use to promote and share quality improvement initiatives with program staff:

6. Human resources

a. What is your current staff vacancy rate?

b. What is your staff turnover rate during the report period?

c. How does your staff turnover rate compare with last quarter/last year?

d. How does your staff turnover rate compare with the same quarter last year?

(Continued)

(Continued)

e. Please share any strategies that you have utilized to increase or impact employee retention or satisfaction?

f. Please state any plans or successful strategies you have used to address staffing challenges:

g. Please state any methods you have used to modify/adapt staffing patterns as a result of changes in program utilization or programming design:

h. Please provide any additional relevant HR information:

7. Financial information

a. What was your program revenue during the last quarter?

b. How does your total program revenue compare with the same quarter 1 year ago?

c. Is program paid on a per diem, contract program, or fee-for-service basis?

d. Referring to item 1e, if you are experiencing a reduction in clients or have not been at capacity during the quarter, how much impact has client reduction had on your budget/financial implications?

e. Referring to item 1e, if you are experiencing a reduction in clients or have not been at capacity during the quarter, what types of marketing strategies have you employed to address program utilization?

f. Please provide any additional relevant financial data:

8. Comprehensive overview and targeted areas

a. After reviewing all the information in the report, what do you believe your program did well this quarter?

b. What do you believe are the primary areas of concern that need to be addressed during the next quarter?

c. Please discuss the methods that you will use to address these concerns:

d. Please provide any additional comments about your findings based on this analysis:

This tool was adapted from one that I originally developed for Spectrum Human Services, Inc. and Affiliated Companies while employed by the agency. The tool continues to be used by all the agency's programs as a critical part of their quarterly and annual comprehensive program review process.

As you can see, the *Quarterly/Annual Comprehensive Data Report* guides the data collection, analysis, and reporting process, promoting a comprehensive picture of the program through which systematic and ongoing program planning can occur. The report covers each of the major aspects of the program. The report is used on both a quarterly and an annual basis to provide guidance and to ensure comprehensive review. Whereas the report itself provides a summary of data, it does not take the place of other data-specific reports that provide additional information about specific aspects (e.g., contract compliance goals, quality improvement plan).

Summary

The collection, analysis, and reporting of data is a critical part of ongoing information sharing and is often essential to the sustainability of a program. Because information is not only powerful but empowering, information-sharing responsibilities must be delegated among multiple levels of program staff. This only serves as another mechanism by which to possibly engage program staff with the program as well as reinforce the role that each staff member has in a program's success (and failures). In addition, collecting data without sharing it with all stakeholders who have a need to know is akin to buying a treadmill and never using it—it's an investment that yields no return. Therefore, if data is collected, it must be shared. Furthermore, information sharing should be systematically guided to ensure that data is getting to all who need it. Particularly in the 21st century, when competition in mental health and human services is fierce and only the strong survive, effective data reporting can only help to ensure a program's sustainability.

CASE ILLUSTRATION

David's semi-independent living program for adults with developmental disabilities had been operating for 1 year. David held a 1-year anniversary celebration with the program staff to mark the occasion, and he invited all the agency's staff and administrators.

David had put a great deal of effort into ensuring that all pertinent information about the program was continuously collected, analyzed, and immediately shared with all the people who had a right to and a need for the information—his staff being one

(Continued)

(Continued)

of the most important recipients. To ensure that his staff were fully aware of all aspects of the program, David had insisted that all the staff collaboratively develop the process evaluation, outcomes evaluation, and initial quality improvement goals. In addition, they had developed the contract compliance plan and a schedule and assignments for regular data collection and reporting.

To ensure that all staff remained personally connected to the data, they took turns collecting and reporting specific data sets and alternated responsibility for developing the program's quarterly report using the *Quarterly/Annual Comprehensive Data Report Tool* and for leading the discussions about the data. By doing so, it appeared that all staff had a firm understanding of exactly what the program was designed to do and what it had accomplished thus far.

Since the anniversary celebration was held to mark the program's success in being operational for 1 year, David thought it would provide a good forum to present the program to the rest of the agency's staff so that they, too, could fully understand the program. Five of the program staff members had volunteered to lead the presentation, and they had completed the *Annual Comprehensive Data Report*. The staff developed a PowerPoint presentation to provide a brief overview of their program and to discuss the results of the process evaluation and initial outcomes. They outlined the program's quality plan and contract compliance goals, providing a progress update on each. They then discussed the costs of the program, their staff turnover rate, challenges that they had encountered in retaining direct care staff, and the steps they had taken to resolve this issue. Finally, the group shared each of the major issues that had been identified through their various analyses and the measures they had enacted to address each, reporting on the progress of each strategy. Finishing their presentation, they took questions from the audience.

Regardless of the nature of the question—be it about the rationale for a quality improvement goal or the cost needed to replace a staff position—the program staff readily provided responses, and David never once contributed to the discussion. There was no need for him to participate, as his staff understood their program in its entirety as well as he did. When asked about plans for exploring new business, since their program was doing well and appeared highly stable, the staff quickly responded that they had just begun revisiting their strategic plan to thoughtfully examine their next steps. But another staff member (sitting in the audience) added that any new planning would be in addition to continuing all the existing monitoring, evaluation, and improvement efforts and that maintaining and improving what they currently had was their primary commitment.

Witnessing this, David knew that he had been successful in ensuring that all his staff were not only well aware of but completely competent about their program and all its various aspects. Allowing himself only a moment to appreciate this, his mind quickly turned to finalizing plans for a similar presentation to his funding source and other stakeholders, which he and his staff had been facilitating each quarter.

DATA REPORT PLAN EXERCISE

1. Review the *Comprehensive Quarterly/Annual Data Report Plan* and identify four additional items that you believe should be included in this analysis.

2. State your rationale for including this additional data.

3. Discuss this with a partner or in a small group.

REFLECTION AND DISCUSSION QUESTIONS

1. How do you determine the types of information to be shared, with whom to share them, and the frequency of such sharing?

2. What have your experiences been related to information sharing and data reporting?

3. In your current work, what are the strengths and/or weaknesses in how data is collected, analyzed, and reported?

4. What do you perceive as the role of data in today's mental health and human services, and what factors do you believe contribute to this?

5. Do you believe types of data can be prioritized in levels of importance, and if so, how would you prioritize the data sets contained on the *Quarterly Program Data Report?*

References

Borelli, B., Sepinwall, D., Ernst, D., Bellg, A. J., Czajkowski, S., Breger, R., et al. (2005). A new tool to assess treatment fidelity and evaluation of treatment across 10 years of health behavior research. *Journal of Consulting and Clinical Psychology, 73*, 852–860.

Byford, S., Leese, M., Knapp, M., Seivewright, H., Cameron, S., Jones, V., et al. (2007). Comparison of alternative methods of collection of service use data for the economic evaluation of health care interventions. *Health Economics, 16*, 531–536.

Gard, C. L., Flannigan, P. N., & Cluskey, M. (2004). Program evaluation: An ongoing systematic process. *Nurse Educator, 25*, 176–179.

Gibelman, M., & Furman, R. (2008). *Managing human service organizations.* Chicago: Lyceum.

Kettner, P. M., Moroney, R. M., & Martin, L. L. (2008). *Designing and managing programs: An effectiveness-based approach.* Thousand Oaks, CA: Sage.

Mai, C. T., Law, D. J., Mason, C. A., McDowell, B. D., Meyer, R. E., & Musa, D. (2007). Collection, use, and protection of population-based birth defects surveillance data in the United States. *Birth Defects Research, 79*, 811–814.

Morris, R., Macneela, P., Scott, A., Treacy, M. P., Hyde, A., Matthews, A., et al. (2010). The Irish nursing minimum data set for mental health—valid and reliable tool for the collection of standardized nursing data. *Journal of Clinical Nursing, 19*, 359–367.

Senge, P. M. (2006). *The fifth discipline.* New York: Doubleday.

CHAPTER 16

Attain Program and Organizational Accreditation

Learning Objectives

1. Increase understanding of both the history and current status of relevant accrediting bodies

2. Compare and contrast the three major accrediting bodies in mental health and human services

3. Differentiate concrete costs and benefits and soft costs and benefits related to accreditation

4. Identify potential benefits of pursuing/attaining accreditation

5. Identify various factors used in considering prospective accrediting bodies

6. Discuss the various steps involved in pursuing accreditation

7. Develop a comprehensive plan for pursuing accreditation

WHY BOTHER WITH ACCREDITATION?

Janet and Eric had been operating their residential program for adults with dementia of the Alzheimer's type for a little less than 2 years. For the past 18 months, the program had been filled to capacity (56 clients), and their capacity had increased from a previous average of 40 clients. The families of their clients had consistently expressed praise for the program, and they had passed each of their licensure reviews with flying colors. The monitoring reviews from their contractors had also been quite positive, and their program had been publicly recognized for its work.

While it was difficult to find cause for concern with the program, during the quarterly board of directors meeting, one of the directors asked Janet and Eric about their plans to pursue accreditation. Janet was familiar with accreditation through her previous experience in hospitals, but Eric was not since the small outpatient clinic in which he had previously worked had not been accredited. Viewing their residential program as quite different from a hospital, Janet responded that she did not see the value in pursuing accreditation at this point, especially in light of their program's success. After a short discussion about hospital accreditation versus accreditation of mental health and human service organizations, the board turned to other orders of business.

Six months later, Eric and Janet's main competitor announced its recently attained accreditation, using it to further market its program. Not long after, a new competitor arrived on the scene and attained accreditation the following year. As both competing organizations continued to market their accreditation status, Eric received more and more calls from families of prospective clients inquiring about their accreditation status, and Janet was specifically questioned during a meeting with contractors about why their organization was not accredited.

After a lengthy discussion spurred on by a great deal of concern for their organization, Janet and Eric decided to begin planning to pursue accreditation. Unfortunately, this decision came at the same time that they were forced to lay off a third of their employees, since their capacity had dropped to 35 clients over the past year.

CONSIDERING JANET AND ERIC

1. When should Janet and Eric have begun pursuing accreditation?

2. What significance does accreditation have today in mental health and human services?

3. What do you believe are the pros and cons related to accreditation?

About This Chapter

This chapter takes up the final step in comprehensive program development—attaining program and organizational accreditation. The reason that both program and organizational accreditation are identified is because, for many accrediting bodies, these are considered two different aspects. And whereas organizational accreditation is typically required in order for a program to receive accreditation, in some cases an organization may be accredited even when one or more of its programs are not.

This step is directly related to Step X (Evaluate the program) and Step XIII (Develop an information-sharing plan), because accreditation is dependent on compliance with best practice standards. However, like all the other steps that compose the comprehensive program development model, this step is also related to each of the previous steps. Accreditation planning and attainment is viewed as the final step because of what it signifies—national recognition for excellence.

In order to fully investigate accreditation and the process by which one pursues it, we must begin with an examination of the history of accreditation and its significance today. We will follow this with a discussion of the major accrediting bodies in mental health and human services today, which include the Council on Accreditation (COA), the Commission on Accreditation of Rehabilitation Facilities (CARF), and The Joint Commission.

We will explore major aspects related to accreditation, including the costs and benefits of accreditation, the relevance of accreditation to clinical program development, and identifying the right fit between program/organization and accrediting body. We will follow this with a discussion of accreditation planning and the development of the accreditation plan to guide this work. A case illustration demonstrates the material covered in the chapter. And finally, an exercise is provided to help you directly investigate and identify the most appropriate accrediting body for your program/organization and develop a plan for pursuit of accreditation.

STEP XIV: ATTAIN PROGRAM AND ORGANIZATIONAL ACCREDITATION

History and Significance of Accreditation

Dr. Ernest Codman's 1910 proposal to standardize health care by tracking every patient's treatment from beginning to end to evaluate its effectiveness

(The Joint Commission, 2009) served as the catalyst for what we know today as accreditation standards. In fact, answering Dr. Codman's call, the first accreditation standards were promulgated by the American College of Physicians (ACP) in 1917. The very small, yet mighty, *Minimum Standard for Hospitals* filled all of one page with requirements. This in turn led to the collaboration between the ACP, the American Hospital Association, the American Medical Association, and the Canadian Medical Association to create the Joint Commission on Accreditation of Hospitals (since renamed The Joint Commission [2009]). The Joint Commission was established in 1951 as an independent, not-for-profit organization whose primary purpose was to provide voluntary accreditation, publishing the *Standards for Hospital Accreditation* in 1953.

It was not until 1966 that an accrediting body was founded to focus on rehabilitation facilities—CARF. And in 1969, The Joint Commission turned its attention to mental health programs. However, without the work of physicians in the early part of the 20th century, the significance of accreditation in mental health and human services would likely not enjoy the stature that it does today. Then, as now, accreditation practices had been guided from within the profession—by professionals seeking to ensure high quality and effectiveness.

> Out of recognition of the need to define standards of quality for the services provided by human service organizations and increase accountability for the outcomes of services, various organizations have evolved to formulate standards in specialized service areas and to enforce them through an accreditation process. (Gibelman & Furman, 2008, p. 83)

Today, it is unusual to find a human service or mental health provider who is not intimately aware of accrediting bodies and accreditation standards. Indeed, many an organization is guided by accreditation standards, seeking this badge of approval and proudly displaying it wherever possible.

Purpose of Accrediting Bodies

Accrediting bodies fulfill a specific purpose: They define quality standards related to operations and administration of organizations, and they monitor compliance with those standards. Accrediting bodies are not unique to human services and mental health programming but, rather, have become a standard (pardon the pun) part of organizational life for a diverse array of industries. Consider ISO, TS 16949, and QS 9000—quality standards for the automotive industry that are commonly displayed on the business flags of automotive companies and suppliers (quite a common sight to those of us living in Detroit). The International Organization for Standardization is a major accrediting body of industry and commercial businesses. In addition, accrediting bodies are a primary aspect of K–12 and higher education, with varying types of state, regional, and national accrediting bodies available as well as accrediting bodies focused in both the institutional and program levels. Accreditation in each of these diverse industries illustrates just how embedded accreditation has become in organizational life.

While accrediting bodies across industries may vary in several key aspects, they also share commonalities. Primarily, accrediting bodies share the following major features:

- They define quality standards.
- They monitor quality standards.
- They require a fee for accreditation and reaccreditation.
- They maintain term-limited accreditation/reaccreditation cycles.

With these four shared characteristics, accrediting bodies assume a position of power in articulating quality definitions, act as accountability agents, require payment for their services, and provide ongoing structure for the accreditation process. As such, they provide comprehensive guidance and serve as external watchdogs for organizations.

Accreditation Process

The accreditation process begins with the organization seeking accreditation filing an application/intent, along with the application fee. This is typically followed by a discussion with a staff person from the accrediting body about the self-study process, guiding documents (e.g., accreditation standards, guidance manual), and time frame for submitting the initial self-study. Once the organization seeking accreditation becomes fully educated about the accreditation process, the organization then devises its own plans for completing the self-study and gathering all the necessary documentation needed as part of the self-study submission. Whereas developing the self-study is often an enormous task, the more significant work lies in ensuring that compliance with each standard is met, developing new policies and/or practices to comply with the standards, or determining what steps will need to be taken to bring the program/organization into compliance with the standards. Completion of the self-study typically requires 12 to 18 months.

Compliance with accreditation standards is the basis on which each organization is evaluated in the accreditation process and is thereby what each organization seeking accreditation aspires to achieve. Compliance with standards is typically verified through two measures: written evidence that is part of the self-study documents (e.g., policies, protocols) and physical evidence that is verified as part of the on-site visit. Physical evidence may be gathered on-site by the peer reviewers through discussions with staff and/or clients to verify that certain practices are in place, through reviewing documentation logs, or through other means.

Following its completion, the self-study and supporting documents are submitted to the accrediting body. The accrediting body typically conducts an initial review of the self-study and composes a team of peer reviewers (the size of the peer review team is determined by the size and scope of the organization seeking accreditation—typically two to five individuals). Travel plans and scheduling of the on-site visit are then coordinated between the accrediting body, peer reviewers, and the organization seeking accreditation, and the on-site visit schedule is developed. Accreditation visits typically extend from 2 to 5 days, depending again on the size and scope of the program/organization seeking accreditation. Whereas accreditation visits are usually packed with activities as peer reviewers seek to obtain the most information as efficiently as possible, a diverse amount of activity occurs. The visit begins with a short introductory meeting between the peer reviewers and administrators and other key staff from the organization seeking accreditation to explain the purpose of the visit, the protocols that will be followed during the visit, and review of the visit schedule. Immediately following this introductory meeting, the peer reviewers may separate or work in teams to gather additional information and verify compliance. Box 16.1 provides a snapshot of a typical on-site accreditation visit schedule.

BOX 16.1

ACCREDITATION SITE VISIT SCHEDULE SAMPLE

Day 1

8:30 am: Introductory meeting

9:00 am: Individual interviews with president/executive director and other key administrators

10:00 am: Interviews with program directors and/or supervisors and interviews with administrative support staff

12:00 pm: Interviews with other key staff

1:00 pm: Lunch on-site

2:00 pm: Review of client records, program documentation, and organizational policies and other documentation

6:00 pm: Reviewers break for dinner and reconvene in hotel to debrief day's events, plan for next day's activities, and begin to develop the on-site visit report of findings

Day 2

8:30 am: Interviews with board members and program and administrative support staff

10:00 am: Visits to residential sites or other administrative office and interviews with staff and clients

12:00 pm: Lunch with program staff and/or clients

1:30 pm: Review of program documentation and policies, review of human resource and finance records, review of information technology and quality policies and protocols, and meetings with additional program and/or administrative support staff

6:00 pm: Reviewers break for dinner

7:30 pm: Reviewers finalize the on-site visit report and recommendations

Day 3

8:30 am: Exit interview between review team and key organizational staff, with review team providing brief verbal feedback

9:30 am: Review team leaves site

Following the site visit, the organization seeking accreditation receives an official report from the accrediting body summarizing the findings of the accreditation process (i.e., self-study and on-site visit) and notification of accreditation status. Organizations may be granted provisional or full accreditation status depending on the results. Whereas provisional accreditation status often requires an interim report (within 1–2 years), full accreditation status may be granted for 1 to 5 years. Once accredited, an organization then must continuously seek reaccreditation by completing a self-study and hosting an on-site visit within the time frames established by the accrediting body.

Whereas the accreditation process itself is somewhat similar for each of the three major accrediting bodies, the accrediting bodies differ in somewhat significant ways. To promote a fuller understanding of this, each of the accrediting bodies is discussed below.

Major Accrediting Bodies in Mental Health and Human Services

Within the mental health and human services, there are three major accrediting bodies:

- The Council on Accreditation (COA)
- The Commission on Accreditation of Rehabilitation Facilities (CARF)
- The Joint Commission (formerly known as the Joint Commission on Accreditation of Hospitals)

Table 16.1 provides a snapshot comparison of these three accrediting bodies.

Table 16.1 Comparison of Major Accrediting Bodies

Feature	COA	CARF	The Joint Commission
Eligible applicants	Private and public organizations	Private and public organizations	Private and public organizations
Major program types/service standards*	Child welfare; juvenile justice; domestic violence; behavioral health; substance abuse; adult services	Rehabilitation services; behavioral health; child and youth services; substance abuse	Hospitals, home care, ambulatory care; behavioral health; substance abuse
Accreditation time frames	4 years	1 to 3 years	Varies based on program/service type
Application fee	$750**	$975**	$1,700**
Annual fees	Individually calculated per organization	Individually calculated per organization	Individually calculated per organization

*List is not exhaustive for each accrediting body but, rather, a sample of major service areas.

**Rates as of April 2010.

These accrediting bodies each emerged or included behavioral health as part of their scope within an 8-year span of one another, with CARF evolving in 1966, followed by The Joint Commission's decision to include behavioral health and the introduction of COA in 1977. Whereas each was initially designed with a specific and limited focus, over the intervening years, they have each expanded dramatically in the scope of programs that they accredit. As a result, today it is much more difficult to identify a particular programmatic focus or theme for any of these three accrediting bodies. This can pose an additional challenge to mental health and human service providers interested in pursuing accreditation. In addition, the scope of administrative and organization-specific standards (e.g., governance, ethics, administrative supports) has continued to become more sophisticated as knowledge regarding organizational structure has continued to increase.

Whereas each of these major accrediting bodies operates as an independent organization with its own employed staff, their operations are primarily driven by volunteer peer reviewers. The peer review process is one of the defining features of the accreditation process. Peer reviewers consist of human service professionals who serve in a volunteer capacity to review their peer organizations. Before delving further into the peer review process, we must first discuss the accreditation process itself by taking a closer look at the three major accrediting bodies.

Council on Accreditation

COA is the youngest of the three major accrediting bodies. It is arguably the most well known by child welfare organizations, particularly those specializing in foster care and other child and family services. According to its website,

> COA is an international, independent, not-for-profit, child- and family-service and behavioral health care accrediting organization. It was founded in 1977 by the Child Welfare League of America and Family Service America (now the Alliance for Children and Families). Originally known as an accrediting body for family and children's agencies, COA currently accredits 38 different service areas and over 60 types of programs. Among the service areas are substance abuse treatment, adult day care, services for the homeless, foster care, and inter-country adoption.
>
> In addition to standards for private social service and behavioral health care organizations, COA has developed separate business lines for public agencies, networks and lead management entities, opioid treatment programs, employee assistance programs, and financial management/debt counseling services. (COA, n.d., paras. 2–3)

At the time of this writing, COA accredits more than 1,800 private and public organizations in the United States, Canada, Puerto Rico, Bermuda, England, and the Philippines—34% with annual budgets less than $2 million and 44% with annual budgets between $2 million and $10 million (COA, n.d.a). Both the breadth of service standards available and the number of accredited organizations that COA counts on its roster reflect the significant growth of accrediting bodies in mental health and human services over the past 20 years.

COA receives varying degrees of support and guidance from a host of sponsoring and support organizations (see Table 16.2; COA, n.d.c). These organizations are specifically invested in COA and, as such, highlight the

Table 16.2 Sponsoring and Support Organizations of COA

Sponsoring Organizations	Support Organizations
Alliance for Children and Families	American Association of Children's Residential Centers
Association of Jewish Family and Children's Agencies	American Network of Community Options and Resources
Catholic Charities USA	Child Welfare League of Canada
Child Welfare League of America	Eagle Program of the United Methodist Association
Children's Home Society of America	Employee Assistance Society of North America
Foster Family-Based Treatment Association	Mental Health Corporations of America, Inc.
Joint Council on International Children's Services	National Association for Children's Behavioral Health
Lutheran Services in America	National Association of Social Workers
National Council for Adoption	National Alliance for the Mentally Ill
National Foundation for Credit Counseling	National Association of State Alcohol and Drug Abuse Directors, Inc.
National Network for Youth	National Association of Therapeutic Wilderness Camps
National Organization of State Associations for Children	National Council for Community Behavioral Healthcare
Volunteers of America	

fact that accrediting bodies are guided by professionals within their major disciplines rather than by external forces.

The breadth of service standards (i.e., accreditation standards for specific types of programs) is quite diverse, as noted previously. Interestingly, of the three major accrediting bodies, COA is the only one that makes its standards accessible to the public at no cost. The current standards, as well as other pertinent information about COA, are available on the organization's website (COA, n.d.d). Finally, and likely as a result of the more recent trend of accrediting bodies to expand their scope, COA (n.d.b) has also published a document comparing COA and CARF.

Commission on Accreditation of Rehabilitation Facilities

CARF historically has been known for its focus on residential facilities, particularly those serving the developmentally disabled and mentally ill populations. Today, CARF continues this focus but also accredits programs in the major areas of aging, behavioral health, child and youth services, employment and community services, medical rehabilitation, and opioid treatment. Some of the specific accreditation standards are for assisted living, adult day services, mental health and alcohol and other drug programs, outpatient and residential medical rehabilitation, child youth protection, and shelter programs.

According to its website, CARF accredits more than 6,000 service providers in North and South America, Europe, Asia, Africa, and Micronesia (CARF, 2010). CARF standards are collaboratively developed with input from consumers, rehabilitation professionals, state and national organizations, and funders (CARF, 2010). The standards are reviewed annually, and new ones are developed to address the changing conditions and current consumer needs.

The Joint Commission

As highlighted previously, The Joint Commission is the oldest of the three major accrediting bodies, having begun in 1951. Unlike COA and CARF, The Joint Commission was founded as an accrediting body for medical health programs and continues to focus primarily on medical health. However, today The Joint Commission also accredits a variety of behavioral health providers. In the area of behavioral health, The Joint Commission currently accredits more than 1,800 organizations, providing such services as addiction treatment, crisis stabilization, and residential facilities and group homes, among others (The Joint Commission, 2010). Behavioral health care composes approximately 10% of the providers accredited by The Joint Commission, while the other 90% are medical and related providers. Whereas behavioral health care is only a very small part of The Joint Commission's focus, the wide range of service standards for medical services includes hospitals, long-term care, ambulatory care, and outpatient medical clinics. And in the medical health field, The Joint Commission is often viewed as *the* accrediting body. The Joint Commission offers both accreditation and certification based on the following definitions:

> Accreditation can be earned by an entire health care organization, for example, hospitals, nursing homes, office-based surgery practices, home care providers, and laboratories. Certification is earned by programs or services that may be based within or associated with a health care organization. For example, a Joint Commission accredited medical center can have Joint Commission certified programs or services for diabetes or heart disease care. These programs could be within the medical center or in the community. (The Joint Commission, 2010, paras. 2–3)

The Joint Commission is going strong after more than 60 years and is credited with initially setting the stage for the current state of accreditation in mental health and human services.

Costs and Benefits of Accreditation

As you likely already know or have gathered through reading so far, accreditation requires a long-term commitment predicated on an appreciation for all that is involved in the process. Once accredited, organizations typically wish to remain accredited; therefore, once accreditation standards have been met, there is often an intense dedication to continued quality. Whereas it is the significance of what accreditation status means that is often sought, there are specific costs associated with achieving such status.

In terms of cost, there are both concrete costs and costs that are much more difficult to quantify, such as the cost related to the development of new policies and procedures. Starting with the easier of the two to define, the primary concrete costs of accreditation include the initial application fee, on-site visit fees, ongoing maintenance/annual fees, and reaccreditation fees. The application fees range from $750 to $1,700, fees associated with the on-site visit may range from $1,000 to $4,000, and maintenance and reaccreditation fees average $2,000. Because the exact fees are based on the accrediting body, the institution seeking accreditation, and the type and scope of accreditation being sought, it is difficult to provide concrete amounts; rather, it is best to inquire about the specific fees with the individual accrediting bodies.

In terms of understanding the long-term concrete costs of accreditation, it is best to think in terms of the cost over a 10-year period, since accreditation requires a long-term commitment. The 10-year annualized fees typically range from $3,000 to $6,000, again varying based on size and scope of the organization. In addition to the accreditation fees, specific purchases are often required to comply with accreditation standards. These purchases might include such items as locking file cabinets, software, hardware, office supplies, and other resources. Therefore, all projected concrete costs associated with accreditation must be specifically accounted for in the annual budget. And in keeping with effective finance practices, it is better to over-estimate costs than to underestimate them, particularly since these costs are extraneous and, therefore, funding for them must be taken from administrative overhead and/or other non-program-specific funds.

Whereas the concrete costs of accreditation may seem substantial, particularly in light of the limited finances associated with most human service organizations, other costs of accreditation are often much greater. I consider these nonconcrete costs, or soft costs—costs that the organization incurs in the way of staff time and other resource use that are difficult to quantify but have to be considered in understanding the total costs of accreditation. Chief among these costs is staff time, which includes the time dedicated to the following major activities:

- Developing the self-study
- Developing new policies and procedures
- Training for implementation of new policies and procedures
- Participating in the site visit and follow-up activities

In addition to staff time dedicated to the actual accreditation activities, the other major cost is related to preparing the organization to initially pursue accreditation. This often means modifying the organizational culture in order to garner support for accreditation. Because accreditation, like any new activity, requires change on the part of organizational staff, such change typically comes with a cost. As a result, a significant amount of time and energy may be needed to familiarize staff with accreditation—the process and significance—and to *sell* staff on investing in accreditation.

Whereas the costs of accreditation cannot be overlooked, they must be examined in relation to the benefits of accreditation. Similar to costs, there are both concrete and soft benefits that may result from accreditation. Especially today, one of the most significant concrete benefits associated with accreditation relates to the contractors' requirement that organizations applying for specific funding opportunities be accredited (see Box 16.2). For instance, a recent Request for Proposals (RFP) that I reviewed was limited to organizations that were currently accredited. This means that for organizations that are not accredited, funding opportunities may be significantly reduced.

BOX 16.2

SAMPLE RFP REQUIREMENT OF ACCREDITATION

State of Michigan Department of Corrections

Residential Substance Abuse Treatment Services

"To be eligible to provide residential treatment services, vendors must hold a Department of Community Health residential treatment license and have a nationally recognized accreditation" (State of Michigan Department of Corrections, 2010, p. 10).

In terms of fully understanding this from a financial perspective, if the potential new funding opportunity that requires accreditation would result in revenue of $250,000 annually for 3 years, this must be considered in relation to the annual concrete cost of accreditation (e.g., $30,000 for the initial accreditation process, including staff time in preparation, and approximately $6,000 in subsequent years to maintain accreditation). This 3-year cost-benefit analysis then is $42,000 in costs versus $750,000 in benefits—with the benefit of $708,000 in potential revenue to the organization. Understood in these terms, this makes the decision about pursuing accreditation fairly straightforward, if not incredibly simple.

To provide another example of the financial impact that accreditation status can have, several studies examined organizational accreditation status and its relationship to the business of substance abuse treatment programs. The findings included the following:

- Accredited agencies provided more treatment hours than their nonaccredited counterparts (Lemak & Alexander, 2005).
- Accredited organizations were more likely to provide medical services than their nonaccredited counterparts (Durkin, 2002).
- Accredited organizations were more likely to provide mental health treatment (Friedman, Alexander, & D'Aunno, 1999).

In addition to this specific type of benefit, other concrete benefits may include preferential evaluation of proposals based on accreditation status (i.e., not required for applications for funding but preferred) and the ability to attract specific partners and/or pursue other business as a result of accreditation status. Soft benefits of accreditation, on the other hand, can be extremely numerous, including such aspects as staff recruitment efforts resulting in staff seeking out organizations that are accredited as potential employers and increased stature among peers. And last, the benefits resulting from the implementation of best practices, comprehensive policies and guidance, and effective operations—each of which is invaluable and should result from accreditation. As a result, the benefits of accreditation greatly outweigh the costs, as is illustrated in Table 16.3.

Table 16.3 Costs and Benefits of Accreditation

Costs	Benefits
Application/intent costs	Potential ability to pursue specific new funding
Self-study costs	Potential preference given to proposals for new programming/new funding opportunities
Site visit costs	Increased opportunity to retain existing funding
Maintenance costs	Recruitment tool for potential employees
Staff costs related to preparation activities	Comprehensive guidance for implementing best practices
Staff costs related to self-study and site visit activities	Improved guidance for program implementation and maintenance through comprehensive policies and procedures
Staff costs related to policy development, practice implementation, and training	Increased stature among peer organizations
Staff time related to preparing the organization for pursuing accreditation	Increased efficiency in overall operations resulting from comprehensive policies and procedures
Resources and supplies needed to comply with accreditation	Improved effectiveness in overall operations resulting from comprehensive policies and procedures

(Continued)

Table 16.3 (Continued)	
	Potential recruitment/marketing tool to attract clients based on commitment to quality
	Increased knowledge and skills among staff as a result of compliance with accreditation standards
	Potential for increased commitment and engagement among staff as a result of accreditation status
	Potential as an employee retention tool

Relevance to Clinical Program Development

One of the many benefits of pursuing accreditation is that accreditation standards provide guidance for implementing best practices. This is because accreditation standards are developed from current research findings and best practices in the field. As stated earlier, accrediting bodies are initially organized by professionals with a specific focus on ensuring quality within their respective field of practice. While accrediting bodies employ paid staff as part of maintaining and handling the day-to-day operations, some, if not most, of the staff are often professionally affiliated in the field as well, and the peer review team is just what the name implies—a team of professional peers. In addition, sponsoring and support organizations that are part of the larger field provide additional guidance to the accrediting bodies, particularly in regard to the development of practice and organizational standards. The development of accreditation standards is then based on this collective knowledge from professionals in the field as well as current research and best practices. By utilizing this comprehensive approach to the development of accreditation standards, standards reflect the current state of knowledge of the given field—which is precisely the intent, to establish current quality standards that are used to guide organizational practices.

This has specific relevance to clinical program development in that accreditation standards can be seen to do a large part of the work for program developers. Because accreditation standards have been designed based on the cumulative review of current and emerging research, program developers are wise to utilize this knowledge in their program design, implementation, and evaluation efforts. For instance, accreditation standards for shelter services for survivors of domestic violence may identify specific community linkages that should be accessed to promote long-term success. By reviewing these standards during the program design process, accreditation standards can provide valuable guidance. As a result, accreditation standards can guide program design and implementation processes and, therefore, ensure compliance with best practice standards during the evaluation process.

Identifying the Right Fit

Determining which accreditation to pursue is largely based on examining which accreditation standards are most relevant to the program and organization. This selection process has become more difficult in recent years, since accreditation bodies have continuously expanded their scope; however, this may simply result in even greater consideration being given to such decision-making processes. For instance, if your organization consists of two programs, an inpatient substance abuse treatment facility and an outpatient mental health counseling center, a review of the three major accrediting bodies would tell you that whereas CARF has specific standards for treatment programs of alcohol and other drugs and mental health, COA has specific standards in both residential treatment services, including services for substance use conditions and outpatient mental health services, and The Joint Commission has specific standards for addiction treatment and outpatient treatment. In addition, each of these three accrediting bodies has opioid treatment programs. Since each has service standards developed for both of your programs, further exploring is warranted to determine which accrediting body to pursue. These decisions must be guided by identifying which body is the best fit for your organization.

Determining the best fit is often a unique process for each organization, since it should be based on many factors. However, to help guide this decision-making process, Box 16.3 provides a list of factors to consider.

BOX 16.3

FACTORS TO CONSIDER IN SELECTING AN ACCREDITING BODY

- The primary identity of the organization and that of the accrediting body
- The history of the accrediting body in your specific areas of programming
- The specific relevance of the accreditation standards to your specific programming
- The number of major competitors accredited by the specific accrediting body

(Continued)

(Continued)

- The number and scope of similar programs/organizations accredited by the specific accrediting body
- The relevance of the specific accrediting body to existing and prospective contractors
- The degree to which the service/program standards are perceived to provide guidance and potentially strengthen/enhance the clinical program
- The degree to which the organizational standards are perceived to provide guidance and potentially strengthen/enhance the organization

As you can see, included in the above issues to consider in determining which accrediting body to pursue is the degree to which the accreditation standards are perceived to potentially strengthen the clinical program and the organization. These are indeed key factors, particularly since accreditation standards should promote more effective and higher-quality programming and organizational operations. Therefore, accreditation standards that do not promote further growth and development may be of lesser value than those that do.

While there are likely numerous other issues that may be considered in determining which accrediting body to pursue, some organizational leaders may choose to pursue more than one accrediting body. This may especially be the case for organizations with multiple and diverse programs. For instance, an organization that provides residential care for adults with developmental disabilities as well as foster care and outpatient substance abuse treatment may pursue CARF accreditation for its programs specializing in developmental disabilities, COA for its foster care program, and The Joint Commission for its substance abuse treatment programs. Pursuing more than one accreditation may also be done specifically to improve organizational functioning. For instance, you may find that the accrediting body that offers the best fit for your program in terms of service standards lacks in the way of organizational standards. Because each accrediting body requires applicants to fulfill both organizational standards as well as program/service standards, you may decide to pursue two accreditations so that you are confident in both key areas.

Accreditation Planning

As you have likely already surmised, accreditation planning requires a significant amount of time and long-term planning. This is largely due to three key activities that are integral to both initially deciding to pursue accreditation and actually pursuing it:

1. Preparing the organization/staff for the pursuit of accreditation

2. Selecting the right accrediting body and standards to pursue

3. Moving forward in the accreditation process

Each of these activities individually requires a significant amount of time. As discussed earlier, making a decision to pursue accreditation in an organization that has not previously done so means that staff need to be prepared for this type of change—understanding why this is occurring and, more importantly, being encouraged to buy in to the purpose and significance of accreditation so that all employees can fully support the entire process. Once an accrediting body has been selected, completing all the activities required to attain accreditation can take more than 2 years. Because of all that must be accomplished as part of pursuing accreditation, a comprehensive accreditation plan is needed to effectively guide the process.

Developing the Accreditation Plan

Similar to each of the other planning tools, the accreditation plan is devised to promote the most effective and efficient accreditation process. Box 16.4 provides a snapshot of most of the elements that should be a part of the accreditation plan.

BOX 16.4

THE ACCREDITATION PLAN

1. Communicate the purpose and significance of pursuing accreditation to organizational staff and other stakeholders (e.g., board members, clients) to promote buy-in.

2. Form an Accreditation Exploratory Committee charged with leading the investigation of potential accrediting standards and bodies.

3. Report the findings and recommendations of the Accreditation Exploratory Committee to staff and other stakeholders.

4. Develop a 5- to 10-year accreditation budget to project long-term concrete costs that can then be integrated into the existing budgets.

(Continued)

(Continued)

5. Form an Accreditation Planning Committee to lead the accreditation process, including identifying an accreditation Plan of Work with an established time-line and all key activities and assignments needed to develop the self-study/survey identified. In addition, the committee provides plans for structuring and guiding the accreditation process (e.g., orientation, meeting schedule, training).

6. Following the attainment of accreditation, design an *Accreditation Maintenance Plan/Quality Improvement Plan* outlining all methods that will be used to continuously evaluate programming and organizational operations for quality and effectiveness, including identifying methods by which compliance with accreditation standards will be integrated into each program and department.

Summary

The importance of accreditation has grown dramatically over the past 10 years and, as such, is an integral part of organizational life in today's mental health and human services. Since the initial evolution of accreditation bodies more than 60 years ago, the guiding purpose of accreditation has not changed nor has the process by which accreditation standards are promulgated. Throughout their history, accreditation bodies have been dedicated to promoting the highest quality of services and are guided and supported by professionals that are part of the larger field. The use of the peer review process promotes a monitoring system *of peers for peers,* and in this way, the profession shares and collectively invests in a commitment to excellence.

While there are specific costs to an organization that must be considered in accreditation decisions, the benefits that accreditation can bring far outweigh any such costs. In fact, now more than ever before, accreditation status is specifically identified as a requirement in RFPs for new or continued funding opportunities, further highlighting the significance of accreditation today. As such, accreditation not only has the potential to improve the service delivery system and organizational functioning, but it may also play a decisive role in sustaining the business.

Making decisions about pursuing accreditation and the act of pursuing accreditation are major processes and, as a result, should not be entered into lightly. Because of the amount of work involved in pursuing accreditation and the long-term organizational investment that accreditation requires, comprehensive planning must be in place to guide the process. By gaining a fuller appreciation of all that accreditation means today and all that is involved in attaining accreditation, you will be prepared to pursue the right accreditation for you and your program in order to ensure the long-term sustainability of your program/organization.

CASE ILLUSTRATION

Kara and Gregory had first discussed accreditation when they were working out the details of starting their own agency. Once they knew they were moving forward with the agency, they had investigated the various accrediting bodies and determined that COA was likely the best fit. During their initial strategic planning process, pursuing accreditation was identified as one of the agency's short-term goals. As a result, it was determined that Gregory would lead this effort.

During their first year in business, the agency had two programs—a community-based program and a semi-independent living program—both of which served juvenile offenders. Gregory had begun discussing the importance of accreditation with all the agency staff and the board members throughout the year and had composed an accreditation team consisting of staff at various levels in the agency to lead the planning effort. The group had met monthly, reviewing all relevant program and organizational standards, developing and implementing new policies and practices, and continuously informing staff and other stakeholders about the reasons for each new policy and procedure.

To further reinforce the purpose of accreditation and the agency's plans, Kara related the accreditation standards back to the agency's commitment to continuous quality improvement and excellence. In addition, she included their pursuit of accreditation as part of fulfilling their mission to ensure that they were able to offer the most effective and highest-quality services to those whom they served. Kara also took several opportunities to provide staff, board members, and other stakeholders with information related to the long-term economics of accreditation and, particularly, its relationship to the agency's future ability to secure funding.

By the time the COA peer review team arrived for their on-site visit, Gregory and Kara not only felt confident that they had successfully met the accreditation standards, they also felt confident that they had successfully created a climate among their staff that not only was supportive of accreditation but fully appreciated the meaning it carried. Gregory had been particularly excited to note how much more comfortable he felt putting certain policies in place, realizing how much he had learned from the accreditation process. Both Kara and Gregory realized that not only had they worked diligently to attain accreditation for their agency, but that as a result of this pursuit, the organization they had built had a much stronger foundation in place, both organizationally and programmatically.

ACCREDITATION PLAN EXERCISE

To increase your own knowledge and understanding of each of the three major accrediting bodies discussed in this chapter and how relevant each may be to your own program development efforts, complete the exercise below. The exercise is designed to provide you with a better understanding of precisely how much and what type of information is available at no cost from each accrediting body—information that is necessary to decision making about which accreditation to pursue.

1. Using the program that you designed earlier, conduct an evaluation of the three major accrediting bodies to determine which offers the best fit for your program.

2. Develop a brief summary of your findings, minimally including the following:

   - Identification of the relevant service standards of each accrediting body (if applicable)
   - Strengths and weaknesses related to the relevant service standards based on information available from each accrediting body
   - Perceived strengths and weaknesses of the organizational standards based on information available from each accrediting body
   - Analysis of the accreditation status of local competitors and other national providers of same/similar services
   - Other information used in the decision-making process

3. Develop a 2-year accreditation plan timeline, identifying each of the key activities that will be needed to ultimately attain accreditation. Include training, meetings, and other support activities that will be used to guide the accreditation process, as well as the time frames by which the self-study/survey will be submitted and the site visit will occur.

4. Identify at least five outcomes that you believe will result from attaining accreditation.

References

Commission on Accreditation of Rehabilitation Facilities. (2010). *The public says: Accreditation matters!* Retrieved April 1, 2010, from http://www.carf.org/consumer.aspx?content=content/About/News/boilerplate.htm

Council on Accreditation. (n.d.a). *About COA.* Retrieved March 31, 2010, from http://www.coanet.org/front3/page.cfm?sect=1&cont=4320

Council on Accreditation. (n.d.b). *COA and CARF: A comparison.* Retrieved April 2, 2010, from http://www.coanet.org/files/COACARFcomp.pdf

Council on Accreditation. (n.d.c). *Sponsoring and supporting organizations.* Retrieved July 1, 2010, from http://www.coanet.org/front3/page.cfm?sect=12

Council on Accreditation. (n.d.d). *List of standards.* Retrieved September 15, 2010, from http://www.coanet.org/front3/page.cfm?sect=55&cont=4191

Durkin, E. M. (2002). An organizational analysis of psychosocial medical services in outpatient drug abuse treatment programs. *Social Service Review, 76,* 406–429.

Friedman, P. D., Alexander, J. A., & D'Aunno, T. A. (1999). Organizational correlates of access to primary care and mental health services in drug abuse treatment units. *Journal of Substance Abuse Treatment, 16,* 71–80.

Gibelman, M., & Furman, R. (2008). *Managing human service organizations.* Chicago: Lyceum.

Joint Commission, The. (2009). *A journey through the history of The Joint Commission.* Retrieved April 1, 2010, from http://www.jointcommission.org/AboutUs/joint_commission_history.htm

Joint Commission, The. (2010). *Facts about Joint Commission accreditation and certification.* Retrieved September 15, 2010, from http://www.jointcommission.org/AboutUs/Fact_Sheets/facts_jc_acrr_cert.htm

Lemak, C. H., & Alexander, J. A. (2005). Factors that influence staffing of outpatient substance abuse treatment programs. *Psychiatric Services, 56,* 934–939.

State of Michigan Department of Corrections. (2010). *Residential substance abuse treatment services* (Request for Proposal No. LC-2010-007). Lansing, MI: Author.

CHAPTER 17

Putting It All Together

Comprehensive Program

Development in the 21st Century

Learning Objectives

1. Summarize the comprehensive program development model

2. Identify the specific knowledge and skills necessary for comprehensive program development

3. Identify methods by which to continue to develop professionally in the area of program development

4. Identify methods by which to promote accountability in program development

Comprehensive Program Development

Engaging in comprehensive program development in mental health and human services is no easy task, nor should it be. Given that the programs we design and implement have the potential to impact the lives of individuals—often those individuals who are most vulnerable—such work should indeed come at a great cost to us.

Unfortunately, we have often failed to understand that what we do is a business and that our work must therefore be treated as a business. Thankfully, much has changed, particularly in the past decade. Chief among the changes that have helped move our field forward have been demands for increased accountability and increased calls for the use of evidence-based practices. Clients, contractors, other oversight organizations, and the general public have continued to become more knowledgeable about mental health and human services, and as each has become better informed, pressure has continued to mount for us to improve our work. In addition, there is increased emphasis on research and other scholarly literature that is outcome-driven—establishing evidence of what works and what does not work. As mental health professionals historically have embraced the scientist-practitioner model, now more than ever before, there are demands to not simply support such a model but, rather, to actively demonstrate this model through our work.

As these changes have been taking place, promoting greater accountability and demanding more effective treatment, the mental health and human service industries have become increasingly competitive. While in many instances funding has increased in specific areas, in other areas, funding has continued to be reduced. This, coupled with a greatly expanded number of mental health and human service providers opening their doors over the past 2 decades, has created a highly competitive marketplace. Today, this marketplace is defined as one in which only the strong survive. What is most telling today is the shrinking number of human service and mental health organizations that has resulted from organizations closing their doors or merging with other organizations.

However, these conditions that have impacted the field so dramatically in recent times have reinforced the essential need for mental health professionals to not only demonstrate their scientific knowledge and skills but to devote equal energy to demonstrating their business acumen. Fully appreciating that mental health and human services is a business and, as such, requires a comprehensive understanding of business planning. This type of knowledge and skill is key not only to competing in today's marketplace but to surviving in today's marketplace.

The comprehensive program development model presented in this text is essentially a business planning guide for mental health and human service professionals. In fact, an alternate title for this book could very well be *Business Planning in the Mental Health Professions in the 21st Century.* Business planning implies a focus on long-term success. It also implies concentrated efforts, both of which provide necessary structure to the planning process. But more importantly, business planning implies due diligence—a commitment to the most thorough examination and analysis of information and data and subsequent use of such analyses in decision making.

In the past, some mental health professionals have at times found it difficult to understand that our work is indeed a business, arguing that such thinking might be incompatible with the concept of helping. I've never quite understood this, since each of us pursues this as a profession (i.e., work) for which we are paid. Moreover, I have taken issue with this line of thinking because on some level, I find it irresponsible to not give our work the respect that it deserves as a business—a business that is focused on helping. We must understand that our failure to effectively operate our practices/businesses may result in the collective failure of our profession to effectively treat individuals in need. Moreover, we must appreciate that the concepts of *helping profession* and *business* are not at all incompatible but, rather, intimately connected.

Fortunately, I believe such distaste for accepting and understanding the business of mental health and human services is largely behind us and has been held by only a very small number of individuals. In fact, when I began teaching master's-level counseling students more than 10 years ago, many students struggled with making sense of helping as a business, often producing some wonderfully vigorous debates. Today, however, most of my students not only acknowledge that they are preparing for a career that is in fact a business, but they are also committed to ensuring that they can most effectively conduct themselves within their business in order to reach their ultimate objectives of improving the lives of others.

While conditions have changed over the past 2 decades, forcing us to rethink mental health and human services, I believe that where we are now is the most exciting place yet. And as a result, now more than ever before, mental health professionals must be well versed in comprehensive program development and each of the major phases that compose it—design, implementation, and sustainability. As a way of summarizing the model, the next section will revisit each of these major phases and the various steps of the comprehensive program development model that compose them.

Design

Comprehensive program development begins with the design phase and involves a tremendous amount of preplanning activities that guide the design process. Like the entire program development model, design is a linear process, beginning with the identification of an unmet need. This is followed by comprehensive data collection and analysis to promote a full understanding of the need and to explore various ways to most effectively address the need. A thorough review of current research and other literature is conducted to ensure that the clinical program design is evidence-based, or empirically guided when a sound evidence basis has yet to be established to treat a specific issue. In addition, various multicultural aspects must be addressed in the clinical program design. A variety of planning tools should be used in the preplanning, planning, and design phases. A list of several of the most common design tools is provided in Box 17.1.

BOX 17.1

DESIGN TOOLS

- Community demography assessment
- Needs assessment
- Asset map
- Timeline
- Gantt chart
- Service specification model
- Logic model
- Organizational chart
- Spreadsheet
- Line-item budget

In addition to the clinical design, all the other aspects that allow a clinical program to be implemented must be designed. This means that the organizational infrastructure must be designed, including the staffing, equipment, facilities, and so on—all that is required for the clinical program to become a reality. In addition, the various supports, including community resources that will be utilized in program implementation, need to be engaged and considered as part of the initial design process. And finally, a detailed financial plan must be developed and specific funding sources must be identified in order to prepare for program implementation.

In sum, the design phase of the comprehensive program development model includes the following eight steps:

1. Establish the need for programming

2. Establish a research basis for program design

3. Address cultural identity issues in program design

4. Design the clinical program

5. Develop the staffing infrastructure

6. Identify and engage community resources

7. Identify and evaluate potential funding sources

8. Develop the financial management plan

Implementation

The implementation phase involves putting most of what has been devised in the design phase into action. Without having conducted due diligence and having developed a sufficient design, program implementation would not be possible. As such, implementation builds directly from design—again, reflecting the linear nature of program development. Because of all the work that has been completed to bring the program to fruition and the stakes that are involved, the implementation phase can be both wildly exciting and highly stressful. Typically, it is at the point of implementation or the beginning days of a program that the program is most highly scrutinized; therefore, mistakes in implementation can negatively mark a program for a long time to come.

During the implementation phase, several activities need to occur that allow you to move the program forward. One such activity is thoroughly reviewing the contract/grant to ensure a full understanding of expectations of the program and organization. Often, additional planning tools are needed to ensure compliance with the requirements of the grant/contract, mapping out time frames for when various activities and documents are due, and providing additional structure to prevent any problems with contract compliance. It is also during the implementation phase that you must work to establish the relationship with the funding source—initiating this contact and becoming familiar with not only the contract manager but any other relevant contract administrators. Again, the tone that is used to initially establish this relationship may play a critical role in sustaining the contract; therefore, the establishment of these relationships should be given great consideration.

Concurrent with implementation of the program itself, the program evaluation must also be implemented. The three major types of evaluation—fidelity assessment, process evaluation, and outcomes evaluation—are simultaneously implemented so that from the beginning of a new program implementation, each of the various aspects of the program are evaluated. Conducting a fidelity assessment allows you to assess the degree to which the integrity (i.e., fidelity) of the clinical model is retained throughout the implementation process, whereas the process evaluation provides more comprehensive information related to the various aspects of implementation, such as staffing, outputs, time frames, etc. While both the fidelity assessment and process evaluation focus on the implementation process, the outcomes evaluation is conducted to specifically assess the impact of the program in fulfilling its intended objectives as well as achieving other outcomes. Together, these three types of evaluation compose a comprehensive program evaluation—providing a significant amount of information with which to fully understand the program.

Also integral to the implementation process is specific attention to the program infrastructure that includes but is not limited to staffing, leadership and administrative oversight, information systems, quality assurance planning, and contract compliance. Plans must be made to ensure that effective leadership and administrative oversight are in place to provide sufficient support to the program and that specific activities (e.g., meetings, reviews) are also in place to provide additional structure to the oversight process.

Information systems, both in the way of hardware and software, as well as data collection methods and information sharing are also critical aspects that must be specifically attended to during implementation. Whereas a client information system may prove fruitful in capturing the most essential information in one place and allowing for easy retrieval of such information (unfortunately, the retrieval process continues to plague many organizations due to how client information systems are structured—and this should be a key consideration when purchasing a client information system), software programs specifically designed for human resource management and finance management (ideally, an integrated human resource and finance system) are also essential. In addition, basic spreadsheet programs, statistical programs, and other data storage and analysis programs are needed to support the program. Information systems typically play a specific role in the collection and analysis of pertinent program data—comprising much of what is necessary for quality assurance efforts and ensuring contract compliance. In addition, structure is needed to guide the quality assurance program, such as leadership for the quality assurance process, methods by which quality assurance activities will be conducted, and supports that will be used to guide the quality assurance process. Quality assurance and contract compliance are both integral to long-term sustainability, and in addition, they each rely on adequate information systems and administrative oversight and leadership. It is in this manner that these specific aspects of implementation interrelate. Box 17.2 provides a brief summary of the various implementation activities.

BOX 17.2

SNAPSHOT OF IMPLEMENTATION ACTIVITIES

- Implementing the program
- Reviewing the contract/grant and setting up systems to ensure compliance
- Establishing the relationship with the funding source
- Implementing the program evaluation
- Ensuring that an appropriate leadership and administrative oversight structure is in place
- Ensuring effective information systems are in place
- Ensuring an effective quality assurance and contract compliance system is in place

---

Sustainability

Just as a successful implementation is predicated on an effective design, sustaining a program is dependent on continuous success in program delivery/implementation. As a result, sustainability is based on the sum of program design and implementation efforts and requires constant attention throughout implementation/delivery in order to be achieved. This is because any deficits related to initial due diligence and preplanning may not prevent a program from being implemented; however, such deficits may indeed prevent a program from being sustained. For instance, if initial data collection efforts were limited—not taking into account any specific factors that might have artificially indicated a more significant problem than actually existed or that did not take into account the long-term extent of the problem—data may have justified the need for the program; however, once implemented, the program may not be sustainable. See the following case vignette for an example of this.

IS PROGRAM EXPANSION JUSTIFIED?

Trudy and Anne had been operating a 24-bed residential substance abuse treatment center for the past 4 years, and over the past 3 months, they had received more referrals than they could handle, necessitating the use of a waiting list for the first time since they had opened. While they were both pleased to be able to maintain their program at capacity—especially since this had been increasingly difficult for them to achieve over the past few years, often running at approximately 80% capacity—they also realized that if they expanded their program, they could eliminate the waiting list.

Anne met with the agency president to explain the need for program expansion, sharing with him the referral data of the past 3 months and expressing that she and Trudy did not want to miss this opportunity to grow the program. After discussing the costs involved with adding six beds and what they would need to do to gain approval from the state for an expanded license, the president agreed to authorize the expansion. He had recently been talking to the agency's directors about his vision of growth, and he wanted to recognize Trudy and Anne for taking initiative in this area.

Within 3 months and after expenditures of more than $200,000, the building renovations were complete and an approval for expansion of their residential substance abuse license had been authorized. Trudy was able to quickly move clients from the waiting list into the program after having hired 14 new staff members. The program remained at capacity for another 9 months, and then Anne began to notice a drop in referrals. She and Trudy were concerned and began contacting their referring agents, but each told them the same thing: They continued to be happy with the services, and they had already referred all the clients who were in need. During a meeting with other providers, one of Trudy's colleagues noted the state's recent move to discontinue its prisoner reentry program. The initiative had resulted in an influx of clients in need of substance abuse treatment, but because it was based on state funding, he had been initially leery of how long it would last; so he had been careful not to make any significant changes in his business for fear the increase in service needs would be short-lived. He was now very relieved that he had followed what was going on at the state level and had not taken any new risks. Sheepishly, Trudy agreed with him about how important it was to stay on top of government spending and other external factors that can significantly influence your business.

Trudy returned to the office and discussed what she had learned with Anne, and both of them vowed to never again conduct a *less-than-thorough* analysis—in fact, they agreed that from here on out, the most effective due diligence would be used to guide all their business decisions. Unfortunately, because the increase in referrals that they had experienced was not sustainable, they were back at their previous level but with excess beds, which meant they were at 60% capacity. Therefore, they had to turn their attention to the most difficult task of remaining fiscally healthy while facing a bloated workforce and a $200,000 loan to repay.

As illustrated by Anne and Trudy, sustainability doesn't require specific attention to only post-implementation activities; rather, sustainability is also dependent on the strength of justification that led to implementation. This can be a costly lesson to learn, both in the case of new program development and in program expansion or program modification.

With solid justification for new program development, effective design, and effective initial implementation, sustainability requires specific focus on achieving quality and preserving key relationships and attention to all that is needed to maintain a program. These needs include building and preserving resources and relationships with community resources in order to ensure additional support and access to information and knowledge about the broader climate. In addition, this involves working with peers and other organizations as part of a broader coalition and working both collectively and individually in various types of advocacy. Whereas program evaluation begins at the point of program implementation, the ability to effectively conduct ongoing evaluations and, more importantly, to use the evaluation results in program improvement, marketing, and contributing to scholarly research, are critical to sustainability. Employing effective data collection, analysis, and monitoring techniques and engaging in effective information sharing is necessary for program sustainability, and without such, it may be difficult to continuously garner support for your program. Finally, pursuing national accreditation and other forms of credentialing is necessary to remain current and to demonstrate a commitment to quality. Moreover, accreditation and other forms of recognition must be part of a broader continuous quality improvement program that characterizes the work of the program. Box 17.3 provides a brief summary of the various sustainability activities.

BOX 17.3

SUSTAINABILITY ACTIVITIES

- Building and preserving relationships with community resources
- Engaging in advocacy efforts
- Participating in coalition building
- Conducting program evaluations
- Effectively communicating evaluation results and next steps
- Engaging in effective information sharing with all stakeholders
- Pursuing accreditation and other forms of credentialing as part of a broader commitment to quality improvement

In addition to the specific sustainability activities that are a part of the comprehensive program development model, sustainability also requires constant attention to external factors that may influence the program's ability to continue. Although knowledge of the external climate is one of the reasons why relationships with colleagues and community resources and coalition building are so important, this issue deserves individual attention. Being fully informed about legislation, national and state trends, and other factors that may impact your business today is critical, but in addition, you must be fully informed about what may be on the horizon. In fact, had Trudy and Anne more thoroughly investigated the reasons behind their influx of clients, they would have understood that the increase may be short-lived, rather than reflective of long-term change.

Required Knowledge and Skills of Program Developers

As you likely have learned from this text, professional counselors and other types of mental health professionals are charged with an incredible responsibility as program developers. In order to be effective program developers, a tremendous amount of knowledge and skill is necessary. In some ways, mental health program developers must be individuals who not only possess the knowledge and skills associated with a master's degree in counseling (or clinical/counseling psychology or clinical social work) but also the knowledge and skills associated with a master's degree in business administration (MBA) and a master's degree in public health (MPH). Whereas the foundation provided by a clinically focused master's degree (from an accredited and highly reputable academic program and university) is most significant, some of the knowledge and skills traditionally associated with an MBA and MPH are also necessary to be a successful program developer today. Specifically, due diligence in business planning, accounting, management, leadership, and organizational development and change—each of which has historically been associated with business degrees—are essential skills for program developers. Evaluating national and local trend data, developing comprehensive response systems, and understanding the various factors impacting need and interventions—often associated with public health professionals—are also critically needed skills in program development efforts. Finally, a strong background in scientific skills—increasingly emphasized in academic counseling programs—is paramount to success as a clinical program developer.

While it is not necessary to possess three graduate degrees, mental health professionals today must have the requisite knowledge and skills that the combination of these three degrees characterizes. This means that specific attention must be paid to developing a broad repertoire of knowledge and skills that allows you to effectively compete as a mental health professional today.

Table 17.1 provides a snapshot of the knowledge and skills required at each of the stages of comprehensive program development.

Table 17.1 Knowledge and Skills Needed in Comprehensive Program Development

Program Development Stage	Knowledge and Skills Needed
Establish the need for programming	Data-collection methods; data-collection tools; data analysis
Establish a research basis for program design	Comprehensive research methods; conducting literature reviews; discriminating among results of data analyses and data sources; knowledge of comprehensive sources of information, including scholarly literature, accreditation standards, and governmental venues
Address cultural identity issues in program design	Deep knowledge of the concepts of cultural identity and cultural competence; inclusive understanding of cultural identity; demonstrated cultural competence skills; research skills related to examining issues of cultural identity and cultural competency; commitment to promoting individual freedom and fighting against any form of discrimination
Design the clinical program	Scientific skills to understand the relationship between needs, interventions, and outcomes; design methods and tools; mission and vision statement development; knowledge of ideological foundations
Develop the staffing infrastructure	Organizational design theory; organizational development; organizational chart; knowledge related to the role of organizational design to work flow and communication; management and leadership theory and practice
Identify and engage community resources	Communication and engagement skills; collegiality and collaboration skills; ability to influence others
Identify and evaluate potential funding sources	Knowledge of comprehensive sources of funding; access to comprehensive sources of funding; evaluation and analysis skills in discriminating among funding opportunities

(Continued)

Table 17.1 (Continued)

Program Development Stage	Knowledge and Skills Needed
Develop the financial management plan	Budgeting; accounting; financial systems; monitoring and oversight; laws pertaining to organizational finances; financial reporting
Develop the proposal	Research; development of a sound argument and plan; writing; ability to garner support from others; financial management
Implement the program	Organizational knowledge and skills; management and leadership skills; knowledge of treatment fidelity, process evaluation, and outcomes evaluation
Evaluate the program	Research and evaluation; evaluation design; statistical analysis; fidelity assessment; process evaluation; outcomes evaluation; training skills to prepare others for evaluation
Build and preserve community resources	Communication and engagement/retention skills; collegiality; leadership skills; ability to attract and retain supports
Develop an advocacy plan	Advocacy skills; knowledge of various advocacy pathways; communication and engagement/retention skills; collegiality; leadership skills; ability to attract and retain supports
Develop an information-sharing plan	Importance of data reporting; data collection and information systems; effective communication skills; reporting time frames; reporting tools and methods; report writing
Attain program and organizational accreditation	Knowledge of the various accrediting bodies; ability to discriminate among accrediting bodies; planning skills; leadership and organizational development; leadership in organizational change; policy and practice development; self-study development; written and verbal communication skills

Where Do You Go From Here?

While the knowledge and skills required to be an effective program developer may seem a bit daunting, understanding the tremendous responsibility of program developers may help put this into perspective. Indeed, the responsibility of another individual's life and livelihood is enormous and, therefore, should require an incredible commitment on our part; however, the commitment is not only to possess the knowledge and skills to engage in comprehensive program development but, rather, to remain current in this knowledge and skill.

Remaining Current and Staying Relevant

A former colleague of mine would ask individuals interviewing for a faculty position, "How do you remain relevant in your work?" I always thought this was a brilliant question—very straightforward and effective in prompting critical self-reflection—and more importantly, one that we should all constantly ask ourselves.

Remaining relevant in the work that we do requires constant curiosity spurred on by a hunger to continue learning and growing. Such hunger is fueled by acknowledgment that there is always more to know—that you will never know it all. Accepting this may be difficult for some, but without this type of humility, it is often challenging to be inspired to seek more knowledge.

The work that we do is ever-changing; in fact, it might be the most dynamic type of work that exists. This is particularly true because individuals are constantly changing, rarely acting according to script but, rather, constantly demonstrating what it really means to be unique. In order to effectively attend to the changing nature of individuals, we cannot tolerate becoming passive. Rather, we must return again and again to the understanding that we can never fully understand one another, but we must be committed to constantly attempting to achieve this. In this regard, remaining relevant means viewing each new encounter as a *new encounter,* not an encounter previously experienced for which you already have the answers. Even after you have treated 200 teenage girls for sexual abuse, you must allow each new client/survivor the freedom to teach you about who she is and exactly what she needs, suspending any preformed judgment based on your prior experiences.

Maintaining relevance also means remaining current in awareness and knowledge. Acknowledging that all knowledge is vulnerable to time is essential to ensuring that you remain current. For instance, when I began my academic training, eating disorders among males was not addressed either in the literature or in the practice setting because it was not yet identified as an issue and, therefore, was not broadly acknowledged or understood. Today, however, we know that this disorder is not at all limited to females. In addition, we now have an emerging body of research on female sex offenders, and I am hopeful that over the next 10 years, we will learn more and more about this specialized population. I would become irrelevant quickly if I continued to ignore the fact that boys and young men are vulnerable to eating disorders and if I failed to acknowledge and learn about female sex offenders. And even though I may have begun with a solid knowledge base, it is my responsibility to continue to develop it.

There are multiple strategies that can help you remain current, most that naturally occur through the use of the comprehensive program development model (i.e., community resource preservation/maintaining collegial relationships, coalition building, advocacy work, accreditation planning and other credentialing, and remaining current with best practices). In addition, being active politically and remaining keenly involved in legislative and other external venues that impact mental health and human services can assist you in remaining current. Reading, conversing, and using other methods to remain fully informed and to gather multiple perspectives are also essential. And, related to this, engaging in healthy skepticism and questioning much of what you hear is often necessary to really digest new information.

Committing to Continued Professional Development

Directly tied to remaining relevant is a commitment to continuous professional development. This means not only learning new knowledge but acquiring new skills as new knowledge develops. Whereas each of the activities listed above as part of the comprehensive program development model is also useful in professional development efforts, other methods are needed to ensure appropriate growth. First and foremost among these methods is continued learning—through reading, training, coursework, and other methods. However, this can also be the most challenging, since the amount of educational and training opportunities is endless and you must be vigilant in discriminating among such opportunities. Questioning information presented, reviewing sources of information, and critically evaluating information provided are each necessary to effective learning. Simply digesting new information without evidence of its value is akin to the old data analysis adage *junk in, junk out.*

In addition to learning and acquiring new knowledge and skills through various venues, you also must force yourself to *stretch.* Stretching in this regard means pushing yourself to be uncomfortable—be it in an activity (e.g., public speaking), confronting one of your perceived weaknesses (e.g., statistical analysis), or forcing yourself to go beyond what you believe you are capable of or what you believe you need (e.g., enrolling in a course on organizational development).

Professional development equals continuous growth. Moreover, professional development may equal professional satisfaction and fulfillment. As a result, professional development can be like beginning your career over and over again—capturing all the excitement and stimulation that learning holds and thereby constantly renewing yourself and your work life.

Ensuring and Advocating for Accountability-Based Practice

Remaining current and relevant in your work and committing to continuous professional development are cornerstones of a successful career in any industry. However, with specific regard to program development, you must also be committed to ensuring and advocating for accountability-based practices. As counselors and other mental health professionals, we are held to the standard of care or the mandate of nonmaleficence (i.e., do no harm). As such, our first responsibility is to ourselves—to ensure that we do not engage in any practices that could potentially cause harm to our clients. At the same time, we also must ensure that we do not engage in practices that we know have not been found to be effective. This level of professional accountability requires that we remain highly knowledgeable about various treatment efforts and their effects, that we attend to treatment fidelity when implementing an evidence-based practice, that we engage in continuous evaluation of our interventions and programs, and that we continue to use our evaluation results to further inform treatment strategies and program development.

In addition, as mental health professionals, we also must engage in advocacy for the use of evidence-based practices and accountability as a defining mandate of our profession. This is because we are collectively responsible for the outcomes of our work, and more importantly, we must be the voices of those whom we serve to ensure that their needs are most effectively addressed.

Summary

Engaging in comprehensive program development can be one of the most meaningful aspects of your career; however, it can also be one of the most challenging. Over the past 20 years, our field has witnessed dramatic changes in how we understand program development and all that it entails. As a result, comprehensive program development today is not simply something engaged in by a few mental health professionals but, rather, a prerequisite for all mental health professionals. The major phases of program design, implementation, and evaluation must be fully understood both individually and as interdependent parts. And the steps involved in each of the phases of comprehensive program development must be attended to in order to ensure success and long-term sustainability. It is my hope that the comprehensive program development model presented in this text will assist you in your own program development efforts. As a result, we may continue to promote greater responsibility and accountability in program development efforts in the 21st century.

Appendix

Web Resources Discussed in Text

Resource	Location	About
Professional Associations for Mental Health Professionals		
American Counseling Association	www.counseling.org	National professional association for counselors
American Psychological Association	www.apa.org	National professional association for psychologists
National Association of Social Workers	www.socialworkers.org	National professional association for social workers
Professional Associations for Organizations		
Alliance for Children and Families	www.alliance1.org	Membership association for organizations working with children and families
American Correctional Association	www.aca.org	Membership association for organizations working in corrections
Child Welfare League of America	www.cwla.org	Membership association for organizations working with children and families
National Association for the Dually Diagnosed	www.thenadd.org	Membership association for organizations working with persons with developmental disabilities

(Continued)

(Continued)

Accrediting Bodies		
American Correctional Association	www.aca.org	Accreditation standards for correctional facilities
Council on Accreditation	www.coanet.org	Accreditation standards for a broad range of human service and mental health programs
Commission on Accreditation of Rehabilitation Facilities	www.carf.org	Accreditation standards for a broad range of human service and mental health programs
The Joint Commission	www.jointcommission.org	Accreditation standards for a broad range of behavioral and medical health programs
Funding Databases		
Community of Science	www.cos.com	Large subscription-based compendium of governmental and nongovernmental sources
Department of Education	www.ed.gov	Listing of current grant opportunities from the Department of Education
Grants, etc.	www.ssw.umich.edu/grantsetc/	Compendium of funding opportunity databases, sponsored by the University of Michigan
Grants.gov	www.grants.gov	Compendium of governmental funding sources
The School Funding Center	www.schoolfundingcenter.info	Compendium of school funding opportunities
Philanthropic Foundations		
Annie E. Casey Foundation	www.aecf.org	Child welfare
Aspen Institute	www.aspeninstitute.org	Public policy

Bill and Melinda Gates Foundation	www.gatesfoundation.org	Education, poverty
Doris Duke Charitable Foundation	www.ddcf.org	Medical research
Ford Foundation	www.fordfound.org	Social change, social issues
Hogg Foundation for Mental Health	www.hogg.utexas.edu	Mental health
Kresge Foundation	www.kresge.org	Health, environment, community development, arts and culture, education, and human services
John D. and Catherine T. MacArthur Foundation	www.macfound.org	Public policy, human and community development
National Education Trust	www.nctm.org	Educational funding opportunities
Public Welfare Foundation	www.nationaleducationtrust.net	Service, empowerment, advocacy-related funding
McCormick Foundation	www.mccormickfoundation.org	Children, community development
Robert Wood Johnson Foundation	www.rwjf.org	Health, health care
Theodore and Vada Stanley Foundation	47 Richards Ave. Norwalk, CT 06857-0000	Mental health program funding
William and Flora Hewlett Foundation	www.hewlett.org	Poverty
William Penn Foundation	www.williampennfoundation.org	Children, families, community development
W. K. Kellogg Foundation	www.wkkf.org	Child development, social services
Technology Grants		
Hewlett Packard Technology Grants	www.hp.com	Technology grants for schools
TechSoup Global	www.techsoup.org	Electronic technology-giving programs for nonprofit organizations

(Continued)

(Continued)

Other Program Development Resources		
National Association of Social Workers	www.socialworkers.org	Indicators for the achievement of the NASW Standards for cultural competence in social work practice
Association for Multicultural Counseling and Development	www.amcdaca.org	Multicultural competencies
Government Accountability Office	www.gao.gov	Governmental performance, accountability standards, and monitoring
National Registry of Evidence-Based Programs and Practice	www.nrepp.samhsa.gov	Searchable database of evidence-based practices affiliated with SAMHSA
National Center for Cultural Competence	http://nccc.georgetown.edu	Resource center for cultural competence in mental and physical health
National Standards on Culturally and Linguistically Appropriate Services	www.minorityhealth.hhs.gov	National cultural competence standards for health care
Office of Juvenile Justice and Delinquency Prevention	www.ojjdp.gov	Logic model development guide; logic model template
Outcome Measurement Resource Network	http://makeadifferenceliveunited.com/outcomes/	Outcomes resources sponsored by the United Way
Responsibilities of Users of Standardized Tests (3rd ed.)	www.theaaceonline.com	Assessment tool provided by the Association for Assessment in Counseling
W. K. Kellogg Foundation	www.wkkf.org	Logic model development guide

Glossary

Administrative support staff: Employees who do not provide direct services to clients but who support the work of those who do; typically work in finance, human resources, information systems, research and evaluation, fund development, and other similar support departments. In addition, individuals who provide office support through secretarial duties, reception, or executive administrative support are also considered administrative support staff.

Asset map: Inventory of assets in the target region; considered a map because it provides additional direction to new program development efforts by identifying various existing strengths and resources that may be used in program design.

Best practices: Practices that are highly regarded as a result of having an evidence basis, being empirically guided, or being identified as a standard that should guide practice.

Breach of contract: An act of noncompliance with a contract. For instance, if master's-level professionals are contractually required to deliver a service and instead these services are provided by bachelor's-level staff, this action on the part of the subcontractor constitutes a breach of contract.

Case management staff: Professionals with either a bachelor's or a master's degree whose primary role is overall case coordination. Case managers work with other professionals, including clinicians and direct care workers, as well as school and other support personnel to ensure the comprehensive needs of the client are being served.

Ceiling: A term often used in relation to the maximum amount of funding available in funding opportunities. For instance, a ceiling of $500,000 indicates that the maximum amount of funding available for a project is $500,000, and therefore, funding requests must not exceed $500,000.

Clinical staff: In mental health and human services, professionals specializing in mental health treatment. These include master's- and doctoral-level counselors, clinical psychologists, clinical social workers, and psychiatrists.

Community assets: Strengths of a community that include process-related issues such as a community's ability to organize, work collaboratively, and meet the needs of its residents, as well as promote safety and a healthy local economy. The term also refers to concrete aspects such as adequate community facilities and support organizations, as well as a thriving business community.

Community demography assessment: A thorough assessment of the target region that examines the various population parameters in order to accurately illustrate the demographic aspects of the community; part of the comprehensive needs assessment.

Community resources: The resources that are available to support the residents of a community, such as human service or other support organizations, services, other treatment providers, libraries, gathering spaces, places of worship, knowledge, and other assets that are available in the community.

Comprehensive needs assessment: Five-pronged data collection and analysis activities that consist of community demography assessment, problem analysis, market analysis, identification of needs, and inventory of assets and that allow for initial decision making in program development.

Contingent/contractual workers: Individuals who are employed on an as-needed basis or to provide a specific and/or specialized function. Unlike part- or full-time employees, contractual workers are not entitled to employment benefits and typically work far fewer and less-structured hours than their part- and full-time counterparts.

Data-based decision making: Results from comprehensive data collection and analysis. This refers to any type of decision making that is based on empirical data and other forms of evidence.

Data layering: Involves the examination of various layers of data in descending order of size in order to further clarify the meaning of data. This process can be useful for conducting several types of data analysis.

Deliverables: Outcomes or specific items that will be provided or submitted in completion of a specific task or project.

Direct care staff: In human services, individuals who provide nonprofessional direct support to clients. These workers often support clients' daily living and other basic activities. They may also be referred to as paraprofessionals. Direct care staff are most often found in residential programs.

Emerging practices: Interventions that have not yet been fully evaluated through rigorous means, practices that have a research basis, or practices that utilize innovative strategies; may also be termed *promising practices*, reflecting that there is more than just a hunch that these practices may be effective and that some preliminary evaluation has likely been completed. In all cases, emerging practices imply the need for rigorous evaluation to effectively determine if they are, indeed, evidence-based.

Empirically based practices: Those clinical practices that are rooted in or guided by empirical research but have not yet been rigorously evaluated to determine if they do, in fact, have an evidence basis.

Evidence-based practices: Practices that have an established basis in evidence—achieved through rigorous evaluation; imply that the results of a rigorous evaluation support positive outcomes or are directly related to client success.

Executive leadership: The organizational structure within a mental health or human service organization, precisely with regard to the top levels of management. Executive leadership typically refers to the top level (i.e., president/chief executive officer/executive director) and the second-to-top level (i.e., chief operating officer/chief financial officer/vice president). The executive leadership team often consists of both operations (e.g., chief operating officer) and support individuals (e.g., chief financial officer). The executive leadership team may vary based on organizational structure; however, the executive leadership team refers to the team responsible for making top-level decisions for the organization.

Floor: Specific to notices of funding opportunities, the minimum amount of funding available to a given project. Opposite of ceiling, the floor may be $100,000, while the ceiling is $500,000. When a floor is identified, it indicates the minimum amount of funding that can be requested.

Gantt chart: A planning tool that is used to identify activities to be completed, time frames for completion, and individuals assigned to an activity; particularly useful in planning, scheduling, and monitoring a wide variety of projects.

Governance structure: The board of directors/trustees or other types of board structures; charged with monitoring the organization as well as representing the organization to the public.

In-kind donation: Items in a proposal's budget that the applicant will contribute to the project. For funding opportunities in which a match funding contribution is required, *in-kind donation* is typically stated next to the dollar amount to indicate that the applicant will support the cost.

Integrated electronic systems: Electronic information systems that are comprehensive and include various types of business data that can interact. For instance, an ideal integrated electronic system would include client information and other program data, finance data, and human resource data and would have the capability to allow the various data sets to interact with one another.

Letter of support: A written statement of support provided by a relevant stakeholder on behalf of an applicant organization. Letters of support are often required by applicants when submitting a proposal for funding. A letter of support is used to provide some degree of evidence that the applicant organization is capable of carrying out the work detailed in a proposal, has had past success with other funding sources, or appears to possess the capability of conducting an effective business.

Managerial and supervisory staff: Individuals who have some supervisory responsibilities for other staff and for part of the business operations or support services.

Market analysis: An assessment and analysis of existing providers that are working to address the identified problems in the region; consists of a thorough examination of the operations and programming of all existing providers; a critical ingredient for decision making in new program development; part of the comprehensive needs assessment.

Match funding: Required funding that must be provided by an applicant for a particular funding opportunity. Match funding requirements are often listed in relation to the total percentage of the funding request and typically range from 10% to 50%. Specific requirements may be placed on match funding, particularly with regard to the types of expenditures that can qualify for match funding (e.g., salaries, rent). On budgets that accompany proposals for programs/projects, match funding expenditures are typically stated as in-kind donations.

Multisystemic approach: Refers to multisystemic family therapy, which was developed by Scott Henggeler and colleagues. The multisystemic approach refers to engaging various systems (e.g., school) that interact with a client in the treatment process. Multisystemic therapy is an example of an evidence-based practice.

Need: An established gap between the identified program and existing services to address the problem.

Partnership: Two or more entities that receive mutual benefits as a result of a relationship; implies equity in a relationship in which each entity contributes and receives.

Philanthropic organizations: Organizations that are developed in order to promote specific interests through the provision of funds. Also known as charitable organizations, philanthropic organizations support specific and/or broad interests.

Preplanning stage of program development: Consists of the identification of a target region and target population and the completion of a comprehensive needs assessment; provides for the first stage of program development: establish the need for programming.

Problem analysis: A systematic data-collection process consisting of review of secondary data sources and various data-collection tools that include surveys, interviews, and focus groups and that is designed to identify existing problems in the target region; conducted following the community demography assessment; part of the comprehensive needs assessment.

Quality indicators: Specific data that indicates quality and, as such, is typically defined as part of determining quality outcomes; part of quality improvement and quality assurance efforts.

Request for Proposal: A notice of a specific funding opportunity in which the funding source is openly inviting proposals. Also known as an RFP, a Request for Proposal may specify exactly the type of project or program that is being funded or may require that the applicant describe the type of project/program for which s/he wishes to receive funding; indicates a competition for funding among eligible applicants.

Request for Quote: A notice of a specific funding opportunity in which the funding source identifies the specific project/program that they will fund and requires applicants to provide a financial quote for which they will implement the project/program; also called an RFQ.

Research basis: The inclusive term I have chosen to use in the text to refer to evidence-based practices, empirically guided practices, emerging practices, and/or best practices. The term *research basis* implies that there is minimally some type of research support for the practice.

Return on investment: The amount and type of benefits received as a result of an investment. ROI may include savings in time and increased efficiency and may result in additional revenue. ROI is sometimes difficult to quantify, but it is an essential part of effective decision making in any business.

Silo: In the context of mental health and human service professions, refers to working in isolation rather than as part of interdisciplinary processes or collaborative efforts.

Staffing infrastructure: The employees and contractual/contingent workers that compose an organization; referred to as an infrastructure because it supports part of the functions of an organization.

Stakeholders: Various individuals such as community members, officials, and various levels of professionals working in the region in schools, law enforcement, human service agencies, and other organizations that are either directly (e.g., living, working) or indirectly (e.g., providing funding) involved in the target region.

Stewardship: Acting effectively on behalf of others. In the case of receiving funding to provide specific services, stewardship refers to one's ability to most effectively manage the funding.

Support agents: Individuals who act as supports to an individual or to the work of an organization. Support agents may provide letters of support on behalf of an organization and may be directly involved in providing services to clients of the organizations. Support agents often work collaboratively with professionals and organizations.

Target population: The identified population in need that is the proposed or actual recipient of new or existing program development efforts.

Target region: Area in which initial data collection is conducted and in which new program implementation is anticipated to occur.

Turf: In mental health and human services, refers to the business that one has and a desire to protect it rather than work collaboratively.

Author Index

Subject Index

Page numbers followed by f or t indicate figures or tables.

SAGE Research Methods Online
The essential tool for researchers

**Sign up now at
www.sagepub.com/srmo
for more information.**

An expert research tool

- An **expertly designed taxonomy** with more than 1,400 unique terms for social and behavioral science research methods

- **Visual and hierarchical search tools** to help you discover material and link to related methods

- Easy-to-use navigation tools
- Content organized by complexity
- Tools for citing, printing, and downloading content with ease
- Regularly updated content and features

A wealth of essential content

- The most comprehensive picture of quantitative, qualitative, and mixed methods available today

- More than **100,000 pages of SAGE book and reference material** on research methods as well as editorially selected material from SAGE journals

- More than **600 books** available in their entirety online

Launching 2011!

 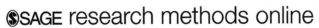 SAGE research methods online

CPSIA information can be obtained
at www.ICGtesting.com
Printed in the USA
LVHW110849110322
713069LV00005B/35